Socio-Economic Status of Widows

Socio-Economic Status of Widows

Dharmendra Kumar

RANDOM

RANDOM PUBLICATIONS
NEW DELHI (INDIA)

Socio-Economic Status of Widows

ISBN 978-93-5111-627-1

Published in 2015 in India by

RANDOM PUBLICATIONS

4376-A/4B, Gali Murari Lal, Ansari Road
New Delhi-110 002
Phone : +9111-43580356, 011-23289044, 011-43142548
e-mail: sales@randompublications.com,
info@randompublications.com, randomexports@gmail.com

Type Setting by : Friends Media, Delhi-110089

Printed at Thomson Press(India) Limited

Preface

Believe it or not, India has over 40 million widows - the highest in the world. It is a paradox that in this nation which has a glorious history with incidents glorifying women, widows are shunned from society. A widow regardless of her age has to don a drab garment and give up other adornments and confine herself to a corner of the house. A widow even has to tonsure her head in certain communities. She is not allowed to attend weddings or other celebrations as her presence is considered a bad omen.

A widower on the other hand does not suffer any differential treatment. Rather he is allowed to remarry even before a year of mourning has passed. Although widow marriages are becoming common in the cities the situation is still dismal in the rural areas. Not only a widow becomes financially dependent but also suffers the indignity of becoming a social outcaste. In Globalized India, where even in wealthy families wives own no assets directly, widows are rendered superfluous and terminally dependent. In poorer families they are just thrown out.

There are many historical evidences to suggest that widow remarriage enjoyed social sanction during ancient period in India. In course of time the practice ceased to prevail increasing the number of widows to lakhs during the 19th century. Therefore, it became incumbent on the part of the social reformers to make sincere efforts to popularize widow remarriage by writing in newspapers and contemporary journals.

Widowhood is defined as the status of an individual who was legally married to someone who subsequently died. Economically, the death of a spouse will result in loss of income and property that the deceased spouse received or owned, unless provision for their continuation and inheritance is made explicit in income programme rules, laws of inheritance, or through the deceased spouse's will. For this reason, it is important to understand how marriage and inheritance rights to income and assets are defined in law and by programmes that provide income to elderly persons.

Prominent among these reformers were Raja Rammohan Roy and Iswar Chandra Vidyasagar. They carried out large scale campaigns in this regard mainly through books, pamphlets and petitions with scores of signatures. In July 1856, J.P. Grant, a member of the Governor-General's Council finally tabled a bill in support of the widow remarriage, which was passed on 13 July 1856 and came to be called the Widow Remarriage Act, 1856. But Vidyasagar pressed on and urged the British to pass legislation that will allow Hindu widows to remarry. To support his request, Ishwar Chandra Vidyasagar collected almost 1000 signatures and sent his petition to the Indian legislative council. The council received thousands of signatures for and against this measure but the members finally decided to support the enlightened minority, The Hindu widow remarriage act was passé in 1856. Although, the value of this act for improving the lives of woman has been questioned, one cannot doubt Ishwar Chandra Vidyasagar's desire to create a more humane society.

This book will definitely prove to be a boon to teachers, students and research scholars

I would like to thank my team for standing beside me throughout my career and writing this book. My special thanks go to "Random Publications" who have published the book.

– Dharmendra Kumar

Contents

1

Introduction to Widow

A widow is a woman whose husband has died, while a widower is a man whose wife has died. The state of having lost one's spouse to death is termed *widowhood*. These terms are generally not applied to a person after he or she becomes divorced from their former spouse.

This term "widowhood" can be used for either sex, at least according to some dictionaries, but the word *widowerhood* is also listed in some dictionaries. Occasionally, the word *viduity* is used. The adjective form for either sex is *widowed*. The treatment of widows around the world varies, but unequal benefits and treatment generally received by widows compared to those received by widowers globally has spurred an interest in the issue by human rights activists.

ECONOMIC POSITION

In societies where the husband was the sole provider, his death could leave his family destitute. The tendency for women to generally outlive men can compound this, since men in many societies marry women younger than themselves. In some patriarchalsocieties, widows could maintain economic independence. A woman would carry on her spouse's business and be accorded certain rights, such as entering guilds. More recently, widows of political figures have been among the first women elected to high office in many countries, such asCorazón Aquino or Isabel Martínez de Perón.

In 19th century Britain, widows had greater opportunity for social mobility than in many other societies. Along with the ability to ascend socio-economically, widows—who were "presumably celibate"—were much more able (and likely) to challenge conventional sexual behaviour than married women in their society.

In some parts of Europe, including Russia, Czechoslovakia, Greece, Italy, and Spain, widows used to wear black for the rest of their lives to signify their mourning, a practise that has since died out. Many immigrants from these cultures to the United States as recently as the 1970s have loosened this strict standard of dress to only two years of black garments. However, Orthodox Christian immigrants may wear lifelong black in the United States to signify their widowhood and devotion to their deceased husband. In other cultures, however, widowhood is much stricter and unarguably more demeaning to women's rights. Often, women are required to remarry within the family of their late husband after a period of mourning. With the rise of HIV/AIDS levels of infection across the globe, rituals to which women are subjected in order to be "cleansed" or accepted into her new husband's home make her susceptible to the psychological adversities that may be involved as well as imposing health risks.

It is often necessary for women to comply with the social customs of her area because her fiscal stature depends on it, but this custom is also often abused by others as a way to keep money within the patriarchal family. It is also uncommon for widows to challenge their treatment because they are often "unaware of their rights under the modern law...because of their low status, and lack of education or legal representation."

As of 2004, women in United States who were "widowed at younger ages are at greatest risk for economic hardship." Similarly, married women who are in a financially unstable household are more likely to become widows "because of the strong relationship between mortality [of the male head] and wealth [of the household]." In underdeveloped and developing areas of the world, conditions for widows continue to be much more severe. However, the United Nations Convention on the Elimination of All Forms of Discrimination against Women ("now ratified by 135 countries"), while slow, is working on proposals which will make certain types of discrimination and treatment of widows (such as violence and withholding property rights) illegal in the countries that have joined CEDAW.

THE STATUS OF WIDOWS

Recently, a national daily published a news report concerning a single woman (widow) who was chased away by the villagers. She was allegedly having an illicit relationship with a man of her locality. About two years ago Degani Devi, a single woman, was burnt alive on charges of practicing witchcraft. In yet another incident, a girl from our neighbourhood lost her husband in a road accident just a few months into their marriage. The trauma and shock she underwent after the sudden and untimely death of her husband cannot be described in words. On top of that, she had to endure all the mistreatment from her in-laws who often tortured her for bringing bad fortune to the family. The stories of these women underscore the plight of widows and the attitude of the Nepali society towards single women. The term 'widow' refers to a woman who has lost her husband by death and has not married again. There are a number of causes such as accidents, conflicts, natural disasters, poverty and diseases that have increased the number of widows. According to National Census 2011, there are around 500,000 widows in the country. Widowhood brings not just shock or trauma, it also pushes a large number of women toward an uncertain future. It also becomes a strong cause of destabilization of families. The widows are most of the time mistreated, marginalised and exploited both at home and in the public sphere. They face discrimination and exclusion. In our society, widows are barred from attending any auspicious occasion. It is because of the misconception that the presence of a widow brings bad fortune. This clearly indicates that the social and family status of widows is very low from every point of view. Moreover, a widow is often deprived of her right to inherit the property of her husband, particularly in cases where they have had no children or have only daughters. In some societies, widows are forced to remarry against their will while there are others that bar widows from remarrying.

In this way, widows undergo numerous circumstances that most of the time they find hard to accept. Despite that, most of them accept family and social diktat killing their own conscience. Mistreatment of widows is a worldwide phenomenon. The only difference is the kind of injustice they are meted out and the type of discrimination they face. Though the Universal Declaration of Human Rights clearly states that no one should be deprived of the basic rights, but in many societies widows have been deprived of their rights either in the name of culture or in the name of religion. Owing to the ever-increasing number of widows and their struggle for survival, individuals and a number of organisations have come forward in support of such hapless women. The motive behind is healing the wounds of the widows by providing financial, moral and psychological support.

Loomba Foundation, an international non-governmental organisation, is one of such organisations which have been working for the welfare of widows worldwide. The foundation launched its campaign on June 23, 2005 for the first time to raise awareness of the plight of widows. The successful campaign drew the attention of the United Nations Organisation. As a result, the UNO passed a resolution in 2010, declaring June 23 as International Widows Day. The day is dedicated to the widows worldwide. According to the foundation, there are around 245 million widows in the world with millions of them leading pathetic lives. Following the recognition by the United Nations Organisation, the issue of widows has been able to draw the attention of the governments. Nepal is not an exception to it.

A number of policies and programmes have been introduced by government aimed at addressing the problems of the single women or widows. The provision of the social security allowance of ₹ 500 per month is one such initiative. The age groups of widows vary. Some are young, some are adults and some are elderly widows. For those who are aged, allowance provided by the government may be of some help but for the others it is paltry. However, it can be taken as a part of their recognition. Besides, there are a number of non-governmental organisations that deal with the issue of widows and single women. The problems and issues of widows are raised seeking needful solutions. In this way, collaborative efforts have been made to tackle the underlying problems. Despite this, the widows continue to suffer. In our context, deprivation of property is one of the most common forms of injustice that a widow undergoes. Apart from that, widows suffer abandonment by the family, mistreatment and public humiliation.

STATUS OF WIDOWS IN AFGHANISTAN

Afghanistan is one of the world's most prolific producers of orphans and widows. The number of widows in Afghanistan is estimated to be from 600,000 to two million (2M), one of the highest in the world when analysed against the overall number of Afghan females falling within the reproductive age bracket of 15 to 49 years old. Some 30 to 50 thousand of them are said to be residing in the capital city ofKabul and the rest are scattered elsewhere in the country. On the average, they were widowed at a very young age of 20 to 30 years old — mainly as a consequence of early marriage, betrothal to exceedingly old men, deaths of men in armed conflict, and the generally low life expectancy of Afghans (45 years old).

A typical Afghan widow is around 35 years old. Around 94 percent of them are illiterate and an estimated 90 percent have 3 to 8 children/off springs. The average period within which a woman remains a widow in Afghanistan is 10 years. Given the lack of employable skills, dire economic options, poor social support, stigmatization, and the extremely low status of women in society, Afghan widows and their families wallow in extreme deprivation and are among the most vulnerable citizens of the country. Studies reveal that they are at least five times more prone to oppression, malnutrition and violence.

ISSUES AND CHALLENGES

Widowhood in Afghanistan is like a death sentence, or worse. A 2006 report of UNIFEM indicates that 65 percent of the widows living in Kabul had attempted to commit suicide at least once. Their dismal situation is an outcome of interlinked socio-cultural, economic, political, and human development factors that evolved through long period of political rifts and armed conflict, giving birth to a life that is perhaps the worst possible the world could imagine for widows, to wit:

Negative Socio-cultural Factors

Afghanistan is a highly patriarchal society whose norms, beliefs, practices and traditions are shaped by extremist values of fundamentalists which regard women as less than a human being. Afghan women are generally viewed as 'un-equals' whose existence is circumscribed by their relationships with men and have no social identity of their own. Before marriage, they are daughters to their fathers; and once married, they assume the identity of a wife to their husband. When a husband dies, the wife's life suffers a major de-stabilizing shock as it marks the sudden loss of her social identity, source of protection and support, and basis for functioning in society.

Widowhood in Afghanistan is like a 'death sentence' because it instantly changes society's perception and attitude towards a widow as a harbinger of disgrace and bad luck, a liability, a drain to family resources, and no more than an economic object whose energies could be exploited in slave-like manner. Afghan widows are either taken back by their original family or the relatives of their husband. Otherwise, they wallow in wretchedness as street beggars. For many widows, death is a sweeter option.

Among the major factors that contribute to the disadvantage of Afghan widows, negative socio-cultural factors are the most pernicious, most recalcitrant, and most difficult to address. As long as society is dominated by men with values that are antithetical to democracy, human rights and gender equality, Afghan widows' empowerment would remain arduous and elusive.

Economic Factors

Afghanistan is one of the least developed countries of the world with a 35.8 per cent national poverty rate and a Poverty Gap Index of 7.9. One third of urban residents require continuous food assistance and the figure is much higher for rural areas where 80 percent of the population lives. Serious economic deprivation exacerbates the social disadvantage of widows. Under the custody of her ex-husband's family, a widow is most likely abused as overworked, unpaid, and under-fed economic laborers and household slaves. Often, they are sexually violated and subjected to physical violence. In the household competition for very scarce economic resources, and given the overall lack of economic opportunities in the country, many widows are left with marginal or no resources at all to subsist in humanely possible way. Combined with negative socio-cultural factors that look at widows as passive victims, general dearth of economic options makes advocacy for widows' empowerment tenuous and unattractive.

Apart from these, it is not unusual for Afghan widows to lose their inheritance entitlements to male in-laws. Denial of property rights - mostly as a result of their limited contributions and control over household income - easily pushes widows and their children to the brink of penury. Without properties, education, skills, and connections, and given society's tight restrictions to Afghan women's mobility in public, it is not unusual for widows to stride into absolute poverty than into economic productivity.

Political Factors

The pursuit of women's empowerment and gender equality in Afghanistan sits in a political time bomb. As the 2014 deadline for the withdrawal of international security support draws to a close, Taliban fighters have started to return to the mainstream of national life and Taliban leaders begin to receive political concessions from government. Against this backdrop, Taliban-style cruelty and criminalities to women have re-surfaced, resulting in increased resurgence of female-directed extra-judicial executions, assassinations of activists, murders, beheadings, and honour killings. Given this context, the plight of Afghan widows will continue to take a back seat. The attention of government to women's empowerment has dramatically declined and this is not about to change in the next five years. Except for Article 53 of the Constitution, which articulates a guarantee that *the rights and privileges as well as assistance to women without caretakers and needy orphans will be ensured,* Afghanistan does not have a clear policy on widows.

The National Action Plan for the Women of Afghanistan (NAPWA) recognizes the disadvantage faced by widows and the Afghanistan National Development Strategy explicitly acknowledges that widows are among the most vulnerable people of the country. Yet, all these policy instruments remain un-elaborated and un-implemented. Many of the interventions for widows are done by non-government organisations and international agencies. Due to the enormity of constraints faced by programming in the country, many of the interventions for widows were palliative, un-sustained, and detached from overall priorities of government.

Human Development Factors

Years of war and the Taliban's policy of prohibiting female education left behind a female population that is overwhelmingly illiterate, contributing to the stunting of their potentials to live a full and satisfying life. Thus, Afghan widows are without economic skills, politically disempowered, physically unhealthy, and excluded from the mainstream of social and political lives. Worse, more of them live with emotional trauma due to the terrors of war and the loss of husbands, relatives, properties and social connections.

Under the Ministry of Labour, Social Affairs, Martyrs and Disabled, widows and their families receive welfare support. However, such interventions do not represent an empowering and enduring response to the situation. There are evidences, however, that appropriate interventions enable Afghan widows to rise above their dismal situation. A number of international organisations and NGOs implemented projects whose results proved that an integrated approach to widow empowerment, such as skills development, building of support groups, livelihood opportunities, counseling, and welfare support restore their social functioning and enable them to get out of their sordid predicament.

OPTIONS

We agree that the initiative to call for a separate UN resolution on the empowerment of widows all over the world stands as the most ideal broad step at the moment. Afghan women will benefit a lot from the surge of international pressure that such resolution would elicit. We have seen from the experience on the CEDAW, Beijing Declaration and Platform for Action and many other international instruments that there is tremendous power in international solidarity. We therefore support this conference and all other conferences leading to such UN resolution and we are ready to do our part in advancing this agenda in every way possible.

Toward this end, we will mobilize our networks, lobby with our government and our international NGOs and diplomatic corps in our country, educate the public about the plight of widows, prepare case studies and gather statistics, and work with media to bring widows' concerns into the realm of public policy. Solidarity and consolidated power will stand as our best defence against the indifference of policy and decision makers. In Afghanistan, there are splintered groups of widows that we could be brought together and empowered to pursue varied forms of advocacy. They need to be engaged, positioned in the frontline, and given skills to speak for themselves and move institutions and officials to action. They need to be recognised as main stakeholders of the peace process and must have a voice on the terms of the peace negotiations. We also need to engage organisations that are dedicated to the empowerment of widows because they have the experiences, resources and knowledge that could bolster our activism.

The widows' network should be aided in adopting a common platform and framework that could be pursued at the international, regional and country levels beginning with very strategic and foundational measures such as institutionalisation of national mechanism dedicated to widows' empowerment, conduct of studies on the situation of widows, adoption of a national law on widows, and allocation of specific funds/budgets for programmes and projects promoting widows' empowerment. Since the plight of widows is differentiated by contexts, we need to be able to harness the resources and support of the more advantaged widows to help uplift the situation of those who are not, in the spirit of global solidarity and sisterhood.

Unfortunately, Afghanistan will have to pursue the advocacy for widows' empowerment in a highly volatile and challenged political context. This is not to say, nevertheless, that we cannot do anything. Back home, there are options that we will try to pursue to strengthen the global campaign for widows' empowerment, such as:

Establishing Baseline Information on Widows

It is important to have a more accurate picture of widowhood in our country because these will inform advocacy, policy making and programming. We will therefore try to put together all existing statistics and studies on Afghan widows, their needs and issues, the strengths and weaknesses of policy and programme measures, available mainstream resources that could be channeled to widows and factors that stand in the way of uplifting their situation, as well as researches and case studies about their lives. Based on this, we will develop and disseminate information materials that could be used by media and other partners in our advocacy and we will input our baseline information to any regional, sub-regional or global database that will be established in this regard;

Multiplying Champions and Raising Accountability for Widows' Empowerment

We find it important to increase the number of influential people who could champion the rights of widows in the realms of law, policy, and action. We need to go beyond ourselves and get other people to own the issues of Afghan widows and recognise that they have a role in transforming their lives. If the government recognises its responsibilities to the casualties of war, it is equally responsible in rebuilding the lives that were destroyed because of war. We will therefore facilitate dialogues among legislators, policy makers and widows to generate organic information that could support policy and action and to motivate as many 'influentials' as possible to advance widows' empowerment. Along this line, we will facilitate the drafting of a law on widows and use it as centerpiece agenda for such dialogues. We will also bring together institutions and organisations mandated to improve the lives of widow to reflect on the effectiveness of their interventions and work together for greater impacts and synergy.

Lobbying for Greater Resources for Widows

Even if the government is engaged in a peace process, the reality is that attacks and killings by Talibans continue. This means more threats of widowhood for wives, and greater number of children running the risk of becoming orphans. We believe that the time to allocate funds for veterans, widows and orphans is not after the war but before the war. The budget for the peace process of my country needs to be re-examined to ensure adequate and timely release of financial and other resources for widows and orphans. If the government is giving huge sums of money to returning Talibans who were responsible for the destruction of many lives, it should give equally huge amount of money to those whose lives were ruined by war. This is a platform that we will advocate with high level candidates in the coming elections and an argument that we will use to motivate more women to run for public office.

WIDOW CONSERVATION

Widow Conservation is a term referring to a practice in Protestant Europe in the early modern age, when the widow of a parish vicar was remarried to her husband's successor to ensure her economical support. This practice was common in particularly Scandinavia (*Änkekonservering*) and the Protestant parts of Germany (*Konservierung von Pfarrwitwen*). At the introduction of the Protestant Reformation, the priests were allowed to marry. However, as the priests did not own the vicarage and property attached to his profession, his spouse and issue were left without means to support themselves after his death. The future support of the widows and children of vicars thereby became a concern for the various churches.

The most common solution was that the successor of a vicar married the widow (or perhaps the daughter) of his predecessor, thereby "conserving" her.

WIDOW CONSERVATION BY COUNTRY

Brandenburg

In Mark Brandenburg, Widow Conservation was common practice in the 17th-century. In 1698, Frederick III of Brandenburg banned Widow conservation by the *Juramentum simoniae* as being a form of purchase of the vicarage office.

East Prussia

Widow Conservation was common practice in East Prussia. The practice is here the centre of the legend of *Ännchen von Tharau*, which was inspired by the widow conservated vicars wife Anna Neander (1615-1689).

Mecklenburg

The first widow conservation of the kind is documented from 1551, and by 1580, it had became a common practice, which was recommended by the church order of 1602. By 1704, one third of all vicars' wives were the widow of the predecessor of her spouse.

From 1623 onward, however, there was also an increasing number of widow funds, which made widow conservation more unnecessary while the widow funds grew. The last widow conservation took place in the mid 19th-century.

Pomerania

In Pomerania, the church synod of 1545 saw no other choice but to tolerate the practice, and in 1572, the conservation of the widow or daughter of a vicar was officially declared the duty of his successor. An attempt to replace it with a dowry provided by the congregations in 1575 failed.

During the 18th-century, the practice started to decrease because of more alternatives, such as the foundation of a fund for vicars widows in Swedish Pomerania in 1775.

Saxony

In the Duchy of Saxony, a strong policy to prevent widow conservation was enforced already when it occurred in the 16th-century, and attempts of having a successor of a vicar marry the widow or daughter of his predecessor were actually prevented and contested when it did occur.

Sweden and Finland

In Sweden and Finland (then a Swedish province), the parish vicars was given permission to marry after the protestant reformation of 1527. The support of vicar's widows quickly became a concern. After the death of a vicar, his widow was entitled to a *Nådeår* (Year of Grace) and live on the vicarage while preparing support for her and her children. During that year, the parish were to select the next vicar.

As the parish and church considered it their duty to support the widow of their former vicar, they normally chose a priest who expressed himself willing to marry the widow of his predecessor.

The vicar's widow herself also seem to have played a part in electing the next vicar by using the influence she had in the parish by her position as vicar's wife. Another way to arrange the support of the widow was for the next vicar to marry her adult daughter, if she had one, or indeed that the son of a vicar succeeded him.

In the church order of 1571, the rules stated that the son or the son-in-law of the former vicar were to be considered first when a new parish vicar were chosen. During the 17th-century, the widow conservation were common practice and the majority of the vicar's wives were the widow or daughter of her husband's predecessor. Between 1686 and 1739, the church law clearly stated that when a new parish vicar were to be employed, the candidates who expressed themselves willing to marry the widow or daughter of his predecessor should be given the place before other candidates.

This statue was abolished in 1739, when the authorities started to place the education of the vicars the main qualification, but the practice continued the entire 18th-century, as the parishes continued to regard it their responsibility to support the vicar's wives, who were often locals and had a strong position in their parishes.

By the end of the 18th-century and the beginning of the 19th-century, however, the Widow Conservation quickly came of use. The reasons were several: a different view upon marriage as more of a love union than a practical arrangement; that the education of the candidates, who were less often the son's of vicars, had became more important; and because the recently established retirement funds for vicar's widows which were founded made the solution less needed. During the 19th-century, widow conservation was hardly longer existent.

There were also parishes which were formally inherited this way. In 1591, King John III of Sweden granted the Annerstad parish in Småland to vicar Georgius Marci, to be inherited on both the male and female line by his descendants: either by a son, or by a successor married to a daughter or a widow of his predecessor.

Upon the death of Marci in 1613, his parish was inherited by his son-in-law by marriage to his daughter, Kerstin Marca (1585-1653), who has been referred to as the first Swedish female to have formally inherited the right to a vicar's parish: the Annerstad parish was on several occasions inherited by females in the same fashion, such as for example by Gunilla Osængius in 1685, until the year of 1780, when king Gustav III of Sweden refused the request of a vicars candidate to marry the twelve year old daughter of the recently deceased vicar Anders Osængius.

2

The Practice of Sati

INTRODUCTION TO SATI

In this age of ascending feminism and focus on equality and human rights, it is difficult to assimilate the Hindu practice of sati, the burning to death of a widow on her husband's funeral pyre, into our modern world. Indeed, the practice is outlawed and illegal in today's India, yet it occurs up to the present day and is still regarded by some Hindus as the ultimate form of womanly devotion and sacrifice.

Sati (also called suttee) is the practice among some Hindu communities by which a recently widowed woman either voluntarily or by use of force or coercion commits suicide as a result of her husband's death. The best known form of sati is when a woman burns to death on her husband's funeral pyre. However other forms of sati exist, including being buried alive with the husband's corpse and drowning.

The term Sati is derived from the original name of the goddess Sati, also known as Dakshayani, who self-immolated because she was unable to bear her father Daksha's humiliation of her (living) husband Shiva. Sati as practice is first mentioned in 510 CCE, when a stele commemorating such an incident was erected at Eran, an ancient city in the modern state of Madhya Pradesh. The custom began to grow in popularity as evidenced by the number of stones placed to commemorate satis, particularly in southern India and amongst the higher castes of Indian society, despite the fact that the Brahmins originally condemned the practice (Auboyer 2002). Over the centuries the custom died out in the south only to become prevalent in the north, particularly in the states of Rajasthan and Bengal. While comprehensive data are lacking across India and through the ages, the British East India Company recorded that the total figure of known occurrences for the period 1813 - 1828 was 8,135; another source gives the number of 7,941 from 1815 - 1828, an average of 618 documented incidents per year. However, these numbers are likely to grossly underestimate the real number of satis as in 1823, 575 women performed sati in the state of Bengal alone.

Historically, the practice of sati was to be found among many castes and at every social level, chosen by or for both uneducated and the highest ranking women of the times. The common deciding factor was often ownership of wealth or property, since all possessions of the widow devolved to the husband's family upon her death. In a country that shunned widows, sati was considered the highest expression of wifely devotion to a dead husband. It was deemed an act of peerless piety and was said to purge her of all her sins, release her from the cycle of birth and rebirth and ensure salvation for her dead husband and the seven generations that followed her.

Because its proponents lauded it as the required conduct of righteous women, it was not considered to be suicide, otherwise banned or discouraged by Hindu scripture. Sati also carried romantic associations which some were at apparent pains to amplify. Stein (1978) states "The widow on her way to the pyre was the object (for once) of all public attention...Endowed with the gift of prophecy and the power to cure and bless, she was immolated amid great fanfare, with great veneration".

Only if she was virtuous and pious would she be worthy of being sacrificed; consequently being burned or being seen as a failed wife were often her only choices. Indeed, the very reference to the widow from the point at which she decided to become a "Sati" (Chaste One) removed any further personal reference to her as an individual and elevated her to a remote and untouchable context.

It is little wonder that women growing up in a culture in which they were so little valued as individuals considered it the only way for a good wife to behave. The alternative, anyway, was not appealing. After the death of a husband an Hindi widow was expected to live the life of an aesthetic, renouncing all social activities, shaving her head, eating only boiled rice and sleeping on thin coarse matting. To many, death may have been preferable, especially for those who were still girls themselves when their husband's died.

Over the centuries, many of India's inhabitants have disagreed with the practice of sati. Since its very foundation the Sikh religion has explicitly prohibited it. Sati was regarded as a barbaric practice by the Islamic rulers of the Mogul period, and many tried to halt the custom with laws and edicts banning the practice. Many Hindu scholars have argued against sati, calling it "as suicide, and...a pointless and futile act"; both abolitionists and promoters of sati use Hindu scripture as justification of their position.

At the end of the 18th Century, the influx of Europeans into India meant that the practice of sati was being scrutinized as never before; missionaries, travelers and civil servants alike condemned official Raj tolerance of the "dreadful practice" and called for its end. In 1827 the Governor-General of India, Lord Bentinck, finally outlawed the custom in its entirety, claiming it had no sound theological basis. James also notes that the outlawing of sati practice was considered the first direct affront to Indian religious beliefs and therefore contributed to the end of the British Raj. However the common people felt about it, many Indian rulers of the 19th century welcomed its abolition.

Most recorded instances of sati during the 1800's were described as "voluntary" acts of courage and devotion, a conviction that sati advocates continue to promote to this day. At the very least, women committing sati were encouraged by priests (who received the best item from the women's possessions as payment), the relatives of both families (who received all the women's remaining possessions and untold blessings) and by general peer pressure. However it appears that at least in some recorded cases the women were drugged.

In "An Account of a Woman Burning Herself, By an Officer," which appeared in the Calcutta Gazette in 1785, the observer describes the woman as likely under the influence of bhang (marijuana) or opium but otherwise "unruffled." After she was lifted upon the pyre, she "laid herself down by her deceased husband, with her arms about his neck.

Two people immediately passed a rope twice across the bodies, and fastened it so tight to the stakes that it would have effectually prevented her from rising had she attempted".

Once the reality of burning to death became obvious, many women tried to escape their fate. Measures and implements were put into place to ensure that they could not. Edward Thompson wrote that a woman "was often bound to the corpse with cords, or both bodies were fastened down with long bamboo poles curving over them like a wooden coverlet, or weighted down by logs." These poles were continuously wetted down to prevent them from burning and the widow from escaping.

If she did manage to escape, she and her relatives were ostracized by society, as is related by the redoubtable Fanny Parkes, wife of a minor British civil servant during the early 1800's, who gives a frank eyewitness account in 1823 of a sati burning and the consequences:

A rich baniya, a corn chandler, whose house was near the gate of our grounds, departed this life; he was an Hindu. On the 7th of November, the natives in the bazaar were making a great noise with their tom-toms, drums, and other discordant musical instruments, rejoicing that his widow had determined to perform sati, *i.e.*, to burn on his funeral-pile.

The [English] magistrate sent for the woman, used every argument to dissuade her, and offered her money. Her only answer was dashing her head on the floor, and saying, 'If you will not let me burn with my husband, I will hang myself in your court of justice.' Theshastras say, The prayers and imprecations of a sati are never uttered in vain; the great gods themselves cannot listen to them unmoved.'

If a widow touches either food or water from the time her husband expires until she ascends the pile, she cannot, by Hindu law, be burned with the body; therefore the magistrate kept the corpse forty-eight hours, in the hope that hunger would compel the woman to eat. Guards were set over her, but she never touched anything. My husband accompanied the magistrate to see the sati: about five thousand people were collected together on the banks of the Ganges: the pile was then built, and the putrid body placed upon it; the magistrate stationed guards to prevent the people from approaching it. After having bathed in the river, the widow lighted a brand, walked round the pile, set it on fire, and then mounted cheerfully: the flame caught and blazed up instantly; she sat down, placing the head of the corpse on her lap, and repeated several times the usual form,'Ram, Ram, sati; Ram, Ram, sati;' *i.e.*, 'God, God, I am chaste.'

As the wind drove the fierce fire upon her, she shook her arms and limbs as if in agony; at length she started up and approached the side to escape. An Hindu, one of the police who had been placed near the pile to see she had fair play, and should not be burned by force, raised his sword to strike her, and the poor wretch shrank back into the flames. The magistrate seized and committed him to prison. The woman again approached the side of the blazing pile, sprang fairly out, and ran into the Ganges, which was within a few yards. When the crowd and the brothers of the dead man saw this, they called out, 'Cut her down, knock her on the head with a bamboo; tie her hands and feet, and throw her in again' and rushed down to execute their murderous intentions, when the gentlemen and the police drove them back.

The woman drank some water, and having extinguished the fire on her red garment, said she would mount the pile again and be burned.

The magistrate placed his hand on her shoulder (which rendered her impure), and said, 'By your own law, having once quitted the pile you cannot ascend again; I forbid it. You are now an outcast from the Hindus, but I will take charge of you, the [East India] Company will protect you, and you shall never want food or clothing.'

He then sent her, in a palanquin, under a guard, to the hospital. The crowd made way, shrinking from her with signs of horror, but returned peaceably to their homes: the Hindus annoyed at her escape, and the Musulmans saying, 'It was better that she should escape, but it was a pity we should have lost the tamasha (amusement) of seeing her burnt to death.'

Had not the magistrate and the English gentlemen been present, the Hindus would have cut her down when she attempted to quit the fire; or had she leapt out, would have thrown her in again, and have said, 'She performed sati of her own accord, how couldwe make her? It was the will of God.'... 'What good will burning do you?' asked a bystander. She replied, 'The women of my husband's family have all been satis, why should I bring disgrace upon them? I shall go to heaven, and afterwards reappear on earth, and be married to a very rich man.' She was about twenty or twenty-five years of age, and possessed of some property, for the sake of which her relatives wished to put her out of the world.

As a result of being outlawed, sati began to decline in the 19th Century but persisted in parts of India, particularly Rajasthan, a state with one of the lowest literacy rates in India. Chimnabai, wife of Sayajirao Gaekwad III, Maharaja of Baroda from 1875 to 1939, was a tireless campaigner for the rights of Indian women. In 1927 in a speech at the first All-India Women's Conference she called sati a curse, but also noted that the practice no longer posed a great risk to Indian women, unlike the practices of girl-child marriage and the institution of purdah.

In the late 1950's, a royal sati took place. Performed in Jodhpur by Sugankunverba, the widow of Brigadier Jabbar Singh Sisodia, her act of self-immolation occurred illegally and supposedly in secret. The Maharani Padmavati Gaekwad of Baroda, her close friend, provided this account of her death in 1984:

About a month before he died she stopped eating and drinking. She went about her household chores, looked after her husband and nursed him, but without letting on she got together all the things required for the last rites. I used to go to their house to cheer them up and one evening just a little before sun-down as I drove into the compound, I heard this very deep chanting of Ram-Ram as if coming from a deep, echoing chasm. He had passed away two minutes earlier and she had already announced that she was going to commit sati when he was cremated at sunrise.

While they attended to his body she went to her bathroom, had a bath and put on the brand new clothes that she had stored in her trunk. For sati we don't wear widow's clothes but wedding clothes, with the ivory bangles and everything.

The colour she chose was a sort of light pink calledsaptalu, which none of the wives of the Sisodias can now wear because they now do puja to that colour. When she had dressed she sat with her husband's head on her lap all night. Twice his body perspired and twice she wiped it down saying, 'Why are you so impatient, I am coming with you.

Be calm. The sun's first rays are still to come.' Morning came and her devar arrived, her husband's brother who was going to perform the last rites. When he doubted her intentions she got up and sat over the lamp which they kept burning near the dead body. She fanned the flames with the hem of her sari and sat there for five minutes until he said, 'I'm satisfied.' Now normally when a sati goes to the pyre she is accompanied by a procession, but the word had spread like wildfire through the whole city and people started gathering. So she said, 'We can't walk, bring cars and a truck,' and in this way they avoided the police who were waiting at the entrance to the big burning ghat.

She had sent for me, but I didn't get the message and got there late and by that time the flames had got too high for me to see her - but I heard her voice saying 'Ram-Ram', which never stopped for a second until she died. She is worshipped today not only by Rajputs but by everybody and so many artis and bhqjans (devotional songs) have been composed about her, and her funeral pyre burnt for almost six months non-stop with all the coconuts that people kept putting on it.

There are many interesting points about this particular sati event. The woman was obviously deeply attached to her husband and devastated at his death. However no attempt was made to dissuade the woman from committing suicide; indeed her brother-in-law was concerned only with whether she would go through with it on the day and not bring shame to the family name. While several thousand people manage to catch wind of the event and attend the immolation, the authorities did absolutely nothing to prevent it, despite its illegal status. And at least up to the mid 1980's when this account was recorded, Sugankunverba was still regarded as a martyr, idolized in poems and songs and worshiped as a saint by the women of her family. If the Indian authorities were serious about stamping out sati altogether, then well publicized voluntary satis such as this one did nothing to remove any lingering glamour associated with the act.

In today's India, sati is rarely discussed openly. Ostensibly, it is considered a shameful practice, particularly by the burgeoning middle class, long outlawed and of interest only as a minor historical footnote. And yet the practice continues, particularly in rural areas of India, with over forty documented cases occurring since the 1950's (The Team, 2006), approximately one recorded incidence per year, with some anecdotal evidence to suggest that there are a much greater number of sucessful and unsuccessful sati attempts. Indeed, pro-sati advocates, generally men, demand the right to commit, worship, and propagate sati. One well documented case, that of 18-year old Roop Kanwar, occurred in 1987 at the village Deorala in Rajasthan.

Eyewitness reports of the incident present conflicting stories about the voluntariness of her death: that she was dragged from a shed in which she had been hiding, that she was sedated, that she herself told her brother-in-law to light the pyre when she was ready. Several thousand people managed to attend the event, after which she was hailed as a "pure mother". Devotees from all over India flocked to her shrine to pay homage, bringing huge revenues and status to the village.

The event produced a public outcry in urban centres and served to pit a modern Indian ideology against a very traditional one. After Kanwar's death, the Sati Dharma Raksha Samti or Committee for the Defence of the Religion of Sati was formed, run and supported by educated young Rajput men who stated that sati was a "fundamental part of their traditions; a refusal to legitimize sati, they said, was a deliberate attempt to marginalize the Rajputs". Kanwar's sati led to the creation of state level laws to prevent the occurrence and glorification of future incidents and the creation of the central Indian government's The Commission of Sati (Prevention) Act 1987. However, of the 56 people charged with her murder, participation in her murder or glorification of her murder during two separate investigations, all were subsequently acquitted.

Other incidents of sati continue to take place. Fifty-five year old Charan Shah's self-immolation in 1999 at Satpura village in Uttar Pradesh is shrouded in mystery as witnesses refused to co-operate with official investigations. Shah's suicide is notable because it led to the publication of a vitriolic article apparently justifying the practice of sati and demanding the repeal of the Commission of Sati (Prevention) Act, by a respected female academic, Madhu Kishwar (published in Manushi, Issue 115). In May 2006, Vidyawati, a 35-year-old woman allegedly jumped into the funeral pyre of her husband in Rari-Bujurg Village, Uttar Pradesh. In August 2006, Janakrani, a 40-year-old woman, died on the funeral pyre of her husband in Sagar district. In October 2008, a 75-year-old woman committed sati by jumping into her 80-year-old husband's funeral pyre at Checher in Raipur.

Following public outcries after each instance there have been various reforms passed which now make it illegal even to be a bystander at a sati event. Other measures include efforts to stop the glorification of the victims, including the erection of shrines over their ashes, the encouragement of pilgrimages to the site of the pyre and the derivation of any income from such sites and pilgrims. However, it must be recognised that the tradition of sati in India is very complex indeed. Despite the existence of state and country-wide laws prohibiting the act and its glorification, incidents continue to occur every year and may be on the increase. As one Indian feminist notes, these occurrences confirm that deeply held and deeply cherished norms cannot be changed simply by enacting laws.

ON THE HISTORY OF SATI: ROOTS AND RUMORS

The ritual of Sati (or Suttee) is the killing a favorite wife on her husband's grave. It is not exclusively an Indian ritual but has been practiced in many parts of the world such as China, Oceania, Africa and Scandinavia from where it arrived in India only late.

While often seen as a part of the Hindu tradition by outsiders, actually there is no statement in the classical Hindu scriptures concerning Sati. On the contrary, according to the funeral hymns in Rigveda (ii), there is a ceremony of a widow sleeping next to the corpse of her dead husband and then being allowed to marry anyone she pleases.

According to some sources, the practice of Sati came to India through the Kushans (iii) in 1 A.D. and was practiced by the Rajputs (iv), a warring tribe living in the north-western parts of India who were in constant battle amongst themselves and the Moslems. An interesting explanation for their practice of Sati is that due to the constant warfare many young men were killed and the young widows were considered a danger to the moral stability of society. The introduction of Sati was thus an extreme measure of eliminating them. (The Moslems, who had the same problem of young widows solved it by allowing polygamous marriages).

Sati, which has never been practiced in Southern India, was abolished by the British in India in 1829 and classified as a criminal offence.

SATI AS A FORM OF SUICIDE

By definition, suicide is the deliberate taking of one's own life. Ideally it is an individual's conscious decision, but as soon as it is a behaviour judged by culture or tradition, the line between social pressure and personal motivation begins to blur. Depending on the time and place, suicide may be regarded as a heroic deed or condemned by religious and civil authorities.

According to the Indian Sati ritual, the widow follows her deceased husband onto the pyre. The following aspects show the similarities between Sati and a comparable Viking Age practice of sacrificing a widow and thus illustrate that the basic concept of this custom lies beyond the traditional Indian context:

(1) A considerable amount of time passes between the death of the man and the cremation of the woman, who die at the funeral ceremonylater
(2) The wives and concubines are allowed to choose whether or not they will accompany their husband or master, but once the decision is made they may not change their minds
(3) The woman who volunteers to die is pampered and treated as a privileged person until the day of (her) sacrifice
(4) The victim is encouraged to face her death by emphasizing her role as wife/concubine, how much she desires to be with the man, and also by the use of calming or narcotic drugs to prevent resistance
(5) Sacrifice or release of birds which may represent the soul or journey of the spirit
(6) An old woman or old women accompany the girl(s)(women) to the Pyre and instruct/encourage/and even sacrifice the girls(women).

Sati is a form of suicide closely related to honour: in committing suicide, the widow not just shows ultimate loyality to her deceased husband, but also transforms herself into a heroine, adding even more to the honour of her husband's family.

However, it is also interesting examinating the aspect of guilt: does the widow feel guilty for her husband's early deceasing? Her Sati then would be also standing in a tradition where suicide was offered to a favored few to save one's face. Hara-Kiri in traditional Japanese society is an example therefore, as it was seen as the appropriate moral course of action for a person who otherwise faced the loss of his honour.

On the other hand the practice of Sati must also be seen under the sociological aspects mentioned earlier, where young widows not just presented a danger to moral stability but were also an additional burden to the family. Because they were not supposed to work outside their homes (which would dishonor the family) they had no means of earning their living. So Sati also shows similarities to suicides as self-regulatory mechanism among pre-industrial peoples where members of society who could no longer contribute to their own subsistence committed self-murder for the welfare of the group. Traditionally these were the elderly; if a young woman acts the same way within her social context it just shows as how little her worth for the group is considered.

Why I choose Sati

What interests me about Sati is that it is in a way a point of culmination; for me it is metaphor for a society, that gives no worth to a woman as an individual, but rather sees her as a man's extension or possession, who's right to live vanishes with the man's passing away. Because the ritual of Sati it is of such cruel and horrendous nature, I choose it as the highest and most symbolic climax of this attitude towards women.

We may easily fall into the attitude of seeing Sati as a exotic however atrocious ritual of a remote society that has nothing to do with us and our culture. But, understanding it as an icon, for me it symbolizes concepts of honour and guilt as well as attitudes towards women that very well exist within our own, including western, industrialized societies.

What is the basic idea of Sati other than a woman defining herself (or rather being defined) exclusively through her relationship to her husband, while forgetting about herself as an individual human being? From this point of view it is a cruel logic that as soon as the husband's life is over, her own life must be over as well, and thus creating the urge to follow him onto the pyre, again adding to his honour.

While this final step is not taken in Western societies, very many women adopt attitudes of a striking similarity to their Indian sisters regarding their own perception as individuals; they sacrifice their life and individuality on the altar of marriage and a husband's career and family and while negating professional success define they themselves to a huge extent through their husband.

And a last questions arise for me: to what extent does the practice of Sati involve the free decision of a free individual? To what extent can an individual ever be free when it is born into a rigid society with rigid attitudes and behavioral codexes? Any individual always stands before the decision to either obey to these codexes and thus loose individual freedom, or to rebel against them and leave the group and the protection it may offer.

A woman committing her Sati, thus obeying the group's codex of honour and moral clearly made a decision against personal freedom and for her integration into this very group. However, death is always the big liberator; in stepping over the line (between life and death) voluntarily, she takes the only route towards freedom that has remained for her. Sati thus is truly a point of culmination; in the moment of deepest incarceration into a traditional society's most oppressing moral codexes a door to total liberation is opened.

SATI PRACTICE IN INDIA

Sati refers to a funeral ritual within some Asian communities in which a recently widowed woman immolates herself, typically on the husband's funeral pyre.

Mention of the practice can be dated back to 4th century BCE. While evidence of practice only appears from the 5th - 9th centuries CE. Practice is considered to have been originated within the warrior aristocracy on the Indian subcontinent, gradually gaining in popularity from the 10th century CE to other groups and becoming generally sanctioned/recommended by the doctrines around the 12th century CE. With the military expansions outside of Indian subcontinent, the practice has been attested to have been practiced in a number of localities in Southeast Asia, such as at Indonesia.

The practice was outlawed by the British Raj in 1829 within their own territories in India (the collected statistics from their own regions suggesting an estimated of 500–600 instances of *sati* per year), followed up by laws in the same directions by the authorities in the princely states of India in the ensuing decades, with a general ban for the whole of India issued by Queen Victoria in 1861. InNepal, *sati* was not banned until 1920. The Indian Sati Prevention Act from 1987 further criminalizing any type of aiding, abetting, and even the glorifying of *sati* practice.

ETYMOLOGY AND USAGE

The term is derived from the name of the goddess Sati, also known as Dakshayani, who self-immolated because she was unable to bear her father Daksha's humiliation to her husband Shiva.

The term *sati* was originally interpreted as "chaste woman". *Sati* appears in both Hindi and Sanskrit texts, where it is synonymous with "good wife", the term *suttee* was commonly used by Anglo-Indian English writers. *Sati* designates therefore originally the *woman*, rather than the rite; the rite itself having technical names such assahagamana ("going with") or sahamarana ("dying with"). Anvahorana ("ascension" to the pyre) is occasionally met, as well as satidaha as terms to designate the process.Satipratha is also, on occasion, used as a term signifying the custom of burning widows alive. Two other terms closely connected to *sati* are sativrata and satimata. *Sativrata*denotes the woman who, after her husband's death, has made the formal vow, *vrat*, to burn herself on his pyre. After her death on the pyre, she achieves the venerated status as a *satimata*

The Commission of Sati (Prevention) Act, 1987 Part I, Section 2(c) defines *sati* as the act or rite itself.

HISTORY

ORIGINS AND COMPARISONS

Earliest Records of Sati

Few reliable records exist of the practice before the time of the Gupta empire, approximately 400 CE. After about this time, instances of *sati* began to be marked by inscribed memorial stones. According to Axel Michaels, the first *clear* proofs of the practice is from Nepal in 464 CE, and in India from 510 CE. In India, the earliest of these memorial stones are found in Sagar, Madhya Pradesh, though the largest collections date from several centuries later, and are found in Rajasthan. These stones, called *devli*, or sati-stones, became shrines to the dead woman, who was treated as an object of reverence and worship. They are most common in western India. According to the Greekgeographer Strabo, Aristobulus of Cassandreia, a Greek historian who travelled to India with the expedition of Alexander the Great, recorded that he had heard that among certain tribes widows were glad to burn along with their husbands. Those who declined to die were disgraced.

A description of *sati* appears in the Greek 1st-century BCE historian Diodorus Siculus's account of the war fought in Iran between two of Alexander the Great's generals,Eumenes of Cardia and Antigonus Monophthalmus. In 317 BCE Eumenes' cosmopolitan army defeated that of Antigonus in the Battle of Paraitakene, among the fallen was one Ceteus, the commander of Eumenes' Indian soldiers. Diodorus writes that Ceteus had been followed on campaign by his two wives, at his funeral the two wives competed for the honour of joining their husband on the pyre. After the older wife was found to be pregnant, Eumenes' generals ruled in favour of the younger. She was led to the pyre crowned in garlands to the hymns of her kinsfolk. The whole army then marched three times around the pyre before it was lit.

According to Diodorus the practice of *sati* started because Indians married for love, unlike the Greeks who favoured marriages arranged by the parents. When inevitably many of these love marriages turned sour, the woman would often poison the husband and find a new lover. To end these murders, a law was therefore instituted that the widow should either join her husband in death or live in perpetual widowhood. Modern historians believe Diodorus' source for this episode was the eyewitness account of the now lost historian Hieronymus of Cardia. Hieronymus' explanation of the origin of *sati* appears to be his own composite, created from a variety of Indian traditions and practices to form a moral lesson upholding traditional Greek values.

In the 1886 published Hobson-Jobson, Henry Yule and Arthur Coke Burnell compiled a few dozen excerpts of descriptions of *sati* ranging from 4th century BCE into the 1870s CE.

Practice of Sati in Hindu-Influenced Cultures outside Indian Subcontinent

The early 14th-century traveller Odoric of Pordenone mentions that in the Hindu Kingdom of Champa, in nowadays south/central Vietnam, burning widows alive was observed. Anant Altekar mentions that *sati* spread with Hindu migrants to Southeast Asian islands as well, such as to Java, Sumatra and Bali Other Hindu-influenced cultures where reports of *sati* has come are from Cambodia and Mergui in present day Burma (Myanmar). A Chinese pilgrim from the 15th century seems to attest the practice on islands called Ma-i-tung and Ma-i (possibly Belitung (outside Sumatra) and Northern Philippines, respectively)

Burning alive of widows is apparently attested from some parts of China, but one scholar thinks it was imported from India, and was anyhow very rare.

Lastly, historian K.M. de Silva reminds us, when discussing how Christian missionaries approached the situation at Sri Lanka (which has a substantial Hindu minority population); "In Sri Lanka, unlike India, there were no glaring social evils associated with the indigenous religions-no *sati*, (...). There was thus less scope for the social reformer." However, although *sati* was non-existent in the 19th century, earlier Muslim travellers do report that *sati* was performed on the island when a king died. This is, for example, related by 9th century merchantSulaiman al-Tajir, 13th century Zakariya al-Qazwini, 14th century Ibn Batuta, as well as by 13th century Christian traveller Marco Polo

Comparable Rituals in Other Cultures

The sacrifice of widow(s) or a great man's retainers at his death is attested for a number of cultures outside of India. As an example where the widows vied for the honour to die with their common husband, the 5th century BCE historian Herodotus mentions the Krestones tribe among the old Thracians. The woman found to have been held highest in the husband's favour while he lived had her throat slit on his grave, the surviving wives reputedly regarding it is a great shame to have to live on. Citing 6th century CE Procopius from his "Gothic Wars", Edward Gibbon notes that among the Germanic tribe of the Heruli, a widow typically hanged herself upon her husband's tomb. The *strangling* of widows after their husbands' deaths are attested from as disparate cultures as the Natchez people in present day US state Louisiana, to a number of Pacific Islander cultures.

Cases of Burning at Funerals Elsewhere, History and Legends

A well known case is that of the 10th century CE ship burial of the Rus' described by Ibn Fadlan. Here, when a female slave had said she would be willing to die, her body was subsequently burned with her master on the pyre.

Such rituals as widow sacrifice/ widow burning have, presumably, prehistoric roots, and early 20th century pioneering anthropologistJames G. Frazer, for example, thought that the legendary Greek story of Capaneus, whose wife Evadne threw herself on his funeral pyre, might be a relic of an earlier custom of live widow-burning.

Andronovo Culture Versus Vedic Age

The archaeologist Elena Efimovna Kuzmina enlists a number of clear parallels between the burial practices of the ancient Asiatic steppe Andronovo cultures (fl. 1800–1400 BCE) and the Vedic Age). In Kuz^mina's archaeological definition, *sati* is understood as a double burial, the co-cremation of a man and a woman/wife, a feature to be found in both cultures. Kuz^mina further considers that in the Androvo culture and Vedic age, the practice "was never strictly observed and suicide was replaced by a symbolic act".

MODELS FOR THE SPREAD OF SATI

Altekar's Chronology on Spread of Sati

The earlier historian Anant Sadashiv Altekar, in his (1938) *The Position of Women in Hindu Civilization From Prehistoric Times to the Present Day* held the position that the Vedic Age saw an *active discontinuation* of pre-historic burning of widows, on basis that a 1000 BCE funerary custom describes that of *symbolic sati*, where the widow lies down by her deceased husband, but is then bidden to rise again, to enjoy the bliss of children and wealth remaining for her In the following, a brief sketch on the *chronology* on the spread of sati, as proposed by Altekar is given.

According to Altekar, there is no mention of actual *sati* in the period of Brahmana literature (c. 1500–700 BCE), and the later Grhyusutras, roughly composed 600–300 BCE on a number of rituals, but *sati* is not described or mentioned. In fact, what is written about funeral customs, is that the widow is brought back from the funeral pyre, typically by a trusted servant. Altekar also thinks it significant that Gautama Buddha, who castigated customs of *animal* sacrifice, and other customs where pain was inflicted, is entirely silent about burning women alive. Altekar takes these elements as proofs that burning widows alive had long ago died out as a practice. Nor do the authors of the

Dharmasutras (c. 400 BCE – 100 BCE) or Yajnavalkya (c. 100 CE – 300 CE) say anything about it being commendable to burn a widow alive on her husband's funeral pyre. Although we have late fourth century BCE evidence from Greek authors and the Mahabarata for the *existence* of the custom of *sati*, Altekar thinks it did not really begin to grow in popularity prior to 400 CE, by the manner of which it is infrequently mentioned in the Puranas of that time. A very early attested case from 510 CE is that of the wife of Goparaja, who immolated herself, another similar case attested from 606 CE. As the custom grew in popularity, Altekar highlights as determined opponents of this aristocratic custom in particular 7th century poet BâG-abhamm-a, but also 9th century theologian Medhâtithi and 12th century Devana Bhatta. In Altekar's view, their crusades against the custom were largely unsuccessful.

According to Altekar, it is the period c. 700–1100 CE that sees *sati* becoming really widespread in India, in particular in Kashmir As the centuries wore on, Altekar provides a few statistics on the spread of the custom. In Rajputana, a later stronghold for *sati* there are two, possibly three reliably attested cases prior to 1000 CE; for the period from 1200-1600 CE, there are at least 20 such cases. For the Carnatic, we have about 11 inscriptions relative to *sati* from 1000-1400 CE, for 1400-1600 CE, we have 41.

Thus, a main view that Altekar espoused is that the spread of *sati* increased over time (with local variations, for example reductions in territories governed by zealous rulers hostile to the practice), and probably was close to a maximum when the British began to intervene in the first decades of the nineteenth century.

Modern Causative Models on the Spread of Sati

How, when, where and why, the practice of *sati* spread are complex issues as borne out by the extended discussion of Anand Yang, in addition to the above discussion by Altekar. The practice of *sati* is not mentioned in any of the earliest religious texts, and our first *literary* reference is from the fourth century BCE, some 800 years before the evidence by memorial stones begins to appear.

The Vedic Age (1700–500 BCE), is often regarded as a *Golden Age* in terms of rights and the status of women. It is only in times after 500 BCE that a decline in the status of women can be discerned. Although Anand Yang does not give whole-hearted support to the characterisation of the Vedic Age as a *Golden Age*, Yang underlines, and points to general scholarly consensus that a decline in women's status occurred in the times *after* the Vedic Age relative to it. One view on the increase in practice of *sati* says that this is merely a consequence of this decline in the status of women.

However, Yang says it would be to *overstate the equation* to say the increase of *sati* depended solely on this declined status of women (or only reflected it), nor can it explain the uneven *geographical* spread of this practice. Citing Romila

Thapar, Yang notes as additional explanatory factors, "the practice may have originated among societies in flux and become customary among those holding property..Once it was established as a custom associated with the Kshatriyas (i.e, ruling military elite), it would continue to be so among those claiming Kshatriya status as well".

According to one model, as referred to by Yang, taking into account the association of *sati* with the warrior elite in particular, *sati* only became really widespread during the Muslim invasions of India, and the practice of *sati* now acquired an additional meaning as a means to preserve the honour of women whose men had been slain. As S.S.Sashi lays out the argument, "The argument is that the practice came into effect during the Islamic invasion of India, to protect their honour from Muslims who were known to commit mass rape on the women of cities that they could capture successfully."

However, the practice of *sati*, again according to Yang, with reference to the memorial stone evidence, was carried out in appreciable numbers in both western and southern parts of India, and in some areas, it seems to have reached *peak level* of incidence in pre-Islamic times.

Although, therefore, some local patterns directly contradict the theory that Muslim invasions was the uniformly principal factor behind the increase of the practice, it is certainly true that within the period of Muslim-Hindu conflict, Rajputs performed a distinct form of *sati* known as jauhar as a direct response to the onslaught they experienced.

Military conflicts between Hindu states seems to have propelled the practice of *sati* into wider use as well, not just wars between Muslim forces and Hindu states; a period of increase possibly due to such internal infighting roughly datable to the end of the 1st millennium and beginning of the 2nd millennium.

Yang also points to two other processes behind the increase of *sati*. Firstly, that of "Sanskritinization" of the lower class aspirants to higher status, where emulation of the valorized practices of the warrior meant that *sati* became adopted among these aspirants. The second process for spreading *sati* is regarded by Yang to have been crucial, namely that the priestly class, the brahmins began adopting the practice. As Yang puts it, "Surely, with the practice rooted in both the kingly and Brahminical traditions, its constituency must have grown rapidly across spatial and social boundaries".

PRACTICE

ANUMARANA

The term *anumarana* was used for a very similar type of widow burning to *sati*, namely that when a woman learnt of her husband's death and cremation, she let herself be burned alive with his ashes or sandals. The practice of *anumarana* was generally banned by British authorities already in 1826, three years prior to the general ban on *sati*.

Anumarana was also used, particularly in the 11th century CE in north/northwestern India as a term for a practice where servants and followers, not just widows, immolated themselves at the death of their lord.

JAUHAR

The Rajput practice of Jauhar, known from Rajasthan and Madhya Pradesh, was the collective suicide of a community facing certain defeat in a battle against Muslims. It consisted of the mass immolation of women, children, the elderly and the sick, at the same time that their fighting men died in battle. Arvind Sharma believes that these particular conditions must lead to a distinction between *jauhar* and *sati*, and regards jauhar as principally as the result a desire to avoid being captured alive by the invading Muslims, rather than being regarded as the meritorious self-sacrifice of the devoted widow.

Chittor is famous for *jauhar* of Rani Padmini, Rani Karnavati and the wives of Maharana Udai Singh. Controversies exist among modern historians whether the most famous case, that of Rani Padmini in 1301, is mythical, rather than historical. The other two cases from Chittor were, reportedly, from 1535 and 1568, respectively.

ROYAL FUNERALS

Royal funerals sometimes have included the deaths of many wives and concubines. A number of examples of these occur in the history of Rajasthan.

Maharani Raj Rajeshwari Devi of Nepal became regent in 1799 in the name of her son, Girvan Yuddha Bikram Shah Deva, after the abdication of her husband, Rana Bahadur Shah, who became a sanyasi. Her husband returned and took power again in 1804. In 1806 he was assassinated by his brother, and ten days later on 5 May 1806, his widow was forced to commit sati.

SATI PRACTICE WITHIN NON-HINDU COMMUNITIES

Despite the condemnation of the practice by 3rd Guru Guru Amar Das (1479-1554) and the other religious leaders within Sikhism, popularity of the custom spread within Sikh aristocracy. Thus, for example, when the founder of the Sikh Empire Ranjit Singh died in 1839, 4 of his proper wives and 7 of his concubines committed themselves to *sati* When Raja Suchet Singh died in 1844, 310 of his wives and concubines committed *sati*.

Within Jain theology, the practice of sati is clearly condemned as suicide, but even so, in the *Epigraphia Carnatica*, two of the 41 cases of sati in the time period 1400 to 1600 CE are those of Jain women. The low numbers of Jains known to have committed sati, it suggest that the practice was uncommon within this particular community.

In certain areas, the *Muslim* widows had notably carried out the practice. Francis Buchanan-Hamilton in his *Shahabad report* has written about the relative numbers of *sati* cases in the Patna district in Bihar: The annual number of victims may be about 25. The contagion of example has even extended to the Muhammadans. The Portuguese missionaries among the ancient, indigenous Christian community of Saint Thomas Christians said that they never practised *sati*, in contrast to the Hindu nobility in the Tamil Nadu.

STANDARD PROCEDURES OF TRADITIONAL SATI

The act of *sati* is said to exist voluntarily; from the existing accounts, many of these acts did indeed occur voluntarily. The act may have been expected of widows in some communities, and the extent to which social pressures or expectations constitute compulsion has been much debated in modern times. However, there were also instances where the wish of the widow to commit *sati* was not welcomed by others, and where efforts were made to prevent the death. Accounts describe numerous variants in the sati ritual. The majority of accounts describe the woman seated or lying down on the funeral pyre beside her dead husband. Many other accounts describe women walking or jumping into the flames after the fire had been lit, and some describe women seating themselves on the funeral pyre and then lighting it themselves.

Variations in Procedure

Although *sati* is typically thought of as consisting of the procedure that the widow is being placed, or enters, or jumps, upon the funeral *pyre* of her husband, slight variations in funeral practice have been reported here as well, for different regions. For example, the mid-17th century traveller Tavernier claims that in some regions, the *sati* occurred by construction of a small *hut*, within which the widow and her husband were burnt, while in other regions, a *pit* was dug, in which the husband's corpse was placed along with flammable materials, into which the widow jumped after the fire had started. In mid-nineteenth century Lombok, an island in today's Indonesia, the local Balinese aristocracy practiced widow sacrifice on occasion; but only widows of *royal* descent could burn themselves alive (others were stabbed to death by a kris knife first). At Lombok, a high bamboo platform was erected in front of the fire, and when the flames were at their strongest, the widow climbed up the platform, and dived into the fire.

Live Burials

In some Hindu communities, it is conventional to bury the dead, rather than cremating them, for example within the minority Pranami sect centered around the Panna district inMadhya Pradesh. Self-sacrifice with the widow being buried alive beside her husband has also been attested, in ceremonies with many of the elements similar to those found within rituals of immolation. As an example of how European travellers have reported upon this particular practice of a widow's self-sacrifice by means of live burial, the 17th century French traveller and gem merchant Jean Baptiste Tavernier gave the following account:

In most places upon the Coast of Coromandel, the Women are not burnt with their deceas'd Husbands, but they are buried alive with them in holes which theBramins make a foot deeper than the tallness of the man and woman. Usually they chuse a Sandy place; so that when the man and woman both let down together, all the Company with Baskets of Sand fill up the hole about half a foot higher than the surface of the ground, after which they jump and dance upon it, till they believe the woman to be stiff'd

The 18th century painter Balthazar Solvyns is another witness of the ritual of being buried alive beside the deceased husband, although he specifies this as limited as a caste distinction within the territories such as Orissa, rather than being a general distinctive feature within a particular geographical region that Tavernier recounts. Solvyns gives expression to an inescapable sense of admiration of the woman who chooses to be buried alive, though he regards the whole rite as "barbarous":

We can not refuse our pity to the poor Hindoo women who are sacrificed to this ancient and barbarous custom; but their courage, firmness, and resignation, entitles them to some share of admiration. While their husband lives they are slaves, when he dies they must be ready to resign in the most cruel manner a life of which they never tasted the enjoyments. In no part of the universe are women born to so dismal a prospect.

Minor variations in how live burial was conducted is also reported. In a letter from 1653 Thanjavur, the Jesuit friar Balthazar da Costa says the woman was buried, earth was shuffled in until it reached her neck, whereupon she was strangled.

Compulsion

Sati is often described as voluntary, although in some cases it may have been forced. In one narrative account, the widow appears to have been drugged either with bhang oropium and was tied to the pyre to keep her from fleeing after the fire was lit. In their eagerness British local press of the time proffered several accounts of alleged forcing of the woman. As an example of this, Calcutta Review published accounts as the following one:

In 1822, the Salt Agent at Barripore, 16 miles south of Calcutta, went ont of his way to report a case which he had witnessed, in which the woman was forcibly held down by a great bamboo by two men, so as to preclude all chance of escape. In Cuttack, a woman dropt herself into a burning pit, and rose up again as if to escape, when a washerman gave her a push with a bamboo, which sent her back into the hottest part of the fire. Apart from accounts of direct compulsion, some evidence exists that precautions, at times, were taken so that the widow could not escape the flames once they were lit. Anant S. Altekar, for example, points out that it is much more difficult to escape a fiery *pit* you've jumped in, than descending from a pyre you have entered on. He mentions the custom of the fiery pit as particularly prevalent in the Deccan and Western India.

From Gujarat and Uttar Pradesh, where the widow typically were placed in a hut along with her husband, her leg was tied to one of the hut's pillars. Finally, from Bengal, where the tradition of the pyre held sway, the widow's feet could be tied to posts fixed to the ground, she was asked three times if she wished to ascend to heaven, before the flames were lit.

A Danish missionary, in a letter published in the *Monthly Magazine* in 1751, writes the following of the harrowing fate of 47 widows leaping into the flame pit the year before outside the walls of the Danish colony Tranquebar:

However intrepid most of those unhappy victims appeared before jumping into the pit, the note was vastly altered when in the midst of the flames: there they shrieked hideously, tumbled one over another, striving to reach the edge of the pit and get out of it; but they were kept in by throwing heaps of billets and faggots upon them, as well to knock them on the head as to increase the fire.

However, although cases are certainly attested where direct force was used to burn women alive against their will, or that preventive steps were taken in order to make the escape of the widow practically impossible once the fires were lit, many accounts exist that show the decision to commit *sati* was a resolution taken by the women themselves, even refusing to active attempts to dissuade her from the act. The respected historian Anant Sadashiv Altekar points, for example, to his *own sister*, who committed *sati* 17 January 1946. She had often, and for a long time said she would refuse to survive her husband; not even having a "suckling child" prevented her from carrying out the act, nor the pressing insistence from her relations to abstain from the act. According to Altekar, his sister remained convinced that committing *sati* was her duty as *prativrata*, *i.e.*, as dutiful and protective wife, even into death. Referring to this highly personal experience, Altekar says he is not disinclined to believe in some of the reports regarding the act of committing *sati* as a voluntary act on the woman's part.

SYMBOLIC SATI

Funeral Custom

There have been accounts of symbolic *sati* in some Hindu communities. A widow lies down next to her dead husband, and certain parts of both the marriage ceremony and the funeral ceremonies are enacted, but without her death. An example in Tamil Sri Lanka is attested from modern times Although this form of symbolic sati has contemporary evidence, it should by no means be regarded as a modern *invention*. For example, the ancient and sacred Atharvaveda, one of the four Vedas, believed to have been composed around 1000 BCE, describes a funerary ritual where the widow lies down by her deceased husband, but is then asked to descend, to enjoy the blessings from the children and wealth left to her.

Jivit tradition

In recent years in India, a tradition has developed of venerating *jivit*, or living saints. These are, supposedly, women who had formed the vow to be burned, but sacrificed her own wish to die, due to the illegality of the ritual. According to the followers and believers in these women, the *jivit* needs neither nourishment or sleep, subsisting on her virtue,*sat*, alone. Two famous *jivit* were Bala Satimata, and Umca Satimata, both living until the early 1990s.

PREVALENCE

In old age if the Zamindar became a widower his family would marry off the old zamindar to a poor upper caste young girl. The girl would as her wifely duties look after the Zamindar through to eventual death. Then the family members would drug the young widow and get her to commit sati to deny her her inheritance of the zamindar's estate. This phenomenon gave rise to increase in sati among the Bengali Upper Classes. Later with the abolition of sati this practice died out and the care of the old Zamindars reverted to the family. This upper class sati increased the pressure on its abolition.

Records of *sati* exist across the subcontinent. However, there seems to have been major differences historically, in different regions, and among different communities. Furthermore, no reliable figures exist for the numbers who have died by *sati*, in general.

Numbers

A local indication of the numbers is given in the records kept by the Bengal Presidency of the British East India Company, the only authority within the Indian subcontinent provably known for having sought to keep statistics of the phenomenon of *sati*. An 1829 reported statistics for the period 1815-1824 yields a total of 5997 instances of sati for the Bengal presidency in that period, *i.e.*, in average 600 per year.

In the same statistics, it is said that the numbers for the same time period in the Madras and Bombay presidencies totalled 635 instances of *sati*.Raja Ram Mohan Roy estimated that there were ten times as many cases of sati in Bengal compared to the rest of the country.Bentinck, in his 1829 report, states that

420 occurrences took place in one (unspecified) year in the "Lower Provinces" of Bengal, Bihar and Orissa, and 44 in the "Upper Provinces" (the upper Gangetic plain).

Social Composition and Age Distribution of Sati

Anand Yang, speaking of the early nineteenth century CE, says that contrary to conventional wisdom, *sati* was not, in general, confined to being an upper class phenomenon, but spread through the classes/castes. In the 575 reported cases from 1823, for example, 41 percent were Brahmins, some 6 percent were Kshatriyas, whereas 2 percent were Vaishiyas, and 51 percent Sudras. In Banaras, though, in the 1815-1828 British records, the upper castes were only for two years represented with less than 70 per cent of the total ; in 1821, all sati were from the upper castes there.

Yang also notes that many studies seem to emphasize the *young* age of the widows who committed sati. However, by study of the British figures from 1815-1828, Yang states the overwhelming majority were ageing women, the statistics from 1825-1826 about two thirds were above the age of 40 when committing *sati*

REGIONAL VARIATIONS OF INCIDENCE

Anand Yang summarizes the regional variation in incidence of *sati* as follows:

..the practice was never generalized..but was confined to certain areas: in the north,..the Gangetic Valley, Punjab and Rajasthan; in the west, to the southernKonkan region; and in the south, to Madurai and Vijayanagar.

Konkan/Maharashtra

Narayan H. Kulkarnee believes that *sati* became to be practiced in medieval days Maharashtra initially by the Maratha nobility claiming Rajput descent. Then, according to Kulkarnee, the practice of *sati* may have increased across caste distinctions as an honour saving custom in the face of Muslim advances into the territory. But, the practice never gained the type of prevalence as seen in Rajasthan or Bengal, and social customs of actively dissuading a widow from committing *sati* are well established. Apparently not a single instance of *sati* are attested for the 17th and 18th centuries CE.

Vijayanagara Empire

The *sati* stone evidence from the time of the empire is regarded as relatively rare; only about 50 are clearly identified as such. Thus, Carla M. Sinopoli, citing Verghese, says that despite the attention European travellers paid the phenomenon, it should be regarded as having been fairly uncommon during the time of the Vijayanagara empire.

Madurai

In Southern India in general, there are hardly any inscriptions attesting to *sati* prior to 900 CE. The Madurai Nayak dynasty, reigning from 1529-1736 CE seems to have adopted the custom in larger measure; one Jesuit priest observing in 1609 Madurai the burning of 400 women at the death of Nayak Muttu Krishnappa.

Princely State of Mysore

Established in 1799, a few records exist from the Princely State of Mysore that say permission to commit *sati* could be granted. Dewan (prime minister) Purnaiah is said to have allowed it for a Brahmin widow in 1805, whereas an 1827 eye-witness to the burning of a widow in Bangalore in 1827 says it was rather uncommon there.

Gangetic Plain

In the Upper Gangetic plain, while it occurred, there is no indication that it was especially widespread. The earliest known attempt by a government to stop the practice took place here, that of Muhammad Tughlaq, in the Sultanate of Delhi in the 14th century.

In the Lower Gangetic plain, the practice may have reached a high level fairly late in history. According to available evidence and the existing reports of the occurrences of it, the greatest incidence of *sati* in any region and period, in terms of total numbers, occurred in Bengal and Bihar in the late 18th and early 19th centuries. This was during the earlier period of British rule, and before its formal abolition.. The frequency increased in periods of hardship and famine.

ATTITUDES OF MUSLIM RULERS

Under the Delhi Sultanate, permission had to be sought from the widow prior to any practice of sati as a check against compulsion. However, this later became more of a formality. Mughals interfered little with local customs, but they seemed intent on stopping sati. Mughal emperor Humayun (1508-1556) was the first to try a royal fiat against sati.

Akbar (1542–1605) was next to issue official general orders prohibiting sati and insisted that no woman could commit sati without the specific permission of hischief police officers. The chief police officers were instructed by him to delay the woman's decision for as long as possible. Pensions, gifts, and rehabilitative help were offered to the potential sati to persuade her from committing the act. Tavernier, writing in the reign of Shah Jahan, observed that widows with children were not allowed in any circumstances to burn and that in other cases, governors did not readily give permission, but could be bribed to do so.

BRITISH AND OTHER EUROPEAN COLONIAL POWERS

NON-BRITISH COLONIAL POWERS IN INDIA

By the end of the 18th century, the practice had been banned in territories held by some European powers. The Portuguese banned the practice in Goa by about 1515. The Dutch and the French banned it in Chinsurah and Pondichéry, their respective colonies. The Danes, who held the small territories of Tranquebar and Serampore, permitted it until the 19th century.

BRITISH INDIA

Early British Policy

The British, following the example of the early Mughals, for a while tried to regulate it by requiring that it be carried out in the presence of their officials and strictly according to custom. Attempts to limit or ban the practice had been made by individual British officers in the 18th century, but without the backing of the British East India Company. The first formal British ban was imposed in 1798, in the city of Calcutta only. The practice continued in surrounding regions. In the beginning of the 19th century, the evangelical church in Britain, and its members in India, started campaigns against *sati*. Leaders of these campaigns included William Carey and William Wilberforce.

These movements put pressure on the company to ban the act. William Carey, and the other missionaries atSerampore conducted in 1803-1804 a census on cases of *sati* for a region within a 30 mile radius of Calcutta, finding more than 300 such cases there. The missionaries also approached Hindu theologians, who opined that the practice was encouraged, rather than enjoined by the holy scriptures. Serampore was a Danish colony, rather than British, and the reason why Carey started his mission in Danish India, rather than in British, was because The East India Company did not accept Christian missionary activity within their domains. In 1813, in a speech to the House of Commons, William Wilberforce, with particular reference to the statistics on *sati* collected by Carey and the other Serampore missionaries, forced through a bill that made Christian missionary preaching in British India legal, in order to combat such perceived social evils like *sati*

The British authorities within the Bengal Presidency started systematically to collect figures on the practice in 1815.

Principal Hindu Reformers and 1829 ban

Sahajanand Swami, the founder of the Swaminarayan sect, preached against the practice of sati in his area of influence, that is Gujarat. He argued that the practice had no Vedic standing and only God could take a life he had given. He also opined that widows could lead lives that would eventually lead to salvation.

Sir John Malcolm, the Governor of Bombay supported Sahajanand Swami in this endeavor.

However, it was largely due to efforts of the Bengali reformer and founder of Brahmo Samaj, Raja Rammohan Roy, who beginning in 1812 started championing the cause of banning sati practice and began a large-scale campaign against the practice. He was motivated by the experience of seeing his own sister-in-law being forced to commit *sati*. Among his actions, he visited Calcutta cremation grounds to persuade widows against immolation, formed watch groups to do the same, tried to gain support from other elite class of Bengal and wrote and disseminated articles to show that it was not required by scripture. He was at loggerhead with certain section, who wanted that Government should not interfere in religious practices and filed a counter-petition for making a law banning sati practice. He appealed toWilliam Bentick, the Governor of Bengal, to pass a law banning sati practice in British India and his persuasion bore fruit and practice was banned by a law passed in 1829 in Bengal Presidency, which was later extended in 1830 to Madras and Bombay Presidency. The ban was challenged in the courts by means of a petition signed by about 800 individuals, and the matter went to the Privy Council in London. The Privy Council rejected the petition in 1832, and the ban was upheld.

Later British Attitudes

Although the original 1829 ban in Bengal was fairly uncompromising, later in the century British laws include provisions that provided mitigation for murder when "the person whose death is caused, being above the age of 18 years, suffers death or takes the risk of death with his own consent".

General Sir Charles James Napier, the Commander-in-Chief in India from 1859 to 1861 is often noted for a story involving Hindu priests complaining to him about the prohibition of sati by British authorities.

"Be it so. This burning of widows is your custom; prepare the funeral pile. But my nation has also a custom. When men burn women alive we hang them, and confiscate all their property. My carpenters shall therefore erect gibbets on which to hang all concerned when the widow is consumed. Let us all act according to national customs."

PRINCELY STATES

Sati remained legal in some princely states for a time after it had been banned in lands under British control. Baroda and other princely states of Kathiawar Agency banned the practice in 1840, whereas Kolhapur followed them in 1841, the princely state of Indore some time before 1843. According to a speaker at the East India House in 1842, the princely states of Satara, Kingdom of Nagpur and Mysore had by then banned *sati*. Jaipur banned the practice in 1846, while Hyderabad, Gwalior and Jammu and Kashmir did the same in 1847.

Awadh and Bhopal were actively suppressing *sati* by 1849. Cutch outlawed it in 1852 with Jodhpur having banned *sati* about the same time.

The 1846 abolition in Jaipur was regarded by many British as a catalyst for the abolition cause within the Rajputana; within 4 months after Jaipur's 1846 ban, 11 of the 18 independently governed states in Rajputana had followed Jaipur's example. One paper says that in the year 1846-1847 alone, 23 states in the whole of India (not just within Rajputana) had banned *sati* It was not before 1861 sati was legally banned in all princely states of India, Mewar resisting for a long time prior to that time. The last legal case within princely states was, indeed, from 1861 Udaipur the capital of Mewar, but as Anant S. Altekar shows, local opinion had then shifted strongly against the practice. All the widows of Maharanna Sarup Singh flatly refused to become *sati* when asked, and the one who was burnt with him was a slave girl. Later the same year, the general ban on *sati* was issued by a proclamation from Queen Victoria.

Some princely states, such as the major Salute state of Travancore was perceived not to ever have sanctioned *sati* within their domains. For example, the regent Gowri Parvati Bayi was asked by the British Resident if he should permit a *sati* to take place in 1818, but the regent urged him not to do so, since the custom of *sati* had never been acceptable in her domains. In another state, Sawunt Waree (Sawantvadi), the king Khemsawant III (r. 1755–1803) is credited for having issued a positive *prohibition* of sati over a period of ten or twelve years. That prohibition from the 18th century may have lapsed, since in 1843, the government in Sawunt Waree issued a new prohibition of *sati*.

NEPAL AND BALI

Nepal continued to practice *sati* well into the 20th century, being formally banned throughout the country by a law passed 28 June 1920.

On the Indonesian island of Bali, *sati* (known as *masatya*) was practised by the aristocracy as late as 1903, until the Dutch colonial masters pushed for its termination, forcing the local Balinese princes to sign treaties containing the prohibition of sati as one of the clauses. Early Dutch observers of the particular Balinese custom in the 17th century said that only widows, themselves of royal blood, were to be burned *alive*, concubines or others of inferior blood lines consenting to die with their princely husband could choose to be stabbed to death prior to burning.

MODERN TIMES

LEGISLATIVE STATUS OF SATI IN PRESENT DAY INDIA

Following the outcry after the *sati* of Roop Kanwar, the Indian Government enacted the Rajasthan Sati Prevention Ordinance, 1987 on October 1, 1987 and later passed the Commission of Sati (Prevention) Act, 1987.

The Commission of Sati (Prevention) Act, 1987 Part I, Section 2(c) defines *sati* as:

The burning or burying alive of –

(i) Any widow along with the body of her deceased husband or any other relative or with any article, object or thing associated with the husband or such relative; or

(ii) Any woman along with the body of any of her relatives, irrespective of whether such burning or burying is claimed to be voluntary on the part of the widow or the women or otherwise

The *Prevention of Sati Act* makes it illegal to support, glorify or attempt to commit sati. Support of sati, including coercing or forcing someone to commit sati, can be punished by death sentence or life imprisonment, while glorifying sati is punishable with one to seven years in prison.

Enforcement of these measures is not always consistent. The National Council for Women (NCW) has suggested amendments to the law to remove some of these flaws. Prohibitions of certain practices, such as worship at ancient shrines, is a matter of controversy.

Current Situation

Sati has occurred in some rural areas of India, reports extending into the 21st century. Some 30 cases of *sati* from 1943-1987 in the Rajput/Shekavati region are documented according to a referred statistics, the official number being 28. A well documented case from 1987 was that of 18-year old Roop Kanwar. In response to this incident, additional recent legislation against the practice was passed, first within the state of Rajasthan, then generally, the central government of India.

In 2002, a 65-year-old woman by the name of Kuttu died after sitting on her husband's funeral pyre in the Indian Panna district. On 18 May 2006, Vidyawati, a 35-year-old woman allegedly committed sati by jumping into the blazing funeral pyre of her husband in Rari-Bujurg Village, Fatehpur district in the State of Uttar Pradesh. On 21 August 2006, Janakrani, a 40-year-old woman, burned to death on the funeral pyre of her husband Prem Narayan in Sagar district. On 11 October 2008 a 75-year-old woman, Lalmati Verma, committed sati by jumping into her 80-year-old husband's funeral pyre at Checher in the Kasdol block of Chhattisgarh's Raipur district.

THE MEANING OF SATI

Lindsey Harlan, having conducted extensive field work among Rajput women, has constructed a model of how, and why, women having committed *sati* are still venerated today, and how the worshippers think about the process involved. Essentially, a woman on the path to become a *sati* goes through three stages, that of i) being pativrata during her husband's life, ii) who, at his death, makes a solemn vow to burn by his side, gaining status as sativrata and iii) finally, having endured being burnt alive, achieving the status of satimata.

PATIVRATA

The dutiful wife, the pativrata, is *not* only devoted and subservient to her husband, but she is also *protective*, ensuring his well-being in many ways. Thus, if he actually dies before her, some *culpability* is attached to her for his death, as not having been sufficiently protective of him. Making the vow to burn alive beside him removes her own culpability, as well as within the afterlife, be able to rescue and protect him from new dangers.

SATIVRATA

In Harlan's model, having made the holy vow to burn herself transforms the woman to a sativrata, a transitional stage between the living and the dead, prior to her ascending the funeral pyre. Once a woman committed herself to become *sati*, popular belief thought her to become endowed with many supernatural powers. Lourens P. Van Den Bosch enumerates some of them. The *sati*would gain the powers of prophecy and clairvoyance, as well as the ability to bless women with sons, who had not borne sons before. The gifts from a *sati* were venerated as valuable relics, and in her journey to the pyre, people would seek to touch her garments in order to benefit from her powers.

Lindsey Harlan probes deeper into the sativrata stage: As a transitional figure on her path to become a powerful family protector as*satimata*, the sativrata dictates the terms, and obligations the family must fulfill in order for her to protect them once she has become satimata, by showing reverence to her by observing the conditions. These are generally called *ok*. A typical example of an *ok* is to place a restriction on the type of colours used in the family members's clothing, or to forbid the use of some particular type of clothing.

What can be termed curses, *shrap* is also within the sativrata's power, understood to be a severe teaching to members of her family in how they have failed. One woman cursed her in-laws when they refused to bring neither a horse or a drummer to her pyre, saying that whenever in the future might have need of either (and many religious rituals requires such a presence), it would not be available to them.

Satimata

After her death on the pyre, the woman is finally transformed into the shape of the *satimata*, an spiritual embodiment of goodness, with her principal concern of being a family protector. Typically, the *satimata* occurs in the dreams of the family members, teaching for example, the women how to be good *pativratas*, herself through her sacrifice having proved she was the perfect *pativrata*. However, although the satimata's intentions are always for the good of the family, she is not averse to let, for example, children become sick, or the cows' udders wither, if she thinks this is an appropriate lesson to the living wife who had neglected her duties as *pativrata*.

SCRIPTURES ON SATI

Brahmin scholars justified the practice, and gave reasonings as to how the scriptures could be said to justify them. Among them were Vijnanesvara, of the 12th-century Chalukyacourt, and the 13th century Madhvacharya. They lauded the practice as required conduct in righteous women, and said that it was not to be considered suicide, which was otherwise variously banned or discouraged in the scriptures. They deemed it an act of peerless piety, which was said to purge the couple of all accumulated sin, guarantee their salvation, and ensure their reunion in the afterlife. In the following, a historical chronology is given of the debate within Hinduism on the topic of *sati*.

THE OLDEST VEDIC TEXTS

The most ancient texts still revered among Hindus today are the Vedas, where the *SaC-hitâs* are the most ancient, four collections roughly dated in their composition to 1500–1000 BCE. In two of these collections, the Rigveda and the Atharvaveda there is material relevant to the discussion of *sati*

Endorsement or Prohibition of Sati in the Rig Veda?

Some commentators claim that the Rig Veda sanctions sati, while others claim that it condemns sati. The argument for condoning is based on verse 10.18.7, part of the verses to be used at funerals. Whether they describe *sati* or something else entirely, is disputed, The hymn is about funeral by burial, and not by cremation. There are differing translations of the passage. The translation below is one of those said to prescribe it.

Let these women, whose husbands are worthy and are living, enter the house with ghee (applied) as collyrium (to their eyes). Let these wives first step into the house, tearless without any affliction and well adorned.

The text does not mention widowhood, and other translations differ in their translation of the word here rendered as 'pyre' (*yoni*, literally "seat, abode"; Griffith has "first let the dames go up to where he lieth"). In addition, the following verse, which is unambiguously about widows, contradicts any suggestion of the woman's death; it explicitly states that the widow should return to her house.

Rise, come unto the world of life, O woman — come, he is lifeless by whose side thou liest. Wifehood with this thy husband was thy portion, who took thy hand and wooed thee as a lover.

A reason given for the discrepancy in translation and interpretation of verse 10.18.7, is that one consonant in a word that meant house, *yonim agree* "foremost to the *yoni*", was deliberately changed by those who wished claim scriptural justification, to a word that meant fire, *yomiagne*.

In Atharvaveda

In the Atharvaveda, the ritual element of a widow lying down beside her husband on his funeral pyre is regarded as "ancient custom", in the very next verse, the widow is bidden to rise up again and come to this world, prayer is offered for her better life with children, and wealth. This type of *symbolic sati*, rather than the actual burning of the widow has led several scholars to regard the Vedic Age as a time for the betterment of widow rights, and furthermore, affirming that the scripture allow widow to remarry.

1ST-MILLENNIUM BCE TEXTS

Religious Texts

The Brahmana literature, holy commentaries on the ancient Vedic texts, dated about 1000 BCE – 500 BCE are entirely silent about *sati* according to the historian Altekar. Similarly, the Grhyasutras, a body of text devoted to ritual, with composition date about the time of the youngest within Brahmana literature, *sati* is not mentioned, either.

What is mentioned concerning funeral rites, though, is that the widow is to be brought back from her husband's funeral pyre, either by his brother, or by a trusted servant.

In the Taittiriya Aranyaka from about the same time, it is said that when leaving, the widow took from her husband's side such objects as his bow, gold and jewels (which previously would have been burnt with him), and a hope expressed that the widow and her relatives would lead a happy and prosperous life afterwards. According to Altekar, it is "clear" that the custom of actual widow burning had died out a long time previously at this stage.

Nor is the practice of *sati* mentioned anywhere in the Dharmasutras, texts tentatively dated by Pandurang Vaman Kane to 600-100 BCE, while Patrick Olivelle thinks the bounds should be roughly 250-100 BCE instead Furthermore, nor do the vast texts of the Aranyakas and Upanishads contain any mention of *sati*.

Thus, in none of the principal religious texts believed composed prior to the Common Era is there any evidence at all for a sanctioning of the practice of *sati*, it is wholly unmentioned, although the archaic Atharvaveda do contain hints of a funeral practice of *symbolic* sati. In addition, the twelfth century CE commentary of Apararka, claiming to quote the Dharmasutra text Apastamba, it says that the Apastamba prescribes that if a widow has made a vow of burning herself (anvahorana, "ascend the pyre), but then*retracts* her vow, she must expiate her sin by the penance ritual called *Prajapatya-vrata*

Valmiki Ramayana

The oldest portion of the epic Ramayana, the Valmiki Ramayana, is tentatively dated for its composition by Robert P. Goldman to 750–500 BCE. Anant S. Altekar says that no instances of *sati* occur in this earliest, archaic part of the whole Ramayana.

According to Ramashraya Sharma, there is no conclusive evidence of the sati practice in the Ramayana. For instance, Tara, Mandodari and the widows of Ravana, all live after their respective husband's deaths, though all of them announce their wish to die, while lamenting for their husbands. The first two remarry their brother-in-law. The only instance of sati appears in the *Uttara Kanda* - believed to be a later addition to the original text — in which Kushadhwaja's wife performs sati. The Telugu adaptation of the Ramayana, the 14th-century Ranganatha Ramayana, tells that Sulochana, wife of Indrajit, became sati on his funeral pyre.

Mahabharata

The oldest portions of this epic is from about 300 BCE, and here, we do indeed, find instances of *sati.*

Madri, the second wife of Pandu, immolates herself. She believes she is responsible for his death, as he had been cursed with death if he ever had intercourse. He died while performing the forbidden act with Madri; she blamed herself for not rejecting him, as she knew of the curse. Also, in the case of Madri the entire assembly of sages sought to*dissuade* her from the act, and no religious merit is attached to the fate she chooses against all advice. In the Musala-parvan of the Mahabharata, the four wives of Vasudevaare said to commit *sati*. Furthermore, as news of Krishna's death reaches Hastinapur, five of his wives choose to burn themselves.

Against these stray examples within the Mahabharata of *sati*, we have scores of instances in the same epic of widows who do *not* commit sati, none of them blamed for not doing so.

Other Secular Texts

Other secular texts from the 1st millennium BCE draw a complete blank on *sati* as well, Simmi Jain mentions the Arthashastra, and the works of PâG-ini, in particular theAcm-âdhyâyî.

PRINCIPAL SMRTIS, C. 200 BCE – 1200 CE

The four works, Manusm(-ti (200 BCE - 200 CE), Yâjñavalkya Sm[-ti (200 - 500 CE), Nâradasm[-ti (100 BCE - 400 CE) and the VicG-usm(-ti (700 - 1000 CE) are the principal Smrtiworks in the Dharmaúâstra tradition, along with the Parasara Smrti, composed in the latter period, rather than in the earlier.

Earliest Phase, c. 200 BCE – 500 CE

The first three principal smrtis, those of Manu, Yâjñavalkya and Nârada do not contain any mention of sati; rather, such as Manu prescribe lifelong, ascetic widowhood for the female

Evolution Towards Acceptance of Sati, 500 CE – 1200 CE

It is in the latter half of the 1st millennium CE that Brahminical debate gradually converge towards a consensus that sati is, indeed, a recommendable act. David Brick, summarizing the historical evolution, writes the following:

To summarize, one can loosely arrange Dharmasastic writings on sahagamana into three historical periods. In the first of these, which roughly corresponds to the second half of the 1st millennium CE, smrti texts that prescribe sahagamana begin to appear.

However, during approximately this same period, other Brahmanical authors also compose a number of smrtis that proscribe this practice specifically in the case of Brahmin widows. Moreover, Medhatithi—our earliest commentator to address the issue—strongly opposes the practice for all women. Taken together, this textual evidence suggests that sahagamana was still quite controversial at this time. In the following period, opposition to this custom starts to weaken, as none of the later commentators fully endorses Medhatithi's position on sahagamana.

Indeed, after Vijnanesvara in the early twelfth century, the strongest position taken against sahagamana appears to be that it is an inferior option to brahmacarya (ascetic celibacy), since its result is only heaven rather than moksa (liberation). Finally, in the third period, several commentators refute even this attenuated objection to sahagamana, for they cite a previously unquoted smrti passage that specifically lists liberation as a result of the rite's performance. They thereby claim that sahagamana is at least as beneficial an option for widows as brahmacarya and perhaps even more so, given the special praise it sometimes receives. These authors, however, consistently stop short of making it an obligatory act. Hence, the commentarial literature of the dharma tradition attests to a gradual shift from strict prohibition to complete endorsement in its attitude towards sahagamana.

Smrtis Approving of Sati

Justifications for the practice are given in the *Vishnu Smriti* (dated from 700 to 1000CE):

Now the duties of a woman (are)... After the death of her husband, to preserve her chastity, or to ascend the pile after him.

Justification for the practice is also found in the later work of the Brihaspati Smriti (25-11). Both this and the *Vishnu Smriti* date from the 1st millennium.

Passages of the Parasara Smriti say:

"If a woman adheres to a vow of ascetic celibacy (brahmacarya) after her husband has died, then when she dies, she obtains heaven, just like those who were celibate. Further, three and a half krores or however many hairs are on a human body - for that long a time (in years) a woman who follows her husband (in death) shall dwell in heaven."

In both passages, given the choice between ascetic celibacy and sati, the latter option, according to both the Parasara Smriti and Vaisnava Dharmaúâstra, is said to yield more otherworldly benefits for all involved parties.

Liberation versus ascension to heaven

Within the dharmashastric tradition espousing *sati* as a justified, and even recommended, option to ascetic widowhood, there remained a curious conception worth noting the*achieved status* for a woman committing *sati*. Burning herself on the pyre would give her, and her husband, automatic, but not eternal, reception into heaven (svarga), whereas only the wholly chaste *widow* living out her natural life span could hope for final *liberation* (moksha) and breaking the cycle of rebirth. Thus, acknowledging that performing *sati*only achieved an inferior otherworldy status than successful widowhood could achieve, *sati* became recommended when coupled with a dismissal of the effective possibility for a widow to remain *truly* chaste.

Rules on Brahmin widows

While some smriti passages allow sati as optional, others forbid the practice entirely. Vijñâneúvara (c. 1076-1127), an early Dharmaúâstric scholar, claims that many smriti call for the prohibition of sati among Brahmin widows, but not among other social castes. Vijñâneúvara, quoting scriptures from Paithinasi and Angiras to support his argument, states:

"Due to Vedic injunction, a Brahmin woman should not follow her husband in death, but for the other social classes, tradition holds this to be the supreme Law of Women... when a woman of Brahmin caste follows her husband in death, by killing herself she leaders neither herself nor her husband to heaven."

However, as proof of the contradictory opinion of the smriti on sati, in his Mitâkc-arâ, Vijñâneúvara goes on to state that, according to Yâjñavalkya Sm[-ti, Brahmin women are technically only forbidden from performing sati on pyres other than those of their deceased husbands. Quoting the Yâjñavalkya Sm[-ti, Vijñâneúvara states: *"A Brahmin woman ought not to depart by ascending a separate pyre."*

Those who supported the ritual, did however, put restrictions upon who could and could not participate. Women who had young children to care for were not allowed to participate, neither those who were pregnant or menstruating. Another way a woman could be removed from the pyre was if someone from her husband's side of the family, usually the brother or male member, removed her before the act began.

A restriction, which is another source of debate, was only allowing certain women to go to the pyre, but restricting others. Brahaman women were not allowed to go to the pyre along with their husbands, but other caste groups were allowed. This loophole has been largely contested and some suggest that if the widow's deceased husband did not participate in anything that could have marred his soul, or was shut out of society, she should go to the pyre with him.

There was a choice that the widow had to make at the death of her husband. She could go to the pyre with him or live a celibate life without him; both would allow her to reach heaven. Though it is a choice, many women were not given much of a say in what they were to do, thus many headed for the pyre

Voices of the Ppposition

As the custom of *sati* grew in popularity from the sixth century CE, and also began garnering Brahminical theological support, opposition to the practice came from several corners.

In particular, vociferous opponents includes the senth century poet Banabhatta, the ninth century scholar Medatithi, the 12th-century scholar Devanadhatta, as well as the mystical Tantric tradition, with its valorization of the feminine principle.

Condemnation by BâG□Abhamm□a

The 7th century poet BâG-abhamm-a was a severe critic of the practice of *sati* as it began to gain popularity. He wrote:

..it is a path followed by the ignorant. It is a mere freak of madness, a path of ignorance, an enterprise of recklessness, a view of baseness, a sign of utter thoughtlessness and a blunder or folly that one should resign life on the death of the father, brother, friend or the husband. If life leaves us not of itself, we must not resign it. For this leaving of life, if we examine it, is merely for our own interest because we cannot bear our own cureless pain.

Medhatithi

Explicit criticisms later in the 1st millennium, included that of Medhatithi, a commentator on various theological works. He considered it suicide, which was forbidden by the Vedas

One shall not die before the span of one's life is run out.

PURANAS

The Puranas have examples of women who commit *sati*; they suggest that this was considered desirable or praiseworthy: *A wife who dies in the company of her husband shall remain in heaven as many years as there are hairs on his person.* (Garuda Purana 1.107.29) According to 2.4.93, she stays with her husband in heaven during the rule of 14Indras, *i.e.* a kalpa.

Passages in the Atharva Veda, including 13.3.1, offer advice to the widow on mourning and her life after widowhood, including her remarriage. Although the Vedas provide this advice to recent widows concerning grief and mourning, there is no mention of sati practices within the Vedas or Dharmaúâstra.

Legend of Goddess Sati

Although the myth of the goddess Sati is that of a wife who dies by her own volition on a fire, this is not a case of the practice of *sati*. The goddess was not widowed, and the myth is quite unconnected with the justifications for the practice.

JUSTIFICATIONS FOR INVOLUNTARY SATI

Julia Leslie points to an 18th-century CE text on the duties of the wife by Tryambakayajvan that contains statements *she* regards as evidence for a sub-tradition of justifying strongly encouraged, pressured, or even forced *sati*. Although the standard view of the sati within the justifying tradition is that of the woman who out of moral heroism *chooses*sati, rather than choosing to enter ascetic widowhood, Tryambaka is quite clear upon the automatic good effect of sati for the woman who was a *bad* wife:

Women who, due to their wicked minds, have always despised their husbands (...) whether they do this (i.e, sati), of their own free will, or out of anger, or even out of fear-all of them are purified from sin.

Thus, as Leslie puts it, becoming (or being pressured into the role of) a *sati* was, within *Tryambaka*'s thinking, the only truly effective method of atonement for the bad wife.

Counter-Arguments Within Hinduism

Reform and bhakti movements within Hinduism favoured egalitarian societies, and in line with the tenor of these beliefs, generally condemned the practice, sometimes explicitly. The 12th century Virashaiva movement condemned the practice. In a petition to the British East India Company in 1818, Ram Mohan Roy wrote that;- "All these instances are murders according to every shastra."

Non-Hindu Views and Criticisms

European artists in the eighteenth century produced many images for their own native markets, showing the widows as heroic women, and moral exemplars.

In her article "Can the Subaltern Speak?" philosopher Gayatri Spivak discusses how sati takes the form of regulating women in pre-colonial India according to Hindu law, and how sati takes the form of imprisoning women in the double bind of self-expression attributed to mental illness and social rejection, or of self-incrimination according to British colonial law. The woman who commits sati takes the form of the subaltern in Spivak's work, a form much of postcolonial studies takes very seriously.

HISTORICAL BACKGROUND OF SATI PRATHA

Sati system is the custom in which the widow is placed on pyre of deceased husband and burnt alive. Sati practie can be found mentioned in several Hindu religious scriptures and epics.

Religious Epics like Naradsmriti *etc.* say that after the death of the husband the widow should be a Sati or live purely single.This shows that Sati was not mandatory in ancient times.Nepal's first authentic inscription found on stone pillar at the Changunarayan Temples proves.. Sati system is the custom in which the widow is placed on pyre of deceased husband and burnt alive. Sati practie can be found mentioned in several Hindu religious scriptures and epics.

Religious Epics like Naradsmriti *etc.* say that after the death of the husband the widow should be a Sati or live purely single.This shows that Sati was not mandatory in ancient times.Nepal's first authentic inscription found on stone pillar at the Changunarayan Temples proves that King Man Dev's mother Rajyawati upon her son's request chose not to be a Sati. Vauma Gupt's mother Aabhiree and Jaya Dev's mother Batsadevi also didn't go Sati. This also proves that Sati wasn't compulsory in ancient Nepal.

Extension of Mughal Empire in India, wrong interpretation of religion, selfishness of Pundits, political rivalry and greed of wealth caused Sati system to spread in the Middle Age Nepal. Initially the custom was limited to the monarchs. Later it got its place in Brahmin, Kshetri and Basya community.

Sati system was so prominent during later Middle Ages that the funerals couldn't take place without a Sati. At a king's death, not only his queens rather servents and mistresses also used to be Sati. In some rare instances deceased's mothers and sisters were also immolated. Sister and wives of the King Mahendra Malla became Sati for him. Likewise, mother of the King of Patan Bishwojit Malla who was slashed by his 6 'Pradhans (Ministers)' became Sati for her son. Nine queens for each King Nripendra Mall and Shree Niwas Malla became Sati. Twenty Four queens were burnt alive with King Parthivendra Malla. In the history of Nepal, the largest numbers of queens to become Sati were of Yog Narendra Malla, the king of Patan. Thirty three queens chose to be immolated with him.

King Prithivi Narayan Shah, the great was against the Sati system. Aming at unification of the country he couldn't do much to abolish the system. Though he was against Sati system, altogether nine women sacrificed themselves on his pyre. Among the nine, one was his widow Narendra Laxmi. Seven female sevents and two of his not legally married (chosen by the kings for live-in relation) wives became Sati. Maiju Rani was one of the not legally married (chosen by the kings for live-in relation) queens to become Sati. When King

Pratap Singh Shah died, Maiju Rani was pregnant. According to the then existing rule, a pregnant lady was forbidden from becoming a Sati. But due to the conspiracy of other members of the palace, she was forced to become Sati (on January 9, 1978) after she gave birth to her son Prince Sher Bahadur Shahi.

After her husband death Queen mother Rajendra Laxmi didn't go Sati, rather she participated in active politics. She ruled the country onbehalf of her child Rana Bahadur Shah. But when Rana Bahadur Shah was killed by Sher Bahadur Shah, sixteen queens including Raj Rajeshori Shah and few servents went Sati.

Prime Minister Bhimsen Thapa didn't allow his relative Lalit Tripura Sundari, the 12 years old youngest queen of Rana Bahadur Shah. When Rana Bahadur Shah was killed, his Queen Raj Rajeswori was in exile at Helambu. Bhimsen Thapa called her back and forced her to become Sati after 11 days of Rana Bahadur's murder.

When Rana Bahadur's eighteen year's old son died Bhimsen Thapa forced two of his queens Siddhi Laxmi Devi and Gorakshya Rajya Laxmi Devi to become Sati. At the time Gorakshya's son King Rajendra Bikram Shah was only aged three. In the history of Nepal, no other queens after those two had to become Sati. During the Shah Regime the Sati system was misused as a tool to acquire the political power. From the timenRajendra Bikram Shah the state power was acquired by the Ranas and the Sati system also made its way from the queens to the Prime Miniter's wives.

First Rana Prime Minister Junga Bahadur Rana was dissident to this custom. After his return from the visit of the United Kingdom, he promulgated the first civil code in Nepal. The law incorporated some restrictions regarding the Sati system but it couldn't totally prohibit the practice.

The codifed law incorporates 15 points provisions regarding Sati system.

Shading light on the practice of Sati system during Junga Bahadur Rana's time, Daniel Wright writes, "The women with small children were not allowed to become Sati. Before this the women were forced to become Sati. If one tries to run then she was beaten with stones and killed."

Junga Bahadur didn't allow his bother's wives to become Sati. He restricted his younger brothers Bam Bahadur, Badri Narsingh and Krisha Bahadur's wives from being Sati. He didn't allow her daughter too. He didn't even allow Colonel Uma Kanta's wife to be Sati.

Three days after the death of Junga Bahadur Rana on 25 February 1877, his three wives became Sati. Junga Bahadur younger brother Ranodip Singh was prime minister at the time. It is said that Ranodip was of religious nature and support the Sati practice, so he didn't prevent his sisters in law to be Sati. On the other hand fear of being intervened by his sisters in law in his rule must have inspired him not to stop them. That is because during his time in 1879, when commander in chief Jagat Shumsher died, his widows weren't allowed to become Sati. Again during his time his younger brother Dhir Shumshers wives were also not allowed to become Sati.

After Ranodip's killing, Bir Shumsher became prime minister. He tried to regulate this system during his tenure. He set the rule that the woman who chooses to become Sati had to have permission from the prime minister and in his absence from the higher judicial and legal authorities. In 1887 Bir Shumsher didn't allow Commander in chief Ram Shumsher's widow to become Sati. Though Bir Shumsher tried crub the Sati system, it was still in practice.

During Chandra Shumsher's rule in 1911, a woman named had applied for permission from the local authorities to become a Sati. This shows that this practice still prevailing in his time.

On December 5, 1829, Lord William Bentick abolished Sati system in India. Nepali rulers didn't imitate the Indians rather the practice exitsted for about ninety more years of its abolition in neighbouring India. Meanwhile, Chandra Shumsher was pressurized by the British-India government to uproot the practice.

Thereafter Chandra Shumsher declared the abolition of this practice on the occasion of his 57th birthday on 8th July 1920. His declaration states that if anybody inspires, facilitates or sets fire to a Sati then he would be sentenced to death in murder charge. Chandra Shumsher put an end the centuries long inhumane Sati system in Nepal.

Sati custom prevailed only in Bhramin, Kshetri and Baisyas castes. The ethic groups like Rai, Limbu, Sherpa, Gurung, Thakali *etc.* residing in northern Nepal had the practice of widow marriage. So, Sati custom was not practiced by them. Rana Prime Minister Chandra Shumsher abolished Sati system formulating law in this regard. Abolition of Sati system only restricted a woman from being burnt with his deceased husband but physical and mental violence against widow is still existent. In many instances widows as blamed of being witch and people say that meeting with them on the way brings badluck. Isn't it a new or different form of Sati system?

Finally, a question arises that when a man died women had to be cremated Sati but when a woman died why didn't the man sacrifice for her? Why he thinks of or marries another woman before the thirteen days death rituals of his late wife aren't over? Is this natural? Definitely not, these are rules set by the mele dominant patriarchal society which has caused the women to suffer. The Sati system was a inhumane and brutal behaviour towards the women.

WIDOW-BURNING

The burning of wives on the funeral pyres of their husbands, widow-burning, commonly known as *sati* ("suttee" in English), has been practiced in India since at least the fourth century B.C.E. , when it was first recorded in Greek accounts. It was banned by British colonial law in 1829–1830 and survived in the native

Indian states until the late 1880s, when it was effectively eradicated, although extremely rare cases persisted into the early twentieth century. Since India's independence in 1947—or more precisely since 1943—there has been a spectacular revival of the phenomenon in four Northern Indian states: Bihar, Uttar Pradesh, Madhya Pradesh, and especially Rajasthan, a former stronghold of sati.

Although the number of women who have committed sati since that date likely does not exceed forty (with thirty in Rajasthan alone), an infinitesimal percentage of the female population, the reactivation of the practice has had considerable social and political impact, especially in the case of the "Deorala affair"—the burning of a young Rajput widow named Rup Kanwar in Rajasthan in September 1987. The nationwide trauma that followed this incident and the media coverage it received (in contrast to the relative indifference shown to the other cases) led the federal government to take legal action, issuing the Sati Commission (Prevention) Act a year later.

Sati was never a universal practice in India, even though the earliest statistics recorded by British officials in the late eighteenth and early nineteenth centuries were at times quite remarkable.

Several reasons explain the high numbers logged in certain periods and regions of the subcontinent. For instance, a combination of external factors such as cholera epidemics and local customs, like the unbridled polygyny of Kulin Brahmans, might account for a portion of the 8,134 cases recorded in the Bengal Presidency alone between 1815 and 1828. Widow-burning is but one of a wide range of religious rituals implying self-mutilation and self-sacrifice observed by Indian men and women alike.

Although death by fire has been the prevalent form of the ritual, cremation being the most common type of disposal of the dead among Hindus, sati could take the form of widow burial whenever the caste or community of the deceased called for it, as for example with the Jogi weavers of Bengal, or with the Jasnathis of Rajasthan, a lost branch of Ismaili Muslims who have reconverted to Hinduism.

The original meaning of the Sanskrit word *sati* was simply "faithful wife"; only later was the term applied specifically to the woman who immolated herself. In any case, it never referred to the rite or custom of widow-burning. It was the British who, at the close of the eighteenth century, officialized the confusion, expressed by many travelers before them, between the immolated woman and the sacrifice of widows. The Sanskrit language knows of no specific denomination for the practice and instead resorts to periphrastic and euphemistic expressions like "going with" and "dying with," when the widow is burned on the same funeral pyre as her husband, or "going after" and "dying after" when she is burnt on a separate pyre, these being the two major facets of the rite.

Also noteworthy is the fact that according to the Hindu belief system, the sati dies as a wife, eschewing the ill-fated, ominous, and impure state of widowhood: The "eye of faith," combined with the "belief effect" of the ritual, makes the joint cremation of husband and wife appear to onlookers (and as far as one can tell, to the sati herself) to be a re-enactment of their marriage ceremony. Through her sacrifice, the sati preserves the bodily and spiritual unity of the couple, affording the Hindu sacrament of marriage its ultimate and truest expression.

Placed in a broader context, widow-burning is but one among a variety of forms of funerary ceremonial, found in many parts of the world, that involve the voluntary death of certain categories of survivors. These people sacrifice themselves (individually or en masse) in the course of the obsequies of a higher-ranking person—a ruler, master, or husband. The belief underlying this body of suicidal practices (termed *altruistic* by Émile Durkheim in his 1897 classical work *Le suicide*) is that the deceased will enjoy the same goods and services in the beyond as he had on earth. He will need his mount and his weapons to wage war, food to assuage his hunger, and finery to set off his beauty and glory. In like manner, he will need to be accompanied by his servants, his counselors, and, finally, his wives.

What seems to lie at the heart of the practice of "following in death" is the settling of a debt of obligation and love (the two go together) binding the various parties to a common master. In ancient China, for example, all the categories of survivors mentioned above were buried with kings or great warlords, together with horses, offerings, and artifacts. Such was also the case in Scythia. According to some authors, the custom would have been introduced into India when Scythians (locally known as Shakas) conquered parts of its territory in the first century B.C.E. It would then have been exported from India to the kingdoms of Southeast Asia—mainly Java, Lombok, and Bali—where Hinduism became the state religion during the first centuries of the common era.

An alternative thesis maintains that widow-burning was indigenous to India but belonged to the same pre-Aryan wild clans and tribes as those that had introduced human sacrifice to propitiate bloodthirsty deities, as well as other equally "loath-some" rituals, into the Hindu canon of practice.

Following the same line of argumentation, the remarkable fact that neither the Vedas, the sacred revelation of ancient Brahmanism, nor such authoritative treatises on dharma as the *Laws of Manu* ever mention widow-burning, is taken as evidence for the repression of this barbaric custom by a civilized Aryan society, in which the widow was enjoined either to lead an ascetic life for the rest of her days or, if she had had no male issue, to cohabit with her husband's younger brother until she begot one. These reconstructions tell readers more about the fantasies and ideologies of the people who conceived them than they do about the history of the practice itself. The aboriginal versus Scythian origin theories seem, in fact, to serve the same purpose: to remove sati rituals from the pure land of the Aryans and exile them into its darkest inner or outer confines. In this way, not only is India's immaculate image as the golden land of spirituality and nonviolence preserved, but also the hard core of "barbarism" found in Hinduism is conveniently expelled and thereby repressed.

The latest version of this convenient scenario is the one used in the polemic following the 1987 burning of Rup Kanwar in Deorala. This was the last and most highly publicized of a series of widow immolations that took place in Shekhavati, a rural region of Rajasthan, one of India's most underdeveloped and conservative states. The "Deorala affair" has been interpreted in a variety of ways according to the different viewpoints of the various actors in the controversy of Himalayan proportions. The proponents of secularism and women's causes declared Rup's immolation to be a patent case of murder in a plot in which the rural illiterate masses had been fanaticized by obscurantist forces and demonic agents belonging to specific castes (mainly the Rajputs and Marwaris) who were backing the revival of an outdated, outlawed practice to further their own interests, whether political, economic, or symbolic.

Commenting on the case and its extraordinary impact on a theretofore indifferent public, the Indian social psychologist Ashis Nandy has offered the following interpretation: The burning of Rup Kanvar became a cause célèbre because of her social milieu. Kanvar was born in a semiurban, well-to-do family from Jaipur, the state capital of Rajasthan, and had received a quite respectable education. The English-speaking and Westernized elite that sought to protect itself from the backlash of acculturation by stigmatizing Hinduism and by conflating tradition with superstition, rural life with social backwardness, and belief with obscurantism—that same elite felt directly threatened by the sacrifice of a young woman whose level of education and social background linked her to an economically emerging social group. Kanvar's death could only trigger a defensive reaction because it demonstrated that the line of demarcation between barbarism and civilization, upon which the edifice of what Nandy has called "a new form of internal colonialism" had been built, had proved very easy to cross.

Nearly nothing is known of sati's origin or of its spread across the Indian territory and social strata during the first millennium of the common era. The general opinion is that sati was originally only performed in Ksatriya milieus—by the women of kings, warriors, and persons who had died a heroic death—and that it was eventually adopted by other status groups of society in the course of the second millennium C.E. as the result of a change of soteriology; this is, for example, the position of the Indian historian Romila Thapar. Many invoke the well-known process of Sanskritisation, as theorized by Indian anthropologist M. N. Srinivas in the 1950s, to account for this imitation of the royal model. It is true that the first accounts experts have—Greek sources from Alexander's time (Onesicritos and Aristobulos)—describe the competition between the wives of the warlord Keteus to burn themselves alive on their husband's funeral pyre. It is also true that widow-burning became, from the seventh century onward, a common feature and thus an emblematic caste-identity marker among the same Rajputs who claim to be the Ksatriyas, the "warrior caste," of modern India.

However, this is hardly sufficient ground for claiming that this custom was originally the exclusive prerogative of the martial castes, especially when numerous early accounts, both textual and epigraphical, of other groups—from Brahmans at the top of the hierarchical scale down to middle, low, and even impure castes—practicing widow-burning.

Another problematic issue is the prevalence of widow-burning in those regions of India in which "Shakta" Tantrism has been the dominant form of religious belief and practice since as early as the ninth century C.E. It is in an area comprising the modern states of Bengal, Orissa, Rajasthan, Gujarat, Madhya Pradesh, Karnataka, and Tamilnadu that are found at village boundaries memorial-hero and sati stones, sometimes stretching like vast funeral grounds as far as the eye can see.

The presence of such memorials is actually the only means specialists have for approximately mapping sati, both geographically and historically. The overlap between Shakta devotionalism and the spread of widow sacrifice raises a particularly difficult question for Indologists insofar as Shakta Tantra—with its transgression and reversal of the fundamental values of orthodox Hinduism—gives primacy to the female aspect of the godhead, the well-known Shakti of which Tantric practitioners and believers are worshippers—whence the term *Shakta.* Because, according to this religious system, every woman is essentially the Goddess incarnate, and her female energy the source of life and salvation, it seems difficult at first to reconcile this worldview and ethos with the practice of widow-burning.

But the first question that arises with regard to widow-burning, a question that casts its long shadow across the entire field of its historiography, is that of knowing whether these immolations were voluntary acts or whether, on the contrary, women were forced to burn themselves—whether their immediate circle (family, priesthood, caste) and the dominant religious ideology they embraced did not force them, at the time of their declaration of intent and a fortiori in their hour of death, to mount the funeral pyre.

This crucial element of the mystery of widow-burning is all the more intriguing inasmuch as the historical data provide as much evidence for the one hypothesis as for the other. According to the view one chooses to adopt, one will interpret widow-burning as a form of suicide, as a sacrifice, or as murder—a murder made all the more odious by the fact that it is also a matricide because it is the closest male relative of the deceased, the son, who lights the pyre on which his mother will be burned alive. When viewed as a murder, sati also takes on the dimensions of a collective homicide, being that thousands of men and women attend such events, and because the responsibility of the society as a whole is deeply implicated in it. At the opposite end of the spectrum, those Hindus who believe in "satihood" will view the ritual as a supreme act of selfless devotion and a manifestation of female sacredness, the sati literally becoming Shakti incarnate at her time of death and her burning a magical phenomenon of yogic self-combustion. In this perspective, her self-immolation is a sacrifice that, according to the Hindu belief system, entails no violence to the consenting victim.

Down to the present day, it is the dire fate of Indian widows in India that is invoked as the primary reason for existence of sati. Although widow remarriage has been authorized by law since as early as 1856, it was and still is rarely resorted to among higher or middle castes, or among groups that follow a strategy of embracing high-caste values and practices to collectively uplift themselves in the social hierarchy. An object of universal repugnance, the widow is required to lead a life of asceticism and self-mortification. In the higher castes, her head is shaved, and she is deprived of every finery, every pleasure, and every comfort. Because she is the bearer of misfortune and impurity, she is excluded from domestic festivities, and even from the wedding of her own children. Her existence is but a monotonous succession of fasts, religious observances, and devotional practices.

It can, however, become a veritable trial, given the fact that the hatred and resentment of her inlaws, legitimized by the belief that the widow has "eaten" her husband—caused his death through her misconduct in previous births or in this life—knows no limits. She is subject to humiliation, insult, and abuse. She can be thrown out into the streets and, if her own family refuses to take her back, have no other recourse than to join a widows' ashram at such holy sites as Vrindavan in Uttar Pradesh, or to make good on her reputation as a *whore* —a commonplace term of abuse for widows.

The young widow is especially execrated, since it is judged that her unhappy fate is the result of abominable sins committed in a past life. Early widowhood was widespread in a society where life expectancy was notably low and where child marriage was common among certain castes and in certain regions until it was outlawed (the custom still persists in some rural areas of Rajasthan). So it is that a number of cases of women who committed sati before reaching puberty have come down to us, such as that reported in the late-seventeenth-century account of the French traveler François Bernier, who witnessed the burning of a twelve-year-old widow from Lahore who trembled and wept so vigorously that she had to be bound to finish the matter.

In sharp contrast to the miserable plight that would otherwise have befallen her, the bright prospect of the glory awaiting the woman who commits sati might have been a strong incentive to newly widowed Indian women; this was at least a widely shared idea. Not only was the sati ensured that her sacrifice—in which she would experience no pain—would bring her eternal bliss with her husband in the beyond, she was also persuaded that she would redeem the sins of seven generations in her father's, mother's, and in-laws' lineages, and never be born again into the "impure" female sex.

In castes and milieus where sati had become the ultimate criterion of a woman's "wifely duty" and an icon of caste purity (and thereby, status), not only would family members, Brahman priests, and bards insist that the widow take the solemn vow to burn herself, but tradition at large—as represented by myths, literature, hagiography, and rituals in which satis were worshiped as deities—and, of late, propaganda and political and caste-based activism, left her little chance to escape her fate.

Once the sati declared her intention to follow her husband in death she had to burn herself, even if the Hindu legal treatises that sanctioned this highly controversial practice allowed her to retract. Very often, the would-be sati would have to prove her resolution by enduring a preliminary ordeal, such as burning her finger in a candle flame without showing any sign of pain. This would be taken as proof of her possession by "sat"—by the essence of her being in her role as the perfect wife, a sati—a supernatural power that enabled her to heal, protect, and foretell the future; to curse and bring misfortune on her community or in-laws; as well as to produce wonders and miracles, such as the lighting of her own pyre.

The utterance of the deadly vow set in motion a process of mythification, and in certain cases of deification, that reached its climax in the burning itself, a sacred event for believers, granting merit to family, performers, and onlookers alike. One may further surmise, on the basis of a number of indications, that the sati no longer perceived herself as a flesh-and-blood woman but rather as some sort of deity at the very least, a Shakti in the making. In demonstrable cases in which no violence was used, this process of objectification within the sati herself might explain, at least in part, how burning oneself alive—an act which continues to be repressed in the recesses of the unthinkable—could actually form a part of human experience.

DISPUTES OVER SATI (WIDOW BURNING) IN CONTEMPORARY INDIA

This chapter aims to make clear the nature of ritual violence through the analysis of disputes over sati in contemporary India, pointing out the difficulties in defying it and investigating the possibilities of overcoming it. Originally, Sati referred to chaste women and the goddess symbolising chastity and not to the custom of Hindu widows being burned or buried with the husband's corpse. It was the British colonial rulers who understood the word sati as the act of burning widows. The idea is that the life on this earth literally comes to an end there and the husband and wife live together for ever in heaven. The British prohibited sati as a brutal custom in the beginning of the nineteenth century. Many researchers have already attempted analyses of sati in those days and of the disputes leading to the prohibition of sati. Here I deal with the sati that took place in India in 1987 and its repercussions. I had visited the village concerned around six months after the incident, but the atmosphere was still such that no research could be conducted openly.

For this reason, newspaper and magazine articles on the incident will be used here as the objects of analysis. The number of articles on this topic comes to about two hundred ranging from those that just report the facts of the sati incident and the names of people arrested to special reports of several pages in length. In addition to these there are many research articles by historians, religious studies specialists and anthropologists that have been published till recently. Ritual violence refers to two things: patterned or formalised violence and violent elements in ritual. In other words this is community violence in the sense that it is socially sanctioned, and it is divine violence in the sense that it is linked to a supernatural being.

As we will see later, sati is also ritualised violence which is worshipped by many people and blessed by the goddess. Widows who can receive the blessings of the goddess are limited. The widow must also show a miracle in the act of sati. Once this is accepted those who oppose the sati are cursed by the divine beings. Thus to reproach sati means the same as criticising the community and its system of belief. This is not just a matter of criticising violence as evil, since in order to criticise it, the community and the supernatural beings have to be reprimanded. Disputes over sati teach us the difficulties in this kind of criticisms of violence.

DEORALA, A SITE OF SATI

On 4th September 1987 in Rajasthan, a state in northeast India, a young woman was cremated along with her husband who had died a few hours ago. To be more accurate, the word cremated applies only to the husband since the woman was still alive when she was burned. The first article in an English language newspaper reporting this incident was only a short one of about a hundred words. In an article "A young woman commits sati" dated 5th September, it is said the police reported that an eighteen-year-old woman has committed sati and that four relatives have been arrested for aiding the suicide. There is no comment in particular.

Let me first present what were reported as facts. The village of Deorala is located eighty kilometres north of the state capital Jaipur and just twenty kilometres off the main road leading to Delhi, the capital city and it is by no means an isolated village in the middle of nowhere. The population is 13,000 and there are 300 households of Rajputs who are the dominant caste and own 70 percent of the land in the entire village. The village is well off, it has five primary schools and the level of education is higher than in other regions. Roop Kanwar's sati was the fourth one in this village as far as it is known and the last sati took place seventy years ago. Thirty-eight people have committed sati in Rajasthan since Independence and all have been in the Shekawati district which Deorala is a part of.

Roop Kanwar was eighteen years old, when she married the twenty-four year old Man Singh on 17th January 1987. The husband did not have a job. He had been trying to become a medical student, and had taken a university entrance examination before and after the marriage. He was taken into hospital on 3rd September with a stomach pain, but he died next morning. This happened eight months after the marriage. Taking into account the period that she had spent in her fathers house after marriage, Roop Kanwar and Man Singhs time together seems to have been much shorter - some say just three weeks. She saw her husband's corpse and expressed her will to perform sati. She immediately put on her red wedding clothes and went with the funeral procession to the cremation ground. This was around one o'clock in the afternoon. As the villagers watched, she sat on the wood piled up to burn the corpse. The fifteen year-old younger brother of Singh lit the funeral pyre as the chief mourner.

There were said to have been four to five thousand spectators. Roop Kanwar parental house got to know about their daughter sati in the newspapers next morning. Roop Kanwar was born in a well-to-do family in Jaipur, the capital city of Rajasthan. Her father ran a transportation business there. She was born and brought up in Ranchi in the state of Bihar, and there was a temple of sati nearby. Speculations that this might have influenced her were also reported. She was educated up to eighth class in Ranchi. She went on to high school in Jaipur, but she gave up her studies for marriage. Her father-in-law was an English teacher in Deorala village.

Roop Kanwar's sati attracted neighbouring villagers and several thousand worshippers visited every day even after the incident. The cremation place was called sati stal and was covered by a yellow canopy mixed with light pink. Four Rajput youths with open swords stood in front of the place and twenty-seven youths circled it without stop, guarding the cremation ashes twenty-four hours a day. The number of participants reached a climax on the morning of 16th September, when the ritual ending the mourning period called the chunari festival took place. A chunari (an expensive gold-embroidered silk shawl worn by a bride at her wedding) was taken along with other items from Roop Kanwar's natal house to her in-laws house and then to the cremation ground. There the chunari was burned in the sacred fire amidst the crowd shouting "Victory to goddess Sati!" and priests chanting the Gayatri mantra. The priests cooled the ashes down, gathered them in a pot and buried it. It was said that the ashes were saturated with sacred power (sakti). A trident was positioned where it was buried, worship was performed and more chunari shawls were placed on top. Around 300,000 people participated and some had even walked barefoot from six hundred kilometres away.

Many souvenir shops were set up and many composite pictures were sold of Roop Kanwar and her husband showing the couple enveloped in flames. Even after the chunari festival, two to three thousand people came to Deorala every day. In Roop Kanwar s house the wedding photograph was displayed on the veranda and in the room where she decided to commit sati, the red and silver sari which she was wearing at the time was spread out on display. Elite members of the village decided to collect funds to build a temple for Roop Kanwar at the place of cremation.

It is said 2,000,000 - 3,000,000 yen was collected just on the day of the chunari festival. Women activists reminded the Chief Minister of Rajasthan of the anti-sati act of 1827, demanding an explanation from him, but were turned away. On 14th September, around three hundred and fifty members of thirteen womens organisations took part in a silent demonstration in Jaipur criticising the government for not taking any action on 14th September. They took the matter to the Rajasthan High Court and on 15th September an order was passed banning the chunari festival.

However, this ban was not implemented, the government remained silent and there were even some members of the state assembly who participated in it. At this point, only Roop Kanwar's younger brother-in-law who had lit the funeral pyre had been arrested.

On 21st September a demonstration was organised in Delhi demanding that the Chief Minister should resign and that the central government should prevent the construction of the temple. On 26th over fifty widows joined a demonstration against sati and government relief measures for widows. Rajiv Gandhi who was the Prime Minister at the time sent a minister on 22nd September for investigation into the incident and statement of the central governments position. The state government reacted under pressure, and on 19th September the father-in-law and three other relatives were arrested for aiding suicide.

Twenty-eight people were arrested by 27th September. Policemen were posted in the village and all souvenir shops were banned by 2nd October. The state government issued a law prohibiting the practice and encouragement of sati on 1st October. On 20th October the police demolished a Roop Kanwar monument and on 31st October they arrested five people belonging to the Association for Protection of the Righteousness of Sati (Sati Dharma Rakshya Samiti) for encouraging the glorification of sati. Against these moves of the anti-sati lobby, the pro-sati groups responded by organising a demonstration of around five hundred Rajput men in Jaipur on 19th September as a protest against the arrests made on that day. They demanded that the government should not interfere in religious matters. On 27th September the first meeting of the Association for Protection of the Righteousness of Sati was held in Deorala, and the core members were the Rajputs living in Jaipur. On 8th October they hosted a pro-sati demonstration in Jaipur of about fifty thousand people, which was the largest demonstration organised after the incident. Kalyan Singh Kalvi who was a central figure in the Association for Protection of the Righteousness of Sati and the leader of the states Janata Party also participated and gave a speech at the demonstration.

The influence of anti-sati movements went beyond Rajasthan and on 2nd October a womens organisation criticised the procession at a festival of a temple dedicated to sati in Bombay. Festivals were also banned in a sati temple in Calcutta. Thirty-six womens organisations demonstrated in Delhi on 4th November demanding the establishment of a law prohibiting sati for the whole of India. In response to this, a new prohibition law was passed in the Lower House and Upper House by 16th December. The Chief Minister of Rajasthan resigned on 18th January, and one of the reasons is said to be his inadequate response to Roop Kanwar's sati incident. However, those arrested were later released without bail and no trials have been carried out. Furthermore, in spite of the legal regulations, eight thousand people gathered in Deorala for the first anniversary of Roop Kanwar's death.

Let me make a brief summary of the points of dispute. First of all, the pro-sati viewpoint sees sati as an honoured tradition particular to the Rajputs or Hindus and is antagonistic to the state. By considering sati as religious, it criticises state intervention. The anti-sati viewpoint held most strongly by womens organisations, criticises sati as savage and emphasises the importance of education and the improvement in status of widows. For them, sati is a womens problem and a custom that symbolises the low status of women in India. There is no question of it being a miraculous divine deed and there is no such thing as voluntary sati. They argue that sati cannot be said to be religious and that it is a means of making money at the expense of women. Their attack is also directed against the government as they declare that the government is not sincerely trying to outlaw sati and that the legal prohibitions are merely a gesture. But what they actually did was to call for government action. They not only demanded the urgent arrest of the relatives involved in Roop Kanwar's sati, but also acted against temples commemorating sati in the past in Calcutta and Bombay, saying that they glorify sati.

SATI AS MIRACLE

Here we would like to consider the beliefs behind sati. The anthropologist, Harlan gives the following explanation. In Rajasthan, the value of a woman is determined by her chastity towards the husband (pati). By this the husband is protected from all kinds of danger. The practice of this value is called pativrata. The woman performs another practice when the husband dies. This is sativrata and by this her body gets hot.

That is why it is said that when she chooses her death on the funeral pyre, she does not feel the heat of the flames at all. When she dies, she is called sati mata (Sati goddess). Sati is the manifestation of the moral goodness (sat) in women. In the newspapers, sat is expressed as something that takes hold of a widow, or it is explained that only a widow who has received a revelation from the goddess leaves everything behind and performs sati (Telegraph 10th October 1987). Let us take a more detailed look at the process between the husbands death and the act of sati. When the widow tells her family of her intension to commit sati, she puts her finger near a candle flame and proves that it does not get burned. Next she takes a bath in a river and changes into her bridal clothes.

If it is raining, it will stop and the suns rays will shine on the funeral pyre. The widow jumps on to the pile of wood. It is said that the husband comes to life for a moment to acknowledge his wife's sati. No one lights the pyre. Flames appear from the heat of the widows body itself, as she receives the goddess's blessing. For the widow, it feels like bathing in water and is literally called "bathing in flames" (agni snana). Roop Kanwar was filled with power and due to this power she was able to perform sati. Then, she became a goddess and gained the power to grant the wishes of other people. People came into contact with this sacred power at the cremation ground and sought for all kinds of worldly benefits. From the point of view of other women, Roop Kanwar's sati signified her exceptional strength. The power of the widow who has decided to perform sati appears as a blessing and at the same time a curse to people. People cannot stop sati in fear of her curse.

It is said that the lineage of the man who tried to prevent the sati in Deorala seventy years ago came to an end after that. It is also said that the policeman who arrested Roop Kanwar's father-in-law fell ill.Whatever the status given to sati in the scriptures, the explanations above seem to be enough to tell us about the beliefs that bring about sati. However, there is a contradiction here. For instance, a woman who commits sati is destined to be so, that means she is a chaste woman who has always been serving her husband. But, if that is the case, why does the husband die before her cannot be explained? Why did she not die before her husband?

This is surely a major contradiction if we take into consideration the fact that a widow is often said to be the cause of her husband's death. Moreover, emphasis on the miracle may also lead to the denial of the sati that actually occurred. As some of the villagers point out, the fact that it was the younger brother-in-law who lit the funeral pyre and that there were some people arrested in Roop Kanwar's sati led to the denial of its authenticity (Times of India 11th December 1987). There is also a view that sat could not have manifested in Roop Kanwar since she was too young. In this way, the logic of the people supporting sati seems comprehensive at first sight if we accept the concepts that are presupposed, such as the existence of sat and its power. But it is by no means so, and even if the beliefs themselves were not denied by facts, the authenticity of each of the incidents would be questioned. Roop Kanwar's sati was also not exempt from this inspection.

Furthermore, it is believed that the one who commits sati takes away not only the sins of her own, but also those of her husband, the ancestors and the descendents. This is a belief that deeply reflects the sacrificial nature of sati. We heard for instance that in the case of Roop Kanwar's sati, there was plenty of rain and abundant crops that year thanks to her. It would not be impossible here to identify the aspect of human sacrifice. There are various aspects to sati that cannot be understood simply as beliefs regarding chaste women.

SATI AS RESISTANCE

Roop Kanwar's father said that he was proud of what his daughter had done. She has made both our family and the in-law's family immortal (Indian Express 11th September 1987). But this was not all. Her death can be interpreted as not only making her family and relatives immortal, but also as being used politically to make the Rajputs and their land Rajasthan immortal. As we have already seen, from the beginning of the sati incident, there was a conspicuous attempt to understand and defend this in relation to the Rajput caste. Demonstrations were organised many times with the Rajputs as the core. Why the Rajputs? If we take note of the fact that sati is a phenomenon particular to the Rajputs of Rajasthan, it is necessary to consider the conditions that the Rajputs are in when thinking about contemporary sati.

Rajputs are a royal caste of northwestern India and were highly regarded as warriors even in the colonial period. They used to rule over Rajasthan, but their power has been weakened in recent years, externally due to the emergence of other castes and internally due to land reforms. This is a crisis for the Rajputs. Sati originates from the act of women committing suicide after losing their husbands in battle to prevent being shamed by the enemy, thus, is a suitable symbol for demonstrating their past glory both internally and externally. Sati can be seen as a means of resistance to overcome the crisis of Rajput identity or tradition.

A member of a pro-sati organisation, Kalyan Singh Kalvi, did not stop defending sati as a part of his (Rajput) tradition, in spite of the criticisms of sati by the Congress party members in the centre (Times of India 16th September 1987). Kalvi later weakened his view a little and said that the Rajasthan state government should have deterred sati in accordance with the law, but it was not right that the government should intervene in the chunari festival, and the construction of a memorial since these were only a part of family rituals (Times of India 29th September 1987). Here the relationship between politics and religion and that between the state and the family are put to question. Moreover, he even went on to state that the actions of the government and the police were wounding the religious sentiments of the Hindus, especially the Rajputs, and to hurt their pride would be very dangerous for the country since the Rajputs are emotional people and it is because of this that they have produced many martyrs as soldiers of the country (Times of India 30th September 1987). Other pro-sati people emphasise similar points. According to them, enforced sati is a crime and should be reprimanded, but voluntary sati cannot be opposed or deterred.

To do so, they say, would be government intervention in religious matters. They state that matters regarding religion should not be decided by the government or the courts, but by religious men such as the Shankararcharyas who head the four most important Hindu monasteries in India. In this way, the defence of sati is reconsidered as the tradition of not only Rajputs but of Hindus in general, and its authority is sought in a sphere outside secular power. Here lies the reason why many articles point to the relationship between defenders of sati and contemporary Hindu nationalism, which calls to make Hinduism the state religion and India a Hindu state.

It is thought that just as religion is only a tool for gaining political power in Hindu nationalism, sati is also only a tool in the power politics for politicians. What I want to emphasise here is the point that it is not only because sati is a custom particular to India that it becomes a symbol. Not only this, but also more generally there is a historical relationship between Indian women and Hindu nationalism in the past. That is to say, in India as the anti-British movements became popular at the end of the nineteenth century, it came to be understood that women were the source and storehouse of Indian tradition. Unlike the men who worked outside, women who stayed at home were transformed into unpolluted beings, who were not influenced by the effects of modernisation and westernisation and were the basis of nationalism dreaming for a future independent state.

Here the women who were idealised belonged to the upper castes observing social segregation (purdah). It was not only the British and Indian men who were put in opposition to this category. Westernised Hindu women and lower caste women who had no choice but to work outside along with men were also compared to these upper caste women. In this way, although it was paradoxical, a discourse was born according to which subjectivity was granted to the very women whose place was inside. A similar rhetoric can be seen the dispute regarding Roop Kanwar's sati. That is to say, sati contains the paradox that it recognises true subjectivity in women who are subjugated to their husbands. Moreover, sati differentiates Rajput women from other low caste women in the region ("Their sati is not real.") and at the same time it functions to negate the urban and westernised women and the secularism that they represent. Sati becomes the ultimate tradition to be observed by Rajput women. This tradition is ultimate for women in the sense that they are its true heirs and thus to prove themselves as Rajput women they have to choose death. Their subjectivity can only be actualised by death.

RESISTANCE AGAINST SATI

Most of the English language newspapers reporting Roop Kanwar's sati criticises it. For instance, Indian Express dated 11th September published an editorial with a title saying that a "barbarian tradition" has come back to life. In the editorial titled "Savage and primitive" published on the fourteenth day after the incident when the chunari ritual came to and end, it pointed out that, despite being an educated man, the father-in-law did not prevent the sati nor think that it was against the law. It also states that Roop Kanwar's death is related to violence against women, such as dowry murders and abortion of female foetuses after testing for its sex. It deplores that this incident proves India to be still very far from the twenty-first century. In other newspapers, sati is seen as "savage act" (Hindu 17th September 1987) and expressions such as "shame" and "inhuman act" are used and the word superstition is repeatedly employed (Hindustan Times 18th September 1987).

The many opinions published in the newspapers were much the same. What is common in these editorials is the significance of education and administrative leadership beyond political interests. They criticise that the state government did hardly anything after the sati occurred in fear of what might happen to the results of the next elections. They also approve of the establishment of the new legal measures, but question the efficacy of the law. Sati was understood above all as the symbol of the pathetic condition of widows in India. The fact that demonstrations by widows were organised points to this. In Hindu society, particularly among upper castes, widows are considered to be most inauspicious. This is because the cause of the husband's death is thought to be the wife who is still alive. Widow remarriage is accepted only among low castes. When a woman becomes a widow, various measures are taken to hide her sexuality which is potentially dangerous.

The widow must shave the long hair which is a symbol of womanhood, take off all her jewellery and wear white or plain light colour sari. She is prohibited from taking her meals with other family members and is not allowed to participate in her own sons wedding. She is considered very inauspicious and so is not fit for an auspicious occasion such as marriage. A married woman who dies before her husband is the complete opposite to the widow. If the couple has a son then she is perfect. A married woman whose husband is alive has important roles in rituals, such as marriage, as an auspicious being. So it was said that if there were no such discrimination against widows, no one would want to commit sati. Moreover, sati is said to be a means of deterring the wife's inheritance right.

Especially in the case of Roop Kanwar who had no children, the large amount of dowry in cash and kind given to the husband at the time of the wedding was supposed to be returned when she became a widow. For this reason it was also interpreted and reported that the in-laws who did not want to do so forced the sati to take place. There was also the criticism that contemporary sati is not a honourable tradition, but merely a religious show put up by the entire village aiming to gain the enormous amount of donations that would come from it. It was argued that this is not tradition but a contemporary phenomenon in a society penetrated by the market economy. Furthermore, there were doubts regarding the incident itself.

In a newspaper dated 25th September, a teacher who had taught Roop Kanwar in Ranchi was reported to have said that she was forced to sit on the funeral pyre and that she did not seem particularly religious when she was a student (Times of India 25th September 1987). But, the fact that she was forced has not been proved. A newspaper dated 29th September expresses doubts whether Roop Kanwar really committed sati of her own accord (Hindu 29th September 1987). According to one view, when Man Singh's body was carried into the house, the members of the household blamed Roop Kanwar that she had brought misfortune to the house and said that even greater misfortunes will befall the house in the future.

It was written that even if she had tried to escape, it would have been impossible due to the way in which the wood was piled up and her screaming would not have been heard due to the cheering of the crowds. Later, on 2nd October, a police report was published saying that Roop Kanwar had been trying to escape from the flames that were burning her body. Reports based on actual statements began to appear only after mid October. First, a report was published by three representatives of the Bombay Union of Journalists (Indian Express 23rd October 1987). There it was pointed out that Roop Kanwar was hiding in a shed. After this, the tendency to discuss Roop Kanwars sati as murder grew stronger. However, even in these reports the truth is obscure. The above criticisms moved the government, but were nullified in the face of enthusiasm of those actually involved.

Those who were against sati were to face some dilemmas themselves. These were the problems concerning the subjectivity of women and the fact that, however justified their argument was, it nonetheless could lead to supporting the control and punishment of minority groups, the Rajputs here, by state power. To totally deny the existence of voluntary sati would be to accept the view of women as being powerless and as victims. In the case of sati the object of violence is a woman. But to criticise sati as the ultimate violence of patriarchal society and to talk of women as victims of evil customs could lead to denying the nature of women as agents from the start. As a result, one ends up supporting the typical view of women in patriarchal society, that they are dependent and cannot decide anything for themselves.

It would then seem that the pro-sati discourse praising the heroism of women who commit sati was recognising the subjectivity of women, though it may not apply to women in general, as it denies the agency of those widows who have failed to commit sati. On the other hand, if they accept voluntary sati, not only would they be unable to deny sati itself, but they would also be strengthening the image of women as being tied to tradition in this case as well. This is because the decision to commit sati is made by a woman who wants to be subjugated to her husband and sacrifice everything for him. This clearly shows that sati is literally the ultimate ideological apparatus which establishes a womans subjected subjectivity.

There is a very fine line between seeing her as the victim of tradition and seeing her as the agent of positive choice, since the latter also aims at voluntary subjection. Thus highly educated urban women try to side with the woman and as a result end up constructing an image of women different from themselves. Moreover, the anti-sati lobby emphasised the need for legal reforms prohibiting sati and the glorification of sati. This signifies the demand for state intervention and hence it differs little from the nineteenth century imperialist view. In the nineteenth century, legal system was prepared as a means to civilise India whose backwardness was symbolised by sati and thus colonial rule was legitimised.

At that time, episodes of British people rescuing widows just as they were about to throw themselves into the flames were often reported. It can be said that in 1987 this picture was replaced by that of urban intellectuals civilising savage rural Indians. In this way, the intellectuals, especially the activists in women's organisations in this case, came to be seen as the enemies of "nationalism". They were criticised as women poisoned by western thought who did not understand tradition, and also as agents of the state oppressing the local community. The Rajputs have come to positively accept the position as a minority opposing the modern nation state.

SATI IN THE WEST COAST OF SRI LANKA

On 5th October 1982, an elder of the Tamil fishing village in the west coast of Sri Lanka where I was staying for my fieldwork died. He was seventy-one years old. A funeral was to take place in his house the next morning. Two barbers were to conduct the funeral. There is a division of labour so that members of the barber caste usually officiate in family rituals such as funerals, which involve impurity, and Brahman priests in those that do not, such as marriage. In the case of funerals too, the Brahman officiates the ritual at the end of mourning when the impurity disappears. First, the corpse is carried out the house on to a platform set up in the courtyard. The male relatives pour water on the corpse to clean it. Then the women do the same. The barber shaves the old mans beard and moustache. Those who are present rub turmeric and sesame oil on the forehead of the corpse. The women then wash the body with soap. After being washed, the corpse is moved on to a wooden bed placed in the courtyard.

There the body is rubbed with sacred ashes and dressed in white waistcloth with gold embroidered borders and white shirt which is the formal wedding attire. The body is sprinkled with perfume and decorated with flowers. Then the old wife who has been inside the house until then appears in the courtyard led by the hand by another woman. She wears a bright red wedding sari. Not only does this seem to be a mismatch for a funeral atmosphere but also the fact that it is an old woman wearing it makes it appear strange. The wife seems ready to collapse at any moment. She goes round the corpse once and throws the paddy in a mortar on to the corpse. She then sits next the corpse. After receiving the blessings of the women, she lies down on the right hand side of the corpse. A white cloth is placed covering the two bodies and the relatives through paddy over it followed by other participants. When this is finished the wife gets up. Then three women cut and take off her gold necklace called *tari* which was presented by the husband at the wedding and is the symbol of married women and hence of auspiciousness. A new plain sari is presented to the wife by a male relative. The corpse is then carried to the burial ground. Only men accompany this and the women stay at home.

What I want point out here is that the funeral for the dead is conducted in such a way as to remind us of a wedding and that the farewell to the dead man is also extended to the wife. Both wear a wedding costume and moreover the wife lies next to the corpse. A white cloth is put over them and the unity of the husband and wife is emphasised in a dramatic way. The people bid farewell to both of them. The wife is thought to die along with the husband. She then becomes a widow. The villagers explained this custom in which the wife lies next to the husband as *sati*.

What kind of an attitude can an anthropologist take towards an alien custom in another country such as *sati*? First he can clarify the beliefs behind *sati*. This is what I have presented in the above accounts of the view on ideal women regarding *sati* and the beliefs regarding blessing and curse. The anthropologist Harlan focused on the word *sat*, and there is a similar word in Tamil called *karpu*. This word is also related to concepts such as chastity, heat and protection of husband. If this point is more generalised, much of it overlaps with the discussion above and can become an explanation of the prominent view on women in Hindu society. In Hindu society, death or funeral has been understood by the concepts impure and inauspicious. Certainly death is impure and the children and the spouse of the deceased have to undergo a certain period of mourning. They accept the impurity caused by death and they are also inauspicious. However, from this point of view, the reason why in Sri Lanka the wife must lie next to the husbands corpse wearing a wedding costume cannot be explained. Wedding dress is a symbol of auspiciousness, and marriage is one of the few life cycle rites that do no cause impurity. Why a wedding dress in a funeral? In order to answer this question we have to take womens sexuality into account. An ideal life of a woman is that in which her mature sexuality is always controlled by her husband.

There are three cases of deviation from this ideal, that is, getting married after menstruation starts, the husband dying before the wife and adultery. Mature sexuality begins with menarche. Therefore an ideal marriage should take place before first menstruation. After first menstruation the woman goes to live with her husband. However, child marriages were legally prohibited by the series of reforms in the colonial period. Today, marriage takes place in most castes after first menstruation, but in cases where first menstruation is ritually celebrated as in South India, the first menstruation ritual itself sometimes assumes a form resembling the marriage rites. Thus first menstruation ritual is also the confirmation and at the same time the control of sexuality, though it is insufficient compared to marriage.

In contrast there are cases as those in North India where the first menstruation is ritually completely ignored. I would like to leave the various interpretations of first menstruation and marriage rites for a separate article, but what is important here is that the husband's death should be seen as the end of this kind of control.

That is to say, *sati* is a voluntary proposal of death by women as a means of resistance against the ending of the control of their sexuality that was completed at marriage. Coming back to the funeral in Sri Lanka, if it were not for the comment that this is a kind of *sati* we might have found a more romantic and positive meaning for the scene where the widow appears dressed in her wedding dress. We might even have overlooked the glimpse of ritual violence in the cutting off of the *tari*.

But we cannot just interpret this as a symbol of the strength of the love between husband and wife. This is because it is precisely this kind of discourse that has been legitimising *sati* and it is because of this that it has been the object of criticism. It is also insufficient to ignore the example observed in Sri Lanka as just being symbolic, since by doing so there is the possibility of misjudging the effect and the extent of the violence that is at work in *sati*. In this way, we can say that the analyses of the funeral in Sri Lanka and the *sati* in Rajasthan make possible a deeper understanding of each. Here I want to point out that in the case of the example from Sri Lanka, even if the *sati* was conducted symbolically, there is no way that the widows status is raised or divinised. It can be said then that the example from the Sri Lankan fishing village is just a poor imitation of *sati*. This brings to mind the discourse that true *sati* is only possible for Rajput women.

Here the discussion goes back to the previous questions. Why is it the Rajputs who bring about *sati*? Why Roop Kanwar? To answer these questions, the explanations such as the misery of widows and control of sexuality seem to be much too general. At the same time, these explanations ignore the nationalist view of women which has been historically constructed in India as I have mentioned above. Analytical perspectives such as comparison, investigation of meaning and holistic view which characterise cultural anthropology certainly can be said to contribute to a deeper understanding by linking Sri Lanka and Rajasthan, by not ignoring the symbolism and by taking into consideration the aspect of women's sexuality.

By doing so, some light can be shed on the relationship between death and sexuality which has been neglected in previous studies of funerals that emphasis impurity and inauspiciousness. However, it might be said that the anxiety of previous cultural anthropological explanations, which emphasise the whole and meaning, lays in the fact that the better the explanations are the more they end up accepting the violence that is the object of analysis. We would like to return to the disputes over *sati* keeping in mind how far it might be possible to break the link between explanation, understanding and acceptance.

FROM BLESSING TO VIOLENCE AND TO PAIN

Sati is violence in the name of blessing exercised by a goddess choosing one woman out of many widows. It is the family of her in-laws, the village, and the Rajputs who actually exercise the goddess violence. Sati is carried out in the name of the goddess and the community. The chosen widow becomes a goddess, blesses the people in turn and chooses another widow. In order to deny this belief and to accuse sati as being murder, one would have to deny the power of the goddess and of the community. This is rationalism and secularism which is anti-religious, and also individualism which is anti-community. This is indeed the anti-sati stance.

It is said that only the spread of education based on these ideals will truly liberate women. However, in reality, those who are against sati have no choice but to appeal to the state to prohibit sati. From the point of view of the sati defenders, this is state interference in religion and against secularism (guarantee of religious freedom) and in so far as sati is seen as a family problem, it is state intervention in the private life. In other words, the pro-sati lobby also happens to respond using the same logic of secularism and individualism as the anti-sati lobby. The dilemma against this violence called sati does not end here. For instance, if sati is seen as murder, the people who lit the fire or were directly involved in the sati would indeed be arrested and judged in the name of the law, but the collective nature of the violence would be ignored. Moreover, if the act of murder were emphasised, the violence at the symbolic level would be missed. The everyday discrimination or violence exercised against widows within the home would remain unseen. Furthermore, the power of discourse that distinguishes and differentiates between widows and married women whose husbands are alive would also be overlooked.

These points can be said to illustrate the difficulties in criticising violence, especially ritual violence that is legitimised by religion (community) and which is usually only one element in a ritual. The way to criticise ritual violence such as that represented by sati would be to deny the discourse that it is a divine blessing, that is to say, to make clear that it is not a blessing but violence, and that it does not involve happiness but pain for the one concerned and sorrow for the close relations. For instance, Asahi newspaper dated 13th October 1987 reports Roop Kanwar's sati as follows. The headline was "A young wife in flames embracing her husband who died from illness". The story begins with the sentence 'Kanwar sat on the wood piled up for her husband's cremation and put his head on her lap. She smiled as her body burned in the raging fire and then fell collapsing'.

The words "in flames" in the headline and "smiling" are indeed none else than expressions that mystify sati. In Japan, which is far away from India, sati was just a convenient incident to satisfy the curiosity about the mysterious country where anything goes. The denial of mystification or of the negation of pain typically found in the word "smiling", that is to say, the complete denial of the legitimacy of the violence by the divine beings is one of the few ways of going against the divine and communal violence.

In other words, we have to ask questions regarding the body of Roop Kanwar which was enveloped in flames and not regarding sati as an institution and Hindu or Rajput nationalism. By doing so we can shift the point of discussion from the problem of rational subject who can make decisions to the problem of embodied subject that feels pain. The dilemma faced by the anti-sati lobby, which emphasises the subjectivity of women, is similar to the dilemma that anthropologists feel when confronted with ritual violence of othercultures such as "female circumcision".

This is because anthropologists cannot find a decisive solution as to how they can talk about the victims of violence, how they can resolve the violence itself, and whether they as anthropologists should really say they ought to do so in the first place. This difficulty lies in the fact that they have the beliefs and institutions legitimising violence as their framework of explanation. As long as cultural anthropology respects other cultures from the point of view of cultural relativism, it is not possible to criticise ritual violence. This is more so if it has to do with the identity making of individuals. It is probably necessary to somehow disengage the connection that to understand violence leads to approving and defending it. To focus on pain here would be to point out that the individual is not necessarily totally bound to the systems of meanings or beliefs and social institutions, and does not necessarily become a completely subjected subject.

The very fact of a body that responds to and resists pain shows us that there are aspects which cannot be subjectified. Desire and pain rooted in the body undermine the ideologically constructed subject. At that moment, the individual momentarily overcomes the subjected subject. We must not overlook this moment. The focus on pain, however, should not mean considering the individual as an isolated body. Rather, we should make clear the "community of sorrow" which is hidden by the mystification of pain. This is not about accusing the relatives of acting out of self-interest and dividing up the pro-sati lobby which emphasises honour. It is rather about looking for people who accept the pain of sati as their own. It is by changing the analytic perspective from blessing to violence and then to pain, from the community of honour to the community of sorrow that the anthropology of violence can overcome many difficulties and open up new frontiers.

SATI - THE BURNING OF THE WIDOW

Sati is described as a Hindu custom in India in which the widow was burnt to ashes on her dead husband's pyre. Basically the custom of Sati was believed to be a voluntary Hindu act in which the woman voluntary decides to end her life with her husband after his death. But there were many incidences in which the women were forced to commit Sati, sometimes even dragged against her wish to the lighted pyre.

Though Sati is considered a Hindu custom, the women, known as Sati in Hindu religious literature, did not commit suicide on their dead husband's pyre. The first woman known as Sati was the consort of Lord Shiva. She burnt herself in fire as protest against her father who did not give her consort Shiva the respect she thought he deserved, while burning herself she prayed to reborn again as the new consort of Shiva, which she became and her name in the new incarnation was Parvati.

Other famous woman in Hindu literature titled Sati was Savitri. When Savitri's husband Satyavan died, the Lord of death, Yama arrived to take his soul. Savitri begged Yama to restore Satyavan and take her life instead, which he could not do. So Savitri followed Lord Yama a long way. After a long way in which Yama noticed that Savitri was losing strength but was still following him and her dead husband, Yama offered Savitri a boon, anything other than her husband's life. Savitri asked to have children from Satyavan. In order to give Savitri her boon, Lord Yama had no choice but to restore Satyavan to life and so Savitri gained her husband back. These two women along with other women in Hindu mythology who were exceptionally devoted to their husbands symbolized the truthful Indian wife who would do everything for their husband and they were named Sati.

The meaning of the word sati is righteous. But as written earlier the women named Sati, in Hindu religious literature, did not commit suicide on their dead husband's pyre. Therefore the custom of burning the widow on her dead husband's pyre probably did not evolve from religious background but from social background.

There are different theories about the origins of Sati. One theory says that Sati was introduced to prevent wives from poisoning their wealthy husbands and marry their real lovers. Other theory says that Sati began with a jealous queen who heard that dead kings were welcomed in heaven by hundreds of beautiful women, called Apsaras. And therefore when her husband died, she demanded to be burnt on her dead husband's pyre and so to arrive with him to heaven and this way to prevent the Apsaras from consorting with her husband. There are also other theories about the origins of Sati.

Even though Sati is considered an Indian custom or a Hindu custom it was not practiced all over India by all Hindus but only among certain communities of India. On the other hand, sacrificing the widow in her dead husband's funeral or pyre was not unique only to India. In many ancient communities it was an acceptable feature. This custom was prevalent among Egyptians, Greek, Goths, Scythians and others. Among these communities it was a custom to bury the dead king with his mistresses or wives, servants and other things so that they could continue to serve him in the next world.

Another theory claims that Sati was probably brought to India by the Scythians invaders of India. When these Scythians arrived in India, they adopted the Indian system of funeral, which was cremating the dead. And so instead of burying their kings and his servers they started cremating their dead with his surviving lovers. The Scythians were warrior tribes and they were given a status of warrior castes in Hindu religious hierarchy. Many of the Rajput clans are believed to originate from the Scythians. Later on other castes who claimed warrior status or higher also adopted this custom.

This custom was more dominant among the warrior communities in north India, especially in Rajasthan and also among the higher castes in Bengal in east India. Among the Rajputs of Rajasthan, who gave lot of importance to valor and self sacrifice, wives and concubines of the nobles even committed suicide, when they came to know that their beloved died in battlefield. In other parts of India it was comparatively low. And among the majority of Indian communities it did not exist at all. A few rulers of India tried to ban this custom. The Mughals tried to ban it. The British, due to the efforts of Hindu reformers like Raja Ram Mohan Roy outlawed this custom in 1829.

There aren't exact figures about the number of Sati incidences. In general, before this custom was outlawed in 1829, there were a few hundred officially recorded incidences each year. Even after the custom was outlawed, this custom did not vanish completely. It took few decades before this custom almost vanished.

But still there are rare incidences in which the widow demands to voluntary commit Sati. In 1987 an eighteen years old widow committed Sati in a village of Rajasthan with the blessing of her family members. In this incidence the villagers took part in the ceremony, praising and supporting the widow for her act. In October 1999 a woman hysterically jumped on her husband's pyre surprising everyone. But this incidence was declared suicide and not Sati, because this woman was not compelled, forced or praised to commit this act.

In different communities of India, Sati was performed for different reasons and different manners. In communities where the man was married to one wife, the wife put an end to her life on the pyre. But even in these communities not all widows committed Sati. Those women who committed Sati were highly honored and their families were given lot of respect. It was believed that the woman who committed Sati blessed her family for seven generations after her. Temples or other religious shrines were built to honour the Sati.

In communities were the ruler was married to more than one wife; in some cases only one wife was allowed to commit Sati. This wife was normally the preferred wife of the husband. This was some kind of honour for the chosen wife and some kind of disgrace for the other wives. In other communities some or all of the wives and mistresses were immolated with the husband. And in some cases even male servants were immolated with the kings. This kind of Sati in which the wives and servants were treated as the ruler's property intensifies the theory that Sati was introduced to India by the Scythian invaders of India. In some very rare incidences mothers committed Sati on their son's pyre and in even more rare cases husbands committed Sati on their wives pyres.

THE COMMISSION OF SATI (PREVENTION) ACT, 1987

(No. 3of 1988)

An Act to provide for the more effective prevention of the commission of sati and its glorification and for matters connected therewith or incidental thereto. Whereas *sati* or the burning or burying alive of widows or women is revolting to the feelings of human nature and nowhere enjoined by any of the religions of India as an imperative duty;

And whereas it is necessary to take more effective measure to prevent the commission of sati and its glorification; Be it enacted by Parliament in the Thirty-eighth Year of Republic of India as follows:

PART I

Preliminary

Short title, extent and commencement.- This Act may be called the Commission of Sati (Prevention) Act, 1987. It extends to the whole of India except the State of Jammu and Kashmir. It shall come into force in a State on such date as the Central Government may, by notification in the Official Gazette, appoint, and different dates may be appointed for different States.

Definitions.- In this Act, unless the context otherwise requires.-

(a) "Code" means the Code of Criminal Procedure, 1973 (2 of 1974);

(b) "Glorification" in relation to *sati,* whether such *sati*, was committed before or after the commencement of this Act, includes, among other things.-

(i) The observance of any ceremony or the taking out of a procession in connection with the commission of *sati*; or

(ii) The supporting, justifying or propagating the practice of *sati* in any manner; or

(iii)The arranging of any function to eulogise the person who has committed sati; or

(iv)the creation of a trust, or the collection of funds, or the construction of temple or other structure or the carrying on of any form of worship or the performance of any ceremony thereat, with a view to perpetuate the honour of, or to preserve the memory of, a person who has committed sati;

(c) "*sati*" means the burning or burying alive of –

(i) Any widow along with the body of her deceased husband or any other relative or with any article, object or thing associated with the husband or such relative; or

(ii) Any woman along with the body of any of her relatives, irrespective of whether such burning or burying is claimed to be voluntary on the part of the widow or the women or other-wise;

"Special Court" means a Special Court constituted under Sec.9;

(e) "Temple" includes any building or other structure, whether roofed or not, constructed or made to preserve the memory or a person in respect of whom sati has been committed or used or intended to be used for the carrying on of any form of worship or for the observance of any ceremony in connection with such commission.

(f) Words and expressions used but not defined in this Act and defined in the Indian Penal Code (45 of 1860) or in the Code shall have the same meanings as are respectively assigned to them in the Indian Panel Code or the Code.

PART II

Punishment for Offences Relating to Sati

Attempt to commit *sati.*- Notwithstanding anything contained in the Indian Penal Code (45 of 1860), whoever attempts to commit sati and does any act towards such commission shall be punishable with imprisonment for a term which may extend to one year or with fine or with both:

Provided that the Special Court trying an offence under this chapter shall, before convicting any person, take into consideration the circumstances leading to the commission of the offence, the act committed, the state of mind of the person charge of the offence at the time of the commission of the act and all other relevant factors.

Abetment of sati.-

(1) Notwithstanding anything contained in the Indian Penal Code (45 of 1860) , if any person commits *sati*, whoever abets the commission of such sati, either directly or indirectly, shall be punishable with death or imprisonment for life and shall also be liable to fine.

(2) If any person attempts to commit *sati*, whoever abets such attempt, either directly or indirectly, shall be punishable with imprisonment for life and shall also be liable to fine.

Explanation.- For the purposes of this chapter, any of the following acts or the like shall also be deemed to be an abetment, namely:

(a) Any inducement to a widow or woman to get her burnt or buried alive along with the body of her deceased husband or with any other relative or with any article, object or thing associated with the husband or such relative, irrespective of whether she is in a fit state of mind or is labouring under a state of intoxication or stupefaction or other cause impeding the exercise of her free will;

(b) Making a widow or woman believe that the commission of *sati* would result in some spiritual benefit to her or her deceased husband or relative or the general well being of the family;

(c) Encouraging a widow or woman to remain fixed in her resolve to commit *sati* and thus instigating her to commit *sati*;

(d) Participating in any procession in connection with the commission of *sati* or aiding the widow or woman in her decision to commit sati by taking her along with the body of her deceased husband or relative to the cremation or burial ground;

(e) Being present at the place where *sati* is committed as an active participant to such commission or to any ceremony connected with it;

(f) Preventing or obstructing the widow or woman from saving herself from being burnt or buried alive;

(g) Obstructing, or interfering with, the police in the discharge of its duties of taking any steps to prevent the commission of *sati*.

Punishment for glorification of sati.- Whoever does any act for the glorification of sati shall be punishable with imprisonment for a term which shall not be less than one year but which may extend to seven years and with fine which shall not be less than five thousand rupees but which may extend to thirty thousand rupees.

PART III

Powers of Collector or District Magistrate to prevent offences relating to Sati

Power to prohibit certain acts.- (1) where the Collector or the District Magistrate is of the opinion that *sati* or any abetment thereof is being, or is about to be committed, he may, by order, prohibit the doing of any act towards the commission of *sati* by any person in any area or areas specified in the order.

The Collector or the District Magistrate may also, by order, prohibit the glorification in any manner of *sati* by any person in any area or areas specified in the order.

Whoever contravenes any order made under sub-section (1) or sub-section (2) shall, if such contravention is not punishable under any other provision of this Act, be punishable with imprisonment for a term which shall not be less than one year but which may extend to seven years and with fine which shall not be less than five thousand rupees but which may extend to thirty thousand rupees. Power to remove certain temples or other structures.-(1) The State Government may, if it is satisfied that in that any temple or other structure which has been in existence for not less than twenty years, any form of worship or the performance of any ceremony is carried on with a view to perpetuate the honour of or to preserve the memory of, any person in respect of whom *sati* has been committed, by order, direct the removal of such temple or other structure.

The Collector or the District magistrate may, if he is satisfied that in any temple or other structure, other than that referred to in sub-section (1) , any form of worship or the performance of any ceremony is carried on with a view to perpetuate the honour of, or to preserve the memory of, any person in respect of whom *sati* has been committed, by order, direct the removal of such temple or other structure.

Where any order under sub-section (1) or sub-section (2) is not complied with, the State Government or the Collector or the District Magistrate, as the case may be, shall cause the temple or other structure to be removed through a police officer not below the rank of a Sub-Inspector at the cost of the defaulter.

Power to seize certain properties.- (1) Where the Collector or the District Magistrate has reason to believe that any funds or property have been collected or acquired for the purpose of glorification of the commission of any *sati* or which may be found under circumstances which create suspicion of the commission of any offence under this Act, he may seize such funds or property.

Every Collector or District Magistrate acting under sub-section (1) shall report the seizure to the Special Court, if any, constituted to try any offence in relation to which such funds or property were collected or acquired and shall await the orders of such Special Court as to the disposal of the same.

PART IV

Special Courts

Trial of offences under this Act.- (1) Notwithstanding anything contained in the Code, all offences under this Act shall be triable only by a Special Court constituted under this chapter.

The State Government shall, by notification in the official Gazette, constitute one or more Special Courts for the trial of offences under this Act and every Special Court shall exercise jurisdiction in respect of the whole or such part of the State as may be specified in the notification.

A Special Court shall be presided over by a judge to be appointed by the State Government with the concurrence of the Chief Justice of the High Court.

A person shall not be qualified for appointment as a judge of a Special Court unless he is, immediately before such appointment, a Sessions Judge or an Additional Sessions Judge in any State. Special Public Prosecutions.- (1) For every Special Court, the State Government shall appoint a person to be a Special Public Prosecutor. A person shall be eligible to be appointed as a Special Public Prosecutor under this section only if he had been in practice as an advocate for not less than seven years or has held any post for a period of not less than seven years under the State requiring special knowledge of law.

Every person appointed as a Special Public Prosecutor under this chapter shall be deemed to be a Public Prosecutor within the meaning of Cl. (u) of Sec. 2 of the Code and the Provisions of the Code shall have effect accordingly.

Procedure and powers of Special Courts.-(1) A Special Court may take cognizance of any offence, without the accused being committed to it for trial, upon receiving a complaint of facts which constitute such offence, or upon a police report of such facts.

Subject to the other provisions of this Act, a Special Court shall for the purpose of the trial of any offence, have all the powers of a Court of Session and shall try such offence as if it were a Court of Session, so far as may be, in accordance with the procedure prescribed in the Code for trial before a Court of Session.

Power of Special Court with respect to other offences.-(1) When trying any offence under this Act, a Special Court may also try any other offence with which the accused may, under the Code, be charged at the same trial if the offence is connected with such other offence.

If, in the course of any trial of any offence under this Act it is found that the accused person has committed any other offence under this Act or any other law, a Special Court may convict such person also of such other offence and pass any sentence authorised by this Act or such other law for the punishment thereof.

In every Enquiry or trial, the proceedings shall be held as expeditiously as possible and, in particular, where the examination of witnesses has begun, the same shall be continued from day to day until all the witnesses in attendance have been examined, and if any Special Court finds the adjournment of the same beyond the following date to be necessary, it shall record its reasons for doing so. Forfeiture of funds or property – Where a person has been convicted of an offence under this Act, the Special Court trying such offence may, if it is considered necessary so to do, declare that any funds or property seized under Sec. 8 shall stand forfeited to the State.

Appeal.- Notwithstanding anything contained in the Code, an appeal shall lie as a matter of right from any judgement, sentence or order, not being an interlocutory order, of a Special Court to the High Court both of facts and on law.

(2) Every appeal under this chapter shall be preferred within a period of thirty days from the date of judgement, sentence or order appealed from:

Provided that the High Court may entertain an appeal after the expiry of the said period of thirty days if it is satisfied that the appellant had sufficient cause for not preferring the appeal within the period of thirty days.

PART V

Miscellaneous

Protection of action taken under this Act.- No suit, prosecution or other legal proceeding shall lie against the State Government or any officer or authority of the State Government for anything which is in good faith done or intended to be done in pursuance of this Act or any rules or orders made under this Act.

Burden of proof.- Where any person is prosecuted of an offence under Sec. 4, the burden of proving that he had not committed the offence under the said section shall be on him.

Obligation of certain persons to report about the commission of offence under this Act.- (1) All officers of Government are hereby required and empowered to assist the police in the execution of the provisions of this Act or any rule or order made there under. All village officers and such other officers as may be specified by the Collector or the District Magistrate in relation to any area and the inhabitants of such area shall, if they have reason to believe or have the knowledge that *sati* is about to be, or has been, committed in the area shall forthwith report such fact to the nearest police station.

Whoever contravenes the provision of sub-section (1) or sub-section (2) shall be punishable with imprisonment of either description for a term which may extend to two years and shall also be liable to fine.

Person convicted of an offence under Sec. 4 to be disqualified form inheriting certain properties.- A person convicted of an offence under sub-section (1) of Sec. 4 in relation to the commission of *sati* shall be disqualified from inheriting the property of the person in respect of whom such *sati* has been committed or the property of any other person which he would have been entitled to inherit on the death of person in respect of whom such *sati* has been committed.

Amendment of Act 43 of 1951.- In the Representation of the People Act, 1951.-

(a) In Sec. 8, in sub-section (2) after the proviso, the following proviso shall be inserted, namely;

"Provided further that a person convicted by a Special Court for the contravention of any of the provisions of the Commission of Sati (Prevention) Act, 1987 shall be disqualified from the date of such conviction and shall continue to be disqualified for a further period of five years since his release";

(b) In Sec. 123 after Cl.(3-A), the following clause shall be inserted, namely:

"(3-B) The propagation of the practice or the commission of sati or its glorification by a candidate or his agent or any other person with the consent of the candidate or his election agent for the furtherance of the prospects of the election of that candidate or for prejudicially affecting the election of any candidate.

Explanation.- For the purpose of this clause, *"sati"* and "glorification" in relation to *sati* shall have the meanings respectively assigned to them in the Commission of Sati (Prevention) Act, 1987."

Act to have overriding effect.- The provision of this Act or any rule or order made thereunder shall have effect notwithstanding anything inconsistent therewith contained in any enactment other than this Act or in any instrument having effect by virtue of any enactment other than this Act.

Power to make rules.-

(1) The Central Government may, by notification in the Official Gazette, make rules for carrying out the provisions of this Act.
(2) Every rule made under this chapter shall be laid, as soon as may be after it is made, before each House of Parliament, while it is in session, for a total period of thirty days which may be comprised in one session or in two or more successive sessions, and if, before the

expiry of the session immediately following the session or the successive sessions aforesaid, both Houses agree in making any modification in the rule or both Houses agree that the rule should not be made, the rule shall thereafter have effect only in such modified form or be of no effect, as the case may be; so however, that any such modification or annulment shall be without prejudice to the validity of anything previously done under that rule.

Repeal of existing laws.-

(1) All laws in force in any State immediately before the commencement of this Act in that State which provide for the prevention or the glorification of *sati* shall, on such comment, stand repealed.

(2) Notwithstanding, such repeal, anything done or any action taken under any law repealed under sub-section (1) shall be deemed to have been done or taken under the corresponding provisions of this Act, and, in particular, any case taken cognizance of by a Special Court under the provisions of any law so repealed and pending before it immediately before the commencement of this Act in that State shall continue to be dealt with by that Special Court after such commencement as if such Special Court had been constituted under Sec. 9 of this Act.

COMMISSION OF SATI (PREVENTION) RULES, 1988

G.S.R. 360(E), dated 21st March, 1988.- In exercise of the powers conferred by Sec. 21 of the Commission of Sati (Prevention) Act, 1987 (3 of 1988), the Central Government hereby makes the following rules, namely:

1. Short title and commencement.-
   (1) These rules may be called the Commission of Sati (Prevention) Rules, 1988.
   (2) They shall come into force on the date of their publication in the Official Gazette.
2. Definitions.-
   (1) In these rules, unless the context otherwise requires,- "Act" means the Commission of Sati (Prevention) Act, 1987 (3 of 1988); "prohibitory order" means an order issued under Sec. 6; "section" means section of the Act.
   (2) Words and expressions used but not defined in these rules and defined in the Act shall have the same meanings as are respectively assigned to them in the Act.
3. Delegation of power to prohibit certain acts.- (1) The State Government may, by order and subject to such conditions as it may deem fit to impose, direct that the powers of the Collector or the District Magistrate under Sec. 6 may also be exercised by such other officers not below the rank of the village officers.

4. Prohibitory orders under Sec. 6, how made.-
   (1) Every prohibitory order under Sec. 6 shall be made by beat of drum or other customary mode, in the concerned village, or in case of town or city, in the locality in which the act prohibited is likely to occur or has taken place.
   (2) The prohibitory order shall be displayed at some conspicuous place in the area or areas to which such acts relates and a copy thereof shall also be displayed in the office of the officer issuing the prohibitory order and such display shall be taken as a sufficient notice to all persons concerned in the area of areas to which such order relates.
5. Manner of making order for removal of temples or structures under sub-section (1) of Sec. 7- (1) Before making any order under sub-section (1) of Sec. 7 for removal of any temple or structure, the State Government or any other officer authorized by the State Government in this behalf, shall give at least ninety days' notice to the person or persons involved in the acts complained of, and also to the owners and occupiers of the temple or structure proposed to be removed.

The notice under sub-rule shall specify-
   (1) The temple/structure proposed to be removed, its location and other particulars,
   (2) The owners/occupiers of the temple/structure, and
   (3) The specific instance or instances or worship or ceremony contravening the provisions of Sec.7.
   (3) The Government or the officer authorized by the State Government in this behalf shall, after giving reasonable opportunity of being heard to the persons specified in the notice, order the removal of the temple or structure through a police not below the rank of the Sub-Inspector.
6. Manner of making order for removal of temples or structures under sub-section (2) of Sec. 7.-(1) After issue of a prohibitory order under Sec. 6, the Collector or the District Magistrate, or such other officer as directed by the State Government by order under rule 3 shall, before making any order for removal of any temple or structure under sub-section (2) of Sec. 7 give at least ninety days' notice to the owners and occupiers of the temple or structure proposed to be removed.

The Collector of the District Magistrate, or such other officer as directed by the State Government by order under rule3, shall follow the provisions of sub-rules (2) and (3) of rule 4 in the case of orders made under this rule.

7. Inventory and forfeiture of the property of temple or structure.- As soon as the order of removal of the temple or structure is executed, the State Government or the Collector or the District Magistrate, or

as the case may be, the officer as directed by the State Government by order under rule 3, shall prepare an inventory of all the material and other property obtained after removal of such temple or structure specifying in it the place where it is lodged or kept, and shall forward the intimation thereof to the Special court for declaration of forfeiture of the said material or property to the State under Sec. 13 , if the Special Court considers it necessary so to do, and shall also give a copy of the inventory to the owners/occupiers of the temple/structure removed.

BENGAL SATI REGULATION, 1829

The Bengal Sati Regulation, or Regulation XVII, A. D. 1829 of the Bengal Code was a legal act promulgated in British Indiaunder East India Company rule, by the then Governor-General Lord William Bentinck, which made the practice of sati or suttee—or the immolation of a Hindu widow on the funeral pyre of her deceased husband—illegal in all jurisdictions of British India and subject to prosecution.

TEXT

Sati Regulation XVII A. D. 1829 of the Bengal Code
4 December 1829

Lord William Cavendish Bentick A regulation for declaring the practice of suttee, or of burning or burying alive the widows of Hindus, illegal, and punishable by the criminal courts, passed by the governor-general in council on 4 December 1829, corresponding with the 20th Aughun 1236 Bengal era; the 23rd Aughun 1237 Fasli; the 21st Aughun 1237 Vilayati; the 8th Aughun 1886 Samavat; and the 6th Jamadi-us-Sani 1245 Hegira.

- The practice of suttee, or of burning or burying alive the widows of Hindus, is revolting to the feelings of human nature; it is nowhere enjoined by the religion of the Hindus as an imperative duty; on the contrary a life of purity and retirement on the part of the widow is more especially and prefera-bly inculcated, and by a vast majority of that people throughout India the practice is not kept up, nor observed: in some extensive districts it does not exist: in those in which it has been most frequent it is notorious that in many instances acts of atrocity have been perpetrated which have been shocking to the Hindus themselves, and in their eyes unlawful and wicked. The measures hitherto adopted to discourage and prevent such acts have failed of success, and the governor-general in council is deeply impressed with the conviction that the abuses in question cannot be effectually put an end to without abolishing the practice altogether. Actuated by these considerations the governor-general in council, without intending to depart from one of the first and most important principles of the system of British government in India, that all classes of the people be secure in the observance of their religious usages so long as that system can be adhered to without violation of the paramount dictates of justice and humanity, has deemed it right to establish the following rules, which are hereby enacted to be in force from the time of their promulgation throughout the territories immediately subject to the presidency of Fort William.

- The practice of suttee, or of burning or burying alive the widows of Hindus, is hereby declared illegal, and punishable by the criminal courts.
- First. All zamindars, or other proprietors of land, whether malguzari or lakhiraj; ali sadar farmers and underrenters of land of every description; all dependent taluqdars; all naibs and other local agents; all native officers employed in the collection of the revenue and rents of land on the part of government, or the Court of Wards; and all munduls or other headmen of villages are hereby declared especially accountable for the immediate communication to the officers of the nearest police station of any intended sacrifice of the nature described in the foregoing section; and any zamindar, or other description of persons above noticed, to whom such responsibility is declared to attach, who may be convicted of wilfully neglecting or delaying to furnish the information above required, shall be liable to be fined by the magistrate or joint magistrate in any sum not exceeding two hundred rupees, and in default of payment to be confined for any period of imprisonment not exceeding six months.

Secondly. Immediately on receiving intelligence that the sacrifice declared illegal by this regulation is likely to occur, the police darogha shall either repair in person to the spot, or depute his mohurrir or, jamadar, accompanied by one or more burkundazes of Hindu religion, and it shall be the duty of the police-officers to announce to the persons assembled for the performance of ceremony, that it is illegal; and to endeavour to prevail on them to disperse, explaining to them that in the event of their persisting in it they will involve themselves in a crime, and become subject to punishment by the criminal courts. Should the parties assembled proceed in defiance of these remonstrances to carry the ceremony into effect, it shall be the duty of the police-officer to use all lawful means in their power to prevent the sacrifice from taking place, and to apprehend the principle persons aiding and abetting in the performance of it, and in the event of the police-officers being unable to apprehend them, they shall endeavour to ascertain their names and places of abode, and shall immediately communicate the whole of the particulars to the magistrate for his orders.

Thirdly. Should intelligence of a sacrifice have been carried into effect before their arrival at the spot, they will nevertheless institute a full enquiry into the circumstances of the case, in like manner as on all other occasions of unnatural death, and report them for the information and orders of the magistrate or joint magistrate, to whom they may be subordinate.

IV. First. On the receipt of the reports required to be made by the police daroghas, under the provisions of the foregoing section, the magistrate or joint magistrate of the jurisdiction in which the sacrifice may have taken place, shall enquire into the circumstances of the case, and shall adopt the necessary measures for bringing the parties concerned in promoting it to trial before the court of circuit.

Secondly. It is hereby declared, that after the promulgation of this regulation all persons convicted of aiding and abetting in the sacrifice of a Hindu widow, by burning or burying her alive, whether the sacrifice be voluntary on her part or not, shall be deemed guilty of culpable homicide, and shall be liable to punishment by fine or by both fine and imprisonment, at the discretion of the court of circuit, according to the nature and circumstance of the case, and the degree of guilt established against the offender; nor shall it be held to be any plea of justification that he or she was desired by the party sacrificed to assist in putting her to death.

Thirdly. Persons committed to take their trial before the court of circuit for the offence above-mentioned shall be admitted to bail or not, at the discretion of the magistrate or joint magistrate, subject to the general rules in force in regard to the admission of bail.

V. It is further deemed necessary to declare, that nothing contained in this regulation shall be construed to preclude the court of Nizamat Adalat from passing sentence of death on persons convicted of using violence or compulsion, or of having assisted in burning or burying alive a Hindu widow while labouring under a state of intoxication, or stupefaction, or other cause impeding the exercise of her free will, when, from the aggravated nature of the offence, proved against the prisoner, the court may see no circumstances to render him or her proper object of mercy.

Bengal Government to the Court of Directors on Sati (4 December 1829)

- Your honourable court will be gratified by perceiving the great preponderance of opinions of the most intelligent and experienced of the civil and military officers consulted by the governor-general, in favour of the abolition of suttees, and of the perfect safety with which in their judgement the practice may be suppressed.
- A few indeed were of opinion that it would be preferable to effect the abolition by the indirect interference of the magistrates and other public offices with the tacit sanction alone on the part of

government, but we think there are very strong grounds against the policy of that mode of proceeding, independently of the embarrassing situation in which it would place the local officers, by allowing them to exercise a discretion in so delicate a matter. To use the words of the governor-general, we were decidedly in favour of an open avowed and general prohibition, resting altogether upon the moral goodness of the act, and our power to enforce it.

- Your honourable court will observe that the original draft of the regulation was considerably modified before its final enactment, and that it was deemed advisable, at the suggestion of the judges of the nizamat adalat, to omit the distinction originally made between misdemeanour and culpable homicide, in being accessory to a suttee, and also in the degree of interference to be exercised by the police-officers. Upon the fullest consideration of the objections taken by the court, we determined that it would be better to leave the apportionment of punishment to be regulated by the commissioners of circuit, according to the nature and circumstances of each case, and that separate special instructions should be issued to the police-officers, as well as to the European authorities, to ensure a moderate and lenient exercise of the powers vested in them respectively by the regulation.
- Finally, also, we were induced by the advice of the nizamat adalat to leave out a provision that the Mahomedan law-officers should not take any part in trials in cases of suttee. We were disposed to think that the attendance of the law-officers might be liable to misconstruction, and afford an opening to objections which it was desirable as much as possible to avoid; at the same time the opinion of the court against excepting the offence in question from the ordinary course of trial, was doubtless entitled to much weight, and upon the whole we were willing to be guided by their judgement in omitting the section altogether.
- We beg to refer your honourable court to the enclosures contained in the letter from the registrar of the nizamat adalat under date the 3d instant (No. 21), for the special instructions above noticed, which have been issued to the commissioners of circuit, the magistrate, and the police-officers for their guidance.
- In conclusion we venture to express a confident expectation that under the blessing of divine providence the important measure which we have deemed it our duty to adopt will be efficacious in putting down the abhorrent practice of suttee, a consummation, we feel persuaded, not less anxiously desired by your honourable court than

by every preceding government of India, although the state of the country was less favourable in former times than at present, for its full and complete execution. It would be too much to expect that the promulgation of the abolition will not excite some degree of clamour and dissatisfaction, but we are firmly persuaded that such feelings will be short-lived, and we trust that no apprehension need be entertained of its exciting any violent opposition or any evil consequences whatever.

3

Status of Widows in India

Believe it or not, India has over 40 million widows - the highest in the world. It is a paradox that in this nation which has a glorious history with incidents glorifying women, widows are shunned from society. A widow regardless of her age has to don a drab garment and give up other adornments and confine herself to a corner of the house. A widow even has to tonsure her head in certain communities. She is not allowed to attend weddings or other celebrations as her presence is considered a bad omen.

A widower on the other hand does not suffer any differential treatment. Rather he is allowed to remarry even before a year of mourning has passed. Although widow marriages are becoming common in the cities the situation is still dismal in the rural areas. Not only a widow becomes financially dependent but also suffers the indignity of becoming a social outcaste. In Globalized India, where even in wealthy families wives own no assets directly, widows are rendered superfluous and terminally dependent. In poorer families they are just thrown out.

In the holy Hindu City of Vrindavan, a place that draws devotees from around the globe, thousands of widows live in shame and poverty. Hindus around the world know Vrindavan for its temples but in India it is known as a city for widows. They flock to the ashrams of Vrindavan, where they are provided with the daily rations of a cup of rice and 7 cents. The majority of the widows are ignorant of their basic rights because they come from rural areas where little has changed for centuries. There are so many Non Governmental Organisations who work for the rehabilitation of widows. But only a small percentage of the widows go to them for any help. There is a fervent need to spread awareness among women especially in the rural areas. They need the assurance that people who care are there to support them no matter what happens.

WIDOWS IN KERALA

There is a slightly higher proportion of widows in Kerala (10 per cent) compared to the Indian average. This may be attributed to Kerala's demographic profile (*i.e.* higher female life expectancy), a greater age differential at marriage, and low remarriage rates among widows. The studies on the welfare of widows have focussed on widowhood in northern India, where they face greater levels of discrimination compared to their southern counterparts in general and Kerala in particular. Women in Kerala are known for their elevated status. The gender bias in sex ratios found in India is absent in Kerala (the female to male ratio is 1,058 and 933 per 1,000 for Kerala and India respectively). While life expectancy for Indian women and men is almost identical (61 years for women and 60 years for men), Kerala reports female advantage (76 years for women and 70 years for men) and the highest female life expectancy in the country.

The gender gap in literacy rates is relatively narrow (88 per cent for women and 94 per cent for men in 2011), fertility rates are low (below replacement levels). It has been argued, however, that these indicators only tell part of the story; patriarchal norms continue to reign over the lives of women, manifesting in various forms, including domestic violence. It is also reported that Kerala has the worst record among the Indian states for economic dependency among the elderly; 76 per cent of its elderly women reporting no financial asset in their name.

While, there is a history of progressive public policies in this state, including public support for vulnerable groups, such as widows, economic opportunities for women are few raising specific concerns for their maintaining a good standard of living—particularly if the husband has passed away prematurely. In this case, a woman may be left with young children and no source of livelihood. Whereas in the case of a husband's death after leading a full life and having grown up children who are shouldering family responsibilities, the impact on a woman's life would likely be much less, particularly if an adequate social security system is in place.

STUDY SETTING

The study was conducted in Kottathara, a *gram panchayat* (the lowest territorial decentralized unit) in the rural district of Wayanad, locale of an action research project, implemented by the Centre for Development Studies and the *Université de Montréal*. The project obtained ethical approval by the *Université de Montréal* Ethics Committee on April 25, 2003. One of the main goals of the project was to develop an evidence base that will contribute to the reduction of inequalities in health care and other basic services. The project has several databases, including a baseline survey (a census conducted in 2003 of the 3,352 households located in the *gram panchayat*, which included information on demographics and socio-economic conditions of the population).

The study site is multi-religious and multi-caste (caste is a hereditary, endogamous, usually localised group, having a traditional association with an occupation and a particular position in the hierarchy of castes; each caste is ranked in a hierarchical order), with a high concentration of indigenous populations, known as Scheduled Tribes (31 per cent). Social inequalities in women's health have been observed across socioeconomic and caste groups. Financial barriers to accessing quality health care have been identified, particularly among the poorest and marginalised groups. There are high levels of unemployment and limited economic opportunities. Most of the population are engaged in agriculture and the majority of workers are cultivators or wage workers. Recent declines in agricultural prices in the state have negatively impacted the economy.

For example, the price of pepper, one of the main crops grown in the region, dropped from ₹ 20, 506 per 100 kg in 1999/2000 to ₹ 7, 814 per 100 kg in 2002/03, now gone up to 5000 (The Indian currency is known as rupees, or ₹, when citing actual costs; 1 USD is approximately 46 rupees, currently 55 rupees). A recent drought had exacerbated the situation and there have been increasing stories of mounting debts of farmers, and incidences of debt-related suicides.

The following information is derived from the baseline survey. There are 759 widows living in Kottathara, 9.3 per cent of all females, compared to only 90 widowers or 1.1 per cent of the male population. The widow to widower ratio is 8.4 and the mean age of widows is 60 years. Significantly, the median age is also 60 years, which is due especially to the large percentage of widows below 60 years among the Scheduled Castes and Scheduled Tribes (53 per cent) and Muslims (42 per cent). Among widows, 68 per cent are the head of the household.

METHODS

Data Collection

Field work was conducted over a period of 2 months in 2004, involving a two step process. First, we interviewed key informants in order to gain an understanding of local constructions of 'widowhood' and the welfare and social opportunities for widows. The key informants included: 2 local government employees, 2 members of a local NGO, and 3 widows from a neighbouring *gram panchayat*. Second, we conducted semi-structured interviews with 10 widows in the community on issues related to health and vulnerability, enabling us to hear perspectives from widows. Using the project's baseline survey, we purposely selected widows that would sample a variety of characteristics, including religion, caste or tribe affiliations, age, and poverty status of the household. We interviewed women ranging in age from 33 to 73 years with diverse religious and caste affiliations, including Muslims, Christians, Hindu women from both forward and low caste groups, and two women were from the Paniya tribe, a marginalised Scheduled Tribe. Six women came from households that were below the poverty line.

The median duration of widowhood was 15 years. All the women surveyed have children, most women have between three and four children (boys and girls); only one participant did not have a son. Most of the participants now live with their adult children and were considered to be the head of the household. Seven women have access to land, three of whom have landholdings in their own name.

The interview guide consisted of open-ended questions, which was designed in conjunction with the director of a local non governmental organisation (NGO), who has more than 20 years experience working with women and development projects in the area. We included a limited number of simple questions in order to ease translation and that were to help prompt more in-depth discussions by encouraging the participants to share their experiences and stories. The guide was pre-tested and revised to ensure that the questions were clear and appropriate. Questions were asked regarding the circumstances of becoming widows, survival strategies used following the death of a husband, health and well-being, and the nature and level of support received from their families, the government, and the community. Interviews were conducted until the point of saturation (N=10), which although it is a relatively small sample, represented 13 per cent of the widows living in the study site. Three women identified for interviews were unable to participate because they were not presently residing in their household.

The interviews were conducted by a local team (two females from a local NGO were trained as interviewers and note takers) under the supervision of the first author, a woman of North Indian descent. Informed signed consent was obtained prior to interviews. The interviews were performed in the local language of *Malayalam* and detailed notes were taken. The first author also participated in the interviews by asking follow-up questions after the interview was completed, with the aid of a local translator. Interviews were conducted at the homes of the participants and whenever possible the interviews were conducted in a private area in order to allow the widow to speak freely, without the presence of family members. Interviews lasted between 30 and 45 min. The interview notes were translated from *Malayalam* to English by a local translator and the transcripts were reread for logical translation by the research team.

Analysis

Data analysis proceeded concurrently with data collection. Debriefing sessions were held following each interview with the field team and the NGO director. Line by line coding of transcripts and field notes were undertaken. Data were analysed for thematic content and emerging patterns. The data was grouped into themes and sub-themes and the interrelations between these sub-categories. A report of the preliminary findings was prepared and circulated among the project team for further discussion. Pseudonyms have been used for the participants of this study in order to protect anonymity. We have also changed the names of the people the women talked about in their interviews (*e.g.* other family members, physicians) as well as the names of institutions and some of the locations mentioned in the interviews.

RESULTS

In response to the first study question (becoming a widow), three themes emerged: debt, shame, and survival. In addition, we identified two distinct 'profiles of widows', based on the cause of death of their husband. Three themes emerged in response to the second study question (opportunities and challenges to leading healthy and fulfilling lives), economic security, social mobility and social exclusion, and access to health care. The results are organised under these themes, with illustrative examples.

Becoming Widows: Debt, Shame, and Survival

During the initial period of widowhood, women faced issues related to debt, shame, and survival. Following a mourning period (which varies across castes and religious groups), the women expressed a sense of hopelessness, related both to the experience and emotional stress of losing their husbands and the challenges in meeting the basic needs of their households. Nine of the widows interviewed had lost their husband at a time when their children were still young. None of them reported receiving substantial support from their in-laws, although the women did speak of receiving at least some support from the community. The women remained in their own households after becoming widows, with the exception of two who had returned to live with their parents. They became the primary breadwinners of the family, assuming responsibilities of household decision-making. This early period was highly stressful in their lives. In the most extreme case, Elsamma, a Christian woman with forward caste affiliations with 5 children talked about contemplating suicide:

"Following my husband's death, all my children were below 12 years, and I had decided to jump in the river and commit suicide. I had attempted suicide in this way three times."

The widows reported having to cope with the specific circumstances surrounding the deaths of their husbands, both prior to and immediately after their husband's death. Two main profiles emerged, women who lost their husband due to a chronic illness and women whose husbands had alcohol-related problems and 'drank themselves to death'. These profiles are described in further detail below.

The Chronically Ill Husband (debt)

Seven widows reported that their husbands had died from a chronic illness, who had been ill for a lengthy period of time before passing away. During this time, the men were often bedridden and had to be hospitalized, at least periodically creating economic and emotional burdens. The women continued to care for young children, met household needs, while struggling to repay debts incurred by the medical costs of their husband's illness. The case of Amina, a Muslim woman, married at the age of 14 and had four children prior to her husband's illness, is illustrative:

""For ten years, my husband had been bed ridden. We spent a lot of money for his health care.During that time I was getting only 20 rupees as a kuli worker [wage labourers working in agricultural sector]. I had to meet all the household expenses. I could send the children to school only up to 4thstandard." "

In cases where there were insufficient funds, care would be delayed or stopped altogether. This was the case for Sumanthi, a Paniya woman, as she recalled:

""My husband died six years ago, the cause was not known. He returned home one day complaining of a problem with his head, shortly thereafter he lost his ability to speak. He was taken to Kalipa College. After one month he was shifted back to his home in Kottathara with some medication. He was able to get back some of his ability to speak. The family became unable to pay for the medicine, and it was discontinued. Previously the community had rallied around the family to help pay for the medical fees. He was in this state for two years before he passed away." "

After becoming widows, the women assumed multiple roles within the household: breadwinner, decision-maker, child raiser, homemaker, and caregivers. Children of widows also had to make sacrifices, helping to take over responsibilities often at the expense of their schooling. And there were still debts to pay: Amina, for example, continued to pay off debts related to her husband's medical care for another couple of years and her children (who as she described above only attended school up to 4th standard) were never able to return to school.

Husbands Who Drank Themselves to Death (Shame)

The second profile that emerged was one of women married to men with alcohol-related problems. Alcohol is consumed predominantly by men and it is generally frowned upon by society – although it is readily available. Geeta, Leela and Usha (widowed at 27, 21 and 31 years of age respectively) reported that their husbands had been alcoholics. The use of excessive alcohol was intertwined with shame. This shame was partly felt by the men themselves (in rural Kerala, public drunkenness is viewed negatively by society), as Geeta, a young Hindu woman, recalled:

""The people were telling me that my husband after having consumed too much alcohol had fallen face down in the vegetable garden. Our neighbour had witnessed the incident and had threatened to report him to the police. It is said that his shame led him to kill himself." "

Feelings of shame, however, extended to the families in general and the wives in particular. In Geeta's case, she was blamed by her husband's family and the community for her husband's drinking—she was even blamed for his suicide and was often taunted and ridiculed by others. For Leela and Usha their shame was exacerbated by their husband's abandonment since social shame is associated with abandoned women in India. Their husbands did not assume any financial responsibility for their families and did not maintain any communication with their wives. Leela was abandoned by her husband only to learn from a friend that he had died:

""My husband was a drunk, who did not look after me. He left me when I was pregnant, and I was 20 years old. I did not know where he had gone. I was told by someone that he had gone for work outside and had been bitten by a snake and died." "

Usha was abandoned by her husband when she had three young children; "one day he left me to go back to Malagy [a *gram panchayat* in a neighbouring district]". Usha spoke more passionately and at greater length about her daughter, Beena, who is also a widow and had begun her marriage with great love and happiness:

""Her husband passed away almost two years ago. Like me, her husband was a drunk. They had a love marriage...Soon after he began keeping bad company and started drinking. He ended up selling the shop and he and Beena moved around Wayanad for work, living in rented houses. He was drinking excessively and was making lots of problems in the home. He was drinking daily and was on occasion beating my daughter and myself. He was good for nothing. The neighbours confronted him and told him to improve his behaviour or leave. He was later hospitalized...where he died of jaundice. She [Beena] received a telegram three days later informing her of her husband's death...Today Beena is not emotionally well she is depressed...she has no friends and only leaves the house to the angawadi [the preschool where Beena works] and then returns home.""

Survival

In both of the profiles of widows, the women spoke about particular hardships during the early periods of their widowhood, having to cope with financial and household matters that had previously been the responsibility of their husband with little to no help. Pata's statement is representative of most of the women interviewed:

""I had met with a lot of difficulties at the death of my husband, especially financial difficulties.There was nobody here to help us." "

The women did feel that they could rely—at least to some extent—on some community support. As Usha put it:

""The community has always helped whenever there is a problem. There is a mutual understanding among my neighbours to solve problems." "

However, community support was generally neither sufficient nor sustainable. Priya recalled:

""I did not receive any support from my husband's family, but the community helped me in the beginning, although this support has been slowly withdrawn." "

Therefore; women were faced to take on their families' survival on their own. A certain level of fear and uncertainty were initially felt. Over time, however, these women assumed their roles in the household with greater confidence and as Priya remarked: "*I feel that my power in the household has been increasing over time*". Most women expressed that household decision-making became important to do *with* their children, especially as the children got older.

Lata, a Paniya woman, stated unequivocally that "*all of my decisions are made in consultation with my children.*" As their children became older and were able to take over some financial responsibilities the women also found life got easier. For Priya, her life got easier when her son married and took on financial responsibilities:

""I consumed little food at that time, [the early period following the death of Priya's husband] but after my son's marriage, my daughter-in-law cooks for me. When my son became old enough he got a job as an auto rickshaw driver, and has been supporting me ever since." "

Among the widows whose husbands abused alcohol, although there may have been some psychological relief with their husband's passing (particularly those who have been abandoned); they reported persistent suffering with "emotional pain" due to the great shame associated with their husbands' death.

Challenges and Opportunities for Living Healthy and Fulfilling Lives Economic Security

Economic security emerged as the key challenge. After losing their husbands, the women claimed that they had no desire to remarry. Only one woman remarried (and was subsequently widowed for a second time), she reported that her second marriage was problematic. The universal reason given for not remarrying was for the sake of their children, in Priya's words: "I did not wish to remarry because my children are precious to me". All the women in the sample had children; the age of widowhood ranged between 21 and 63 years of age with most women widowed during their late 20s or 30s. Elsamma, for example, had 5 children by the time she was widowed at the age of 27 years. Without remarrying, the widows had to secure their economic well-being in other ways.

Three women had adult children – sons and daughters – who supported them; one of these women, Jamila a Muslim woman widowed at the age of 63, was also receiving her husband's retirement pension. Jamila, despite having some health problems, reported the least problems among the participants:

""My husband had been a school teacher. I am getting his pension. My children are taking care of me. I am receiving treatment from Dr. Jayla at Salka Hospital. I take ordinary food. I receive everyone's respect as an elder." "

Without family support, the other respondents talked about their struggle to make ends meet. Three women were receiving the widow pension, which entailed Rs 110 per month, received in two lump sums each year. Other respondents were not eligible, as a woman needs to meet three criteria: belonging to a household that is below the poverty line, have no living son aged 18 years or older, and has not remarried. The main drawback for these criteria is among women whose adult son does not care for the family. For example, Sumanthi discussed how her son does not provide any financial support for her and the family despite the many health problems faced by her and the family:

""My son does not provide any financial support. A few days ago he visited us then left the household without assisting us even though I asked for money to pay for medicine for myself and his sister.""

Sumanthi does collect the widow pension, which she said was facilitated by political connections as her husband had been working with the Communist Party of India (Marxist). But for other women, they complained about the difficulties faced in applying for the widow pension, such as travelling alone to the office and handling the administrative requirements. As Geeta recalled:

""I had a bad experience with the Panchayat offices. I went for documents and the staff of the office asked me to come back in the evening and it was for bad intentions, I felt that they would harass me." "

Shantha eventually received the widow pension, but only after a ward councillor intervened on her behalf:

""I have been receiving the widow pension for the past three years. I applied a number of times for it but did not receive it. They say that they do not know the reason. Finally, my ward member applied for me and now I have it." "

Six women work in low paying jobs as agricultural labourers (generally known as *kuli* workers who engage in wage labour), domestic workers, and child care providers. At the time of her husband's death, Usha was not able to meet the needs of her and her three children as an*anganvadi* assistant:

""I received an honorarium of ₹50 per month, which was not sufficient to support my family. I took on additional work. I would work at the angavadi from 9:30 to 3:00, and in the evenings I would clean houses. On Saturdays and Sundays I would work as a kuli worker making 10–12 rupees per day." "

Today, Usha's life is easier because her children have grown up and are supporting her including her eldest daughter Beena. Leela had previously travelled to another district, finding work as a domestic help. She has since returned to live with her parents and is a *kuli* worker. We were also informed of the two women who had left the *panchayat* after becoming widows that one had gone to find work in a nearby district and the other had joined a convent.

One opportunity for economic security was to participate in a self help group, a form of microcredit programme. Three of the respondents took loans from self help groups. These women talked about how these loans have helped them. In one case, Geeta had previously gone for wage work, but she was often taunted by men for travelling outside the house. After joining a *kudumbrasree* group (a self help group supported by the local government) she was able to purchase two milch cows with a loan:

""I have been a member of Kudumbrasree for two years. I took a loan and bought a milch cow. I also have a second cow, both of which recently had calves. From the two cows I am able to extract 10 litres of milk a day. For each litre of milk I will receive about ₹10 selling to the Milk Society. I am happy with this, I am now self-sufficient." "

Geeta further explained that her new job enables her to stay at home to care for her children. Jamila and Lata took loans to purchase chickens, which were used to supplement other sources of income. Other respondents, however, did not reap similar benefits from self help groups. Usha, for example, reported having to withdraw from a self help group due to time constraints:

""Two years back I joined a self help group. I enjoyed being a member but I had to withdraw because of lack of time. I was working morning till evening six days a week. On Sundays I would clean and take care of my own home. I was also unable to participate in any of the activities outside of the meetings.""

Social Mobility and Social Isolation

The second key challenge was related to social mobility and social isolation. Among the younger respondents, they voiced their difficulty with new restrictions in their social mobility. This included attending certain religious and social activities, but also seeking health care, as illustrated by Geeta:

""I am not allowed to go free and travel free. It is better to have a husband just for name sake at least. In this way others will not comment on me. The people are not allowing me to wear a decent dress in the absence of a husband. When my husband was alive I was taken care of very well and if I was ill, he took me for treatment at the hospitals.... Now I am not able to attend festivals and such activities because of the way people talk." "

The older respondents talked about feelings of isolation. Elsamma, an elderly widow has five living children, yet she lives alone in a house provided by the government. She received few visitors and cooked for herself. Jamala lives with her son and his family, but still expressed feeling lonely. This situation improved for some women, however, after they joined a self help group. For Priya, becoming a member of a self help group opened up new social networks:

""I joined RASTA [a local NGO] self help groups 7 years ago, replacing my daughter as a member in one group following her marriage. At that time I was quite lonely in the house and found self help groups gave me friendships." "

For Priya, who did not take a loan (because she was not in need of a loan), it was also the social dimensions of the SHG that she felt was important for her. Leela has also continued as a member of a self help group because of the social aspects of the group, having no interest in taking a loan (because she was worried that she would not be able to repay the loan). Social networking and social support was cited by other women who had taken loans as an additional benefit to their membership.

Access to Health Care

The third key challenge voiced by the participants was related to health. The respondents talked about a range of health problems, the most common being respiratory problems, joint and body pain, and mobility difficulties. Despite facing health problems, most respondents revealed that they had difficulties meeting health care costs for themselves or for a family member. This is illustrated by Usha's story:

""I have some problems in my back and shoulders, bone disintegration, causing a great deal of pain. I think this is caused by pulling water from the well at the anganvadi. I visit the public hospital. The doctor told me that if I pay ₹2000 I could have a ring put in my back to help ease the pain. I cannot find the money for this. I also have uterus pain. At times I cannot urinate, I will then go for treatment from the doctor who will prescribe medicine. I will take this medicine until the urine comes back. After this, the pain and urinal dysfunctions will come back. The doctor has suggested she remove her uterus, for which I have not even questioned the cost." "

Sumanthi needed to take care of her 35 year old daughter with a mental disorder requiring medicines costing ₹ 42 for five days. At the time of the interview, the condition of her daughter had worsened as the family did not have the money to purchase her medicine. Only Jamila, who had both her husband's pension and the support of her children, was able to access the health care she needed.

DISCUSSION

Widows in Kerala

Martha Chen, who has conducted pioneering research on widows in India, recalled her experience in Kerala where she was told by a well-known Communist leader that: "There is no such thing as widowhood in Kerala". The women in this study were not exposed to some of the more extreme forms of suffering and discrimination experienced in other regions of India, but their experiences illustrate their vulnerability to poverty, social exclusion, and ill health. In the following section, we develop a conceptual framework by synthesizing our findings with theoretical understandings of vulnerability and Amartya Sen's entitlements approach. We also draw on findings from research undertaken in other parts of India to promote a wider applicability of the framework.

THE CONCEPTUAL FRAMEWORK

Vulnerability and the 'shock' of Becoming a Widow

Although vulnerability has been defined in various ways, it is generally meant to signify that there is a capacity for harm by an individual or group in response to a stimulus or risk. Definitions have tended to vary across disciplines, diverging according to the focus on different aspects of risks. We focus on vulnerability *to* poverty and ill health as a response to a 'shock', specifically the characteristics of a person or group in terms of "their capacity to anticipate, cope with, resist, and recover from" a shock. To be vulnerable entails a sense of fragility, although one is still 'intact'. Fragility encompasses both the occurrence of a shock (or a stress) and the incapacity to cope with this shock, which we argue is attributed to insufficient entitlements.

Based on our findings in this study, we argue that becoming a widow appears to operate similarly to other 'economic shocks' or 'health shocks' in poor countries. In the case of a health shock, such as death of a working age household member or a chronic illness requiring long term care, households can face a double financial burden due to the loss of income of a breadwinner and the burden of health care expenses. What is particular about widowhood is that financial burdens tend to fall entirely upon women.

This is especially challenging in a society, such as India, where the employment opportunities for women are limited (and wage differentials are high; women are often paid half the wages of men) due to both the dynamics of the labour market and social norms. Health care expenses have been observed to be a major factor in the downward mobility of households. Costs may operate as a barrier to accessing the necessary care, a situation found among some of the husbands who could not access appropriate care. Women who were married to men who abused alcohol faced economic hardships as their husbands' diverted income from household needs to alcohol consumption. Even among those women with a husband, who abuses alcohol creates a situation in which they are essentially living as widows.

Stages of Widowhood

The vulnerability of widows may be characterized into three phases. The initial phase occurs prior to her husband's death. During this time, she may be confronted with caring for her husband (if he is ill) or dealing with his alcohol abuse. In both cases, women may need to assume financial responsibilities due to medical bills (in the first case) and the shedding of any financial responsibility from the husband (in the second case). Women may face other challenges during this stage. Women with husbands who abuse alcohol may also be victims of domestic violence. Although we did not explicitly explore this issue, as it is an extremely sensitive topic requiring special ethical and methodological considerations, physical violence did arise as a consequence of alcohol abuse in the cases of Beena and Usha. Moreover, there is a growing literature demonstrating alcohol to be a determinant of domestic violence in India. Additionally, while the prevalence of HIV/AIDS and other infectious diseases is relatively low in Kerala, in other parts of India, women may face the additional burdens of being infected themselves. It is less clear how the loss of a husband due to an accident or non-stigmatising illness may influence the characterisation of this first phase, but will likely depend on the immediacy of these causes of death (*e.g.* a lengthy period of care giving in the case of a debilitating accident versus an accident that caused immediate death).

The second phase occurs when a woman's husband dies. At this time, women must not only cope with the loss of their husband but also are faced with the challenges of ensuring the livelihood of their children, while coping with financial debts incurred from medical bills if the husband was ill for a long period of time or the social stigmatisation if the husband committed suicide, or died from alcohol-related causes or socially stigmatizing diseases, such as HIV/AIDS. During this period, there appears to be little support beyond assistance from community, which the women in our sample felt was an important albeit temporary source of support, thereby increasing the vulnerability of widows and their children to impoverishment and poor health. Again, it is unclear from our study how the loss of husband from an accident or non-chronic illness may influence this phase; however, the sudden and unexpected loss of husband will likely exacerbate the intensity of the 'shock'—both emotionally and financially—experienced by the woman and her family.

During the third phase, women may begin to learn to assume greater decision-making roles in their households. Enhancing women's decision-making agency has been advocated as one approach to improving women's status. However, some researchers have cautioned that we should not assume that this should translate into women making individualised decisions; 'joint decision-making' when women make decisions in partnership with their husbands should also be considered a sign of women's control. While we did not explicitly study decision-making as part of this study, including not having information on women's decision-making agency before and after becoming a widow, our results suggest that women found the initial period of having to assume all major household decisions to be stressful due to the competing demands that they faced. But over time, the women acquired more confidence in their decision-making skills, especially when they could integrate their children into the decision-making process, which suggests that individualised decision-making is not necessarily the ideal situation for all women. During the third phase, women were also taking on the role of the main breadwinner. In the absence of family support, widows enter the labour force or expand their activities, usually working long hours and often in less than ideal conditions. Widows, particularly younger widows, face social stigmatisation and restrictions in their social and occupational mobility, limiting their employment opportunities as well as their participation in social and community activities.

Set of Restrictions

As widows, women face a set of restrictions that increases their vulnerability. The *shame* of becoming a widow, which is compounded among certain causes of death (*e.g.* suicide; HIV/AIDS) where they may be blamed for their husbands' death, can be debilitating for a woman, Such shame can have a strong psychological impact, restricting her from appearing in public and engaging in social activities. For Geeta, taunts and the negative talk about her—being blamed for her husband's suicide and being a widow—prevented her from attending social and cultural activities in addition to making it difficult for her to seek health care.

As a widow, a woman faces *social stigmatisation* and *social exclusion*. The level of stigmatisation may vary according to the social norms of the particular society, ranging from a 'social death' in certain parts of North India to experiencing ridicule and taunts in Kerala, as discussed by the women in our study. Widows are restricted in their social mobility, confining her to her household. They may also be excluded from attending social and religious events.

Restrictions in remarrying are conditioned by social norms and can be linked to a woman's caste and class status. In our sample, there was also a preference by women for not remarrying for the sake of their children; mothers would like to protect their children from possible neglect from a new husband who may not care for her children. Since all of the women in our study had children their opportunities for remarriage were substantially lowered.

Responsibilities

As women lost their husband prematurely, they were faced with a heavy burden of responsibilities, which increased their vulnerability. This study identified numerous responsibilities. First, women were charged with the responsibility of *caring* for their chronically ill husband. (While in the Kerala context, chronic illness is the major cause of mortality, similar responsibilities for women would be found in societies that continue to face high levels of communicable disease.) Second, women who have had a husband with a lengthy illness are often faced with *paying off debts* incurred through medical bills. Third, women must often *make up for lost income*, due to the loss of the main breadwinner before the death of their husband. This may occur when a woman has a husband, either whose illness or injury prevented him from working, or who spends his money on alcohol instead of on household needs. Fourth, as widows, women (in the absence of an adult breadwinner) must take on the role of the *primary breadwinner*. This may mean either taking up employment or working additional jobs. Fifth, women are faced with becoming a *single parent*, often without additional family support. In our study, among the women who remained in their husbands' village, there was no family support for the husband's family in child rearing. Finally, in the absence of an adult son (or daughter) women are charged with assuming *household decision-making*, which can be very stressful, especially if they had not been part of household decision-making in the past, by either taking joint decisions with their husband or being responsible for certain household decisions (*e.g.* education of children).

Endowment and Entitlement

Sen's work is useful in helping to *explain* the vulnerability of widows. In the entitlement approach, Sen defines 'endowment' as encompassing the resources of a woman that condition her 'entitlement exchange', that is her command to exchange what she owns for a bundle of commodities, such as food or medicine. Her entitlement set is the set of all potential combinations of goods and services that a woman can legally secure given her endowments. While the entitlement approach has been typically used for famine analysis, it is also a useful framework for understanding women's rights in securing resources, both from her household and society, in order to increase her opportunities for health and well-being.

Widows tend to have a relatively small endowment (economic resources, social resources, social security), which increases their vulnerability by limiting a widow's capacity to cope with the shock of becoming a widow. While the distribution of capital, land, and income will vary according to a woman's caste and class, the restrictions placed on a widow may impede her claim on land and other resources. Strengthening *property rights* among women in India has been argued to be one of the key strategies to improving women's status in general and widows in particular.

The lack of property rights has restricted women from securing their husband's land following his death – often his family will reclaim the land. In general, widow's inheritance of land from their husbands have been much higher in the south than in the north, although considerable diversity in widow's claims have been found across northern states, which have been attributed to differences in public policy and ancient legal treatises. In Kerala, property rights for women are among the strongest in the country. In our sample, most of the women owned some land which was predominantly passed onto them from their husband. However, this land was mostly house plots. Among the two women who had substantial land plots, both with forward caste affiliations, the land was not being used for any productive purposes. It is not clear whether women with larger landholdings did not use their land due to the quality of the land or limited capacities to earn income from their land.

Employment restrictions limit widows' capacities to survive and to support their children. These limitations may arise, notably in the north, due to caste restrictions in working outside the household. In Kerala, work opportunities are limited, especially for women, due to the labour market in which there are few employment opportunities outside the agricultural sector. There is little job mobility to improve one's job status and therefore extend her entitlement exchange. Employment opportunities in India are further restricted, especially among younger women, who face limited social mobility and threats of physical and sexual harassment in the workforce.

A social network, which may facilitate entitlement exchange, may be diminished upon widowhood as a woman faces greater restrictions on her social mobility and social stigmatisation. Social security in India for widows is predominantly through the widow pension, which can provide some relief. Although, there have been critiques that the pension is insufficient and fraught with bureaucratic challenges. Moreover, the presence of an adult son, even if he does not provide for his mother, will generally preclude a woman from claiming the widow pension.

In sum, widows face a high set of restrictions, high set of responsibilities, and limited endowment. This, in turn, constrains a widow's capability to live a healthy and fulfilling life, particularly during the early stage of widowhood. Evidence from this study, supported by other research, indicates that widows suffer from high levels of *material deprivation*, *limited job opportunities*,*social isolation*, *social exclusion*, *limited social mobility*, and *poor physical health*. We also identified high levels of stress lowering her *mental peace*. This stress is not only linked to losing a spouse, which has been well documented in the literature on the health of widows in other contexts, but also related to having to cope with the circumstance of the death of a husband (*e.g.* shame, blaming, debt) and the new responsibilities.

To be able to become and live a good life as a widow requires a capacity to cope with harsh and multiple challenges or *resiliency*. Three factors identified in our survey appear to promote resiliency.

First, the support of adult children made a marked difference in the economic and social well-being of the women. While sons are generally viewed as the main source of support, we also found that daughters contributed to improving the lives of their mothers, which has been observed in other contexts. Second, the widow pension was found to offer some relief, providing women with an independent source of income; also, confirmed by Dutta. Third, self help groups provided economic and social opportunities for several women in the study. Self help groups, which are widespread in

Kerala, may also help protect against exclusion from health care and the promotion of mental health.

CASTE AND CLASS DIFFERENCES

Women who are wealthier and have higher caste affiliations are often at an advantage in society, tending to have higher levels of education and greater landholdings. However, in our study becoming a widow appears to have eclipsed differences across women. Irrespective of one's caste or economic status, widowhood has a profound impact on a woman's life raising many challenges. Caste norms can place restrictions upon forward caste women, limiting their opportunities to work or to take on certain economic activities. This appears to be confirmed in our study.

Higher levels of education may not necessarily be an advantage, especially in Kerala, where there are few job opportunities. The gap between education and opportunities to use this education has been found to have negative consequences for women, such as mental distress. Land ownership might not translate into a reality of utilising that land.

Limitations

This study included a small sample of women from a single *gram panchayat* in Kerala, which did not provide an opportunity to glean a portrait of widows across Kerala, given the internal diversity of the state. However, as this study builds on other research we have undertaken in the community, we have been able to provide an in-depth understanding of the realities of widows, who have been an understudied group in population health and human rights research. One of the benefits of building on our prior research was that we were able to use our census to select a sample based on a variety of socio-demographic characteristics—although since our selection was based on current marital status data, we were not able to identify any widow who has remarried. This lacuna is, however, negligible since once widowed, women tend not to remarry (which was confirmed by the women in our sample).

Our sample did not include any woman whose husband died from a cause not associated with either alcohol or a chronic illness, such as an occupational or road accident or an infectious disease, which may have yielded different or modified profiles and requires further investigation.

CONCLUSIONS

The women interviewed in this study face similar issues to other women in their community, such as exclusion from health care and restrictions in their social mobility, but their status as widows make them particularly vulnerable. Moreover, widows' vulnerability—especially during the early stages of their widowhood— stems from an *accumulation* of challenges: limited resources, high levels of restrictions and responsibilities, and a lack of entitlements. Given that our research was undertaken in Kerala where women's status is known to be relatively high and the provision of public services more equitably distributed than elsewhere in India, it suggests that advancing the agenda for improving health and rights of widows is of even greater importance at the national level. Our study supports policy suggestions that have been proposed by others working in India, notably recommendations stemming from workshops and conferences that brought together activists, scholars, lawyers, and widows themselves.

They advocated a multi-pronged approach that would simultaneously address material needs and social identity and respect. Family support is often insufficient to ensure an adequate living standard, there is a need to improve her (and her children's) material opportunities by securing women's property rights, expanding employment opportunities, and ensuring adequate social security benefits. Government interventions specific for widows have been sparse and the impact of available interventions inadequately analysed. In our study, while some women who were eligible for the widow pension did receive it, the process to claim the pension was not always straightforward and tended to be facilitated in those cases where women had political connections. Programmes should address short term health and welfare needs (*i.e.* the period immediately following the loss of their husband) of widows, as well as their longer term needs, since the majority of widows do not remarry and continue to face economic hardships and social stigmatization. The development of these programmes should be done with the participation of widows (who are often excluded from policy dialogues) in order to ensure that they are appropriately tailored to their needs.

Improving widow's social standing and ensuring they have their own identity will require another set of strategies, including public debates and campaigns, government initiatives that ensure that widows are protected from abuse and violence, and creating spaces for widows to organise and develop their own strategies for change. In addition, international and domestic human rights treaties should be applied to address the various challenges that women face when their husband dies and to help protect the rights of widows.

We further propose a need for population level interventions that will address the underlying causes of the vulnerability of widows. The specific interventions may vary according to the particular health issues prevalent in a community (*e.g.* HIV/AIDS, chronic disease). Two key issues that emerged in the context of Kerala are inadequate social protection against health care costs and the negative consequences of male alcohol use. Community-based health insurance could help reduce the financial burden of health care of households, protecting against catastrophic health care costs and the incurring of debts that can impoverish households. Moreover, removing financial barriers to health care among poorer households can help to increase access to care, improving the chances and speed of recovery and the restoration of good health. These programmes, however, need to be gender sensitive "as gender bias in treatment-seeking can persist even after the removal of economic barriers to access".

To address the causes and consequences of male alcohol abuse, community health promotion programmes appropriate to the community context can be implemented. These programmes could "tie-in" with successfully established self help group programmes, helping to produce spill over effects. Several pathways have been suggested linking women's participation in microcredit and their health. Implementing complementary interventions that address underlying causes of women's ill health could enhance the effectiveness of these programmes. The social solidarity of a woman's organisation can help to address particularly sensitive issues, such as male alcohol use.

More research on widows in India and other countries will help to both elucidate the challenges faced by widows and encourage potential solutions. There is a need to undertake research in other contexts with diverse health challenges (*e.g.* HIV/AIDS), and socio-economic conditions (*e.g.* worsening economic deprivation), and cultural beliefs and practices. The framework outlined in this paper could help serve to guide future research.

SOCIO-DEMOGRAPHIC AND HEALTH PROFILE OF WIDOWS IN INDIA

With its focus of attention on widows, the present study provides a demographic overview of their living arrangements and their health status in various states and country as a whole. A more comprehensive picture of the recent conditions and characteristic of widows' households in India was lacking, though relatively some data sources are available. Drawing data primarily from National Family Health Survey 1998-99 and National Sample Survey Organisation 1995-96, supplemented by evidence from National Census, 1991, the main task of the report is to synthesize comparable information about how the widows live and what is the health status of them, and where unprecedented social, demographic and economical changes have been taking place.

Our country has witnessed a declined trend of proportion of widows to total female population, since 1961 Census. However, comparison with census report 1991 with different national survey reports at different points of time indicates that there is an increasing trend since 1991. How far the survey data is reliable can be substantiated with 2001 census data which is yet to come. We have to wait till the socio-cultural tables series of Census 2001 are made public. Higher percentage of incidence of widowhood in southern states suggests that occurrence of rapid demographic transition in one hand and higher life expectancy of women on the other hand.

The proportion of widowhood increases, as they grow older. According to NFHS-2 (1998-99), in the age group of 60 and above, fifty eight percent are widowed among the total female population. According to Census 1991, among females in the age group of 60 and above, more than 65 percent of widows are in the states of Goa, Assam, Karnataka, West Bengal, Andhra Pradesh and Tamil Nadu.

Among widows surveyed 78 percent are in the age group of 50 and above. And 22 percent belongs to the reproductive age group of 15-49 years (NFHS-2). Of those widows surveyed, 78 percent are illiterate, close to 14 percent have completed up to primary education and 7 percent have studied up to secondary school and only 1.4 percent of them have studied beyond secondary school. It is seen that more than three-fifths are illiterate in the age group of 20 to 49 years. Illiteracy is mostly common in the age group 60 and above, among rural residents, among tribals and those with low standard of living (85 per cent-90 per cent). Illiteracy rates for widows are highest in Bihar (91 percent), Rajasthan (90 percent), Uttar Pradesh (87 percent) and Orissa (86 percent). Around 80 per cent of the households in rural areas do not have toilet facilities and live in semi *pucca* and *kachha* houses. On an average, in India 80 per cent of widows live in households with low or moderate standard of living. However, in some states like Tripura, Orissa, Nagaland and Bihar more than 90 per cent are living with lower economic status (low to moderate standard of living condition).

Female headship is likely to appear at a later stage of life cycle, compared with male headship. It may relatively be short lived because of its late occurrence and also the headship may be transferred to a male member on remarriage. Female headships are higher in urban areas than their rural counterpart (46 per cent and 37 per cent). Females head 40 percent of the households and the remaining are headed by are males in those households where at least one widow lives. As was observed, only 9 percent males in the age group of 60 and above are heading the households, while 40 percent of females of the same age group are heading in the households. However, the proportion of female-headed households are higher than male-headed households in the states like Meghalaya (more than 70 percent) and Goa, Kerala, Sikkim, Nagaland and Mizoram (more than 60 percent).

Only 6.5 percent of widows live alone. More widows in rural areas (7.2 per cent) than urban areas (4.8 per cent) are living alone. Mean household size of male-headed household of *dejure* population where widow inhabits is 6.4 persons whereas; in the female-headed households the mean household size is only 4.4 persons. Important finding from the study indicate that higher proportion (48 per cent) of households headed by females belongs to low standard of living group. This implies that female-headed households are by and large poorer than male-headed households. In female-headed households one in seven widows live alone. Majority (three-fourths) of the widows are living with three related adults. It implies that they live in joint families in India and the average size of the families is 6.5 persons.

However, one-tenth of the households are single adult (widow) household. While comparing with various states, it shows that in state like Tamil Nadu, 20 per cent of the households are single adult (widow) households and 15 per cent of widows in the state live alone. Again in Tamil Nadu, average household size of female-headed household is only 3. Among the widows surveyed, 35 percent of them are heading the households in India and 47 percent widows are mothers to the head. A significant percent (5.7 percent) of widows are mother in laws to the head of the household. Around 2 percent each of widows live as daughters or daughters-in-law or sisters in relation to the head of the house hold. Six percent of widows live with other relatives. Also it is seen that in states like Kerala and Goa, some states from northeastern states such as Meghalaya, Mizoram, and Nagaland, more than 55 percent are heading the households. A widow who lives alone, is either from lower economic status or is working outside home or belongs to the older age group (60+).

About ¼th (26 percent) of widows are working outside home. Those working outside home, only one percent are professionals, 5 percent are in clerical jobs including housekeeping and 20 percent are working as agricultural labourers in farm or casual labourers. About one-fourths of workers are from older age group (60 years and above) and around 78 percent of them are illiterate. Work participation rate among widows are higher in the small household size as against large size. The work participation rate among widows is much higher in the range of 30 to 40 percent in the state of Tamil Nadu, Andhra Pradesh, Madhya Pradesh, Karnataka and some parts of northeastern regions. The possible reason of higher work participation is that higher proportions of widows either are head of the household or they live alone.

According to National Sample Survey Organisation (1995-96) data, among widows, 45 percent widows are in the age group of 60 and above and 77 percent are in the age group of 50 and above. Educational level of widows varies widely between place of residence and age group. Illiteracy rate is quite high among widows in India. Nine in 10 widows are illiterate in rural areas. In urban areas literacy status is better *i.e.* close to 37 percent are literate. At 60 year and above, 93 percent and 68 percent of widows are illiterate in rural and urban areas respectively in India.

It is seen that 37 percent of widows are heading their households. Half of them are parents or parents in law. Only 2.2 percent and 1.3 percent are living as daughters and daughters in laws respectively in the households and 7.2 percent are living with other relatives. There is not much urban rural difference existing regarding the headship status of widows. The highest of 63 percent widows are in the age group 35-49 years who head their own households. Close to one fourth of widows are heading the households in the age group 60 years and above. Close to 68 percent mothers (in the age group of 60 and above) live with their own children households. Among those 37 percent heading the household, more than one third of them are in the age group of 50-59 years. At the old age group of 70 and above, 10 percent of them are heading the household.

A little more than one-third of the widows in rural areas and one-fourth in urban areas are engaged in economic activities. Majority of widows who were engaged in labour force, are casual laborers in agriculture (13 per cent) or self-employed in their own farm (10 per cent). However, women who were engaged themselves in non- agricultural sector for self-employment and casual laborers are 4 percent and 3 percent respectively. Only 3 percent are engaged in regular employment. Yet 8 percent elderly widows in urban areas and 15 percent elderly widows (60 years and above) in rural areas, were in the labour force during the reference year. In rural areas, about 71 percent in the age group of 20 –34 years and 66 percent in the age group of 35-49 years are working outside home.

Among the major states, Himachal Pradesh, Kerala, Punjab, Haryana and Goa, more than 10 per cent are elderly widows of 80 years and above. In, majority of the states, the literacy level among widows are quite poor except in Goa, Kerala, Delhi, Mizoram, and Meghalaya. There is a wide variation among states with respect to the working status of widows. More than 40 percent of widows are employed in their own farm in the states of Himachal Pradesh, Mizoram and Nagaland. In the states like Karnataka, Andhra Pradesh, Orissa, Maharashtra and Tamil Nadu, more than 20 percent are working as casual laborers, the highest in Tamil Nadu (31 per cent). Participation in the labour force is least in the states of Punjab and Goa

Among elderly widows, almost 93 percent in rural and 68 percent in urban areas are illiterate. It is very interesting to note that nearly 80 percent live with their children and 8 percent live with other relatives (other relatives include brother, sister, grand father *etc.*). However 10 percent are reported to be living alone, of which 1.4 percent are living in old age home. In the old age too, 13 percent are working outside home. Only 2 percent of the elderly did not have their own children, of them 34 percent lived alone. The work participation rate among elderly widows decreases, as they grow older. In spite of being 80 and above, still 2 percent from urban areas and 4 percent from rural areas work outside home. It is found that as the women grow older, proportions living alone decreases marginally from 11 percent in the age group of 60-69 years to 7 percent in the age group of 80 plus. However, at the age group of 80 plus, 13 percent are living with other relatives.

NFHS-2 (1998-99) collected data on four major morbidity conditions of each member of the households *i.e.* asthma, tuberculosis, jaundice and malaria. In India, 2468 persons per 1,00,000 population *i.e.* 2.5 percent were reported to be suffering from asthma at the time of survey. However, relatively the prevalence rate among widows is much higher *i.e.* 7.4 percent. The prevalence is considerably higher in rural areas than in urban areas for all the diseases. Age differences of prevalence are marked, with the prevalence of asthma increasing from 2.2 percent at age of 20-34 years to 8.8 percent at age of 60 and above.

The prevalence rate of tuberculosis is much higher (10 per1000) among widows than general females (4.6 per1000). The prevalence of tuberculosis increases rapidly with age. However, there is no significant difference between widows as a whole and general population in India with respect to prevalence of this disease. The prevalence of malaria among widows is highest in the age group of 35-49 years (6.7 per cent) in rural area. Prevalence of asthma among widows varies considerably by state, from a low of 41 per 1000 in Delhi and Tamil Nadu to a high of 210 per 1000 in Sikkim. Other states with relatively high prevalence rates *i.e.*, more than 100 per 1000 are Arunachal Pradesh, Nagaland, Mizoram, Bihar, Kerala, Rajasthan and Tripura.

Tuberculosis prevalence rates are also noticeably high in Bihar, Orissa, Andhra Pradesh and Uttar Pradesh among widows. Malaria was most commonly reported in Nagaland, Meghalaya, Arunachal Pradesh and Madhya Pradesh, where10 to 16 percent of were reported to have malaria during 3 months preceding the survey. One-fourth of widows are reported to chew *paan masala* or tobacco. However, this proportion rise from 2.7 percent at age of less than 20 years to 27.2 percent and 24.3 percent at age of 60-69 years and 70 years and above respectively. Chewing *paan masala* or tobacco is as common in rural areas as in urban areas. Chewing tobacco is much higher among widows in households with a low standard of living than in households with a high standard of living.

Only 3.6 percent of widows are reported to drink alcohol. The proportion of widows who drink alcohol uniformly varies across the age distribution. Drinking alcohol by widows is inversely related to the educational status and standard of living index of the household.

The rural widows are more prone to disability than the urban counterpart. Half of widows in rural areas and 43 percent in urban areas have at least one disability with them. Disability with respect to vision (eye sight) is more pronounced and one -third of the total elderly widows have problems regarding eyesight. The prevalence of chronic diseases among aged widows (suffering from at least one chronic illness) is seen higher in urban areas (61 percent) than in the rural areas (56 percent).

'Problem of joints' and 'cough' happened to be the most severe diseases for the aged widows. High or low blood pressure comes next in order of occurrence. In Uttar Pradesh, 40 percent of elderly widows have visual disabilities followed by Andhra Pradesh (39 per cent). The prevalence of smoking biri/cigar/hukka *etc.*, tobacco chewing and alcohol drinking is much higher in rural areas than in urban areas. One-fifth of them chew *pan masala* or tobacco in rural areas where as 13 percent chew the same in urban areas. Alcohol drinking is higher in rural areas than in urban areas.

Policy Implication:

- Widowhood is not a comfortable situation in life. From the living arrangement it is observed that nearly 7 percent of widows are living alone. Being a women, in the kind of social culture we are in, living alone is a task for which there is a strong need for better coverage of social security.
- Female headship of household is one indication, but it has to consider the of poverty along with headship and more particularly widows in early age. Both the government and the philanthropic organisation can give a focus for empowering them.
- The NSSO data reveals that 13 percent of elderly widows (60+) work outside. Though it is encouraging to know that women even at this age are still working, but they are involved in occupation which requires excessive physical labour. Special programme may be targeted to them.
- Old widows also report that they work though they are in older ages (80+). This clearly shows that they may be forced/ compelled to work. An insight to this is desirable.
- The NFHS-2 shows that widows are more prone to prevalence of tuberculosis and asthma. This shows that special coverage of health schemes may be made for them, more so in the high prevalent states, in particular.

Living arrangement analysis has revealed that majority of the widows live with one of the family members, but 10 percent are staying alone. They needs a special care particularly those in advance age.

THE VOICELESS MILLIONS OF WIDOWS IN INDIA

In India, as in many parts of South Asia widowhood is viewed not as a period in the life cycle of a woman, but as a personal and social aberration, to be devoutly wished away.

This attitude to a great extent governs the social, cultural and even economic implications of widowhood. In the Indian psyche, there is acceptance of the inevitability of death, but the natural inevitability of the death of a spouse (husband) is often glossed over.

This inherent contradiction motivates the cultural non-acceptance of widowhood. In a society totally governed for centuries by patriarchy, discrimination on the basis of sex exists in almost every political, economic social and legal institution. In such a situation the Indian widow is triply discriminated against, as a woman, as a widow and as a poor widowed woman. The principle of equality and non discrimination which reflects the spirit of CEDAW is really the touchstone of the Indian Constitution. Article 14 of the Constitution of India states that: "The State shall not deny to any person equality before the law or the equal protection of the laws within the territory of India." Article 15 prohibits discrimination on the grounds of religion, race, caste, sex, and place of birth or any of them.

But the noble spirit of the Constitution is ignored, contravened, contradicted and forgotten in the actual implementation of laws and policies. The Preamble to the Convention for Elimination of All Forms of Discrimination against Women underpins the responsibility of the signatory nations to eliminate this violation of human rights by the phrase "inadmissibility of discrimination" This implies that a constitutional affirmation of the principle of non discrimination does not suffice. Governments have to take proactive role in ending discrimination.

OBLIGATIONS BREACHED BY STATE PARTIES WITH SPECIFIC REFERENCE TO WIDOWHOOD

Article 2 b: To adopt appropriate legislative and other measures, including sanctions where appropriate, prohibiting all discrimination against women.

Move Towards Non Discrimination

Ownership/control of assets, namely property is the greatest protection for widows from deprivation and the consequent discrimination. Even though the property rights of Indian women have grown better with advance of time, they are far from totally equal and fair. There is much that remains in Indian women's property rights that can be struck down as unconstitutional and certainly not in keeping with the spirit of "Non discrimination" As a wife the woman is maintained by her husband, but as a widow she is left totally at the mercy of a patriarchal family or a maze of confusing laws which she neither understands nor can take advantage of. Compounding the misery is the fact that the laws are skewed against her assertion of right as a widow.

- Traditionally a woman in a joint Hindu family, had a right to sustenance, but the control and ownership of property did not vest in her. In a patrilineal system, a woman, was not given a birth right in the family property like a son.
- By the Acts of 1937, 1956 daughters and widows can inherit the self acquired property and the husband's share in the joint family property as Class I heirs after son, daughter.
- Further the Amendments to the Hindu Succession Act in 2005 bring male and female rights in agricultural land on par for all states,

overriding any inconsistent state laws. This can potentially benefit millions of women dependent on agriculture for survival.

- The 2005 act makes all daughters, including married ones, coparceners in joint family property with the same birthrights as sons to shares and to seek partition.The 1956 Hindu Succession Act had distinguished between separate property and joint family property.
- The 2005 amendments give all daughters (including those married) the same rights as sons to reside in or seek partition of the parental dwelling house.
- The legislation removes a discriminatory section which barred certain widows from inheriting the deceased's property, if they had remarried.

Gaps that Emphasize Discrimination

By the amendments, daughters will now get a share equal to that of sons at the time of the notional partition, just before the death of the father, and an equal share of the father's separate share. However, the position of the widow vis-à-vis the coparcenary stays the same

- The widow not being a member of the coparcenary, will not get a share at the time of the notional partition. The widow will not inherit any share in the joint family property in her own right but she is entitled to an equal share with other Class I heirs only from the separate share of the husband computed at the time of the notional partition. In effect, the actual share of the widow will go down, as the separate share of the father will be less as the property will now be equally divided between father, sons and daughters in the notional partition. Daughters' right by birth will enhance the share of daughters by making them coparceners on the same basis as sons. But in doing so it will alter the shares of other Class I female heirs of the deceased, such as the deceased's widow. It will actually disadvantage widows, as the share of the daughter will increase in comparison to the widow. On the one hand the law will not discriminate against woman as a daughter but will discriminate against her as a widow.
- Very often daughters are persuaded by the family and by the mother herself to will away her share so that she can continue her association with the natal home. The argument given is that the natal family had acquired huge expense to give a dowry (On which her husband has control) at the time of the marriage. Most women do require the emotional support from the natal family. But this support comes with a rider of willing away her property right. So when the daughter becomes a widow her deprivation is only enhanced. These inequalities would remain unless the entire coparcenary system is abolished totally since it has folds within folds of inequalities which cannot be dealt

with in a piecemeal manner. However the Government seems reluctant to do so right away.

- Section 4(2) of the Hindu Succession Act allows for special State laws to prevail over the Hindu Succession Act to address the issue of fragmentation of agricultural holdings, fixation of ceiling and devolution of tenancy rights in these holdings. Thus, State laws exist which deny women equal rights of succession in tenancy rights. Agricultural land is the most important form of rural property in India as in the whole of South Asia and ensuring gender-equal rights in it is important not only for gender justice but also for economic and social advancement. Gender equality in agricultural land can reduce not just a woman's but her whole family's risk of poverty. A widow on the death of her husband can be legally barred from asserting her right as a tenant, and so may be deprived of her livelihood. By and large judgements under this Section have upheld laws under Section 4 (2) of the Hindu Succession Act and have mostly denied women equal rights in agricultural land. Possibly because of strong pressures from the agricultural lobby and an apprehension of political fallout, Government has tended to drag feet in granting true realisation to women of their equal rights.
- A man has full testamentary power over his property including his interest in the coparcenary. The equal sharing of the father's property applies in cases where he dies intestate — that is, without making a will. Given the bias and preference for sons and notions of lineage, discrimination against daughters in inheritance through wills is bound to remain. In most cases, the terms of the will would favour the son. In today's context, most property is self-acquired and that property must follow principles of succession under the different succession laws. Moreover, its owner can dispose off such property during his lifetime by gift. It can be bequeath by will to anyone of his choice. The proposed amendment notwithstanding, a Hindu father can disinherit his wife or daughter by will, in his self-acquired property. The law in failing to lay down a ceiling on the amount that can be willed away has emphasized the discrimination against women particularly widows.
- The amendments do not curtail the right of any heir to claim partition of a dwelling house till the settlement of widowed mother's rights in case the deceased male is intestate. This is further example of the insensitivity of the law makers to the plight of widows. On the death of a man, the heirs immediately clamor for partition of the property including the dwelling house. In such a situation the widow is often left homeless, or dependent on the son. Even though by the law of

the land she can claim maintenance from her children, in actuality, she prefers to suffer in silence since she had neither the money nor the knowledge or the support to get into a legal wrangle

- The Christian widow's right is not an exclusive right and gets curtailed as the other heirs step in. Only if the intestate has left none who are of kindred to him, the whole of his property would belong to his widow. Where the intestate has left a widow and any lineal descendants, one third of his property devolves to his widow and the remaining two thirds go to his lineal descendants. If he has left no lineal descendents but has left persons who are kindred to him, one half of his property devolves to his widow and the remaining half goes to those who are of kindred to him.
- In Islam the share of the wife is one-quarter in the absence of a child or agnatic grandchild and one-eighth in the presence of a child or agnatic grandchild. Two or more wives share equally in this prescribed share. Sharia has placed two restrictions on the testator. Firstly, to whom he can bequeath his estate and secondly, the amount that he can bequeath. The majority view is that a bequest in excess of one-third of the net estate is invalid unless consented to by the legal heirs as is a bequest in favour of a legal heir.

Despite the rather egalitarian law of inheritance as stipulated by the Sharia, the condition of widows in predominantly Muslim countries like Pakistan or Bangladesh is no different. In any patriarchal society, women are second class citizens and widows third class. Added to this is the inaccessibility to the resources of education to legal services, to material resources *etc.* Legal reforms so far have not been adequate to give all Indian women a right to property on the same terms as men. Even where law has given a right, conventions and practices do not recognise them. There is no single body of property rights of Indian women. The property rights of the Indian woman get determined depending on which religion and religious school she follows, if she is married or unmarried, which part of the country she comes from, if she is a tribal or non-tribal and so on. Ironically, what unifies them is the fact that cutting across all those divisions, the property rights of the Indian women are immune from Constitutional protection; the various property rights could be, as they indeed are in several ways, discriminatory and arbitrary, notwithstanding the Constitutional guarantee.

Article 2c: To establish legal protection of the rights of women on an equal basis with men and to ensure through competent national tribunals and other public institutions the effective protection of women against any act of discrimination

Cultural Discrimination of Tribal Widows

Between 1987 and 2003, 2556 women were killed after being branded as witches. Witch hunting has been reported in many states of North and Central

India and in Nepal. The peculiar thing about the violence is that, the most victims are widows, aged women and mainly women who are unprotected and closely related to the accusers. The Property right of tribal women is the root cause of this horrifying custom. The Santhal is the tribal community, which awards property rights even to widows. This very right becomes their death warrant. In many cases the widow who owns land is asked to give up her right by the husband's family. When refused they bribe the village healer to brand her as a witch. Often the village panchayat is a silent and helpless spectator.

It is very depressing that in India, only a handful of states have laws against witch-hunting. Because of lack of laws that specifically targets this practice, the people involved with witch hunting are booked under article 323 of the Indian Penal Code. This means that the law now equates the crime of witch hunting with crimes where a person tries to voluntary cause hurt like slapping or physically abusing somebody. Under this law, the maximum punishment for this offence is a jail term up to one year and a fine of 1,000 rupees.

There is a specific law "the prevention of witch practices Act (2001) but this ordinance also comes with a package of drawbacks as the punishment for witch killing is nominal. According to the sections 3, 4, 5 and 6 of the Act, a person who identifies witches can be punished with imprisonment for a term which may extend 3 months or with fine of ₹ 1000. Any person who commits such heinous crime would be punished merely with imprisonment for 6 month or with fine of ₹ 2000 or both. The law has failed to make any impact on culprits as it is seldom practiced and conviction rate for crimes related to witch hunting is as low as 2 per cent.

It is very evident that there is very little effective legislation on a crime that is only rising with the paucity of available tribal lands. The enforcement machinery is inept to convict a complete family, or a village that abets and aids witch hunting. The rather sanguine approach of the Government under pins the discrimination that happens to tribal widows.

Article 2 f. To take all appropriate measures, including legislation, to modify or abolish existing laws, regulations, customs and practices which constitute discrimination against women.

Absence of a Uniform Civil Code

Due to the geo-political nature of the country, various cultures and religions flourished in the country and as a result, we have various personal laws in place. Women have equality of status under the country's Constitution. However, many anomalies remain under different personal laws. Despite the Hindus Succession Act and its Amendments, widows do not have the same right as the sons. This is in keeping with the principles of patriarchy. Similarly the Christian widow is discriminated against in inheriting the husband's property and it is always less than the lineal heir. Unless specifically mentioned in the will the heirs can ask for partitioning of property including the dwelling house thus dispossessing the widow of a roof over her head. Personal laws that govern many minorities in India is also subject to the vagaries of interpretation which given the gender bias in India is likely to discriminate against the women.

Despite The Supreme Court having talked time and again about having a uniform civil code as per Article 44 of the Constitution of India the government has been singularly reluctant to address the issues of minority women's rights. The efforts to conceptualize a common civil code have been largely unsuccessful since there have been attempts to impose Hindu law in the name of a Uniform Code and to ignore even the positive aspects of Personal Laws of other communities. There are various ambiguities within the Hindu laws itself. Therefore, there is a real need to evaluate and revaluate the Hindu code itself along with the Christian and Muslim personal laws so that they are in consonance with the constitution and other codified laws like IPC, Cr.P.C. *etc.* Whenever there is a talk of formulating a Uniform Civil Code in the country, some minority fundamentalist organisations come together protesting that it poses a threat to their religious identity

Despite the secular nature of India and the Indian courts citing by and large the national secular character of the state as justifying the insistence on the right of women to equality, personal law is a barrier to intervention. The politics of vote bank takes precedence over the Government's commitment to a common civil code. In the meanwhile women particularly widows face discrimination on property matters in the name of cultural and religious freedom.

Article 5: States Parties shall take all appropriate measures:

To modify the social and cultural patterns of conduct of men and women, with a view to achieving the elimination of prejudices and customary and all other practices which are based on the idea of the inferiority or the superiority of either of the sexes or on stereotyped roles for men and women

India's Reservation to Article 5a

Even though India ratified the CEDAW in 1993, it made a declaration on its reservations on Article 5(a) and 16(i) in conformity with its policy of non-interference in the "personal affairs" of any community without its initiative and consent. Assuming that this position is valid, the flip side is the general understanding of "community" is limited, confining itself to the notion of male leadership only. Gender identity is based on the behaviour patterns imposed on women and men by culture and religion. In a traditional patriarchal society like India there is institutionalized domination of women by men, and of women's exclusion from the dynamics of power.

Very often cultural patterns of conduct, are at variance with the human rights culture and the maintenance of the status quo patriarchal norms conflict with gender equality. Many of the practices defended in the name of culture that impinge on human rights are gender specific; they preserve patriarchy at the expense of women's rights. In the context of widowhood forced marriage as child brides (resulting in early widowhood) paying to acquire husbands for daughters through the dowry (resulting in depriving widows of any share in the natal property) patriarchal inheritance systems in which daughters inherit less

than sons and the widows' right to property is at variance with customary law, marriage arrangements allowing the husband control over land, finances, (leaving the widow with very little knowledge or resources to assert her right) witch-hunting; compulsory restrictive dress codes, diet code and behaviour code that institutionalize the ostracism and discrimination of widows. The most harmful cultural practice is the stereotyping of widows that serves to underpin their victimized status.

To comprehend this there is the need to understand the cultural customs of the dominant Hindu society in India. In the Hindu society a widow was physically alive but socially dead. The Hindu patriarchy assigns only a secondary role to a woman. In the Hindu ethos the woman with her husband performs rituals and begets sons. This is her social identity and for both, her husband's presence is imperative. Without the husband a woman has no social or religious identity. In this role of a wife is rooted the attitude towards a widow. The widow's social death stems from her alienation from reproduction and sexuality; following the death of her husband. Even though the widow had no social identity she continued to be part of society. So there was the need to place her on the margins of society and institutionalize her marginality and this social marginalization was emphasized by obvious symbols.

From this emerges the pattern of ostracism of widows in India and may parts of South Asia, particularly in Nepal. There is a dress code (widows are expected to wear white and shun all colored garment and jewellery) a diet code (they are pressurized to adopt a vegetarian diet, avoid garlic, onions etc) a behaviour code (restricted movement, not to be actively seen seeking male company, a psychological pressure to lead an actively religious life) This restrictive life is further worsened by the systematic ostracism that widows face. They are discouraged from attending social functions and are considered to be inauspicious. Their very presence can lead to misfortunes. Widows belonging to the minority religions are not as systematically marginalized as Hindu widows. But it is to be noted that prevalent customs often get adopted, particularly when it can translate into control of women's rights.

Skewed property laws, the inability to put a common law regarding inheritance makes the Government responsible for the discrimination that widow's face in India Further the Government has no proactive strategy in place for a change in the social mind sets either through legislation or education.. It is horrifying to note that some religious leaders support the retrogressive principles of widow discrimination. Media continues to stereotype the Indian widow as emaciated victim at the mercy of her male relatives, thus validating the already existing social ostracism. On the principle of "non interference in individual culture" the Government of India turns a blind eye to the prevalent customs and traditions of widow discrimination. There is the need for a truly participative debate on the issue to educate, to inform and to change prevailing mindsets.

By adhering to the principle of non interference in cultural norms, and by expressing reservations to Article 5a of the Convention, the Government of India fails in its responsibility to uphold the human right to a life of dignity for widows. The Government of India puts the onus of change in prevailing cultural norms on community intervention. This is a near impossibility in patriarchal societies where discrimination of women is the accepted norm.

Without a transformation of religious/cultural patriarchy by a decree of the constitutional system, women cannot gain full equality.

The betrothal and the marriage of a child shall have no legal effect, and all necessary action, including legislation, shall be taken to specify a minimum age for marriage and to make the registration of marriages in an official registry compulsory.

India's Declaration Under Article 16 2

The same logic, more or less, of non interference in individual cultures has been extended to India's declaration under Article 16(ii). This CEDAW Article stipulates that child marriage will have no legal affect and mandates and enjoins state parties to make the registration of marriages in an official register compulsory.

The Indian government's stand is that in principle it supports fully the compulsory registration of marriages, but to implement it is not "practical in a vast country like India with its variety of customs, religions and level of illiteracy". Child marriages at best can be regulated, not banned. India's latest position, as articulated in the 37th session of the CEDAW committee, continued to be the same making it obvious that there is a discrepancy between the constitutional provisions of equality and the prevalence of unequal and gender-biased customary practices.

Despite a law stipulating child marriages, on the day of Akha Teej, children as young as 5 are married off in the state f Rajasthan in India. The Enforcement machinery as been unable to eradicated the practice mainly because of the ignorance of the long term harm and the inherent human right violation that the practice entails. The inability of the government to ensure that marriages are registered reinforces the deprivation faced by widows. Absence of registration of marriage affects women more than men. Property inheritance is often denied due to lack of proof of marriage. Registration of marriage is essential for joint registration of property. So it becomes a further tool in the hands of patriarchal forces to deprive widows of their rights. The Government of India's inability to ensure registration of marriages speaks very poorly for the capabilities of the enforcement machinery. Local elected bodies (the panchayat) can be made legally responsible for marriage registration. Effective dissemination of information can further reinforce the need for registration. An expressed inability does not absolve the Government of its responsibility to prevent discrimination practiced against women and widows.

INADEQUATE ACTION BY STATE PARTIES ON THE OBLIGATIONS WITH SPECIFIC REFERENCE TO WIDOWHOOD

Inadequate measures on the part of the Government, non implementation of policies, ineffective programmes invariably affect the poor. Since poverty has a feminine face, women are most affected. In this category widows are the most vulnerable so consequently the South Asian Governments' inadequate policies affect widows most. But there are certain inadequacies that deprive widows even more and these need to be highlighted.

Article 10 (e) The same opportunities for access to programmes of continuing education, including adult and functional literacy programmes, particulary those aimed at reducing, at the earliest possible time, any gap in education existing between men and women

The literacy rate for women in India has shown significant improvement between 1991 and 2001;a growth of 14.8 per cent to show a literacy rate of 54.1 per cent for women.. But despite the gains, disparities in terms of gender, rural and urban women exist. For example of the 304 illiterates in India 192 million are women. Despite this the allocation for adult literacy is only 0.2 per cent of the education budget. This is the only large scale non formal education programme for poor rural and marginalized women but receives very little priority. The full realization of rights is possible only by competent assertion of rights. This is not possible for the large number of widows who are not literate to access the legal aid or programmes for the poor. Illiteracy often puts the widow at the mercy of male relatives who in turn take advantage of her thus further reinforcing the widows' deprivation

States Parties shall take all appropriate measures to eliminate discrimination against women in the field of employment in order to ensure, on a basis of equality of men and women, the same rights, in particular:

The right to social security, particularly in cases of retirement, unemployment, sickness, invalidity and old age and other incapacity to work, as well as the right to paid leave.

Only 28 percent of the widows in India are eligible for pensions, and of that number, less than 11 percent actually receive the payments to which they're entitled. Some states in India have instated the destitute widows' pension. A widow is considered destitute if she is without any regular income or source of income and if she has no relations of 20 years of age or above, particularly a son, or a grandson or if she had not remarried. Widows without any relatives and who do not own land or a house worth Rs 1,000, who do not have any form of regular employment, or who do not have supportive relations are also treated as destitute.

A destitute widow needing assistance is required to apply on a prescribed form to the tehsildar (revenue-cum-administrative officer in charge of a cluster of villages) of the taluk (cluster of villages) in which she resides. The enquiry is conducted by the revenue staff in the village in the presence of the pensioners, village officers and other elderly persons. After sanction by the tehsildar, the pension amounts are dispatched by postal money order. Payments are generally made not later than the second week of every month.

The success of the scheme in reality falls woefully short of expectations. Firstly the application forms are not easily available at the Panchayat offices or if they are, then the concerned officer gives it as a kind of favour. Secondly the forms are not user friendly. The widow is required to furnish proof of age, authentication by the prescribed authority *etc.* Foe the average illiterate widow, this is a Herculean task. Thirdly the forms are to be submitted at the taluk offices, which is difficult and often impossible for poor widows living far away. Follow up requires a couple of more visits. Fourthly verification of the forms is a lengthy process. Most widows do not have birth certificates to prove their age. Often the widow has to pay private doctors to get a certificate.

This is an added expense. Fifthly there is a great deal of arbitrariness in the assessment whether a widow is truly destitute or not. For example if a widow has an adult son or grandson living then the application can be summarily rejected without taking into consideration the fact that the son may not be supporting her. Finally after all the effort the pension obtained is grossly inadequate. It is now ₹ 200 ie about 2 dollars a month.

The Government of India has to make a comprehensive and uniform pension schemes for widows. The procedure has to be made user friendly keeping ground realities in mind.

States Parties shall take into account the particular problems faced by rural women and the significant roles which rural women play in the economic survival of their families, including their work in the non-monetized sectors of the economy, and shall take all appropriate measures to ensure the application of the provisions of the present Convention to women in rural areas. (No data available particulary on rural widows)

Parties shall take all appropriate measures to eliminate discrimination against women in rural areas in order to ensure, on a basis of equality of men and women, that they participate in and benefit from rural development and, in particular, shall ensure to such women the right

Plight of the Rural Widows:

According to the National Rural Employment Guarantee scheme introduced by the Government of India, one adult per BPL household is guaranteed 100 days of work. This immediately is skewed against the widows who are living in a household but not necessarily being supported by the male members.

The assumption is that as a widow she is heading a household. This need not be correct. The widow could be living in her marital/natal home. In such a situation she is not liable to be allowed to avail the scheme. The widow like all rural, under privileged women is the victim of a corrupt system, the former more so by virtue of her vulnerability. All those who are eligible to work under the scheme have to register with the village panchayat (the lowest elected body). The panchayat will make enquiries verify and then will issue a job card. Knowing how male dominated panchayats treat the unorganized poor particularly the women, the widow is immediately at a disadvantage. Like many schemes of the Government the spirit is willing but the implementation is weak. This is a structural weakness which will have to be rectified. In the meanwhile widows continue to be on the lowest rung of the vulnerability scale.

Farmer Suicides

More than 20,000 farmers in India have ended their lives since 1997.This is the most horrifying crisis of survival of the Indian farmers. The crushing burden f debt is quoted as the single most important reason for the mass suicides. Two factors have transformed agriculture from a positive economy into a negative economy for peasants: the rising of costs of production and the falling prices of farm commodities. Both these factors are rooted in the policies of trade liberalisation and corporate globalisation.

In 1998, the World Bank's structural adjustment policies to which India was party forced the economy to open up its seed sector to global corporations which changed the input economy overnight. Farm saved seeds/subsidized seeds were replaced by corporate seeds, which were expensive, needed fertilizers and pesticides and cannot be saved. As a result, poor peasants have to buy new seeds for every planting season and what was traditionally a free resource, available by putting aside a small portion of the crop, becomes a commodity. This new expense increases poverty and leads to indebtness.There is also a shift from biodiversity to monoculture in agriculture.

The district of Warangal in Andhra Pradesh used to grow diverse legumes, millets, and oilseeds. Now the imposition of cotton monocultures has led to the loss of the wealth of farmer's breeding and nature's evolution. Monocultures and uniformity increase the risk of crop failure, as diverse seeds adapted to diverse to eco-systems are replaced by the rushed introduction of uniform and often untested seeds into the market. When Bt Cotton was introduced in 2002, the farmers lost 1 billion rupees due to crop failure. Instead of 1,500 kilos per acre as promised the harvest was as low as 200 kilos per acre. Instead of incomes of 10,000 rupees an acre, farmers ran into losses of 6,400 rupees an acre. The region in India with the highest level of farmers suicides is the Vidharbha region in Maharashtra — 4000 suicides per year, 10 per day. This is also the region with the highest acreage of Bt cotton.

The second pressure Indian farmers are facing is the dramatic fall in prices of farm produce as a result of the WTO's free trade policies. The WTO rules for trade in agriculture are, in essence, rules for dumping. They have allowed wealthy countries to increase agribusiness subsidies while preventing other countries from protecting their farmers from artificially cheap imported produce.

The Government of India has failed to insulate the farmers from the impact of globalization. Added to this is the decreasing investment of the Government into the agricultural sector thus squeezing subsidies and agricultural loans. The end result ar the large number of farmer widows. They have no clear titled right to the land. They are already under a crushing debt. The male earning member is dead leaving behind children who need to be clothed fed and educated. For all this the widow is financially, emotionally and educationally ill equipped. The Government has been making ex gratia payment, but this dole will not help the widow. The approach from welfare has to change to empowerment, so that the widows are supported to till their land, the debts to be waived, their land rights to be recognised. Above all the Government has to address the root cause of such mass suicides. Till then the numbers of rural widow will keep increasing.

Inadequate Data on Widows

The differing forms that violence against widows takes are known. Yet there is astonishingly very little data available. The fact that they do not appear in statistics is: "not attributable solely to technical difficulties, it reflects, above all the lack of interest and consideration from which they suffer, as a result of which they do not yet enjoy the fundamental right to be included correctly in censuses."

Another reason is the myth that widows are taken care of by the familial households and so the deprivations of widows are well hidden in economic and social statistics. Since the poorest segment of a population is usually comprised of female-headed households, it is probable that households headed by widows face greater economic hardships than most. Regrettably, for most countries, the lack of income data desegregated by headship and marital status prevents the direct documentation of the economic vulnerability of widow-headed households. Without adequate data it will be impossible to underscore the economic, social and political vulnerabilities of widows. The UN must itself promote the collection of data by conventional and alternative methods. CEDAW should ask member governments to respond to the questions in its Guide to Reporting under the Convention *etc.* on issues relevant to widows

Need for comprehensive reporting procedures that are transparent, and inclusive

States Parties undertake to submit to the Secretary-General of the United Nations, for consideration by the Committee, a report on the legislative, judicial, administrative or other measures which they have adopted to give effect to the provisions of the present Convention and on the progress made in this respect:

(a) Within one year after the entry into force for the State concerned;

(b) Thereafter at least every four years and further whenever the Committee so requests.

Reports may indicate factors and difficulties affecting the degree of fulfillment of obligations under the present Convention.

The present reporting procedure ensures that State Parties submit a detailed report on the progress made and adherence to the articles of the convention. Governments tend to focus on policies that exist on paper but gloss over ground realities. The NGO report focuses on grass root reality without amplifying the road blocks. A correct assessment would be a combination of both. Perhaps there is need to put a process in place by which Governments and civil society can give a holistic report. It seems like an ambitious plan. But the need of the hour is a verified and correct assessment to ensure that the articles of the Convention are adhered to. A correct assessment only can lead to the complete and actual realisation of women's equality and freedom from all forms of discrimination.

4

Socio-Economic Status and Conflict of Widows

CONSEQUENCES OF CONFLICT

As one of the consequences of conflict, displacement has serious negative impacts on people's lives. Many civilians caught between Maoists and the state security forces are forced to flee their homes for protection and security. Internally displaced persons (IDPs) were targets of killings, forced recruitment, abductions, extortions and other human rights violations. In particular, the killing of people was one of the terrible consequences of the conflict and in the process many adult males were killed, leaving behind their wives who thus became widows.

Maoists suddenly came to her house at midnight and killed her husband. They destroyed her house by bombing it and forced the family to leave, threatening them to kill them all. This led to the end of her married life – she was just 22. Today she is living with her family as a displaced single woman (widow) in Kathmandu after leaving her place of origin in Bardiya. Currently she is working as staff in one organisation because she is literate however she finds it really tough to survive. She is worried about the nurture and education of her daughter and struggling for her survival.

IDPs are overwhelmed by economic, social and psychological problems. They are often traumatized due to the loss of their homes, property and death of or threats to family members. In addition, they are settling into new and often hostile surroundings (temporary or permanent) and typically face no immediate relief of rehabilitation and have to contend with the difficulty of adaptation. Every day is a battle for survival without food and proper accommodation. The impact of conflict on women and girls has been noticeable greater than the impact on men and boys, largely due to gender specific violence and various forms of discrimination, which is multiplied in conflict situations. While women experience marginalized status in Nepalese society, women IDPs are even more marginalized in terms of socio-economic and cultural conditions.

Displaced women, and especially female heads of households such as widows, are at increased risk of abuse, exploitation, coercion and manipulation because of their gender and status. Girls and women are more vulnerable than boys and men to mistreatment and recruitment by traffickers and armed factions. These women IDPs may lack the assertiveness required to stand up for themselves and say "no" to risky situations. Due to the Nepali social structure these women tend to see older men as protectors and providers without understanding the risks involved. Women who stay in their place of origin also suffer due to the conflict. Emigration and recruitment of men into Maoist cadres or security forces as well as the killing of male family members by Maoists and security forces have increased the burden on women. Some of the tasks that are traditionally performed by men have fallen upon women, many of which have become the heads of households.

Indeed, children and women are the worst affected. As a result of the massive migration of men abroad in search of jobs or due to the death of husbands during the conflict, many female- headed households are emerging. Many of these women are turning to prostitution, being trafficked or are performing menial jobs to look after their family. In addition, they face discrimination and harassment on a daily basis due to their single (widow) status in a society that remains conservative and patriarchal.

In most communities affected by conflict, the displaced often find it difficult to go back and restart their lives as most have lost property and income. Single women (widows) and female-headed households may find returning and restarting even more difficult due to limited economic rights of women and lack of legal documentation. Displaced single women (widows) living in urban centers face significant risks to their safety and well-being. Their mobility further decreases due to discriminating social and cultural norms.

Women for Human Rights single women group (WHR) has registered more than 800 conflict affected displaced single women (widows). WHR since its establishment had well documentation of the reports and survey through various projects, workshops and research. The flyer produced by WHR documented that 67.9 per cent of these women are displaced to a different community, thus severing ties from their cultural backgrounds. 35.7 per cent are between the ages of 25-30 years old. These women are often forced to share a small room with 3-4 children, living in unhygienic conditions with inadequate clean drinking water and sanitation. 82.9 per cent of these women are living in economic crisis, having extreme difficulty feeding themselves and their children.

Findings from a study conducted by myself with 28 displaced women in Kathmandu also showed that the number of respondents in the capital were victims of human rights violations from both the Maoists and state security forces. The majority of respondents were single women (widows) whose husbands had been killed in the conflict situation. It was found that out of the total respondents 60.7 per cent were single women (widows). Most of the respondents followed Hinduism and a minority were Christians. A minority of women did not follow any religion stating that they did not trust any religion after the incidents that had occurred and the suffering they faced. The study also revealed that after displacement, the cohesion among family members disintegrated resulting in the dispersion of the family although most remained as nuclear families.

The killing of family members was the major cause of immediate displacement while severe threats to family members belonging to the army, police and government officials also resulted in a high rate of displacement. Following these, the killing of family members, severe threats, abduction of self or family members, physical and sexual violence or confiscation of property were also listed as causes of displacement. It was found that single women (widows) in the urban centre following their displacement faced numerous difficulties including their security, social status, economic opportunities, and cultural adaptation, among others. Furthermore, the compensation they receive is not uniform or equitable and indeed, it is not sufficient. The compensation differs in range and type based on whether a family belongs to the security forces, is civilian, *etc.*

The death of the husband rated as the highest number of incident causing displacement. Displaced single women (widows) in the urban centre have the most difficulties meeting their basic needs for themselves and their families, including affording education for their children. In addition, they face societal harassment. When respondents were asked whether they would like to return to their original community or settle in a new place, half of them wanted to return to their original community. They face many hardships living in the city and since most of the respondents have property back in their place of origin they wanted to return, stating that survival is easier there. The other half of respondents who stated that they did not want to return to their villages cited reasons such as a lack of proper schooling and education provisions, the absence of adequate infrastructure, insecurity and the society within the village. Indeed, the problems women face are far more difficult in comparison to those faced by men.

Respondents listed educational support for their children and employment opportunities for themselves as the most urgent support required. Basic needs, housing and security were also a priority. Some respondents stated that they do not have awareness regarding the legal provision and thus they needed legal service without any difficulties and counseling to boost their confidence. After being displaced, the single women (widows) respondents were engaged in some sort of livelihood, however a number reported difficulties relating to their work. At the time of the interview, 18 per cent complained that they did not receive sufficient revenue for their services, 22 per cent had to endure physical harassment, 11 per cent faced sexual harassment, and 18 per cent faced other problems. The following story highlights some of the difficulties displaced single women (widows) face.

A group discussion with displaced single women (widows) from civilian families and security force families reveals the feelings and thoughts of these women on the pressing issues."Only sending IDPs to their origin is not the solution the concerned authority especially the government should guarantee about their livelihood and security."

"We were taught to drive, I possess license also but almost all of us with license do not have any job of driving. Training is not the remedy we need to get job for the livelihood." "First economic ability to fulfill basic needs, then only we can think of cultural preservation through practicing of rituals. Mental stress and economic burden provides us no time to think about the preservation of culture."

"The government is biased regarding the treatment and services towards family of civilians unlike the family of security forces whether Police or Army."

"I wish the family of the displaced civilians also get the facilities like ours because the pain and agony of displacement due to various reasons is similar. I know the compensation we are getting is not enough at all but it is of great support in this hard time."

These statements clearly indicate that the situation of former IDPs can no longer be ignored but rather should be dealt with using proper mechanisms. Government level policies and those organisations working with IDPs have varied definitions and areas of work. The government policy clearly discriminates between IDPs who have been directly affected by conflict. However, the reasons why people fled from their homes and villages are varied and not necessarily because of the killing of family members, forced abductions or compulsion to leave home. Many left home out of fear of prosecution by both sides in the conflict. A number of organisations working for IDPs also define IDPs as victims of conflict or conflict affected person. Moreover, the range and variation of what constitutes an internally displaced person (IDP) differs among various independent studies carried out by different organisations. However, the full magnitude of the problems and necessities can be known and explored only after the number of the IDPs has been established. From such data the number of women IDPs could be derived, and more specifically the marital status of these women. This is particularly important given that the statistics of WHR reveal that there are 3,907 single women registered within the single women networks who are widows as a result of the conflict and a significant number are living the life of internally displaced persons (IDPs).

According to Head of Department of Compensation and Rehabilitation of the Ministry of Peace and Reconciliation, the government has made policy on different package for displaced persons, orphans, single women who lost husband to conflict, injured persons and those with lost/damaged property. However he mentioned that this information is not in published form and is still under the process. The other fact is the support and provision was not made in consultation with related to civil society or the person concerned.

The allocation and disbursement of funds to IDPs is questionable. Both the government and organisations express the need for systematic and detailed research regarding identification and location of IDPs. It is clear that the increasing number of IDPs is not just short term on the basis of several years of displacement. The support provided should not just support for namesake rather it should be incorporated with skills and proper livelihood. Special attention should be given to female IDPs who are without education or skills and are still bearing the chief responsibility of making a livelihood in urban centers. Many single women (widows) have been unable to access education chiefly due to geographical inaccessibility but also because of societal barriers. Further, geographical inaccessibility often results in poor economic condition and increased vulnerability.

For effective responses to displacement, recognition of the reality of displaced people and the formulation of successful programmes, women's concerns need to be incorporated. Indeed, in the design of programmes to rehabilitate and resettle IDPs who are also single women (widows), more consideration needs to be given to women generally and single women specifically. There is certainly a strong need for greater participation of displaced single women (widows) in public life. Bottom of Form

CONTEMPORARY SOCIAL POSITION OF WIDOWHOOD AMONG RURAL AND URBAN AREA

Across Indian societies, women continue to struggle for gender equality and women's rights issues. Particularly, Widows in India are facing a lot of problems and hardships in the family and society because of traditional norms, cultural practices and beliefs in the society. In the patriarchal Hindu society in which women derive their status from their husbands, widows have always been regarded as symbols of misfortune, and their presence was thought to be inauspicious at happy occasions.

They were forced to withdraw completely from the social life of the community and were made to follow a severe discipline which made their existence a virtual social death. Efforts were made during the early colonial period to work towards reforms to improve the condition of widows in India. Yet, glaring gender discrimination exists in India over the centuries. Women, particularly widows in India are the victims of social stigma. Discrimination of widows is a common phenomenon which is deep rooted in the traditional values and beliefs of the community. Widows are found to have abundance of problems all over the world due to the doctrine of patriarchy and social debasement.

Among the widows, the most vulnerable groups are those who have been living alone or staying with unmarried children. Some of the major problems they face are, responsibility of child-bearing, lack of companionship, violence against widows, hindrances in remarriage, control over sexuality, victimization, and psycho-social adjustment with her own family and society. In all the developing countries, millions of widows and their children live in the condition of acute insecurity, deprivation and violence. Even though we have Civil laws of inheritance, customary laws relating to marriage and inheritance, land ownership and child custody there exists is a large gap between the legal measures and practices due to the rigid patriarchal attitude towards women.child custody there exists is a large gap between the legal measures and practices due to the rigid patriarchal attitude towards women.child custody there exists is a large gap between the legal measures and practices due to the rigid patriarchal attitude towards women.

In India and probably elsewhere irrespective of religion, caste, class and education, millions of widows are deprived of their universally acknowledged human rights. Their essential needs like food, shelter and cloth are forbidden. A few women are forced to face sexual harassment from their in-laws. Widows' needs are marginalized in Indian society and they are not taken into mainstream. Even in an educated civilized society, they are isolated and placed under several restrictions.

Because of the question of control over their sexuality, widowhood is insisted on women to confine them in their homes. They are not allowed to attend any social and religious functions and so they restrict their right to live in public sphere. Gender hierarchy is deep rooted in Indian culture. Compared to widowers, widows have much more restriction in the society. Widowers have the freedom to move everywhere as well as to participate in social functions. Due to patriarchy, women are considered as a secondary object and this gender hierarchy is observed in family as well as in society too.

Widows are discriminated even by their family members and they are restricted physically and socially. They are not allowed to wear coloured sarees, bangles, forced to wear unattractive attire, ornaments, hair style, *etc.* These kinds of restrictions were very rigid in the community. Further their presence is prohibited in social, cultural and religious ceremonies. Society does not permit them to re-marry, which is a violation of human right. Even though the Indian Constitution guarantees equality to all, discrimination against widows is still prevalent, and widowhood is overwhelmingly a woman's problem. In India, there are three times as many widows than widowers. Child-marriage, polygamy, the wide age-gap between men and women, war and increasing rate of AIDS have greatly increased the number of widows, especially young ones. The sample is 500 respondents have been taken in this research of this 8 respondents were HIV/AIDS positive among this 3 respondent admitted that they have HIV/

AIDS positive. Total by there are more than 40 million widows in India and majority of their life has been described as a "living sati", a reference to the now outlawed practice of widow burning. outlawed practice of widow burning.

STATEMENT OF THE PROBLEM

While women had a chequered growth transcending spatial, temporal, religious and caste barriers, widows have undergone a lot of suffering. The traditional religious society had imposed severe sanctions on widows. The widow undergone physical, mental, moral and spiritual agony, by the cruel hands of the society had inflicted unbearable pain on them. As a result, widows were forced to live a socially ostracized, economically dependents and physically austere and spiritually pious life. A widow's public presence was not considered as auspicious one; therefore she had to live in seclusion.

By realizing the untold misery undergone by the widows, several social thinkers and reformers had champion the cause of widows and advocated several remedial measures like abolition of *'sati'*, child marriage restriction and widow re-marriage during the last 200 years. In order to prevent inhuman practices to widows, social legislations like abolition of Sati Act 1829 and Abolition of Child Marriage Act 1929 were passed. The social activists in different parts of India had implemented a number of projects with a view to improve the welfare of widows. Both Central and State governments as well as many NGOs have introduced various schemes to protect widows from the social on slaughter and to promote their welfare.

This study examines the socio-economic condition of widows, particularly widows belonging to rural and urban in Dindigul District. The overall objective of the study is to analyse their contemporary issues and suggest measures for their betterment.

FEMINIST RESEARCH METHODOLOGY

Methodology is the study of the methods and practices in research investigations, the gathering of evidence in the process of knowledge and theory formation. Feminist research methodology critiques the theoretical principles and applications of traditional methodology from a variety of perspectives. Semi-structured interviewing has become an important element in feminist qualitative methods for its ability to record women's thought, beliefs and values employed in the development of feminist theory.

Tools for Data Collation

In the present study data were both 'primary' as well as 'secondary' sources. The dates were collected primary sources constituted of the widows of 18 years and above and were victims of abuse and neglect by Participatory scientific observation, Interview schedule, and Secondary sources include census reports, articles, newspaper reports, journals and books. As the study was qualitative in nature, an in-depth interview was the primary tool for data collection; The interviews were conducted according to 'Interview Topic Guide' which consisted of two broad items like: personal details, Socio condition.

Sample Size

The study has been drawn by using random sampling method. Total sample selected for the study are 500 respondents, out of 9,850 widows as according to recorded in Department of Women and Welfare as on 31.03.2013 in Dindigul District.Women and Welfare as on 31.03.2013 in Dindigul District.Women and Welfare as on 31.03.2013 in Dindigul District.

The Contents of Data Analysis

The data obtained during the interviews were in the form of 'linguistic narration'or was of a qualitative in nature. The content of each interview was carefully analysed on the basis of the responses given by each respondent. The writer of analysis were how individuals recounted their histories - what they emphasize and omitted their stance as protagonists or victims, the relationship the story established between the teller and the audience – all shape what an individual can claim of their own lives. Personal stories are not merely a way of telling someone (or oneself) about one's life; they are the means by which identities may be fashioned.

Design of the Study

Here, descriptive design will be used to describe the data. Descriptive research design is a scientific method which involves observing and describing the behaviour of a subject without influencing it in any way.

Scope of the Study

A widow is a person who is subjected to innumerable miseries not due to her fault but due to ignorance, superstition and the social custom followed by the patriarchal society, her agony and sufferings have not been reduced even after the passage of time. Due to the deep recorded operation of patriarchy, widows have been silently suffering in the society.

The problem of widowhood has elicited considerable interest in the minds of researchers in recent times. In the Indian context, the problems assume considerable importance, as the age difference between husband and wife is higher and widow–remarriage is highly restricted. Hence, in order to understand the complex phenomenon of widowhood, a systematic study of various problems faced by widows, the causes, the consequences and the effects on the personality of widows, the difficulties in adapting widowhood and how they will manage to overcome the problems, patriarchal society creating new gender roles and socially and culturally restricted socialization practices against widows, and the devaluation of widow's life.

Several legislative and social programmes have been launched during the last five to six decades with a view to liberate widows from their predicament. The present study of widows in Dindigul District in particular urban 250 respondent and rural 250 respondent gives sufficient insight into the changes brought to the status of widows and analyses help giving the current position of widows. The present study to place the problem in proper perspective and to decide the frame work for analysis.

Precise definition of the concepts would enable both the collection of relevant data, and meaningful interpretation of the results of analysis. Widowhood may be perceived as a position involving major change in a woman's role both in the family and in the society. The familial and societal lives of widows are also marginalized them due to rapid development of modernization, liberalization, technological advancement *etc.* Widowhood can lead to intense frustration among widows resulting in stress, depression and other forms of adaptive behaviour. If their pattern of reactions is to frustration is not appropriate, it becomes imperative to look into the individual psychological factors of the widows. These psychological factors determine the pattern of reaction to frustration among widows in comparison to married women and the difference in the reaction pattern of widows and married women.

In India's ritualistic, male dominated society, widowhood has been projected as a form of discrimination to devalue women. As per popular social practice a widow is often blamed for her husband's death. Upon attaining widowhood, most widows in India are subjected to economic decline, social isolation and related deprivation. They are restricted about how and where they live and in terms of inheritance, remarriage, and employment and the kind of social support they can receive from relatives and to community.

Even after decades of struggles by social reformers and passing of progressive legislation's like Sati Abolish Act 1829, The Hindu Widow Remarriage Act 1856, *etc.* Widows are still one of the marginalized sections of the society with least importance in public and private spheres. The problem of widowhood in India is critical both in terms of its emotional depth as well as sheer number of person's caught in the cruel practice. As per the 1991 census Pondicherry had the highest proportion of widows (67.7 per cent) in India. In view of the fact that when of consider whole Tamilnadu is also not far behind than Pondicherry in the care the researcher has made a study on the current status of widowhood in Dindigul district. Researcher has selected 500 widow respondents among rural and urban area in Dindigul district.

WIDOWHOOD ACROSS CULTURES

Human behaviours generally are guided by the dominant prescriptions and proscriptions embedded in particular societies, and this is reflected in wide cross-cultural variations among those who have lost a spouse through death.

For example, the situation of Hindu widows in India has undergone numerous changes, ranging from extremely harsh treatment in the past to slow but steady improvement in the modern era. The custom of suttee—the wife's self-immolation on her husband's funeral pyre—has long been outlawed but periodically reappears, especially in rural areas. Even today, widows in that highly patriarchal, patrilineal, and patrilocal society experience isolation and a loss of status.

Their remarriage rate is very low. Widows often face a difficult life that is influenced by vestiges of patriarchal and religious dogma and exacerbated by economic problems that force them to become dependent on sons, in-laws, and others. Widowers, by contrast, are encouraged to remarry soon and add progeny to the patriarchal line. Israel is another place where the society and religion are strongly patriarchal and women lose status in widowhood. Jewish mourning rituals "tend to isolate the widow and tie her to the past rather than providing means of creating a new life". Moreover, women who lose husbands through civilian causes of death encounter greater difficulties than do those whose husbands are killed in the military. War widows and their families receive preferential treatment through government policies that give them special recognition, numerous benefits, and many more alternatives for improving their status and prestige than is possible in more traditional societies. Remarriage, for example, is is a much more acceptable alternative for women in Israel than it is in India.

All societies are undergoing various degrees of transition. Korea is a society whose transitional problems are dramatically reflected in the situation of widows. Earlier in Korean history, widowhood resulted in a loss of status and remarriage generally was prohibited. Husbands tended to be much older than their wives and to have a higher mortality rate, and a large number were killed in wars. Moreover, widowers remarried, whereas most widows remained single. All these factors contributed to a widening ratio of widows to widowers over the years. Under the impact of modernization, including increased urbanization and industrialization, Korean society is being transformed, and with it the conditions surrounding the status of widowhood.

This transformation includes a shift from authoritarian societal and familial system in a primarily rural environment towards systems based on more equalitarian norms. Widows began to move to the cities, and this had advantages and disadvantages. On the one hand, they could accompany their sons and take advantage of urban services and the possibility of new friendships. On the other hand, the move removed them from their extended families and neighborhood friends and the communal supports in their rural villages. Living with a son in the city often strained the daughter-in-law relationship. In addition, being distanced from the relatively stable and integrated life of their villages and lacking friendship networks in their new environment often left them vulnerable to loneliness, especially in the case of the elderly widowed. Presumably, succeeding generations with greater personal resources will encounter fewer adaptational requirements.

While survivors face certain common problems and role strains both within and outside the immediate family, it is difficult to specify a normative course of adjustment. This is the case because the widowed are a heterogeneous group characterised by wide differences in social and psychological characteristics. It also is due to the fact that spousal loss evokes a panorama of emotional and behavioral responses from the survivors, depending on factors such as the timing and circumstances of the spouse's death. For example, a wife whose husband was killed in a military battle will respond differently than she would if he had committed suicide or suffered a long terminal illness. Many other antecedent conditions, such as the quality of the marital relationship, affect the bereavement reactions and coping strategies of survivors.

THE DEMOGRAPHICS OF WIDOWHOOD

Census data for the United States show that at the end of the 1990s there were more than 13.5 million widowed persons, 85 percent of whom were women. However, people in the widowed category may leave it through remarriage. Hence, the number of people who have ever experienced spousal loss is much greater than is indicated by these data.

For some decades, the widowed female has outnumbered her male counterpart by an ever widening margin. Three factors account for this: (1) Mortality among females is lower than it is among males, and therefore, greater numbers of women survive to advanced years, (2) wives are typically younger than their husbands and consequently have a greater probability of outliving them, and (3) among the widowed, remarriage rates are significantly lower for women than for men. Other factors that contribute to the preponderance of widows include war, depressions, and disease pandemics.

For several reasons, widowhood has become largely a problem of aged women. Each year in the United States, deaths of spouses create nearly a million new widows and widowers. Among people 65 years of age or over, roughly half the women compared with about 14 percent of the men are widowed. (U.S. Bureau of the Census 1997).

Advances in medical technology and the pervasiveness health programmes have extended life expectancy. The probability of mortality before middle age has decreased, and for the most part widowhood has been postponed to the later stages of the life cycle. Gains in longevity have been more rapid for women than for men. Thus, the growing proportion of elderly females accents their higher rates of widowhood. About one-fourth of all married women will become widows by age 65, and one-half of the remaining women will be widowed by age 75. During that age span, only one-fifth of men will lose their wives. It is projected that the ratio of widows to widowers will increase dramatically from nearly six to one currently to ten to one over the next quarter century.

Because the large majority of the widowed are women, most studies have concentrated on them, while the social consequences for men who lose their spouses has remained a comparatively unexplored area since Berardo (1970) called attention to this gap three decades ago. Widowers, although fewer in number, face many of the same adjustments that confront their female counterparts. At the same time, there is ambiguous evidence that suggests that widowers have greater vulnerability compared to their female counterparts, while other studies present the situation of widows as more problematic. This disagreement in findings results in part from the failure of many studies to control for the confounding influences of factors such as age, social class, income, health, and retirement.

RESEARCH FINDINGS ON WIDOWHOOD

In making the transition from marriage to widowedhood, the bereaved often are confronted with a variety of personal and familial problems and are not always successful in adapting to those circumstances. This is reflected in the findings that compared with married persons, the widowed consistently have higher rates of mortality, mental disorders, and suicide. While there is a consensus that bereavement is stressful, research on its effects on physical health has yielded inconsistent results. The evidence shows that the widowed experience poorer health than do the married, but the reasons for this difference are unclear.

Because widowhood is most likely to occur in the elderly, research has focused on that population. However, there is some evidence that the transition to widowhood varies by developmental stage. Older widows adapt more readily because losing a spouse at an advanced age is more the norm, making acceptance of the loss easier than it is for those who are young when widowed. Grieving over the death of a husband or wife at older ages can be exacerbated if additional significant others also die, requiring multiple grieving. This can cause bereavement overload, which makes it difficult for the survivor to complete the grief work and bring closure to the bereavement process. There is a consensus that the distress associated with conjugal bereavement diminishes over time. Grief becomes less intense as the years pass, but this is not a simple, linear process. The emotional and psychological traumas of grief and mourning may recur sporadically long after a spouse has died.

Gender differences in adaptation to widowhood have been widely debated. The evidence suggests a somewhat greater vulnerability for widowers. Men are less likely to have same-sex widowed friends, are more likely to be older and less healthy, have fewer family and social ties, and experience greater difficulty in becoming proficient in domestic roles. Higher mortality and suicide rates also suggest greater distress among widowers. Continuous widowhood has been associated with a loss of income and an increased risk of poverty. Two-fifths of widows fall into poverty at some time during the five years after the death of their husbands. Female survivors, for example, have dramatically higher proportions in poverty than do their divorced counterparts, although both groups experience economic risk resulting from the ending of their marriages that may impede their and their families' adjustment to a new lifestyle. There is some evidence that widowers also suffer a decline in economic well-being, although to a lesser degree than do their female counterparts. Poor adjustment to widowhood thus may be related to a lack of finances. Elderly individuals often have below-average incomes before the death of a spouse. They may be unwilling or unable to seek employment and are likely to face discrimination in the labour market. The younger widowed are more likely to have lost a spouse suddenly and therefore may be unprepared to cope with a lower financial status.

Life insurance has become a principal defence against the insecurity and risk of widowhood in urban industrial society with its nuclear family system. It is a concrete form of security that may help a bereaved family avoid an embarrassing dependence on relatives and the state in the case of an untimely death. However, the amount of insurance obtained is often insufficient to meet the needs of the survivors. Even in instances in which adequate assets have been accumulated, many surviving wives are not prepared to handle the economic responsibilities brought about by a husband's death. Presumably, in the future, a better educated and occupationally experienced population of widows, especially those who were involved in a more equalitarian marital relationship of shared responsibilities, will be better able to cope with their new single status.

Widowhood often leads to changes in living arrangements. Reduced income may force surviving spouses to seek more affordable housing. They also may choose to relocate for other reasons, such as future financial and health concerns, a desire to divest themselves of possessions, and a desire to be near relatives or friends. Most often, survivors living alone are women, usually elderly widows. Isolation and lack of social support can lead to deterioration in their physical and mental well-being. Compared with elderly couples, they are much more likely to live in poverty and less likely to receive medical care when it is needed.

WIDOWHOOD AND DIVORCE

Similarities and Differences. Early epidemiological analyses suggested that more deleterious effects were associated with separation and divorce than with widowhood. However, later surveys found higher levels of physical and psychological distress among the widowed than among the divorced. These contradictory findings have not been reconciled. However, for many decades, researchers also have perceived a number of similarities in adjustment between the two groups. For both, there are accompanying disruptions in lifestyle related to changes in income, social interactions, definitions of self, lost emotional attachment, and general psychological well-being. For example, similarities in adjustment have been noted with respect to mode of death or cause of divorce, including the amount of prior warning or preparation a person has before either event, the degree of responsibility felt, and the cause of the event. The more unexpected the loss is, the more responsibility one feels for the loss and wonders whether he or she could have prevented it or helped the spouse and the more difficult the adjustment is.

Another similarity is that whether a spouse is lost through divorce or widowhood, the length of time for adjustment shows considerable variability. The degree of emotional attachment affects the degree of anxiety and depression associated with the loss of a partner, and in both cases the attachment declines as time passes. Emotional attachment is a normal outcome of the tendency for people to form strong affectional bonds to significant others and is not pathological. However, the accumulative changes that occur with the loss of a partner make those who are divorced or widowed more vulnerable to psychological and physical illness, suicide, accidents, and death. While most partners return to their former level of functioning within a couple of years after the loss of a spouse, some never recover and continue to have poor levels of functioning.

There are also specific factors that make adjustment in widowhood or divorce more difficult, including age, gender, race, and socioeconomic status. Adjustment to the loss of a spouse in either case appears to be more difficult for younger women. Some analysts argue that age is a confounding factor because younger women are more studied as divorcees and older women more studied as widows and because divorce is more common among the young and widowhood more common among the old. The latter factor means that one's adjustment is somewhat dependent on those who have gone before and can help socialize a person to the new role. However, more recent research suggests that younger women still face more adjustment problems. Analyses suggest that the young and the old bereaved differ in both the intensity of grief and patterns of grief reactions, especially with respect to adverse health and psychological outcomes within the first two years after the demise of a husband. It appears that younger widows experience a different adjustment than do older widows, in part because they have fewer cohort friends who are also widows.

Younger survivors are developmentally "out of sync" with their cohorts, and this exacerbates their sense of loneliness and need for companionship. Their expectations may be different because they have more years ahead and more potentially eligible marital partners in the future than do older widows. Blacks appear to have an easier time adjusting to the loss of a spouse through divorce than do whites, and black females, who may receive more familial support than whites do, appear to adjust more easily than do white females. Finally, income and financial security play a major role in adjustment: Those near poverty have the most difficult time coping with the loss of a spouse. Female survivors have more problems coping with the loss of income than do their male counterparts, often because their incomes are tied to health insurance, retirement, and other benefits that accompanied the husband's occupation. Men have more difficulty than do women handling the household chores that were often the responsibility of their wives. Future male cohorts may have less difficulty with this because of changes in the socialization of male children and the rising age at first marriage, and the fact that young men have to cope with household responsibilities on their own before marriage.

WIDOWHOOD AND REMARRIAGE

The probability of remarriage is significantly lower for widows than for widowers, especially at the older ages. It appears that while a large majority of older widows remain attracted to and interested in men in terms of companionship, for a variety of reasons only a small minority report a favorable attitude towards remarriage. Some may feel they are committing psychological bigamy and therefore reject remarriage as an option. There is also a tendency to idealize the former partner, a process known as sanctification. This makes it difficult for widows to find a new partner who can compare favorably with the idealized image of the deceased. Widows also remarry less frequently than do widowers because of the lack of eligible men and the existence of cultural norms that degrade the sexuality of older women and discourage them from selecting younger mates. Many women manage to develop and value a new and independent identity after being widowed, leading them to be less interested in re-entering the marriage market.

There are other barriers to remarriage for the widowed. Dependent children limit the opportunities of their widowed parents to meet potential mates or develop relationships with them. Older children may oppose remarriage out of concern for their inheritance. Widowed persons who cared for a dependent spouse through a lengthy terminal illness may be unwilling to risk bearing that burden again.

WIDOWHOOD AND MORTALITY

The increased risk of mortality for widowed persons has been widely reported. Men are at a greater risk than women after bereavement. The causes of these differences are unknown. Marital selection theory posits that healthy widowers remarry quickly, leaving a less healthy subset that experiences premature mortality. Other factors, such as common infection, shared environment, and lack of adequate daily care, also may influence the higher mortality rates of the widowed.

Studies of whether anticipatory grief or forewarning of the pending death of a spouse contributes to adjustment to bereavement have yielded conflicting results. Some suggest that anticipation is important because it allows the survivor to begin the process of role redefinition before the death, whereas unanticipated death produces more severe grief reactions. Survivors who have experienced unexpected deaths of their spouses report more somatic problems and longer adjustment periods than do those who anticipated the loss. Anticipatory role rehearsal does not consistently produce smoother or more positive adjustment among the bereaved. It appears that the coping strategies employed by survivors vary with the timing and mode of death, which in turn influence the bereavement outcome.

SOCIAL SUPPORT AND REINTEGRATION

It has been suggested that social support plays an important role in the bereavement outcome and acts as a buffer for stressful life events, but the research is somewhat inconclusive, partly as a result of difficulties identifying those support efforts which produce positive outcomes and those which do not and the fact that support needs change over time. Nevertheless, there is evidence that the extent to which members of the social network provide various types of support to the bereaved is important in the pattern of recovery and adaptation. Available confidants and access to self-help groups to assist with emotional management can help counter loneliness and promote a survivor's reintegration into society. The social resources of finances and education have been found to be particularly influential in countering the stresses associated with the death of a spouse. Community programmes that provide education, counseling, and financial services can facilitate the efforts of the widowed and their families to restructure their lives.

For many older widows, a substantial period of future living alone remains: on average, another fourteen years or more. Borrowing from occupational career models, some researchers have suggested that adopting a "career of widowhood" orientation may facilitate the recovery and well- being of these survivors: "That is, for most persons, widowhood need not be considered the end of productive life, but rather the beginning of a major segment of the life course, and one that should be pursued vigorously in order for it to be successful and fulfilling". In this perspective, the widowed are encouraged to seek control over their existence by actively construing their own life courses. The assumption is that they will adapt better if they plan for where they want to be at different potential stages during the entire course of widowhood. This plan might include the following phases: "a time for emotional recovery; a time for taking stock, re-establishing or restructuring support relationships, and formulating personal directions for the future; a time for discovering a comfortable and satisfying independent lifestyle, and for determining an approach to maintaining economic, psychological, and social functioning; perhaps a time for personal growth and change; and a time for reasoned consideration of one's last years and assertion of a degree of control over the arrangements surrounding one's own decline and death."

There is considerable heterogeneity among the survivor population and thus in their ability to implement a successful "career in widowhood." They differ, for example, in relational competence, that is, characteristics that help them acquire, develop, and maintain personal relationships that are essential for social support. Establishing a new and satisfying autonomous identity after the loss of a spouse is never easy. The probability of achieving that goal can, however, be enhanced through counseling strategies designed for individual circumstances and programmes that help survivors avoid desolation coupled with meaningful social and familial support systems.

ECONOMICS OF SINGLE-PARENT FAMILY LIFE

The most profound effect of divorce is economic deprivation for mother-only families. For example, in the United States, the custodial mother's and children's standard of living is reduced by 30 percent on average while the noncustodial father's standard of living increases by 15 percent. The typical pattern for both middle-class and working-class newly divorced mothers in Western societies is to move into inadequate apartments in undesirable neighborhoods due to the scarcity of affordable housing that will accommodate children.

The result is that they often leave their social networks and sources of support at the same time that they are forced to enter the labour force or increase their working hours. For single parents the housing/employment issue is one of affordability and geographic proximity and access to jobs that pay a living wage. In addition, teenage mothers face economic adversity with the interruption of their education. As teen mothers move into adulthood they often remain unskilled, unemployed, and unemployable.

Child support, money paid by the noncustodial parent to the custodial parent towards the support of the children, does not offset the economic deprivation experienced by single-parent families. Since mothers retain custody in the majority of cases, fathers are typically ordered to pay child support. However, award levels have consistently accounted for less than half of the expense of supporting a child, representing about 10 percent of the noncustodial father's income. According to one study, a father's child support payments average less than his car payments.

Despite recent U.S. legislation, many fathers do not pay court-ordered child support payments. In 1997, 68 percent of custodial mothers with children under the age of eighteen received full (42 per cent) or partial (27 per cent) child support payments, leaving a third without any payment. The average amount received by U.S. mothers in 1997 was $3,700, an increase of $400 from 1994. Women below the poverty level are the least likely to be awarded or to receive child support. Black and Hispanic mothers are even less likely to be awarded support or to benefit from payments.

When the situation is reversed and custody is granted to the father, mothers are ordered to pay lower child support awards since fathers tend to have higher incomes. Mothers still pay an average of $3,300 to custodial U.S. fathers, although only one-third pay in full. Compared to noncustodial mothers who do not pay support, mothers who pay support earn a higher income, have more regular visitation with their children, are consulted more by the fathers, and have more positive feelings about their arrangement.

The economics of single-parent family life mean that single mothers are disproportionately represented among the poor. Among U.S. households headed by single mothers in 1998, one-third lived below the poverty line, compared to 12 percent of male-headed families. In 1999, 42 percent of children living in female-headed families were poor, compared to 18 percent in male-headed families, and 8 percent in couple-headed families. Overall, women with dependent children comprise two-thirds of the poor population, a phenomenon referred to as the "feminization of poverty." This is especially pronounced for African-American and Hispanic women who head families, with 43 and 51 percent, respectively, living below the poverty line, compared to 31 percent of white mothers who head families. African-American (14.7 per cent) and Hispanic (16.8 per cent) single fathers are also more likely to be living below the poverty line than their white male counterparts (10.8 per cent).

Around the world women make up the majority (70 per cent) of the 1.3 billion people who live in poverty. The United Nations Commission on the Status of Women (1996) estimates that women constitute almost 60 percent of the world's population, perform two-thirds of all working hours, receive only one-tenth of the world's income, and own less than 1 percent of the world's wealth. The poverty of families headed by women can be attributed to the fact that women's roles are primarily domestic (mother, homemaker), undervalued, and unpaid. In addition, when women work for wages they make significantly less than their male counterparts.

Even full-time employment does not guarantee financial security, given the structure of the labour force, the lower wages paid in female-dominated occupations, and the lower human capital investment of single mothers (education, training, and work experience). However, even when controlling for education and work place experience, women earn less than men, a global pattern that holds true across all racial and ethnic groups throughout the occupations. In the developed world, the United States and Canada have the highest wage gap (75 per cent) and the Scandinavian countries have the lowest (80 per cent to 94 per cent).

Gender differences in earnings are exacerbated by race; in 1995, the median income for full-time year-round work in the United States was $22,900 for white women, $20,700 for African-American women, and $17,200 for Hispanic women. Whereas the majority of single mothers worked for wages in 1997 (79 per cent), one-third were employed part-time or part-year only. Single fathers, on the other hand, were more likely to be working full-time (77 per cent), with only 17 percent working part-time or part-year.

In addition, single mothers are more likely than other employees to experience layoffs, they receive fewer fringe benefits, and they pay higher expenses for childcare (Kinnear 1999). In developing countries, families are often disrupted as parents leave home to find work. For example, Filipina women regularly migrate to Hong Kong to work as domestics on multiple-year contracts managed by the government. They leave their children in the Philippines and send money for their support since the wages earned in Hong Kong ($325 month) exceed what they could earn at home ($125 month).

The income of mothers heading families, supplemented by child support and transfer payments, is used to support the family. In the United States child support and alimony together account for about 10 percent of the total income of white mothers and for about 3.5 percent of the income of African-American mothers. However, alimony or spousal support is awarded in less than 15 percent of all divorce cases, is received in less than 7 percent, and has been virtually eliminated in marriages ending in fewer than five years.

Another source of support essential to the ability of single parents to manage the demands of work and home is child care. A disruption in child-care arrangements can be stressful for any family in which both parents work; for the single-parent family, it can create an immediate crisis. Single mothers report that childcare is one of the most difficult obstacles in their efforts to provide for their families through paid employment. European and Scandinavian countries are ahead of the United States in developing government subsidized comprehensive childcare programmes. France and Sweden, in particular, provide a model of supporting working mothers, with resulting low rates of poverty among mother-only families, along with modest levels of public dependency. Japan also provides high-quality, affordable day care for working mothers; poor families receive the service free.

PUBLIC ASSISTANCE FOR SINGLE-PARENT FAMILIES

An alternative or supplement to paid employment for U.S. single parents is public assistance in the form of Temporary Aid to Needy Families (TANF), formerly Aid to Families with Dependent Children (AFDC). This means-tested programme, established in 1935 as part of the Social Security Act, was originally designed to support mothers and children who had lost a male earner in the family, allowing the mother to stay at home. Historically, welfare policy was based on a distinction between worthy women who were dependent through no fault of their own (widows) and undeserving mothers who were divorced or never married. Programme regulations were developed in ways that reflected this distinction, along with racist assumptions about the role of immigrant and African-American women within both the family and the paid labour force.

Welfare reform and the resulting TANF programme represent a change in societal views about women's roles in the family and at work. The assumption is that mothers can and should work to support their families and that public support should be temporary and supplemental. TANF placed a lifetime limit of five years on welfare eligibility, required that within five years one-half of a state's caseload was to be enrolled in jobs or jobrelated activities, and excluded college education from the list of qualified work and training activities. As a result, the welfare rolls dropped dramatically from 14.2 million in 1994 to 7.6 million in 1998, a decline of more than 40 percent. At the same time the number of children living at the lowest levels of poverty (less than $6,401 in 1997) grew by 400,000 between 1995 and 1997.

Only about half of all mother-only families receive welfare benefits at any given time. In recent years the rate of participation in at least one public assistance programme plummeted from 45 percent in 1993 to 38 percent in 1997. Regardless, public assistance, including non-cash transfers, maintains families well below the U.S. poverty line.

Other developed countries, particularly those in Western Europe, have maintained the goal of supporting mothers to stay at home if they wish. In Great Britain, for example, mothers are not pressured to find work outside the home, and child allowances, national health services, and access to public housing are provided. In Norway single parents receive a child allowance, a child care cash benefit, an education benefit, a housing allowance, and transitional and advanced cash benefits. While most single parents (90 per cent) have incomes less than half the median family income, only 9 percent of all children in single-parent families fall below the poverty line. Developing countries are less likely to have formalized assistance programmes in place, although there are grassroots efforts such as the AIDS Support Organisation in Uganda to aid widows and their children and Dwip Unnayam Sangstha in Bangladesh to help divorced and widowed women and their children.

Views of Single-Parent Families

Societal views about single-parent families are expressed in social policies and agendas. U.S. policies, especially those relating to welfare, child care, and family/work support, reflect disapproval of families needing public support, single-parent families in particular. Divorced or "broken" families as they are sometimes called are seen as deviant and a threat to the social order. Other Western countries support the wellbeing of children regardless of the number of parents with programmes such as guaranteed child-support payments, health insurance, child care, maternity and parenting benefits, and housing subsidies. Although all families are well-supported, couple-headed families are valued over other family forms.

In many areas of the Third World single mothers are socially ostracized and seen as having inferior status. In the case of widowhood, women are not allowed to inherit property or possessions in many countries where other sources of support are not provided. In the past, unmarried women (with or without children) would have been cared for by the family system, which has been weakened as a result of urbanisation. In these patriarchal societies men and women do not share equally the limited resources available to families. Development, especially strategies based on capitalism, worsens the situation for women.

Societal views are also expressed in public discourse about women living outside of marriage and family who fail to live up to the ideals of motherhood imposed through legal and public policies. Feminists argue that efforts to control women's sexuality and enforce mothers' economic dependence upon men are part of a backlash designed to limit women's mobility and freedom. Rather than attempt to force women into a traditional mold, more institutional support for the new type of dual-earner and single-parent family prevalent today is needed.

CONFLICT AMONG RIGHTS CONFLICT AMONG RIGHTS

The expanded assertion and recognition of rights, and the dimensions to rights that are emerging, have given rise to situations of conflicts among rights, and consequently, among rights activists. Choices are being made, and a prioritisation of rights occurring in a range of areas. The neglect of women's rights in the human rights arena for decades after the Universal Declaration on Human Rights and the Constitution of India, has had the women's movement demanding, and acquiring even if partially, recognition of women's rights as human rights. There were some among our respondents who held that human rights are those which are asserted against state action and inaction. A human rights lawyer, on the other hand, saw human rights as a strategy which ought not to be confined within an inflexible definition.

For people in the women's movement, however, human rights are about patriarchy and systemic oppression and violence; domestic violence and death in the matrimonial home could not, clearly, be excluded from the universe of human rights issues. As a civil liberties' activist told us, in a pamphlet they prepared in 1990, she compared statistics in dowry deaths with encounter killings: it was 2000:300. Though it stoked a lot of controversy, the women members of the organisation were very happy that the issue had been raised, she said. The emergence of women's rights in the human rights universe has also brought with it some contradictions which demand to be addressed.

A MORE JUST DEAL FOR WOMEN AND FAIR TRIAL STANDARDS

In cases of violence against women: registering a case; getting effective investigation underway; the ordeal of trial for the victim, particularly in situations of rape; the difficulty in obtaining evidence in offences within the home, as also in cases of rape; and the low rate of convictions had women's groups, and on occasion, the National Commission for Women, demanding changes in the law to deal with these issues. Over the years the demand has been for -

- The recognition of certain actions/practices as actionable offences - domestic violence, cruelty in the matrimonial home and 'dowry death'. While the first is under consideration of Parliament, the latter two now find a place in the law. Section 498-A IPC, which makes punishable a 'husband or relative of husband of a woman subjecting her to cruelty' has become contentious. On the one hand the extent of violence in the matrimonial home is undeniable, and restraining the perpetrators and protecting the victim-woman is imperative. On the other hand, the experience of abuses of this provision which defines an offence that is cognisable and non-bailable, which may land families in prison pending bail, is said to have caused resentment against, and distrust of, this provision. Those who would not drop the provision because of the occasional misuse, point out that there are hardly any other protective measures to help a woman battered in her marital home, nor any other deterrent provision to add caution to offending members of the matrimonial family.
- Enhanced punishment for certain offences against women. The introduction into the law of 'minimum sentences', and higher sentences has also happened. Implicit in the demand for prescription of higher penalties is the need to secure deterrence - if the low rate of conviction takes away the possibility of deterrence, it is sought to be reintroduced through a higher penalty where conviction does result. It has also been a measure of the state's, and popular, perception of the seriousness of the offence. The conflict lies in this, that it comes at a time when the virtues of imprisonment are in serious question. It is not evident that the conditions in prisons, and the violations of the rights of prisoners which is now common knowledge, has been reckoned with while asking for enhanced sentences. But the conflict became most apparent when death penalty for the offence of rape was mooted. When it was first suggested in the mid-1990s, there was very little by way of audible objections from women's groups; some women's groups extended it support. It was when the issue was raised again in 1998, that there was an avalanche of protest from women's groups. The NCW

too released a report of a study it had done which showed that most of their respondents opposed the prescription of death penalty for rape. For some in the women's movement, the opposition to death penalty for rape appears to have been a pragmatic position - since it would only make the women more vulnerable if the penalty were so severe. For others, the pragmatic argument was a means of opposing the spread of death penalty into areas where it is not, already. What is disturbing is the persistence of the Home Minister in holding out the death penalty as a promise to women, as a statement of seriousness about the problem.

In this context the failure to challenge the prescription of the death penalty for offences in the Commission of Sati Act 1987 also becomes an area that needs to be re-visited.

- Shifting the onus of proof. This has already been introduced into the Evidence Act 1872 in 1983 and 1986. Section 113 A raises a presumption as to abetment of suicide by a married woman where she commits suicide within seven years of her marriage, and it is shown that her husband or in-laws or a relative of her husband had subjected her to cruelty. Section 113 B raises a presumption of dowry death where it is shown that soon before her death she had been subjected to cruelty or harassment by the accused for, or in connection with, any demand for dowry. Section 114 A presumes absence of consent in certain prosecutions for rape. A respondent reasoned that she had opposed this shifting of onus of proof because it would open the gates for the state to extend the shifting of onus to other areas; see what has happened in TADA and such laws, she said. Also, while the violations are certainly heinous, the criminal justice system is structured to require the prosecution to prove guilt; it is often not possible for an accused to rebut an accusation, she said, even where the accused may be innocent. Further it is a dilution of fair trial standards. The contrary position is that there are offences where such a presumption is not necessary if justice is to be done to the woman.
- A separate criminal code for women. This was a proposal that emanated from the NCW and was widely discussed in 1995-96. This was intended to make the trial less traumatic for women, speed up the criminal judicial process, and it was expected to raise the conviction rate. There were discussions of making some inroads into the rights given to an accused under the law. This proposal, however, appears to have been shelved.

It was suggested to us that child sexual abuse being of an extraordinary nature, there should be a relaxation of fair trial standards in dealing with it.

HIV, AIDS AND DISCLOSURE

The two conflicting positions on disclosure by a hospital/doctor about the HIV+ status of a person has been set out supra while mapping human rights issues. To that discussion of the issue may be added that the view on disclosure seems to have been influenced by the context of the proposed marriage of the petitioner in that case. It may be appropriate to consider the reach of the principle of disclosure while weighing the rights content of the court's decision.

AIDS AND HIGH RISK GROUPS

The AIDS campaign has given visibility to women in prostitution who had so far been unable to requisition public spaces. There are few who deny that women in prostitution need to be empowered to prevent their becoming ready victims of HIV transmission, as also of passing the virus on. However, the programme of intervention to protect from AIDS has re-introduced the idea of high risk groups, and women in prostitution as constituting such a group - a notion that was contested in the 1980s as discriminatory, and with the potential of leading to victimisation of targetted groups.

Abortion in the context of Women's Health and Sex Selective Abortion

When Parliament passed the 1971 law legalising abortion under certain conditions, the statement of objects and reasons listed three reasons for passing the law:

- As a health measure - when there is danger to the life or risk to the physical or mental health of the woman;
- On humanitarian grounds - such as when pregnancy arises from a sex crime like rape or intercourse with a lunatic woman, *etc.*; and
- Eugenic grounds - where there is substantial risk that the child, if born, would suffer from deformities and diseases.'c

By 1995, when the Maternity Benefit Act 1961 was amended, the insertion of population control provisions into the law was being acknowledged, and resisted. The 1995 amendment, however, did give a renewed emphasis to placing the onus for family size on the woman when it incorporated 'leave with wages for tubectomy operation' as a 'maternity benefit', even as it gave medical termination of pregnancy the same position in law as miscarriage.

This is a statement of the adoption of abortion as state supported policy. The question of abortion as a right, and abortion as a population control measure may need to be re-visited. There was also a proposal to limit the provision of maternity benefit under the Act to women workers up to the second child; this however seems to have been dropped, perhaps because of the protest that met the proposal at almost every turn. The Pre-natal Diagnostic Techniques Act 1994, which was modelled on an earlier Maharashtra law, was enacted expressly 'to prohibit pre-natal diagnostic techniques for determination of sex of the foetus leading to female foeticide. Such abuse of techniques is discriminatory against the female sex and affects the dignity and status of women.' The punishment for transgressing the prohibition of the law is intended to be deterrent. Yet, in the seven years since the law was enacted, there have been no prosecutions of which any of our respondents made mention. The conflict inherent in asking for abortion as a matter of right, and believing that sex selective abortion needs to be curbed requires to be squarely addressed.

SEXUAL HARASSMENT IN THE WORKPLACE

After the Supreme Court's Vishaka guidelines, demands for translating them into policy and practice are being made. The allegations of sexual harassment by persons in positions of leadership within the human rights community, and the lack of procedures prescribed in Vishaka even within the human rights community, has been raised as an area of conflict in the context of human rights.

FREEDOM OF EXPRESSION, PRIVACY AND CENSORSHIP

The depiction of women, as also of violence against women, has raised difficult questions of censorship and of free speech and expression. The control that capital has over the media has been recognised, and it is not the free speech rights of corporations that is in issue here. Feminists worry that the power to determine what is 'obscene' or 'indecent' could curtail the use of media to interrogate, for instance, rape: for the depiction of rape could be viewed as 'obscene' and explicitly addressing the issue proscribed. Even as feminists, and women, find public spaces for their speech and expression, the space could get restricted and reconstructed by censorship. The Miss World contest organised in Bangalore in 1996 gave rise to similar, uneasily quietened questions.

The responsibility of the researcher, and the impact of publishing research findings, has been in issue in the Almora case, where research published in September 1999 became a subject of singular controversy in April 2000. The research, on AIDS and the local community, used the responses from a sample of respondents who spoke about the sexual practices in the area, from where male migration for work is very high. Promiscuity and adultery were spoken of. The protesters were angry at the depiction of the community in the report. That the research was funded by a foreign donor agency added a dimension to the protest.

The NGO later apologised, and withdrew the report. By then, three activists had spent 45 days in jail. In the meantime the state had moved in to impose the NSA on them. This last deed was roundly condemned, and much of the human rights community spoke as one to attack the state action. The questions raised by the research and the report, however, continue to hang in the air.

PROSTITUTION

There has been considerable movement in public perception. Most significant though has been the openness with which the practice, proliferation and problems of prostitution are now discussed. Inevitably, perhaps, there have been conflicts that have surfaced in this area of women's rights. On the one hand is the demand that sex work be recognised as real work. In the mid-'90s this was articulated as sex work being seen as labour. There was also a demand that labour laws be applied to sex work. That appears to have been gradually amended to the demand that sex work be accepted as labour in terms of the dignity that labour commands. A collective of women in prostitution identified three R's - Respect, Recognition and Reliance. The women in the collective also spoke about the right to say 'No' in the course practice of their profession, and said they had to be given the right of 'self-determination'.

While there was no demurring about the need to protect women from exploitation - from the police, the pimp, the madam and the client - there were dissenting voices on recognising prostitution as sexual labour. As one respondent said it: 'Feminists are being included in a much larger agenda. They are giving patriarchy and sexual exploitation a sugar coating by calling it work. Earlier patriarchy oppressed women by calling them 'mother goddess' and curbing her freedom. Today patriarchy oppresses her by calling her the 'bread winner'.

She continued: 'I accept that today the state is doing little to stop trafficking. But the day sex work is seen as work under law, that will be the end of all efforts to stop trafficking.' A woman from the collective, however, said: 'Trafficking can only be stopped by us. Only we know what is happening in our areas. We are telling the government they should give us the right to act.' She however conceded that not all areas where prostitution is practised and trafficking occurs were yet capable of being so monitored. We see ourselves as workers, she said, and we want a union that will give us a base. A 'mela' which was organised by the collective in Calcutta in March 2001 reportedly met with stiff resistance from some women activists, while others stood up for the rights of the women to organise themselves. It is sometimes depicted as an issue of 'agency' of the woman as against those who see women in prostitution as victims, and subjects of exploitation. Six aspects which a woman in the collective adverted to if they were to be considered to be 'labour', and their association recognised, were:

- Police raids would not happen.
- Mental torture in the rescue homes would cease. Also, when the girls are released by pimps, they say they have paid huge amounts when they actually pay far less in bond. Bonded labour is therefore rampant in the present dispensation, she said.
- A self-regulatory examination board, with a multi-sectoral member composition would be able to prevent the entry of minors into

prostitution. The two criteria of age and willingness would be applied by them. Now, we don't have even the right to stay where we are, she said.

- The right to say 'No' would get established.
- Teasing to demean women in prostitution would reduce.
- When they retire, they are not even able to go back home; once they are declared to be labour, that will change. That would be real rehabilitation, she said.

There was some conceptual confusion about 'decriminalising' and 'legalising' prostitution. While most of our respondents saw a need to decriminalise to prevent them from being a vulnerable group, the mix up with legalising prostitution - which many among our respondents were unable to accept - dogged our discussion. A proposal that the travel of single women across political borders be controlled, which was under discussion with the NCW, was dismissed by some respondents as being a prescription for obstructing freedom of movement of women and as likely to serve no other end.

The children of women in prostitution are seen by the law as being potentially in 'moral danger'. The Juvenile Justice Act 1986 and its successor legislation - the Children in Need of Care and Protection Act 2000 - allow for their children to be taken over by the state. A judge of the Supreme Court had even said that the women should be 'coaxed, cajoled or coerced' to give up their children. This clash of a complex of rights and of perceptions needs to be more fully understood.

THE SOCIAL AND POLITICAL CONTEXT

To understand shortcomings in implementation of women's right to land and resources, it is important to consider the social and political context within which land and property laws are applied. Land distribution laws in India are often implemented in a context of weak and inaccessible political infrastructure, which in turn engages with a thick web of social values that directly impact the laws' efficacy in facilitating women's access to land and resources. Furthermore, women's agency and political empowerment is circumscribed by social relations. Issues of social values and customs vary widely from one region to another, increasing the inconsistent nature of implementation and impact on women's access to resources.

Until recently, the analysis and data collection of issues on food security and poverty levels remained at the household levels. Without looking at poverty and hunger at the level of individuals within the household, gendered needs and roles of women in providing food security, and sustainable livelihoods, their contribution and participation remain invisible in statistical data. Therefore while the contribution of women to the sustenance and survival of South Asian economies is immense, it has historically remained formally unmeasured and thus unaccounted for and undervalued. This chapter attempts to give glimpses into this 'invisible' context of women's access to land and resources. In India there are three sources of land for women: land transferred from government, from the market, and through family inheritance. Most often land is acquired through inheritance, as 87 per cent of land is privately owned. As in many other parts of the world, land structures social relations as it holds symbolic meaning for one's social status. Land is thus deeply tied to survival, dignity and social values for much of the rural poor.

Economic globalisation and privatisation is directly impacting these aspects of land ownership by distorting equitable distribution of land, and creating pressures for the livelihoods of small and marginal farmers. Land is being acquired more and more by multinational corporations, the political and social elite for purposes such as entertainment complexes, natural reserves, industry, tourism, commercial agriculture and other industries.

Often the interests of those with political and social status are linked to the interests of multinational corporations. For example, in much of urban India, the social elite tend to be industrialists, and in rural India, the social elite tend to be landlords most belonging to upper caste. Often the social elite have acquired more land than legally permitted under the Land Ceiling laws. At the same time, when lands are distributed to rural landless peoples, they usually receive wastelands which require substantial human and financial capital to convert into productive lands. This process can take years and most men and women succumb to the pressure to mortgage the land or take loans against their property instead of using it for sustainable livelihoods.

The present socio-economic context renders rural women especially vulnerable, as most women are not experienced in managing resources. Many rural women are illiterate or are not familiar with money lending practices. They are vulnerable to illegitimate moneylenders who charge exorbitant interest rates casting people into debilitating amounts of debt. Often landless labourers in this situation sell their land back to the landlords for extremely low prices, only to end up working on the land as free or bonded labourers. Thus placing land and other resources in the hands of the rural poor is not enough. They also need skills and inputs to manage and keep their resources.

LABOUR ISSUES FOR WOMEN WORKERS

Throughout South Asia, with the exception of Pakistan, women are generally concentrated in low-waged work. The call for minimum and equal wages for women has been made by women within the trade unions and unorganised sector movement in India. Little heed has been paid to amend existing practices of discrimination. Constraints on mobility due to reproductive responsibilities and social norms imply that women tend to be absorbed at the lowest end of the labour market, in low-wage, casual and flexible jobs. With structural reforms and the expansion of global value chains, the social valuation of men as 'workers' has contributed to men getting better jobs than women in the informal sector to. The feminisation of labour here refers not then to greater female employment, but rather the devastation of working conditions for men as well.

The recent National Rural Employment Guarantee Scheme gives a guarantee of 100 days of unskilled labour work to the poor. While it is a positive step to assure wage labour it does not ensure that people own and are engaged in developing their productive assets. The call for increasing the asset base of the poor can be supported by the ongoing labour movement in India by implementing the demand of tripartite labour boards. The labour boards can have women workers resource committees that work upon ensuring that demands for women's land and resource rights is met by building productive assets, in the name of and under the control and management of women.

FOREST - DEPENDENT COMMUNITIES

Tribal people traditionally held land and forests as a community resource for their sustenance and livelihood needs. Mining is degrading the quality of the land, destroying forests and bio diversity in this region, which in turn degrades agricultural land and limits the agricultural activities of local communities who are so dependent on these lands. The demand, as per the Samatha Judgement of 1996, is that local people are made share-holders and proper attention is given to rehabilitation, jobs to the local people, and services.. In the forest areas the pattern of industrialisation is restructuring social relations. Labour roles are changing with the transition from traditional land- and forest- based livelihoods to miningbased.

With this shift in labour roles and traditional livelihoods, gender roles are shifting as well. Where men and women had previously worked together in agricultural activities, now men are working daily in the mines to earn cash income, whereas they would have previously worked to support their families through agricultural production. Women are staying at home to carry out only household duties with the degradation and alienation of lands. Recent research indicates that violence against tribal women is increasing while kinship bonds are decreasing. The practice of eliminating widows through " witch hunting" has been condemned throughout the country. Nutritional intake is decreasing due to decreased traditional cultivation and agricultural activities, and as a result peoples' immunity and health is declining as seen in the increasing incidences of diseases like tuberculosis and malaria. Among tribal and rural peoples this has not been supplemented with the provision of primary public health serves.

On the contrary, attempts are being made to privatise the health services making it inaccessible to the marginalised and poor. The availability of home-based cures, traditional medicines and medicinal herbs has declined, as they cannot be grown as easily due to reductions in the quality and availability of land. The traditional health care system has thus deteriorated and in the absence of adequate state health care facilities, people are turning more and more to baseless 'magic-religious rituals'.

The increasing vulnerability of land- and forest- dependent people in rural India has conflated pressure to retain what remaining land and resources they do hold. Now tribal women are prohibited from owning land without the support of their father, husband, son or brother, so that if a woman is married to a non-indigenous person, the land can stay with the male relative and with the tribal community. Livelihoods of forest-dependent peoples, especially women, are adversely affected by forced evictions. Non-timber forest produce forms a major source of income for many tribal communities. Women are almost exclusively involved in collection, storage, processing and marketing of minor forest products such as fodder, thatching, and medicinal herbs. However increased government control of forests and minor forest products are adversely affecting livelihoods choices of Tribal and forest-dependent women. The recent Forest Rights Bill considered by Government of India from the Ministry of Tribal Affairs takes steps towards placing forests in the hands of tribal peoples.

WOMEN'S ORGANISED STRENGTH

Many land rights movements and women's groups have showcased successful interventions where women have come together as a group to manage a common resource for the sustenance of the community. Due to their traditional roles and reduction of vulnerability with a collective approach, rural women have proved themselves to be better skilled and more efficient at managing common resources than the men of the community.

In areas where forests have been devastated, women have been better able to manage and rehabilitate forests than men due to their traditional roles and skills as fuel wood and fodder collectors. Furthermore women formed into Self Help Groups can collectively expand livelihood options for the community through investing their assets into land ownership and rehabilitation. In Shankergarh, Allahabad the Mahila Samakya Federation of women's groups has acquired fish ponds and mining areas on group lease. As a group, these women are collectively managing these resources and retain ownership.

HUMAN RIGHTS AND SEXUALITY MINORITIES

The founding document on which most human rights organizations base their advocacy is the Universal Declaration on Human Rights. From this initial document has emerged a whole series of human rights declarations, conventions and treaties pertaining to the rights of various marginalized groups and communities such as children, women, indigenous people, disabled people, prisoners, religious and ethnic minorities, refugees, *etc.* However, one significant absence in international human rights law has been an express articulation of the specific interests of sexuality minorities. This silence is dismaying, for the focus on human rights is often justified by invoking the Nazi holocaust and resolving to prevent another such genocide.

What is forgotten in this invocation of history is that the Nazis not only systematically persecuted Jews, communists and disabled people, but also went about eliminating homosexuals. In fact thousands of homosexuals lost their lives in Nazi concentration camps. It is only in the final decade of the 20th century that the gay/ lesbian/ bisexual/ transgender movement brought to the fore the rights of those discriminated against because of their sexuality. In 1991, Amnesty International for the first time came out with a policy to support the rights of people imprisoned because of their sexual orientation or because of engaging in homosexual activity in private. In the mid 1990's, the Human Rights Committee held that the anti sodomy law of Tasmania violated the right to privacy and the right to non- discrimination guaranteed to all persons under the International Covenant on Civil and Political Rights.

In Scandinavia, the provision of equal rights for sexuality minorities, including marriage rights, was an important breakthrough. The other major development has been the South African Constitution, which for the first time expressly prohibited discrimination on grounds of sexual orientation. But while the scope of human rights has been extended to include hitherto marginalized communities at the global level, a similar movement is yet to take place in India. In fact, most human rights organisations in India have not begun to address the question of rights of gays, lesbians, bisexuals, transgender, hijras and others who are oppressed due to their sexuality.

Sexuality is sometimes viewed even in liberal and radical circles as a frivolous, bourgeois issue. In such a context, homosexuality is seen implicitly as something deviant and unnatural that is at best defended as an individual freedom but not a matter of priority for the human rights movement. Generally, issues of poverty and gender, class and caste oppression are seen as more important than that of sexuality. But this ignores the fact that sexuality is integrally linked to ideologies and structures of social oppression such as patriarchy, capitalism, the caste system and religious fundamentalism. Hence, the struggle for sexuality rights cannot be separated from the broader human rights struggle for economic, political and social liberation.

THE STATUS OF SEXUALITY MINORITIES IN INDIA

As reported in various studies, homosexual orientation is common in almost every culture and every society. However, homophobia is chiefly the product of a Judeo Christian morality spread to various parts of the world through European colonialism, which exported its laws and its morality into other local contexts. It has to be noted that homosexuality also finds a mention in the various precolonial laws. Homosexuality is seen as an offence in Manusmrithi, which however can be expiated. Lesbianism by contrast merits more serious punishment. Islamic Shariat law treats homosexual conduct as a serious offence, though it is being argued by some recently formed gay Muslim organisations that Islamic law can be interpreted in a non-homophobic fashion. It was with the enactment of uniform criminal laws in India, in 1860 that there was a uniform proscription of homosexual behaviour.

Though sexuality minorities have always existed in India sometimes in forms, which are culturally sanctioned and at other times in invisibility and silence, their issues have never seriously been articulated. It is only recently that the rights of sexuality minorities as an issue have been taken seriously in India by various civil society organisations. With the founding of India's first gay magazine Bombay Dost in the late 1980's and the starting of a lesbian collective in Delhi called Sakhi, lesbian, gay and bisexual issues were first articulated in a public forum.

Since those early beginnings, the fledgling sexuality minority rights movement has grown increasingly vocal and articulate. Today there are organisations, helplines, publications/newsletters, health resources, social spaces and drop-in centers in most of the major cities in India like Delhi, Mumbai, Calcutta, Bangalore, Hyderabad, Pune, Chennai, Patna and Lucknow.

There has also been a branching out into smaller cities and towns like Akola, Trichi and Gulbarga. In spite of this, the support structures provided are painfully inadequate with few or no such organisations for lesbians, bisexuals and hijras. What is more, many of the newly emerging organisations die out silently while even the more established ones have been able to reach out in concrete terms only to a small section of the sexuality minority population due to lack of resources, personnel, government support and extreme societal/state discrimination.

CONTEXT AND METHODOLOGY

It is in these twin contexts of the global movement for recognition of sexuality minority rights and the increasing assertiveness of sexuality minority voices at the local level that the present report is located. PUCL-K has been receiving reports that there has been a sharp increase in attacks on sexuality minorities in Bangalore, including harassment and illegal detentions by the police of gay and bisexual men in public recreational areas. All sexuality minorities, *i.e.*, gays, bisexuals, lesbians, transgender, transvestites, hijras and other homosexual men and women, suffer in different degrees social and political marginalisation due to their sexuality and/ or gender. To mobilize against these police violations, the Coalition for Sexuality Minorities' Rights, comprising sexuality minority organisations, lawyers, women's organisations and social activists, was formed.

This coalition approached PUCL-K to investigate reports of human rights abuses against sexuality minorities, and to help mobilize public opinion against such abuses. The PUCL-K invited ALF, Manasa and PDF to join in the investigation. A team was formed for the purpose comprising Arvind Narrain, Sharada, Venkatesh, Ramdas Rao, and Laxminarayana. This team met on 2nd July 2000 to investigate reports of widespread police harassment of sexuality minorities in Bangalore. It was able to meet representatives of various organisations supporting rights of sexuality minorities such as Sabrang; Sangama; Good As You; Swabhava and Snehashraya.

However, as the team sat to hear the testimony of members of the affected communities, it became apparent that it was impossible to discuss police harassment without understanding the deeper structural roots of homophobia. For example, police harassment builds on and is reinforced by the fact that society looks at sexuality minorities with disgust and hatred and values them as less than human beings. It is felt quite acceptable to violate the human rights of people who the majority has never really considered as human beings worthy of the same respect as 'normal individuals'. Hence in order to understand the oppression of sexuality minorities one needs to examine the various forms of oppression, both societal and state. It is only within this larger framework that one can comprehend the kinds of violence that sexuality minorities are subject to in our culture and society. Due to the law, societal values and mainstream culture being unfavourable towards sexuality minorities, very few can afford to be open about their 'illicit' sexual orientations. Therefore, we would like to thank those who came forward and testified before the team.

This report is a record of such testimonies and conveys something of the pain, anxieties and hopes of the people we met. It is an attempt to break through the invisibility and the silence that society has tried to throw over people simply because of their sexual orientation. In spite of our best efforts we could speak to only gays, bisexuals and one hijra person. However we were able to remedy the lack of an adequate hijra voice by having an extended meeting with some hijra people on 8 October, 2000. The absence of lesbians in the hearing is itself an indication of the kind of oppression that they face, both as women and as non-heterosexual people and the infinitely greater silence that surrounds many issues pertaining to lesbians. We tried to make up for this absence by meeting a small group of lesbians separately on 16 December 2000.

We also circulated a questionnaire on issues, which emerged in the course of the testimony to gays, bisexuals and lesbians. Apart from members of the community, the team also met Dr. Shekhar Seshadri of NIMHANS and other prominent physicians, as well as a reputed homeopathic doctor. We also met the ACP Cubbon Park circle, Mr. Santosh Hegde and Mr. Mariswamy Gowda, Inspector of Upparpet Police Station. In this report, we have put together the testimonies of at least 25 people we met both in the office of Sangama and in other public spaces, as well as the information we gathered through questionnaires, interviews and a review of existing documentation.

The names of those who testified at the hearings have been changed to protect their confidentiality because of fears expressed about police and societal victimisation. We would also like to apologize for the relative sketchiness of certain sections of the report, such as the ones on the workspaces, household spaces and impact on the self — areas in respect of which information is not readily forthcoming. We hope that the next organisation, which takes up this issue, will fill in these gaps and produce a more comprehensive report.

FOCUS OF THE REPORT

This report examines the human rights violations suffered by sexuality minorities in India under two broad heads, namely the state and society, as two sites from which violence against sexuality minorities is perpetrated. The violations by the state can be further subdivided into violations by the law and by the police. Societal violence is inflicted through the various sites like the family, the medical establishment, workspaces, household spaces, public spaces and popular culture. Both societal and state violence impinge strongly on the individual person's dignity. The report then goes on to document issues of further marginalization among sexuality minorities, namely the position of lesbians, bisexuals and sexuality minorities from low income/non English-speaking backgrounds and hijras. Finally, we conclude by putting forth a series of recommendations on how both state and societal violations of the basic human rights of sexuality minorities can be combated.

DISCRIMINATION BY THE STATE DISCRIMINATION BY THE STATE

The state is one of the powerful institutions through which discrimination against sexuality minorities is encoded, institutionalized and enforced. The prime means through which discrimination becomes a structural feature of everyday living of sexuality minority populations is through use of the law and the police.

THE LAW

Legal discrimination against sexuality minorities operates through the criminal and civil law systems. The regime of discrimination can be analysed under the following heads:

SEC 377 OF THE INDIAN PENAL CODE

Legal Discrimination against the sexuality minorities takes many forms, the most notorious being Section 377 of the Indian Penal Code, a British colonial legislation criminalizing homosexual behaviour, that continues to be in the Indian statute book although it has long since been removed from the British statute book.

- Section 377 reads: Of unnatural offences: Whoever voluntarily has carnal intercourse against the order of nature with any man, woman, or animal, shall be punished with imprisonment of either description for a term which may extend to 10 years and also be liable to fine.
- Explanation: Penetration is sufficient to constitute the carnal intercourse necessary to the offence described in this section.

Section 377 is repugnant on a number of counts, the main ones being:

- It does not distinguish between consensual and coercive sex. Thus cases of abuse and voluntary sex between two consenting adults can be prosecuted under this provision. This would violate the constitutionally protected right to privacy under the expanded definition of right to life.
- The definition of "unnatural offences" is obsolete. It invites questions such as what is " the order of nature"? As conceived by whom? Previously, it was considered that the order of nature was that the sexual act be performed only for the sake of reproduction. But today it would not be considered "against the order of nature" if people have sex mainly for pleasure. Moreover, empirical evidence easily shows that homosexuality and bisexuality is widespread in the Indian society covering a large section of people belonging to different regional, linguistic, and religious backgrounds and social strata. Section 377 denies these people a right to their sexuality.
- It is also important to note that this chapter does not prohibit homosexuality, but only prohibits certain sexual acts, which both homosexuals and heterosexuals, married and unmarried people, might engage in. However this chapter is almost always used to target sexuality minority populations as they are erroneously seen as the only ones to perform 'carnal intercourse against the order of nature'.
- It serves to legislate into being a new morality, a morality that condemns many forms of sex between two consenting adults including oral sex and anal sex and other kinds of sex, which the judges might decide, fall within the definition of "carnal intercourse against the order of nature" .
- In the entire history of the statute from 1860 to 1992, there have been very few reported cases under 377 in the higher courts, with most of the persecutions being for non-consensual acts of sodomy. In fact, currently Section 377 exists only to be used by the police mostly to victimize gay and bisexual men whom they catch in public areas to extort money and blackmail, despite the fact that blackmail and extortion are criminal offences. Section 377 has also been used to intimidate lesbian women, particularly in the cases of women who have run away together, or if they make their relationship known..

However, since Section 377 has also been used to prosecute cases of child sexual abuse, any demand for its repeal will have to go hand in hand with the enactment of a law on child sexual abuse.

OTHER FORMS OF LEGAL DISCRIMINATION

- Section 46 of the Army Act notes that "Any person subject to this act who is guilty of disgraceful conduct of a cruel, indecent or unnatural kind... can be removed from service". There are similar provisions in the Navy Act that subjects all employees of the Indian Navy to the disciplinary requirements under a similar enactment.
- The legal provisions relating to obscenity, the concept of moral turpitude as a ground for dismissal from service, and provisions in the various state Police Acts can also be used to target same sex behaviours and identities. Thus, the only way homosexuality figures in Indian law is as a conduct to be prohibited.
- There is no recognition of the rights of sexuality minorities in law. For instance, same sex unions do not even have legal recognition, let alone any of the economic and legal rights/benefits available to heterosexual marriage contracts. Same-sex couples are deprived of, among other things, the right to common property and inheritance, "next of kin" privileges in the event of illness or death of their partner, and custody maintenance and adoption rights. Given the fact that all cases of same-sex union in India that have appeared in the media are those of women from smaller towns, their economic and social vulnerability makes the legal and social acceptance of their relationship vital..
- Homosexual relationships are not recognised when it comes to defining the family for the purposes of insurance claims, compensation under the workman's compensation act, gratuity benefits and for the purposes of nomination.
- The constitution, while it contains certain prohibited grounds of discrimination such as race, caste, creed, sex, etc, does not specifically include sexual orientation. Thus the position of the law includes aspects which both empower the police to harass and reduce sexuality minorities to non-entities in the eyes of the law. In other words, sexuality minorities are subjects who have become fit to be harassed, but are invisible when it comes to themselves being right holders.

THE POLICE

In the testimonies we heard, oppression by the police turned out to be one of the major concerns of the gay, bisexual and transgender people. The oppression took the following forms.

EXTORTION

This appeared to be one of the most common forms of oppression. The police often stop gay/bisexual men in the cruising areas, threaten them saying we know what you are doing, take their names and addresses and extort money from them. It is difficult to estimate the number of cases of extortion suffered by the community, as there are obviously no police records. Since FIRs are almost never recorded it appears to be one of the easiest ways for the police to make easy money as the gay/bisexual men are so scared of being 'outed' to wider society that they will part with whatever they have with them.

ILLEGAL DETENTION

Another technique used by the police is illegal detention. The police in this case take people in for questioning and detain them in the lock up for periods of time varying from overnight to a few days. They do not file a First Information Report and keep no documentary evidence of the person's detention. Due to the lack of such evidence, these cases do not come to the attention of the public.

ABUSE

Members of the community spoke about police abuse as another form that oppression took. The police often abuse the men using filthy language, beat them up and even subject them to sexual abuse. When this happens there is no recourse for the largely underground population of male gays/bisexuals as any reporting would mean that the anonymity is shattered. The systematic abuse suffered by sexuality minorities is brought out in a revealing remark like "the police were very nice they beat me only once". Such a remark shows the degree of internalization of self-hatred wherein the person believes that he actually deserved to be beaten up. This is a serious psychological consequence of abuse.

OUTING

The police have also on occasions outed gay/bisexual men to their families. In the recent testimony we came to know about a recent case when the police got to know about the sexual behaviour of a gay/bisexual person and revealed the same to the family. In an environment wherein not only is homosexuality/bisexuality as an orientation a matter of deep public ridicule, but also a matter of private shame, outing by the police is a definite form of oppression. The following incidents document the forms of police oppression outlined above:

- Recently there have been a number of reports of the police in Bangalore targeting people who are presumed to be homosexual in public recreational areas such as Cubbon Park and Krishna Rao Park.
- On 23 February 2000, 3 men in Cubbon Park were taken to the local police station and illegally detained for a day after being forced to pay ₹100/- each as extortion.

- On 27 March 2000, 3 men who were chatting in front of the High Court building were taken to an isolated place in the park, verbally abused, harassed and warned against visiting the place again. In all these four instances, FIRs were not filed against these men and no receipts given for the money taken.
- On 22 April, 2000, 10 men were picked up in the same area and taken to Vidhana Soudha police station where they were verbally abused, some badly beaten up, all their money taken, and their addresses were taken with threats to inform their families and embarrass them.
- In another incident at Coles Park, a policeman beat up and chased away a number of people on the mere suspicion of being homosexual; when a bystander protested, he was told to mind his business.
- On 8 June 2000, the police arrested Narayana, a self-identified kothi on suspicion of theft. He was not informed of the charge against him, neither was there any implicating prima facie evidence. He spoke to members of the team about the abuse meted out by the police. "I kept pleading that I was innocent, but was kept in the lockup was then taken by a public bus to Hubli for investigation and shamefully handcuffed to the seat. Even after the real thief was arrested on the third day and the goods recovered, I was still not released. The activists who came to demand my release were informed that I was not under arrest but was co-operating with the police investigation. The police then seized my diary, which contained the addresses of my kothi friends. Subsequently I was taken handcuffed to the cruising areas and told to identify the other kothis. When I complained to the Station House Officer about my continued detention I was told that I would be released only if I provided information about other kothis. I was finally released after eight days of verbal abuse and public humiliation and was threatened with serious consequences if I did not frequently report to the police station."

These are just a few examples of a widespread pattern of police extortion, physical, verbal, and sexual abuse, and blackmail perpetrated on gays/bisexuals by Hoysala teams and the beat constables in parks and other recreational areas. Since gay/bisexual men have no acceptance and no social space in society, these cruising areas are the few spaces available to them to informally network and socialize with other gay/bisexual men.

Ironically, these public areas, lacking the privacy and protection of a home, are also places where gays/bisexuals are most prone to attack not only by the police but also by goondas and hustlers who take advantage of their vulnerability and stigmatized existence, to freely hound and rob them. Given their social invisibility, information about such attacks does not easily become public and hence is difficult to investigate and act upon. Nevertheless, the documented cases of police highhandedness towards gays/ bisexuals are serious enough to warrant a thorough investigation into such charges. It appears that instead of protecting the citizens and upholding the law, the police themselves are violating laws relating to extortion, assault, wrongful confinement and wrongful restraint.

EMERGENCE OF SEXUALITY MINORITY ACTIVISM

One welcome development is the formation in April 2000 of a coalition of sexuality minorities to resist these increasing police violations against gay/ bisexual men in parks and other recreational areas. The coalition has been able to bring about some public awareness and support for the issue, leading in turn to the admittedly minimal empowerment of a hitherto powerless minority to be able to at least report instances of police harassment to a sensitive group. The coalition comprises several Bangalore-based organisations, such as ALF, Good As You, Manasa, Sabrang, Sangama, Snehashraya, and Swabhava, which are involved with the rights of sexuality minorities.

According the members of the coalition, police atrocities on the homo/ bisexual and transgender people have increased alarmingly in the months spanning February to April 2000. " They are actively harassing, blackmailing, physically and verbally abusing the gay and homosexual group of people," alleged members of the Coalition. " There have been several such instances of abuse. A week ago, we saw a person being beaten up in a public area under the Fraser Town Police Station by cops belonging to the Hoysala team No. 36. Similarly two weeks ago 11 persons were beaten up in two separate incidents in Cubbon Park."

THE POLICE RESPONSE

- In the last week of April, members of CSMR met the Police Commissioner T. Madiyal on this issue and he assured them he would look into the matter. In the second week of May, the coalition was invited for a discussion by the Cubbon Park police inspector and sub-inspector. They thanked the coalition for reporting cases of police excesses to them. The group was told that the cops in Hoysala team No.36 had been changed.
- When the Joint Commissioner of Police Dr. Ajai Kumar Singh was asked what the police view was on the subject of gay rights, he said: "Homosexuality is an offence under Section 3 of The Indian Penal Code and it is the duty of the police to prevent any kind of offence from happening. If the cop on duty questions or prevents any form of crime, he is only doing his job. Where is the question of harassment or atrocity? These are not cases of human rights violation because these groups are not legally recognised. Let them repeal the IPC

Act, which bans homosexuality. Even if the Act were changed, people would still be penalized if they continued to attract or encourage obscenity in public places. They can carry on with their activities in their homes, but not outside• . Singh also added that the police was under tremendous pressure from the general public for taking money from gay groups and turning public spaces, particularly Cubbon Park, into a park for people with alternative sexuality. "The allegation is from both the sides. The police will obviously have to take the side of law and make sure that public places were not misused. So far we have not received any notice from the National Human Rights Commission on police atrocities on gay and transgender people."About the complaint of the coalition that the police are guilty of extortion, abuse and illegal detention of sexuality minorities, his response was: "If the allegation is against extortion, physical abuse or illegal detention, then the aggrieved should immediately lodge a formal complaint in the said police station and as suggested, look into the matter. Justice will be done." .

- The PUCL team met the Assistant Commissioner of Police of the Cubbon Park Circle, Mr. Santosh Hegde, on 29 November 2000 to find out if the police having jurisdiction over Cubbon Park are following any specific policy with respect to sexuality minorities. Denying that there was any such policy, he said that in his entire career there was not a single case booked under Section 377. He maintained that the police do not normally arrest men on the suspicion of being homosexual in a public park, which is frequented by people from all sections of society. Hence it is not possible to arrest someone merely on suspicion of being homosexual, because a defence lawyer could easily shoot it down. However if a homosexual act did take place, and proof was available the police would definitely arrest the perpetrator. About extortion, Mr. Hegde admitted that policemen are not all 'Satya Harishchandras' and it was possible that some of them do extort money from homosexuals but the problem was that homosexuals do not come forward to lodge a complaint due to social stigma. As regards the nature of homosexuality, Mr. Hegde was quite clear that it was an animal-like behaviour.
- Mr. Mariswamy Gowda's comments to our team were guarded and cautious but sufficiently revealing about how the police deal with sexuality minorities. He admitted the difficulty in booking cases under Section 377 of the IPC; unless one of the sexual partners complains that he was coerced into a homosexual act it is almost impossible to book a case against a homosexual. In fact, according to the officer, to the best of his knowledge not a single case has been booked against

homosexuals in Bangalore, at least in the last 20 years. Like other officers, this officer believed that homosexuality is an unnatural offence under Section 377, although it was clear from his account that he was referring not to homosexuality *per se* but to homosexual acts. When asked about if the police go on clean up drives against sexuality minorities, he guardedly admitted that the police did on occasions chase away hijras and those suspected of 'indulging' in homosexual acts as it amounted to a public nuisance.

CONCLUDING COMMENTS

From the above statements, it is clear that police regard homosexuality as an aberration and an instance of animal-like behaviour. Despite these prejudices regarding homosexuality, they still have to adhere to a certain rule of law framework laid down in the Indian Penal Code and the Criminal Procedure Code. Thus as Mr. Hegde noted, it was not possible to arrest merely on the suspicion that someone was a homosexual.

In cases of extortion, illegal detention and physical abuse, the police are obliged to look into the matter if a complaint was lodged. This however is easier said than done due to the fear on the part of sexuality minorities of being 'outed' to their families, fellow employees and wider society. Hence unless further steps are taken to guarantee the confidentiality of the complainant, it is unlikely that sexuality minorities would be able to lodge FIR's in the police station. The existence of a rule of law framework can also be a space that human rights organisations and sexuality minority organisations should claim in order to protect the basic human rights of sexuality minorities.

However the extent of ignorance among the top levels of the police with respect to Section 377 is shocking and inexcusable. As noted before, what is penalized in Indian law is homosexual acts and not homosexuality, which is a wider concept and can be defined as 'same sex attraction'. Further Mr. Singh is wrong in asserting that groups that support gay rights are illegal. This convenient elision from sexual behaviour to sexual orientation serves the police well during the so-called " clean-up drives" against the sexual minorities. Despite the Police Commissioner's explicit denial, Mr. Mariswamy Gowda asserted that the police under his jurisdiction periodically round up a number of people whom they identify as gays and release these people only after ensuring that they don't reappear in the area; hijras whose sex work makes them "a public nuisance" face a similar eviction.

During these " clean-up drives," no charges are pressed, no legal procedures are followed by the police; obviously, the police are aware that their actions are untenable as it violates the rights of free association and assembly guaranteed to all citizens under the constitution of India. In operating entirely outside the ambit of law, the police are confident that they have the support of the dominant culture. This makes it well nigh impossible for sexuality minorities to emerge from the pall of invisibility. While Sec 377 provides the legal sanction to arrest people who engage in the sexual acts forbidden by law, cases under this provision rarely come to court.

Thus what is clear is that the police have no clear policy on sexuality minorities. The law is more often used by the constables to extract money and favours from the affected people. While the police officers at the top-level claim that they follow the norms with regard to sexuality minorities, the average constable feels at liberty to misuse Section 377 to extort, harass and abuse sexuality minorities. Organisations dealing with sexuality minorities should use this gap between the claim and the practice to hold the police force accountable for the violations of the rights of sexuality minorities.

VIOLENCE AGAINST THE OLD VIOLENCE AGAINST THE OLD

Singh defines elder abuse as "harm to an elder person caused by someone in a position of trust, who may have control over the victim". This includes material abuse such as financial exploitation, physical abuse, such as pushing, physical assault, psychological abuse, such as chronically threatening, swearing at or insulting the older person, and neglect or failing to provide necessary help such as meal preparation, housework or personal care.

In the past few years, the aged have frequently been the target of gang robberies or brutal killing by servants or outsiders. Old are attacked frequently due to their inability to put up a fight. Elders normally have to face up to the facts that, their energy and authority is eroding. To add to their woe is the death of any one of the spouse. In the past few years, the aged have frequently been the target of gang robberies or brutal killing by servants or outsiders. Old are attacked frequently due to their inability to put up a fight.

Elders normally have to face up to the facts that, their energy and authority is eroding. To add to their woe is the death of any one of the spouse. Widows have to be dealt with specifically, as the death of a spouse for a woman in any age is a tragedy in itself, because of the norms and tradition and the manner in which she is treated after the death of her husband.

VIOLENCE AGAINST WIDOWS

Closely linked with Sati and harassment of widows, is the custom of child marriage producing number of child widows, but not child widowers. Widow remarriage is not common and not sanctioned by society, however, men were allowed to remarry. Sati idealized as sitting on the funeral pyre of the deceased husband; and those widows who did not go through this had to make themselves physically unattractive and absent from public functions. Widows are called inauspicious and are avoided, whenever possible. Sati, according to Giri, was recommended after 500 AD in the *Dharmashastras* and spread across the country around 1,000 AD. There are three kinds of widows. One is a young girl with no children, a woman who becomes a widow after some years of marital span and has children. The third is case of a woman who is widow of 50 years and above of age.

Giri mentions three options for a widow woman according to orthodox tradition:

- Sati,
- Ascetic widowhood or,
- Remarriage.

Widows are expected to lead an ascetic life by the society with restrictive codes of dress, diet and demeanour and of social ostracism from the religious and social life of the community. She is expected to remain in perpetual mourning, and give up eating "spicy food", in order to cool her sexual energy, and remain celibate, devout and loyal to her husband's memory. To Dreze J., the well being of widow is not just a question of economic security, but also one of dignity, self-respect and participation in society. Many widows in the Chen sample suffered from different forms of social isolation, psychological abuse or emotional distress. To Dreze J., the social marginalised of widows was frequently found to take one or more of the following forms:

- *Rumours and Accusations*: Widows are often accused of being responsible for their husband's deaths, regarded as sexually threatening, and generally considered as inauspicious by the society. Widows are also accused often of immoral relations.
- *Enforced Dress and Behaviour Codes*: Many widows are under strong pressure to observe restriction in codes of dress, appearance and behaviour. Some of the traditional restrictions have become quite rare, even among the upper castes, but others remain widespread.
- *Social Ostracism*: A widow is often excluded from the religious and social life of the community, due to her perceived in auspiciousness.
- *Physical Violence*: violence against widows primarily takes the form of sexual harassment (young widows being considered as sexually vulnerable and/or promiscuous) or property related violence (because widows are seen as unwanted claimants on ancestral, property).
- *Emotional Harassment*: Sarcastic remarks in the presence of others, verbal abuse, beating and illtreatment of her children are some of the forms of emotional harassment. There have also been reports of houseowners sexually abusing widows who are living alone and cannot pay rent.

Not all widows, Dreze J. face these type of mistreatment. Many older widows who live with their sons (and their families) enjoy their respect and love. Some older widows are happily integrated in their daughters households. If is young widows who are most vulnerable to mistreatment, unless they have the support of their parents or brother.

Table. Incidence of Widowhood (Percentage of Widows by Age group –1991)

Age group	Widowed differenc e	Widowed	M - F			M	F
All ages	1.94	6.50	4.56				
0-9	0	0	0	10-14	0.04	0.06	0.02
15-19	0.07	0.18	0.11				
20-24	0.31	0.59	0.28				
25-29	0.61	1.15	0.54				
30-34	1.01	2.32	1.31				
35-39	1.32	3.94	2.62				
40-44	2.32	7.71	5.39				
45-49	3.17	11.16	7.99				
50-54	5.58	21.93	16.35				
55-59	6.85	23.76	16.91				
60-64	11.16	45.24	34.08				
65-69	13.39	48.10	34.71				
70-74	18.70	66.51	47.81				
75-79	22.13	65.06	42.93				
80+	25.39	69.78	44.39				

Percentage of total widows to total female population is 6.5 for women and 1.94 for men. The percentage of women widows is much more than men from age group 40 onwards to 80+. The highest male female difference (47.81 per cent) is in the age group 70 to 74, where the percentage of female widows is 66.51 and male widows is 18.70 per cent. Some of the essential factors that account for high levels of deprivation among Indian widows include limited freedom to remarry, insecure property rights, social restrictions, on living arrangements, restricted employment opportunities and lack of social support. The system of patrilocal residence, which has the effect of isolating women, is a fundamental source of gender inequalities in many parts of rural India and also plays a crucial part in the deprivation of widows. Patrilocality in the narrow sense refers to the norm, prevalent in most Hindu communities of India, according to which a woman has to leave her parents home at the time of marriage to join her husband in his home. In a broader sense, especially in most Hindu communities of North India where marriage rules dictate marriage outside the clan and village.

If could also result in drastic alienation from her parental family. In North India, widows are expected to remain in their husband's village, and most of them do so. At the same time they are unlikely to receive much support from their inlaws. On the contrary, the relationship between a widow and her in-laws is typically quite tense (property rights being one of the most common sources of tension). Widows are thus denied both the freedom to leave their husband's village, and the support they need to live there happily. Limited freedom to remarry, in some communities, particularly in northwest India, ascriptive leviratic unions (*e.g.*, between a widow and her brother-in-law) remain quite common.

Elsewhere, the standard pattern is that most childless widows remarry, but only a small proportion of widowed mothers does so. Out of 562 respondents in the Chenix sample of widows, 510 women had lost their husbands and did not remarry; 35 women, who had lost their husbands, remarried and then became widowed again by losing their second husbands, and 17 women who had lost their husbands, remarried, and were still married at the time of the survey. In the Chen sample of 562 ever-widowed women, 13 per cent in North India had remarried compared with only 6 per cent in South India. The lower probability of remarriage in South is due in part to the practice of levirate in the North.

The issue of remarriage, according to Srivastava, is linked to property issue. Widow remarriage is not allowed so that part of the property does not pass into another family's hands. Some section of the population encourage leviratic relationships (where the widow marries the brother of her deceased husband), to ensure that the property stays with the family. In cases where she gets into a "*nata*" (live-in relationship with another man), the relationship is formalized by the village community and she loses right to her first husband's property. She has a lower status in a '*nata*' than a remarriage. Aside from these general restrictions, widows face specific difficulties in seeking gainful employment opportunities.

These include: lack of access to indivisible productive assets owned by the deceased husband's family (*e.g.*, wells, ploughs and bullocks); weak bargaining power vis-à-vis male partners in economic transactions, frequent absence of a literate member in the household; limited access to institutional credit, and, particularly in the case of widows with young children, the burden of domestic work.

One of the clearest and most important findings of Chen's and other studies is the overwhelming dependence of widows on themselves and their own sons. The proportion of widows who live in households headed either themselves or by one of their sons are well over 85 per cent in the Chen sample. The proportion of widows who live in a household headed by a brother-in-law or parent-in-law is below 3 per cent and the number of widows who live in a household headed by a brother of the father is also below 3 per cent. Legal.

Formally according to contemporary Indian law, a widow has an unequivocal right to a share of her husband's property, including his land. This is in addition to the legal rights she has irrespective of her marital status to a share of her parents' property.

Field studies, however, indicate that these legal rights are comprehensively violated, and that a large majority of widows have very limited and insecure property rights. This deprivation of property rights not only represents the loss of a potential source of independent income, but also diminishes the bargaining power of a widow vis-à-vis her in-laws, sons and other potential supporters. Singh has mentioned urbanization and modernization and consequently the erosion of the traditional form of care of the elderly people, which was prevalent in India like joint family. There is an emotional estrangement between the young and the old in nuclear family. Even if the old has money to fend for themselves, many are unable to do so due to the lack of loyal domestic servants.

Some of the other indicators of violence against the old and widow could be symptoms of withdrawal, mental deterioration, cessation of activities, felling of inferiority, inadequacy and frustration. Old and widows are victimized by relatives, informal care providers, house-owners, friends or formal caregivers in institutional settings. They are abused almost by anybody who has power over them.

5

Plight of Widows in India

A glaring gender discrimination among Hindus exists in India over the centuries. Whereas a widower can remarry as many times as he likes, a widow cannot remarry irrespective of her age. Since child-marriages were common, position of child-widows was pitiable, since their very existence or seeing their face early in the morning was considered a bad omen.

The unfortunate women who could not commit or were prevented from Sati were doomed to lead the most austere life. Among the brahmins and some higher castes, their heads were shaven, they were made to wear red or white sari without ornaments and eat single meal. Their presence at family public functions were totally forbidden.

The widows slogged in joint families, died unwept and unsung. Many social reformers in different parts of India tried to better the lot of such women by educating them and making self-reliant. Child marriage was forbidden by law in early 20th century and this act alone reduced the suffering of women substantially.

The Hindu codes of conduct tried to bring in parity with men regarding ownership and property. With the spread of education and especially the awareness during India's freedom struggle, there was a national awareness regarding the condition of women. Many widows took active part in constructive programmes laid down by Gandhi and were forefront leaders.

After independence of India (in 1947) and the subsequent reforms that followed, the dress-code for widows became less rigorous and has disappeared. In cities, at least among middle class, no child-widows are seen. However, widow remarriages are not common.

Widowhood is considered still considered a curse and family support is missing at times. But the humiliation of facing a barber for tonsuring the head belongs to history. It goes to the credit of widowed women that they face life bravely and try to be cheerful believing in fate or the karma theory. They tried to lead a pious and austere life presently to earn auspicious existence in next birth.

THE PLIGHT OF WIDOWS MEETING IN INDIA

The four square hall filled with over 120 widows in Mallampall village of Warangal, india was serene when we arrived. The women sat on the ground in their usually manner by folding their legs. Some of us sat on the ground with them to give them a sense of belonging. Part of the experience learning of the Community Driven Development Training was a visit to the widowhood meeting. We have been informed of the plights of the widows in india and how the women will cry because of the ill treatment they received from the society and their late husband's family.

After the warm welcome with a song in telugu, the coordinator started to ask some questions. They have been told to close their eyes as they answer the questions by raising their hands. She also spoke in teluge but Sunitha was there to interpret to the CDD team. More than half of the women are between the age of 18 - 30years, they raised their hands to indicate. They were very young indeed. She asked so many questions and these women raised their hands with their eye closed. They all have children, some one, two and more than three. Only one had no child. Their husbands had dead of out drinking alcohol, sudden death, committed suicide, illness including AIDS and other reasons.

Many of the women were crying as their raise their hand to each question; some CDD participants also had drops of tears in their eyes. Surprisingly, many of the women wants to committee suicide because of their situation, they raised their hands to indicate. Almost all of them are do not have money to take care of their children and have not been able to pay all them owe.

...........I did not understand the words of the song, the coordinator sang in telugu in a very sorrowful tone and slowly. Almost all the women seated on the ground cried the more. I was very troubled as she sings, what is she saying to them that make them cry more and more, I said to myself? I wanted to stop her from singing; I hate to see women cry. These women are already hurt and in pain. What they need is a joyful song that will raise their hope for the future, I thought to myself. The woman beside me wept more and more, that I opened my bag and brought out my little towel to wipe her face. Her weeping started even when the coordinator was asking the questions. She raised her hand severally to the questions as it concerns her. I just wanted to be strong at least for one person - to consoling her.

Those who were courageous, yet in pain and sorrow still came forward to share their stories of agony as a widow. One of the women said, her husband died when her son was 9 months. Now he keeps asking of his father because other children at school also talk about her father. The little always ask why she does not decorate herself like our women. She feels so bad when her boy ask so many questions.

The children of the widows also had sorrow in their heart, they wept as they share their own side of the story for their mother. They have wonderful dreams - to be a nurse; police officer which she said is her mother's dream to make her happy. Finally, my tear dropped as Sunitha explained in English what the little girl said,........she will treat her mother as her daughter when she makes money because her mother has suffered so much for them to go to school.

Life situation of widows in the rural areas is quite deplorable. They are ill-treated and are forced to accept and live sub human existence. They face social exclusion and harassment. They are discouraged from wearing good clothes or applying any make up. Though legally they have equal rights, society shows disparity, restricts their social behaviour and does not approve of their remarriage.

"Widowhood is a state of social death, even among the higher castes," says Mohini Giri, a veteran activist in the fight for women's rights who was nominated for the Nobel Peace Prize in 2005. "Widows are still accused of being responsible for their husband's death, and they are expected to have a spiritual life with many restrictions which affects them both physically and psychologically."

Although widows today are not forced to die in ritual sati (burning themselves on their husband's funeral pyre), they are still generally expected to mourn until the end of their lives. Whether young or old, widowed women leave behind their colorful saris, flowers on her hair and her bands are broken by force after her husband's death. Widows seem to follow rules based on tradition because they have internalized them. They keep doing what other widows did without asking, resigned to a kind of fate—such as placing restrictions on their own diets. In much of Indian society—across caste and religion—a widow is often perceived by family members to be a burden and sexually threatening towards marriages. They are not allowed to participate in occasions – parties, wedding. They are not allowed to bless the couple even their own children because of the believe that long exist.

The widows are coerced to live a life devoid of any happiness, comfort and companionship. The option of remarriage is eliminated and ceases to exist for them. They have to spend their entire life singing bhajans and eating insipid food as spices are supposed to arouse sexual desire.

Bala Vikasa PDTC has over 15,000 widows in more than 8,000 villages in Warangal, india. They bring about an attitudinal change in the society to end social disparity, stop suicides among widows and ensure social justice to them. They also ensure that the women are not called with the name "widow". Special sessions for widows were held to help them face life bravely and to move forward in life confidently. They were encouraged to live normal lives, like other women. They also distribute money and food to all widows present at the meeting.

WOMEN IN WHITE: INDIA'S WIDOWS

Janaki was a young inmate of a widows' home in Benaras. The home was run by a widow who supplied the younger inmates to zamindars and seths.

Janaki was one of the widows forced into prostitution. Chuhiya was the youngest widow at the ashram. All of eight. The madam offered Chuhiya for gangrape. Chuhiya survived the rape, but only just. Janaki managed to make her way out of the ashram. But even outside it, she came to grief. She killed herself.

Bina was six when she was married off to a man who was 32. Her brother sold her to the bridegroom for Rs 300. For three years her husband beat her, locking her out of the house for days at a stretch. Then one day he died. At nine, Bina was a widow. Her brother-in-law and sister-in-law then began abusing her, beating her. They wanted to drive her out of the house: she was unlucky, they said. When she grew up, she would demand her share of the property. Finally, when she was in her late teens, her sister rescued her and took her to an ashram in a nearby town.

A funeral procession was about to leave for the cremation grounds. The widow sat cringing in a corner. No one would touch her. Three women from the barber caste were summoned. They pounced on her and tore her ornaments off. In the procession, she had to follow 200 feet behind the rest, lest her shadow fall on a married woman and she be widowed too. No one approached her all day — even to give her water. For 13 days after the cremation she was made to sit on the ground in the same clothes. On the 13th day she was allowed to bathe and change. The barber women came and shaved her hair off. The brahmin came to collect his dues. Then she was sent off to the Ganga on pilgrimage. Who knows if she ever came back..........

Which of these stories is fact, and which fiction?

Which of these stories is set in the 19th century, which in pre-independence India, and which in contemporary India? Give yourself 10 points for each correct answer: The first is the bare bones of the plot of Water, Deepa Mehta's controversial film set in 1930s Benaras, now abandoned, following a storm of protest last year.

The second is the real-life story of a girl who lived in a village 22 kms from the town of Madhubani in Bihar. Bina is now around 30. She lives in the Abhay Ashram in Madhubani, is literate, and manages a handicrafts emporium in the town. She earns Rs 550. "My life was played with as though it were a doll's," she said recently. "But we will make progress. We will show the kind of revolution that widows are capable of if harassed." The third is as real as it can get too. It is based on an article by an anonymous writer titled 'The Plight of Hindu Widows as Described by a Widow Herself' published in April 1889.

Only the first story, therefore, is fiction. But even that, a West Bengal government-sponsored study released recently reveals, reflects the facts. Widows from West Bengal, the northeastern states and Bangladesh still make their way to the ashrams of Vrindavan, Mathura and Varanasi, in the hope that in the holy cities, god will not allow anyone to starve. Young widows are still being brought in by sex traffickers and sold into prostitution. The 'sevadasi' system, in which the 'service' done to rich and powerful pilgrims is seen as an act of piety, is still prevalent. Sexual exploitation still exists at the bhajanashrams.

In September 2001, a high-level meeting of the National Human Rights Commission, representatives of the Department of Women and Child Development, Human Resource Development Ministry, and Governments of Uttar Pradesh and West Bengal was held. At this meeting, Justice JS Verma said: "It is unfortunate that nothing substantial seems to have happened to elevate the status of women who hence come to Vrindavan despite the philanthropic attitude of the people in the country to help others. The need of the hour is to take concrete steps to stop the flow of women to Vrindavan and simultaneously carry out rehabilitation programmes whereby the overall plight of these women can be improved."

The NHRC, it was decided, would be the facilitating agency that would take these concrete steps, coordinating efforts of the government and NGOs. Justice Sujata V Manohar, NHRC member who visited Vrindavan to study the plight of widows, stated that facilities such as free and clean accommodation, financial assistance and proper health care should be provided to these destitute women. She suggested that a fund be set up for their dignified cremation, distribution of pension, establishment of self-help groups for income-generation, provision of LPG connections for group cooking, ration cards, group housing scheme and suitable security measures.

Whether these "concrete steps" will make any difference at all to the widows of Vrindavan remains to be seen.

An earlier study, commissioned in 1992 by the National Commission for Women and conducted by Deepali Bhanot, corroborates that "the flesh trade flourishes in Vrindavan and Mathura in the full knowledge of the police, administration, holy men and politicians." Amongst the several widows interviewed, Chapla Desi, 27, is quoted as saying, "All men lust after our bodies." Baldly stated, but essentially what the Adi Parva of the Mahabharata recorded centuries ago: "Just as birds flock to a piece of flesh left on the ground, so all men try to seduce a woman whose husband is dead."

Of the 2,910 women surveyed in the West Bengal study, 2,113 were from West Bengal, 297 from Bangladesh. Over 500 were below 30. Fifty per cent of them depend on the doles at the bhajanashrams and on begging. There is no other way to make a living. No wonder they turn to prostitution. The NCW study stated that women are paid Rs 2 plus 250 grams of rice and 50 grams of dal for singing bhajans eight hours a day. Scams in various institutions ensure that sometimes they don't get even that. With rents skyrocketing from Rs 3 to Rs 350 per month, most widows outside the ashrams now live 30-40 to one squalid tenement. A few jute sacks constitute their bedding. Diseases such as tuberculosis, dysentery and STDs are common, but medical help is virtually non-existent. From their meagre earnings the widows must save to take care of their own last rites.

In spite of this miserable existence, only 436 widows of the 2,910 would go home given the chance. This is perhaps the saddest part of their story. For in these temple towns at least the widow is free to live her own life with others like herself. Back home it is her own family that does her out of her property, obliterates her identity and ordains for her a kind of social death.

The problems of the destitutes in temple towns is only one visible end of the white sari. According to the 1991 Census there are 33 million widows all over India — 8 per cent of the total female population and 50 per cent of the female population over the age of 50. In terms of prevalence of widowhood, India ranks among the highest in the world. The incidence of widowhood rises sharply with age: 64 per cent among women aged 60 and above, and 80 per cent among women aged 70. An Indian woman who survives to old age is therefore almost certain to become a widow. In contrast, only 2.5 per cent of Indian men are widowers, and even in the older age groups only a small minority of men are widowed. The main reasons for this are the much higher rate of remarriage for widowers, and the fact that male mortality rates are higher than female.

The story of the daily deprivations of these 33 million widows is never told. Deprivations that cause mortality rates for widows to be a shocking 85 per cent higher amongst widows than among married women.

Most Indian states do have pension schemes for widows above a certain age. While the pension is less than Rs 150, the bureaucratic requirements are bountiful: the applicant must have no children capable of supporting her, she must earn less than Rs 100, she must be physically unfit to work, she must not beg, she must not own a house....But she must have the ability to apply for a pension, make several trips to the taluka office etc! No wonder less than 10 per cent of all widows actually receive the State's largesse.

Apart from the economic problems, widows even in educated, middle class families continue to be placed under immense psychological and social pressures. Martha Alter Chen's extensive survey of widows across seven states reveals that even today widows are accused of being 'responsible' for their husband's death. They are pressurised to observe restrictive codes of dress and behaviour. They are excluded from religious and social life. They are physically and sexually abused. And they are done out of their property. In theory, 51 per cent of widows have rights to a share in their husband's land. But these rights are often violated in practice by brothers-in-law. It is ominous that in the Jharkhand region of Bihar, of the 46 Santhal women persecuted and killed as `witches' in recent years, 42 were widows with land rights.

What isn't entirely accurate is the popular conception that widow remarriage is prohibited in Hindu society. Only the upper castes prohibit the practice. In most other cases, widows are allowed to remarry — including levirate marriages to their brothers-in-law — but often don't choose to, either because of their children, or because a man agreeing to marry a widow is generally impoverished, looking for a second wife, or old.

Also, most widows today are not forced to undergo the rituals that marked the renunciation of a woman's sexuality amongst the Brahmanical upper castes. The Brahmanical tradition especially after 700 AD saw women as "sites of conflict between a demoniac stri-svabhava — their innate nature, which is lustful — and their stridharma, a woman's duty.

There (was considered) no greater delight and no more destructive urge for women than sex," writes Uma Chakravarti in Widows in India: Social Neglect and Public Action, edited by Martha Alter Chen. Early marriage was the only way to channelise her lustful sexual energies. "Through marriage and wifely devotion, the biological woman - a wild, untamed and disorderly entity — can be converted into a 'cultured' woman, a social entity who has vanquished all the demoniac force within her."

With her husband dead, a widow's riotous passion is the cause of moral panic. She must therefore be completely neutered, desexed. The Laws of Manu laid down that she must give up ornamentation, observe fasts, emaciate the body, eat only one meal a day, and sleep on the floor. She must not eat 'hot' foods or betelnut which heats up the body. The orange haldi applied on her before marriage to heat it up for intercourse and the bloodred kumkum and sindoor that marked her out as a sexually potent female were to be substituted by the ash of the funeral pyre. And after the 14th century, her hair — the site of all sin and pollution — was to be shaved off. If a widow did not shave her head, it was believed, every drop of water which fell upon her hair would pollute her husband's soul as many times as the number of hairs upon her head.

Widows in India may no longer be required to shave their hair off. But the mindset that sees a woman's identity only vis-à-vis the males around her has not really changed. As Meera Kumar, a women's activist who has written extensively on the subject of widowhood says, "The traditional Hindu blessing for a married woman is 'Sadaa Sowbhagyawati Bhavaa,' thereby implying that marriage is the only desirable state for a woman." No wonder the widow is marginalised and reduced to a social non-entity. "On the one hand society reveres the mother as a demi-goddess. But she cannot be a goddess unless she sports sindoor and bangles. There is an absolute dichotomy in the attitudes to the woman as pativrata and as widow."

6

Economic Issues of Widowhood

WIDOWHOOD: ECONOMIC ISSUES

Widowhood is defined as the status of an individual who was legally married to someone who subsequently died. Economically, the death of a spouse will result in loss of income and property that the deceased spouse received or owned, unless provision for their continuation and inheritance is made explicit in income programme rules, laws of inheritance, or through the deceased spouse's will. For this reason, it is important to understand how marriage and inheritance rights to income and assets are defined in law and by programmes that provide income to elderly persons.

WIDOWHOOD

When a marriage comes to an end by the death of a spouse the impact of this loss on the living spouse and his/her ability to cope is influenced by the social ambience in which they live. The acceptance of and sympathy for widowers, but not for widows, is a situation that leads to the rejection of these women. Sometimes this rejection is mitigated by the extra-ordinary circumstances of widowhood, for example, war-widows, but it is never excused. The hardship they face may be different but it still exists. What informs this mass psyche is the memory of sati, where a woman would die with her husband rather than live without him.

If divorce is looked upon as the betrayal of one's promise, then widows, it must be assumed, have done no wrong. They have remained in the marriage till the death of their spouse. One would therefore presume that the social and legal system would do everything to ensure that the rights of widows would be made secure and accessible. However, the response reserved for the widow is one of outright rejection that unless she has a son, her life is not worth living. We should note that the statistical data for this chapter is rather old, most of it being from Martha Alter Chen's book 'Widows in India', published in 1981. While revising this report, we made an effort to find more up to date information to incorporate, however we found that little research has been done on this topic in recent years and the information that was found was not as helpful as Chen's original tables.

ECONOMIC EFFECTS OF WIDOWHOOD

Widowed older women, on average, report lower incomes and are more likely to be poor than are other groups of elderly persons. This is true in the United States and in other countries as well, though the difference in the United States is greater overall than in other developed countries.

In the United States, over 48 percent of the poor elderly are widows, even though widowed women account for only 26 percent of all persons age sixty-five and older. Compared to the slightly more than 4 percent of couples age sixty-five and older who are poor, about 20 percent of widowed women are poor. This poverty rate is considerably lower than the 50 percent of widows who were poor in 1970, reflecting gains in earnings for both men and women, as well as improvements in pension and Social Security benefits. Nevertheless, on average, married women in the United States experience a decline in income when their husbands die. Although widowers (men whose wives have died) are somewhat more likely to be poor than are married couples, data that follow couples over time do not show a decline in average economic well-being for men when wives die.

The decline in economic well-being upon widowhood is somewhat of a puzzle. There exists a well-functioning life insurance market that sells products that insure against the loss of income upon widowhood. In addition, legislation has increased the rights of spouses to spouses pension benefits. While the timing of death is uncertain for a given individual, death probabilities can be predicted with considerable accuracy, permitting the estimation of probabilities and length of widowhood. Information that is readily available on Social Security benefits, and requirements that pensions provide annual reports on workers' accrued benefits, would seem to provide the information necessary for couples to protect against any loss of income upon one spouse's death.

One explanation for the difference between the economic status of married couples and widows is the association between death probabilities and economic status. Poorer men are more likely to die than higher income men. This is partly because individuals with chronic health problems generally have lower lifetime earnings (and lower retirement income) and die at younger ages than healthier individuals.

For these individuals, low wages and early death are both due to long-term health problems. On the other hand, individuals who work in lower-paying jobs may be engaged in more hazardous tasks, have no employer-provided health insurance, and be less able to pay out-of-pocket for health care. Their low earnings are a cause of poorer health and consequent higher mortality. Whatever the reason for the association between lower earnings and poorer health, the lower income of widows can be attributed in part to widows being drawn from couples who were economically worse off when married than were women of the same age whose husbands are alive. This, however, is only a partial explanation. Husbands in higher-income couples do die and, on average, a decline in economic status is measured for their widows as well.

For some couples the out-of-pocket costs of health care associated with a spouse's terminal illness or nursing home stay can diminish resources. However, there is little evidence that uncovered health care expenditures are a major contributor to higher poverty rates among widows. The concern that some spouses were left impoverished by payments to long-term care facilities for the care of the other spouse led to the 1988 amendments to the Social Security Act, which permits a community spouse to retain assets and incomes above the limit that previously had been allowed for nursing home reimbursement under the Medicaid programme.

Currently, the institutionalized spouse's eligibility for Medicaid reimbursement of long-term care costs is assessed after a specified share of the couple's income and assets (approximately half, up to a maximum amount) is allocated to the community spouse. The remaining share is allocated to the institutionalized spouse, and it is only this share that must be spent-down in order for the institutionalized spouse to be deemed Medicaid-eligible. While these provisions are important to some couples, their influence on widows' well-being is limited. Married men have a low probability of nursing home entry. That a similar decline in economic resources is not observed for married men when wives die suggests that the expenses of a terminal illness *per se* are not a major contributor to the lower economic status of widows.

There is stronger evidence that widows, in contrast to widowers, are more likely to suffer income declines due to the loss of the deceased spouse's Social Security and pension benefits. Why this happens, despite the availability of survivor benefits from Social Security and employer-provided pensions, is described below.

While couples could insure against the loss of this income through the purchase of life insurance, research shows that many elderly couples are underinsured against probable income loss, and that life insurance is most likely to be purchased by relatively wealthy and healthy couples. The limited evidence available on asset change upon widowhood suggests that some decline in assets occurs upon widowhood. While it is expected that the growth in financial resources owned by women will reduce the financial consequences of widowhood, the persistent association between health, low income, and low assets means that the wives in couples with low lifetime earnings may remain vulnerable to economic insecurity as widows.

A final source of measured income differences between married and widowed women deserves mention. In surveys, some individuals identified as widows may not, in fact, have experienced the death of a marriage partner. This occurs for two reasons. First, it is known that divorced women whose former husbands die often describe themselves as widowed, an identification encouraged in part by the availability of divorced survivor benefits from Social Security. Second, it is also likely that women long separated from their husbands or in common-law marriages may term themselves widows after those partners die. The lower incomes and assets of these individuals may be due to their ineligibility for the benefits provided to widows by laws and programmes. Their classification as widows not only exaggerates economic differences between widows and married couples, but also obscures the reasons these women are worse off. This situation may deter policy aimed at improving the economic position of divorced, separated, and never-married elderly women.

Survivor Benefits: the U.S. Social Security Programme

The 1939 amendments to the Social Security Act provided benefits to wives and widows of retired and deceased workers. These benefits were initially paid to wives and widows age sixty-five or older. In 1950, widowers were made eligible for benefits, provided financial dependency on their wives prior to death could be established. In 1956, spouse and widow benefits were made available to women sixty-two to sixty-four years of age, and in 1961 to widowers in this age group.

The age of eligibility for survivor benefits was reduced to sixty for widows in 1965 and for widowers in 1972, the same year that the dependency requirement for widowers was eliminated, making all Social Security survivor benefit provisions gender-neutral. Survivor benefits are payable to divorced spouses if the marriage lasted at least ten years. If each meets all eligibility rules, both a surviving spouse and divorced surviving spouse may receive benefits based on the deceased spouse's earnings record.

Survivor benefits are equal to 100 percent of the deceased worker's primary insurance amount, but may be reduced if the deceased worker had received retired-worker benefits prior to age of full benefit eligibility; if the survivor receives benefits early; if the survivor is eligible for other social security benefits (the *dual entitlement* provision described below); if a pension from noncovered work is received; or if the survivor reports other earnings (but only prior to the age of full benefit eligibility when the earnings limit is lifted). Some of these are described here, but programme details are available at the Social Security Web site.

Survivor benefits are payable at age sixty or, for disabled survivors, at age fifty-five. However, receipt before the age of full benefit eligibility reduces the amount received. As that age rises from age sixty-five to age sixty-seven (for those turning age sixty-two in 2022 or later) the monthly reduction will be adjusted such that 71.5 percent of the full survivor benefit is always payable at age sixty. A maximum and minimum payable amount applies to some survivor beneficiaries. For survivors who first receive survivor benefits no earlier than the age of full benefit eligibility (currently sixty-five, but increasing to sixty-seven) the survivor benefit can be no more than what was, or would have been, paid to the deceased worker.

This means that a survivor of a retired worker who received benefits that were reduced for early retirement can receive no more than that amount, even if the survivor was older than age sixty-five (or, in the future, age sixty-seven) when survivor benefits were first received. Concern that the cap on benefits for widows of workers who received benefits early contributes to the lower income of widows and may lead to a lifting of the cap. The *Social Security Handbook* provides greater detail on specific programme provisions.

Survivor benefits for which an individual is otherwise eligible may be reduced by the dual entitlement provision that, in effect, leads to the payment of the higher benefit for which an individual is eligible. The consequence is that survivors of one- and two-earner couples with identical retired-worker benefits may be paid quite different amounts, with the latter experiencing a larger decline in Social Security income than the former. The monthly benefits paid to two hypothetical couples, illustrates this (the higher hypothetical amount approximates the primary insurance amount of males awarded retired-worker benefits in 2000). Couple A is a single earner couple, while spouses in Couple B have identical covered work histories and benefits.

The retired-worker benefit of the single earner couple ($1,200) is equal to the combined retired-worker benefits of the two-earner couple. Each spouse is also eligible for a spouse benefit equal to one-half of the other spouse's retired-worker benefit. The nonworking spouse in Couple A will be paid an $800 spouse benefit, but, because only the higher of any two benefits is paid, neither spouse in couple B will receive an incremental benefit (the $300 spouse benefit would be less than each spouse's $600 retired-worker's benefit). Thus, when one spouse in each couple dies, the survivors are paid very different amounts. The survivor benefit is larger for couple A and equal to two-thirds of the pre-widowhood amount, compared to only one-half, for survivor B.

Differences in benefits paid to couples with identical earnings histories have motivated proposals for changes in Social Security survivor benefits. Most reform proposals call for the payment of a given percentage of a couple's combined benefits.

This would increase the survivor benefits of Couple B, and for all couples that share earnings responsibility. Some proposals include the reduction or elimination of spouse benefits, a change that would equalize predeath benefits paid to couples such as A and B, but leave the survivor benefit differences intact. However, savings from their elimination would help finance the higher cost of uniform survivor benefits for all couples.

Survivor Protection: Employer-Provided Pensions and Individual Accounts

Widows may also experience a decline in income when their spouse receives a single life annuity, a benefit that ceases upon the death of the annuitant. The 1974 Employee Retirement Income Security Act (ERISA) was passed in part to increase the chances that a survivor would receive a benefit from a deceased worker's pension. ERISA requires both that private-sector, employer-provided pensions offer a *joint-and-survivor*benefit (*i.e.*, one that pays some share of the retired-worker's benefit to the designated survivor) and that the default payment to a married worker be at least a *joint-and-one-half survivor* annuity, unless the worker chooses otherwise. The 1984 Retirement Equity Act amended the ERISA survivorship provision to require a spouse's notarized signature when the default joint-and-survivor option is rejected or another beneficiary designated.

Unlike Social Security, which does not reduce retired-worker benefits for a married worker with probable survivors, employer-provided pension plans (and other annuities) will reduce the amount paid to a worker when a joint-and-survivor benefit is chosen. This is because the pension is expected to be paid out over the longer period of time that includes the years when the survivor alone is alive.

A survivor annuity is a specified percentage of the reduced benefit paid to the worker. Thus, a joint-and-one-half survivor benefit will pay an amount to the pensioner that is less than the single life annuity, and pay a benefit to the survivor, should the pensioner die, that is equal to 50 percent of this reduced amount. Unlike Social Security, which may pay survivor benefits to more than one surviving (or divorced, surviving) spouse, pensions are obligated only to consider one survivor.

Public employer-provided plans are not covered by ERISA, including its survivorship provisions. Although the majority of public plans offer joint-and-survivor benefits, they are not always the default, and they less frequently require notarized approval by the other spouse if a single life pension is selected. Further, the survivor provisions need not be met by retirement savings plans that are not employer-provided benefits.

About two-thirds of married male pensioners select some type of survivor benefit. For some women the loss of a husband's pension income (because they chose a smaller survivor percentage or no survivor benefit) is a major cause of a decline in resources.

Men with smaller pensions, men with other sources of income to share with their potential widow, and men whose wives had their own pensions are more likely to choose a single life pension. This last finding suggests that the increase in retirement security for women due to their own pension coverage may be offset by reductions in the probability of husbands selecting survivor benefits.

STATE LAW AND WIDOWHOOD STATUS

State law can influence resources of surviving spouses in two important ways: (1) by defining marriage, and, (2) by specifying property ownership and property inheritance rights. Generally, the Social Security programme recognizes an individual as a survivor for purposes of receipt of survivor benefits if the courts of the state in which the deceased spouse was living at the time of death would recognise the union as a valid marriage or would recognise the survivor as having the same status as a widow for purposes of sharing in the distribution of personal property when the deceased left no will. Uncertainty under state law about the legal status of a marriage may arise if the relevant state does not recognise the marriage—even if performed legally elsewhere—if a prior divorce was not completed or filed, or if common-law marriage is not recognised in that state. Because Social Security does not obtain or maintain records on marital status prior to benefit application, the documentation of marriage, divorce, and death of a spouse is an important part of establishing eligibility for survivor benefits.

State property and inheritance laws are important in determining the assets inherited by survivors. In so-called community property states, assets and income acquired during marriage are considered equally owned by each spouse, and a surviving spouse has ownership rights to half of all property acquired during marriage, even if the deceased spouse had willed more than their share of property to another person.

In so-called common-law property states, assets and income are considered to be owned and controlled by the income-earning spouse, although a spouse may still be able to claim a share of a deceased spouse's assets under the principle that a working spouse has an obligation to provide for the economic well-being of the other spouse.

OTHER NATIONAL EXAMPLES

Income in the later years of life, including during the period when only one spouse survives, is a result of life-long earnings and savings. In most developed countries, widowed women report lower incomes and are more likely to be poor than are other groups of elderly persons. In part, this is because they are drawn from poorer couples. But the larger explanation lies in the way in which public and private income and assets are, or continue to be, paid to surviving spouses.

National social security systems can and do smooth out the consequences of earnings differences. While most developed countries provide survivor benefits (althoughSweden has eliminated them), variations in rules about the share of inherited benefits, offsets for other income, minimum age of benefit receipt, minimum guarantees in public programmes, and the role of the private sector in retirement income are all thought to contribute to differences in the well-being of widows. Clearly, the generosity and security of the underlying benefits paid to married retired workers provides the first layer of economic protection to surviving spouses. Survivor benefits build on this relative generosity.

The survivor benefits payable in Germany would seem less generous than in the United States, but they build on a more generous retirement base. During the first three months of widowhood, women receive 100 percent of the insured's pension. Thereafter, 60 percent of the pension is paid if the widow is age forty-five or older, if she is disabled, or if she is caring for at least one child. Otherwise, only 25 percent of the insured's pension amount is paid. These benefits are generally not taxed but they may be offset by other income. When the additional income exceeds a limit (equal to about one-third of the maximum benefit), benefits are reduced by 40 percent of the excess amount.

In contrast, the British national insurance system allows for inheritance of benefits with few offsets. Widows age forty-five and over without children get an age-graded share of the Basic Benefit, and at fifty-five they receive the full grant. While widows are eligible only for the higher of their own or their husbands' Basic Pension benefit, they may inherit their husbands' State Earnings Related Pension Scheme without offsets for other income or earnings. For widows of men who would have reached pensionable age before October 2002 (age sixty-five) the percentage inherited is 100 percent of the benefit, although it is scheduled to decline gradually to a maximum of 50 percent by October 2010.

In Canada, surviving spouses are eligible for a benefit consisting of two parts: a flat-rate benefit and an earnings-related benefit that is equal to a percentage of the benefit for which the deceased spouse would be entitled were he or she age sixty-five. After age sixty-five, this percentage is 60 percent, regardless of the age at which benefits were first received. Survivors may receive both the survivor benefit and their own benefits, subject to limits which may reduce their total below the combined benefits.

WIDOWS AND THE ECONOMY

One of the most consistent findings by various authors with regards to African widows is the degree to which they are economically self-reliant (Potash 1986:27). Like African women generally, they contribute substantially to household economy and often provide most or all of the support for themselves and their children. In some African societies, women are the primary subsistence producers and men in others. The type of and degree of female and male economic interdependence relates to labour organisation, the requirements of the productive technology and the pattern of income distribution. Men and women in some cases control their own income. But in many, resources are pulled together. This type of income control has implications for the widow. For one, the widow may not differentiate her personal income and property from that of the husband. Furthermore, since the influence of the kin group, the inheritance rules, and kinship ties are strong among many African societies and are often more emphasised than marital ties, a widow stands the chance of loosing access to property jointly acquired with her husband. The result is that the widow may have to start a new economic life on the death of the husband.

How does the above picture apply to the rural Igbo widows studied here? The assumption was that they will substantially differ from urban widows in terms of their economic survival strategies. They will invariably be dependent on agriculture and as such ownership and rights to inherit and use land will be very important to them. One would expect that the widow should inherit her husband's property and estate and sustain herself and her family from there. But this is not the case for these widows.

My focus in the interviews were what economic activities widows undertake. I further looked at the following: How significantly were widows' economic activities different from when their spouses were alive? What prompted the choice of economic activity which these widows undertake? What support, if any, do widows get from the extended family, children, levir and lovers (*iko*)? How is land, a major factor in a predominantly agricultural economy controlled in the family in terms of its allocation, use and inheritance? Since widows are not guaranteed part of their husband's wealth including land, we shall examine what economic activities they undertook.

Of the 80 widows interviewed, 28 were traders. 16 were farmers. 17 combined farming and trading. Apart from farming and trading, 7 of the widows were engaged in various types of civil or public service. 4 were self employed in the service industry. 6 of the older widows were not engaged in any economic activity and two are apprenticed in a skills acquisition centre. Since my informants are rural widows, this percentage cannot be representative of Igbo widows. It cannot also be representative of the educated and urban elite widow. We assume however that they derive their major income from the civil and public sectors. The study concentrated on those widows who lived off farming, trading or a combination of both.

AGRICULTURE

The importance of agriculture in Igbo economy cannot be overemphasised. Nwachukwu (1989) argues that up till 1900, a typical Igbo was in the main a farmer. Being the head of a household, he was the owner of productive resources and planned what to do, how to do it and the size of land to be cultivated. Labour consisted of the members of the family, neighbours, friends, in-laws and relations. Nwachukwu argues that there appears to have been a positive correlation between the number of wives, children and friends, and in-laws in

Igboland and the size of his farm. Agriculture was the main economic activity of the Igbo for a very long time. Aside from assisting men in yam production, women had their own crops. These ranged from cassava, coco yam, maize, pepper, various types of vegetables and legumes which were exclusive to women. Agriculture and local trading went hand in hand for women. They sold the excess produce in the local markets and substantially provided food for the family.

Cassava was the major agricultural product for women. It was introduced by the Europeans into Igboland after 1914. Since it was looked upon as inferior to yam - the prestige staple crop and generally regarded as a man's crop, cassava thus became virtually women's crop. Its production and marketing devolved essentially on women. Ekechi noted that the adaptation of cassava as a food crop tended to enhance the economic position of women in society. Phoebe Ottenberg writing about Igbo women and cassava cultivation noted;

Women's acceptance of cassava meant not only the alleviation of the traditional famine period preceding the yam harvest but also a profound alteration in the economic and social relationship between husbands and wives. In pre-colonial times, if a woman's husband did not give her food, she was in a sorry plight; now she can subsist without her husband.

Besides cassava offered a potential for capital accumulation and ultimately the assertion of some degree of independence. An Afikpo woman reportedly told an interviewer in 1952 that if a woman has any money she buys land and plants cassava. The year after she does this, she can have a crop for cassava meal which she can (also) sell and have her own money. Then she can say, "*what is man? I have my own money*". The introduction of cassava provided women an opportunity to have a special agricultural product.

Agriculture was also important for women in other ways. The Igbo lie in the palm belt of southern Nigeria. Agricultural output especially palm produce contributed substantially to the GDP (Gross domestic Product) of Nigeria as a whole. These palms grew wild in farm lands and who owned the land also owned the palm trees. Its processing however was the woman's duty. The palm oil belonged to the man while the palm kernel belonged to the woman. Agricultural export has been important and more pronounced in the fifteen years following the Second World War, when earnings from it were buoyant, and constituted the economic foundation of migration to the towns.

From the 1960s an even stronger influence was exerted on the composition of the GDP. The volume of palm kernel in thousand tons were 409 in 1964-6; 213 in 1970-2 and 172 in 1976-8. For palm oil it was 146 for 1964-6; 10 for 1970 and 2 for 1976-8. Palm produce for a long time constituted a major source of income for men as well as women. But it has over the years declined as a major source of income for rural dwellers. After the 1960s, agricultural export seized to be a major export earner. Petroleum emerged as the major export earner for Nigeria. Its volume was greatly increased after the Biafra secession was overcome in 1970. Although earnings for a woman were enhanced by income from palm produce, her inability to control the land and its resources as a widow also means a substantial loss of income from the palm trees.

Women raise various agricultural products for food and cash. Indeed profit from sale of agricultural products especially palm produce was the largest single source of capital for investment in trading.

INHERITANCE

When an Igbo woman becomes a widow, it would be preferable for her to continue to work the land. But inheriting land is impossible for an Igbo widow. She will be subjected to one of two legal system: statutory law or customary law. According to statutory law, a widow is allowed to inherit part of her husband's property and estate including land. Section 36 of the Nigerian Marriage Act provides for the widow in the following ways:

(a) A widow with children is entitled to one-third of her husband's estate;

(b) Where the widow has no child, she is entitled to half of her husband's estate.

The above provision therefore, indicates that on paper, a widow is entitled to inherit from her husband on his death. Similarly, his children are entitled to inherit from his estate. Where the deceased is survived by both widow and children, the nuclear family is the sole beneficiary. But how does this apply in practice? In many cases, the applicable rules are difficult to discern. Even where they are known, the provisions are not really subject to precise interpretation. Evidence suggests that the widow's rights of inheritance under the Marriage Act are completely ignored by the deceased's relatives who regard the deceased's estate as their birth right.

It also indicates that courts do not follow statutory law but customary law. One rule which most traditional African societies are unanimous about is that in the customary law of intestate succession, the widow has no place in the sense that she can never inherit from her husband. This is in line with the customary practice among the Igbo. In a case reported by Omiyi for example, portrays the inability of a wife to inherit property from the husband. The court held in this case that;

The native law and customs alleged here is, briefly, that property can not be allotted and descend through a wife. If such native law and custom existed, it would mean that on the death of the childless wife, not of the same family as her husband, property vested in her would pass away from the husband's family, from whom the wife became entitled to it, to the wife's family.

In a 1959 case which Omiyi also reported in her study, the husband was survived by three customary law widows. There were no children. Before his death the deceased instructed his senior wife to administer his property and use the income to maintain herself and the other wives, and to continue staying in the compound with the hope that they might have children for him. The senior wife attempted to carry out the wishes of her husband but was challenged by his nephew, the plaintiff in this case. He claimed not only that he was the rightful administrator of his uncle's estate but also that the widow should be expelled from the late husband's compound. It was held that a widow can neither inherit her husband's estate nor administer it.

Another case which illustrates this customary rule that a widow cannot inherit property was demonstrated in a 1988 land dispute. In this case, a widow from the research area, had sold a piece of land. Her son challenged her mother's right to sell any part of his father's land. In his judgement the traditional ruler of the town noted;

The Eze who is the custodian of the customs and traditions of this town in no equivocal manner condemn the practice of purported purchase of landed property from women or housewives. Such purchase is disallowed by the customary laws of the town particularly in a case such as this where the woman, a widow for that matter, has a grown up son who is the automatic heir to the estate of the deceased father.

In an appeal in the above case at the Customary Court in Ahiazu Mbaise in 1989, the court held that;

It is unheard of that a woman with a grown up son can sell her husband's land in the absence of the son...It would be uncustomary if this court were to find for a defendant claiming that he bought a piece of land of a man with a son from his wife.

I attended the proceedings of a case during field work in 1995. In this case, a widow who had no surviving son had given all the land belonging to her late husband to a family member whom I would call 'A'. 'A' had taken care of the widow before she died. The extended family brought a case against 'A' in the village council. They claimed as follows;

1. That the widow had no right to give her husband's land over to one member of the family.
2. That although 'A' looked after the widow, he had no customary right to inherit the land alone.
3. That the land should be joint property. They based their claim further on the fact that the extended family had the customary right over the land since their brother had no son.

The village council decided that;

'A' could not inherit from the late widow as she had no right under customary law to transfer land to him That 'A' be compensated with the plot of land given to the woman when she was married into the family. That the other family members should pay back to 'A' some part of the money spent on maintaining the widow.

'A' refused the judgement and has taken the case to the customary court. This case is not yet finished, but it is reasonable to believe that the customary court will uphold the judgement of the village council. In these cases, the provisions of section 36 of the Nigerian Marriage Act are grossly neglected both by the courts and village council.

A similar case reported by Omiyi from a Ghana Law Report shows how wide-spread this practice was across many African societies. In this case a customary law widow sued her deceased husband's family claiming one-third of her husband's intestate estate basing her claim on two grounds. Firstly, she asserted that she helped the husband to acquire the property in question. Secondly she claimed that she was a lawful customary law widow and therefore was entitled under customary law to a share of her husband's estate. The court dismissed her claims although it was found out that she actually helped in the acquisition of the property. It was held that under customary law a widow does not become a co-owner of property she helped her husband to acquire. All over Igboland and indeed many parts of Africa, the customary law that a widow cannot inherit her deceased husband's property was notorious by frequent proof in the courts that it became judicially noticeable. In this context, the wife was deprived of inheritance rights in her deceased husband's estate because under the prevailing native laws and customs, the devolution of property follows the blood.

The facts given here raise one major problem, namely that of the economic survival for a widow in a rural Igbo society. The widow's position, her right to inherit property, use and alienate land is constrained by customary and cultural practices.Although comprehensive data are difficult to obtain, it is evident that informal mechanisms have evolved to give widows some access to productive resources.

Although a widow cannot inherit land, most widows gain some kind of access to their husband's land. They have this access as long as they have sons and continue to live in their husband's family. The farm land was to enable the widow to provide some support for herself. Generally such allocation was regarded as temporary since the land belonged to the children as a right. The widow looses control of such land when her sons get married and share their father's land. Mother-son relationship can go sour as a result of who should control land.

Except under special circumstances, widows and in fact most women have access to productive resources especially land only through husband-wife relationship. Although husband's were important sources of farms for widows, some were also fairly independent in the means by which they acquire farms. Widows are not prevented by customs from buying land. This they did through a male proxy or their adult sons. These practices have remained largely unchanged in Igbo society.

Customary Right to Land

A widow lacks the flexibility to manage land and its resources since it theoretically belongs to her children or the kin group. This imposed limitations to what the widow can do with the land. But to understand the widow's peculiar position, we must also examine the peoples' spiritual and ritual attachment to land. We must also examine their understanding of land as the only means of maintaining a cosmological balance between themselves, their ancestors and the generation yet unborn. For the people land is an affair for men. Three explanations may be offered here: (i) women lack customary right over land, (ii) women cannot own land and (iii) the spiritual value of land. To understand why women lack customary rights to land, it is important to know under which circumstances access to land may be gained. Meek, (1937:30) has classified land into the following categories; (i) land which are sacred or taboo, (ii) virgin land, (iii) farmland held in common by the members of a village, kin group, or extended family and iv) individual holdings.

The first class of lands include sacred groves surrounding the shrines of public cults (such as *ala*, the earth-deity and *ekwensu,* the spirit evil) It also includes the taboo lands or evil forest known as *ajo ohia.* These lands do not belong to the individual but are regarded as belonging to the deities or spirit and no one could normally attempt or be allowed to use any fraction of such land for farming purposes. Although some of these sacred groves have been tampered with as a result of the advent of Western religion, they are still in existence in many communities today.

The virgin forests are land which have remained unused for farming purposes because nobody has required it or because the village has forbidden farming there, lest it should lose its use as a means of defence or shade or a source of supplies of wood. If a piece of uncleared forest is of no obvious use to the village, any one is at liberty to clear it for farming purposes, and the land so cleared becomes his private farmland. He cannot be deprived of it, and he can pledge it or transmit it to his children. But if there is any uncertainty as to whether the village may require the uncleared land, the would be farmer must first obtain the permission of the local elders. Such opportunities of having access to land must have been the practice a long time ago. Even when this was the case, women and particularly widows would have no right to clear or lay claim to any of such plots. Customs and traditions as well as the rituals attached to land will prevent them from having such access to land.

The next class of land is farmland held in common by an entire village, kin group, or extended family. This is one of our major area of concern here. This land is formally apportioned out afresh each time it is to be farmed. It is held in reserve for the benefit of the whole group (in addition to individual holdings) and cannot therefore be pledged without the consent of the group as a whole. This land is regarded as *ala ozuzu* (land held in common). Land in some instances are held in common on behalf of the kin group or the extended family. This type of land is usually allocated to married males in a particular family for farming. Individual holding is a very important practice today. These lands are usually handed on from father to son, or acquired by clearing virgin forest or in return for a loan or sales. Among the Igbo, population pressure has made land very scarce. Land so held belongs to a man and his immediate family and can be pledged without reference to anyone. In this way, those who can afford to, acquire additional land in perpetuity for themselves and their family. In some instances, it may be leased and the land could be redeemed when the cost of lease has been refunded. In all classes of land, a woman does not fit any of the categories through which land may be acquired.

In terms of this customary right to land, let us view this right from the perspective of a married and an unmarried woman. An unmarried daughter has like her brothers, the right to live in her father's house subject to all the normal incidents of local tenure. But since a woman does not actually undertake to cultivate land as of her own right, she is not usually given any farmland. An informant answered when asked why women could not inherit land;

why should a woman be allocated land? She does not belong to this community. She marries away from this village and can only have access to land where she marries. Her access to land will be through her husband and her children.

This implies that rights over the use of land depends primarily on agnate descent, and secondarily on local residence. Women do not fit into this arrangement since marriage is basically exogamous. As a result, the head of the family never revolves on the woman. She never expects to become head of the family, nor to inherit land when the husband dies.

With regard to family property, also, the position of the head of the family is inherited by the most senior adult male child. Failing that, the eldest adult male member of the family would inherit the property but never the woman. Thus a woman of what ever status is not allowed to inherit landed property.

Eze and Nwebo cited court cases which further clarify the above notions. They gave instances of such cases which took place in 1963 and 1967, indicating that women were not allowed to inherit landed property from their father and consequently have no *locus standi* to bring an action in respect of family property. In the 1963 case in particular, the supreme court of Nigeria held that;

By the customary law predominant in Igboland, a widow has no right to succeed to personal or real estate of her deceased husband. Of course, it would be absolute nonsense in the circumstances for a widow who is herself regarded as property to turn round to claim the property of her late husband. In such a case the only right available to her will be to be accommodated by the person who inherits the husband's estate until she remarries or becomes financially independent or dies.

Citing Obi's '*Manual of Customary Law*', Eze and Nwebo observed further that in some areas within the Igbo society, a widow without a son has no right to remain a member of her late husband's family. The husband's heir or relative might even expel her from the husband's compound and other lands. Moreover, her limited rights in the family are subject to 'good' behaviour. Furthermore, the testamentary powers of the women are also restricted under the Igbo custom. In some communities in Igboland, a married woman or a widow who is living in her husband's family cannot as of right dispose of her landed property or economic crops by will, except to her own children or to members of her husband's family.

Land Ownership

The same mode of thinking about customary right over land also created the atmosphere in which it was felt that a woman could not own land. Land ownership among the Igbo confers certain rights which are the same whether under statutory or customary law. But ownership is subject to differing interpretations. According to Lord Cohen, the meaning of the word 'owner' is not always clear. In his opinion,

...the term 'owner' is loosely used in West Africa. Sometimes, it denotes what is in effect absolute ownership; at other times is only to rights.

Chubb (1961:6) in his study of land tenure among the Igbo, pointed out also that:

in the main, the term, ownership, hardly connotes the exact relationship between such an occupier and his land. He has full right to its produce and may build and plant permanent crops as he pleases, but he regards himself as holding it in trust for the next generation.

Collaborating the above, an informant noted:

Land was here before our fathers were born. They did not own the land but merely farmed on it. But as population grew, people became more acquisitive. They had to acquire more farm land for their family...men acquired the land and women only helped to farm on it.

Also, the Pivy Council noted in a case brought before it at the beginning of the century that;

the notion of individual ownership is quite foreign to native ideas. Land belongs to the community, the village, or the family, never to the individual

Communal ownership was the system when population densities were small and no one man could own or lay exclusive claim to any piece of land. However, when a community, kin group or family migrated to a new region and cleared it for settlement, it could lay claims to it. This action according to Chubb conferred the strongest of all titles to the land. In such cases, the land holding passed on to descendants. I could not establish when individual holdings become very important in land ownership. But oral evidence suggests that this must have been long ago. Even though Nwabueze argues otherwise (that is that family or communal land amongst the Igbo may have its origin in an individual founder who first acquired the land), he also recognises the possibility of a new settlement being founded by an entire community or family. They then entrust titular ownership to a strong patriarchal head or leader. This however, developed from customary rights of occupancy, into real ownership after many generations of continuos occupation. Due to abundance of land in the past perhaps, there was little or no friction and dispute over pieces of land until population pressure turned individuals into petty capitalists.

As Wigwe contends, in Igbo customary law, ownership is in the sense outlined above. But whatever meaning is attached to ownership denotes who has right to control and benefit from it. The right, however, has been challenged. Some are of the opinion that the idea of an absolute property in land is incompatible with the limits which society places on the use of land. Such titles, leases, and mortgages merely express man's desire for orderliness. In the above circumstance, women have no customary right to own land as members of a village group since they are expected to marry. Furthermore, they do not have such rights as married women or widows since they are theoretically strangers in the community.

The Spiritual Value of Land

There is still a third explanation for widows problem in getting access to farm land. This can be sought in the spiritual value attached to land. In approaching the subject of land ownership in Igboland and its impact on the widow's economic existence and survival, it is important to emphasise that land is sacred. In the context of traditional religion, land is the basic matrix of existence. Land is described adoringly as 'mother earth' or earth goddess *ala* and is generally regarded as the arch-divinity of every locality in Igboland. Chubb described land as the *fons et erigo* (fountain and origin) of human morality, productivity and fertility.

Actions which constitute desecration of the land or abomination include suicide, homicide, stealing of farm products especially yam and coco yam, giving birth to twins (in the past), incest, a widow getting pregnant during the period of mourning and a host of other actions. Ilogu (1974) has itemised about twenty-four 'abominations' or ethical and social prohibitions and taboo of Igbo moral code associated with land. Any violation of these prohibitions is considered moral, spiritual and social pollution of the land. They therefore require appropriate ritual purification of the offender(s) and the community in order to appease the earth goddess. Echeruo (1978) has further emphasised the pre-eminence of *ala* among the other divinities and noted that;

one divinity, however, was beyond the capriciousness of Igbo men: that divinity is neither 'Igwe' nor even Chukwu, but Ala, the goddess of the earth. She was the one divinity which no man nor woman and no community could afford to offend, much less discard. If ever there was a supreme god among the Igbo, it was ala.

In cases of abomination against the land, it has to be sanctified, placated and purified of the sacrilege (*ikwa ala*) by special rituals through the office of the appropriate priest (*onye isi ala*) using appropriate cult objects (egg, fowl, kola nuts) as advised by the oracle. It is true to say that the cult of the ancestors or ancestor worship is closely linked with land. In traditional Igbo society, *ala* has a special shrine established by the competent priest including the *eze-ala* (priest of the land) and marked out with special shrubs or trees. It is perhaps because of conceptualisation such as the above that land ownership is a special privilege and a matter of prestige in all cultures, and especially among the Igbo.

The myth, rituals, taboos, beliefs, sanctions and emotional commitment that this worship engender on the Igbo becomes an instrument of social, political and economic control. It also imposes some degree of conservatism and constraint on Igbo land utilisation and ownership. The priest of *ala* for example is subject to many taboos. Thus they are forbidden as a rule to eat in another house, to eat food cooked by a menstrous woman, or to sit or have sexual intercourse on the ground. In some communities, widows and tattooed persons are forbidden to enter the house of the priest of *ala.*

From the reflection on *ala*, it must be mentioned that any research into the foundations and principles of Igbo land use, inheritance and taboos associated with it must understand the people's moral and religious attachment to it and not only its utilitarian value as a means of production. This of course, has implications for women and widows especially since control of land and its use fall outside the area of women's domain in Igbo society.

The religious traditions help to explain the existing customary law practices as they relate to widows. Even in the case of statutory married women, it is difficult to see how she could inherit her husband's real property, especially if it is part of family property. In the main, land was not easily accessible to widows. Men dominated land through their religious and spiritual control of it. The ownership and inheritance system, the religious meaning attached to land ownership and other customary practices place women in a different position. It was therefore impossible for the widow to survive entirely from farming. As a result of these constraints, we can understand why widows take to trade and other economic activities.

OTHER PROBLEMS FOR FARMING WIDOWS

Many of the widows presented the issue of land as the major problem which they face in farming. This state of affair is wide-spread for many widows. A woman who was widowed in 1960 had this to say about her husband's farmland.

When my husband died, I was in real trouble if I touched his yam, palm trees or land. I have been a very miserable widow especially after his brothers took away my seven children. The girls were given away in marriage without my consent and the younger ones were given away to distant people where I could not see them. I had to go to my father's house to stay. On one occasion, I came to my husband's house to collect my goats which nobody was taking care of. They beat me up, took me to the police and bribed the magistrate to jail me. I was sentenced to three months and I served it because I could not pay the option of fine.

In spite of these constrains, these rural widows engaged in one form of subsistent agriculture or the other. Two major additional factors come into consideration. These are the question of the number of plots that can be put under cultivation as well as the labour requirements for the production of certain crops. Land continues to be scarce due to the population pressure on available land. In the early 1970s for example the Food and Agricultural Organisation (FAO) estimated that the total area cropped in Nigeria (including bush fallow) was less than two-fifths of the area suitable for agriculture. The low ration, along with the widespread practice of shifting cultivation, suggest a favourable relationship of land to population. The impression is somewhat misleading. For Green and Rimmer (1981:70) notes that in some parts of the southern forest which includes Igboland, pressure of population has reduced fallow periods to interval too short to restore soil fertility. If we go by Leith-Ross's estimate of the fallow period in the 1930, she recorded that a farm in the Igbo area could lie fallow for four or five years during which time the land regains possession of its fertility. This was because of the abundance of land. Today however, a land in the Mbaise area cannot be left fallow for more than one year. Population pressure in this area has always been higher than most parts of Igboland.

As a result of this pressure on land, every effort is made by anyone who had the means to keep all available land in his or her possession. No wonder customary rules have persisted among the Igbo since they give men advantage in the control of land. This is critical for the widow considering that agriculture was the main occupation of over 60 per cent of the rural population including the Igbo.

In terms of the labour requirements, there are certain crops which the widow cannot cultivate. There is also a significant reduction in the number of plots a widow can put to use after the death of the husband. The widow may not pull together the labour needed to farm large plots of land. 62 of the informants have access to between 4-6 plots of their former husband's total agricultural land. In the past, a family's total cultivated land could be as many as 10-12 plots. Some of the widows still have access to all their former husband's lands because they have not been shared between their unmarried children. With their status as a widow, they will not be able to put the land to effective use alone. The labour requirement and the traditional division of labour along gender lines also dictate what crops the widow can plant. Yam cultivation, for instance, is labour intensive and requires a lot of attention from planting to harvest. Basden (1966:147 ff.) called yam-the Igbo staff of life and noted as follows;

The cultivation of yams absorbs such a great proportion of time and energy that it deserves appropriate attention when writing about the occupation of the Ibos...the planting of yam is a serious and important business to the native, and under the old system of government any infringement of the farming etiquette led to grave consequences.

This of course limited the woman's ability to engage in yam cultivation. An informant widowed in 1995 answered when asked what crops she cultivates;

After my husbands death, I was instructed by his relatives to sell his yam tubers and take a little which I can manage alone. I plant cassava, and coco yam.

Another informant noted;

I had to sell my husband's yam tubers because people believed that since the owner is dead, the yam will continue to diminish yearly through poor harvest. The yam was sold in a far away market where buyers will not know that the owner was dead. My children took the yam to the market. They had to put on cloths that are not their normal mourning dresses. We sold the bulk of the yam because I could mot manage it without help. Today, I plant coco yam, maize, groundnut and vegetables".

Only 3 of the widows cultivated yam on an average scale. They could afford to buy the labour, had assistance from their male sons and in some cases were helped by relatives.

To continue farming the land she worked as a wife, certainly is no easy solution for an Igbo widow. No wonder many combine farming with trade and some even entirely replace farming by trade.

TRADE

By trade, we mean everything that is connected directly with buying and selling, and more especially the functions of marketing. Trading fills up the lives of many Igbos. Trade was of two kinds; local as well as regional (or long distance) trade. Trading activities provided an alternative occupation for many widows who could not make a living through farming alone. Local trade in particular has been important for women in many ways. It provided avenue for the sale of excess farm produce such as coco-yam, palm produce, vegetables, groundnut, maize, pepper *etc.*

Basden (1966:194) describing traditional Igbo society stated that it might be affirmed that the whole of the native trade was on the hands of women and by them largely the markets were controlled. Trading became more important for women especially during the early twentieth century.

Women especially have responded to increasing level of trade during the later part of the century by turning to marketing goods and services to help sustain themselves and their family. Basden confirmed that in former times, the women had direct transaction with the trading posts. These were the produce buyers who bought palm oil and kernel from women, but there sprang up a class of middlemen who worked on commission, a source of women's agitation in later years.

Ordinarily, no Igboman took part in the actual buying and selling in the local market. He may occasionally assist in preparing the goods for the market and may, occasionally assist in carrying to and fro, but there his activities usually ceased. Seen against this background Ekechi noted that it was not surprising that women strongly resented any attempt to challenge their dominance in the cassava trade.

Thus in 1938 women complained vehemently "against unfair male competition in the sphere of women's crops, especially cassava". What seems clear according to Ekechi is that not only did men intrude into spheres of women's economic activity, but also they ultimately dominated it, especially its long-distance trade sector. Several factors seem to have made this possible. The infrastructure developments (roads and rail ways) as well as the introduction of bicycles and motor lorries had facilitated the expansion of trade. Thus while women still dominated the cassava trade at the local markets, men had very likely ventured into long-distance trading using bicycles and motor lorries as mode of hauling cassava. And since these new modes of transport afforded increased opportunities for bulk trading as compared to the traditional head loading, they increasingly helped to promote higher profit. It is therefore reasonable to assume that prospects of a lucrative trade must have provided the impulse for men to engage in the cassava trade.

Equally important are cultural factors which also may have given men a decisive communal advantage over women. For example by the 1930s and 1940s few women, if any, ventured into long-distance trading. Besides, long distance trading entailed being away from home. In fact social and cultural (sexual) constraints tended to prohibit women from engaging in long-distance trade in the traditional economy. Women who habitually returned home late from even the local markets invariably incurred the displeasure of the elders as well as reprimands from their husbands.

Furthermore, until recently, there were few women indeed who could afford to transport cassava by bicycles or motor lorries. Thus from the 1940s noted Ekechi, the marketing of fermented cassava in far-away markets seems to have devolved largely on men. In fact, by the 1950s and early 1960s, some informants noted that men dominated the long-distance trade in cassava to various parts of the Igbo hinterland. The cassava was sold in bulk to women who then retailed it in the local markets.

The commercialisation from the 1920s of the market which implied greater emphasis on a money economy, colonial exaction (such as taxation) and the drive towards self-improvement may have all combined to induce men to intrude into the sphere of women's business. It can be stated that colonialism and its impact on the larger society altered the economic and political position of women in Igboland. Mba (1982:69) summed it up as follows: *The position of women in Southern Nigerian Society was both diminished and enhanced under colonialism. In government and administration, there was almost total loss of their traditional areas of responsibility and participation because they were excluded from all levels of administration. In the economic realm, while colonialism provided increased opportunities for some women in trade, it also led to a take over by men of many areas formally reserved for women and to a gross under-utilisation of women in their traditional roles in agriculture.*

From all indications, it appears that this was the state of affairs till the period of the Nigerian - Biafra Civil War between 1967 and 1970. The civil war had the Eastern region as the theatre of war. The Igbo economic and commercial activities were paralysed. Agriculture during the period was disrupted as people planted in fear or never planted at all. However, agrarian economy especially food production faired well in some rural areas of Igboland such as Udi, Ohaozara, Abakiliki, Afikpo. Beyond some of the Igbo boundaries, areas such as Etche and other parts of the present Rivers State became sources for procuring food. To a large extent the war changed the economic position of women in Igbo society once again.

Research in the Mbaise area indicate that regional trade outside the town and state boundaries increased during the war in addition to local trade. An informant noted that most women during and after the Nigeria-Biafra civil war were active traders. The civil war like colonialism led to a sexual reversal in inter-regional trade once more. Men could not freely engage in this trade during the war and the war created opportunity for most women to once more take control of the cassava trade.

AHIA ATTACK: WOMEN ON THE ECONOMIC WAR FRONT

On the Igbo side teenage boys and men of up to 50 years and more were recruited or conscripted into the army. The war, according to one informant created a large widow population and poverty among the Igbo but liberated women in many ways. Women fought on the economic front. Asked why she took to trading during the war, this widow replied;

Before the war, I was dependent on my husband's income. When he died in the first year of the war, I had to start trading to save my children from hunger. We went to various places which would have been impossible if my husband was alive. In our group of ten, six were widows. The war changed things and it is difficult to reverse it now.

Changes during the war modified the position of women in general and widows in particular. Women became more involved in regional trade during the period of the civil war. This remained attractive for many women even after the war. I gathered from oral sources that a large percentage of women who are engaged in long distance trade today remain predominantly widows.

Certain factors were responsible for this change. In the main, the social constraints within the society which prevented them from undertaking long-distance trade beyond the local areas as married women, became less important for the widow. Moreover, the widow had to survive. Survival for others during the war was also more important that the social constraints which prevented women from taking part in the trade in the past. Thus over many of women involved in such trade today are widows. The remaining are usually older women who have reached menopause.

At the end of the civil war in 1970, one would have expected that men would take over the long distance trade from the women once more. This did not appear to have been the case since women still dominate the trade. This can be explained by the following reasons: First, easy means of transportation by lorries which reduced time required for the trade made it possible for groups of women to engage in long distance trade.

Women therefore do not have to be away from home for long periods of time. The labour requirement in the form of driving, loading and off loading of the goods were still being done by men. In addition, cassava trade has been traditionally looked upon as a female area of activity and men were ready to give it up for migration to the urban centres after the civil war. For the widow in particular, she had to fend for herself and was not obligated to be at home at any particular time.

It must be noted however that Igbo women in most cases combined farming and local trade. It was typical to hear many widow's say that they are both traders and farmers. Farming for many is a way of life and not just an occupation. A lot of women would therefore farm some piece of land available to them in addition to trading. The fact that the society does not look kindly on a woman who buys all that she needs from the market makes it imperative that every one sees herself as a farmer also.

KIN GROUP AND COMMUNAL ASSISTANCE

But farming and trading were not the only means of survival for widows. In purely traditional society and by the custom of widow inheritance, the heir succeeds to the wives of the deceased as regards the duty to maintain his widow. But the degree to which the heir or those who have inherited the widows provide maintenance and support for them depends on what the widow did. If she leaves her deceased husband's family and remarry there is no support. The rules governing inheritance are consistent with the general character of the social organisation.

At the same time, they are so elastic and based on such equitable principles that they can be easily modified to meet changing conditions, such as the progressive tendency towards individualisation. The Igbo custom of widow inheritance, whereby the heir or successor steps into the shoes of the deceased kin as regards the deceased's rights and obligation to his wives, was perhaps one of the most effective ways of providing for her in an intact traditional society. This was well and good for the bygone days. But today traditional obligations are easily evaded. They have become very burdensome and most people are no longer interested in widow inheritance. These arrangements have become unattractive to men for several reasons. In the past, a woman and her children increased a man's pool of labour for farming. As agriculture looses its importance as the means of sustenance, labour requirements also become less important.

Related to the above is the shortage of land for agriculture which implicitly reduces the number of plots that could be put under cultivation. Monogamy which increased with adaptation of western religion and culture has contributed to this decline. For the widow, there is increased tendency towards individualism. The widow, therefore, has to look else where for support and sustenance. A widow commented when asked what assistance she gets from the kin group.

I sustain myself by farming. I sell some of my products for cash. The extended family does not assist me in any way.

For one widow, the case was different. She said;

Since my husband died, his property has been in my care though I placed some in the care of my in-laws. I have not had any problems. My in-laws are unique. They take good care of me and my children.

According to some informants, widow's children in some cases are shared among relatives and at times co-wives. At times, kinsmen involve widows in life sustenance such as share cropping.

The statistics indicate that the kin group play less role in assisting the widow. 69 of the informants indicated that they had no form of assistance from the kin group. 4 had some assistance from the kin group. 2 widows got assistance in the form of training their children from the extended family. However, in most African societies where rules of seclusion, as among the Hausa of Northern Nigeria or limited access to resources as among the Swahili prevent widows from being self-reliant, widows depend partly on natal kin or either a new marriage. Older widows among most rural communities also rely on the support provided by their children, especially by their sons. Daughters in-laws, co-wives, sons and occasionally daughters provide substantial assistance to the widow. In-laws in many instances provided assistance for the widow especially if her daughters married wisely and successfully. They provide for the widow in cash and in kind as well and protect her from undue maltreatment within and outside her home. Widows may also be protected by their own parents and their matrilineal kin. Brothers and sisters in most parts of Igboland supported the widow in various ways. Some of the informants noted the assistance from their children;

After my husbands death, my survival depended on what I could do for myself. But today, my children and in laws assist me. I thank God that I have these children to take care of me at old age. There is much difference now and when my sons were not yet married. Initially, they cared for me, but now, their attention is divided between me and their own families I do not expect much any longer. I farm my husband's land since all my children live in the city. They are yet to share their father's land.

One informant said she had assistance in cash from her lover and his wife. The lover also paid school fees for her children. In exchange, she rents part of her husband's land to her lover's family.

This was the only example of assistance from a lover did not come to my notice. But I assume that other cases exist since many of the widows were not willing to answer such questions.

A final source of assistance could be found in the rural banking system and friendly societies. Widows who had guarantors were given small loans from the rural banking systems known as *isusu* and *otu* (triff and loans groups). Some of the informants indicated that they took loans from friendly societies for trading.

The virtues of friendly societies were thrift and self-help, inculcation of the spirit of cautious husbanding of funds, a determination to save some amount however meagre, for the rainy day.

NEW POSSIBILITIES

Wage earners have never formed part of the Igbo social system in the traditional or rural societies. But with the introduction of colonial rule and education for women, salaried work has become an important part of Igbo economic life especially in the urban areas. It is increasingly becoming a possibility for rural women. Among the 80 widows interviewed, 7 used these possibilities to survive economically.

Western institutions and a variety of openings are available in this area. Teaching for women stands first; then comes, nursing in hospitals dotted about the rural areas. Those informants who have acquired western education find themselves in these professions while others are self employed in the service sector. This is an emerging trend and the possibilities open to widows in this sector will continue to increase.

Although I identified a case of prostitution among the informants, I could not establish how many women who get involved in the practice. I think however that there may be more cases than meet the eye. At least, this is an option for young widows in many other societies.

We may conclude that the social system determines what widows can do in the economy. The support system which formed the basis of widow sustenance in the past has given way to a more individualised survival system.

But the customary rules which determined the system of inheritance of assets and property have not changed. Customary rules of inheritance as well as right to use property places the widow in a difficult position. Rules and regulations relating to the use of land for agriculture have remained unchanged over time. This is more pronounced if the widow has no male children who can inherit their father's land.

The result is that the majority of widows in Igbo society have no secure land rights and are unable to ensure sustenance for themselves and their family through agriculture alone. Consequently, trading became an important supplementary source of income, in some cases even an alternative to farming. These two economic activities are also in many cases combined with assistance from nearest kin.

7

Widows in Third World Nations

In many traditional communities of developing countries (especially on the Indian subcontinent and in Africa), widowhood represents a "social death" for women. It is not merely that they have lost their husbands, the main breadwinner and supporter of their children, but widowhood robs them of their status and consigns them to the very margins of society where they suffer the most extreme forms of discrimination and stigma.

Widows in these regions are generally the poorest of the poor and least protected by the law because their lives are likely to be determined by local, patriarchal interpretations of tradition, custom, and religion. Unmarried women are the property and under the control of their fathers; married women belong to their husbands. Widows are in limbo and no longer have any protector.

Across cultures they become outcasts and are often vulnerable to physical, sexual, and mental abuse. It as if they are in some way responsible for their husband's death and must be made to suffer for this calamity for the remainder of their lives. Indeed, it is not uncommon for a widow—especially in the context of the AIDS pandemic—to be accused of having murdered her husband, for example, by using witchcraft.

The grief that many third world widows experience is not just the sadness of bereavement but the realization of the loss of their position in the family that, in many cases, results in their utter abandonment, destitution, and dishonor.

In some African cultures, death does not end a marriage, and a widow is expected to move into a "levirate" arrangement with her brother-in-law ("the levir") or other male relative or heir nominated by his family. The children conceived are conceived in the name of the dead man. In other ethnic groups she may be "inherited" by the heir. Many widows resist these practices, which are especially repugnant and also life threatening in the context of AIDS and polygamy. Refusal to comply may be answered with physical and sexual violence. While in earlier times such traditional practices effectively guaranteed the widow and her children protection, in recent decades, because of increasing poverty and the breakup of the extended family, widows discover that there is no protection or support, and, pregnant by the male relative, they find themselves deserted and thrown out of the family homestead for good.

Widowhood has a brutal and irrevocable impact on a widow's children, especially the girl child. Poverty may force widows to withdraw children from school, exposing them to exploitation in child labour, prostitution, early forced child marriage, trafficking, and sale. Often illiterate, ill-equipped for gainful employment, without access to land for food security or adequate shelter, widows and their children suffer ill health and malnutrition, lacking the means to obtain appropriate health care or other forms of support.

However, there is an astonishing ignorance about and lack of public concern for the suffering of widows and their families on the part of governments, the international community, and civil society, and even women's organisations. In spite of four UN World Women's Conferences and the ratification by many countries of the 1979 UN Convention on the Elimination of All Forms of Discrimination against Women (CEDAW), widows are barely mentioned in the literature of gender and development, except in the context of aging. Yet the issues of widowhood cut across every one of the twelve critical areas of the 1995 Beijing Platform for Action, covering poverty, violence to women, the girl child, health, education, employment, women and armed conflict, institutional mechanisms, and human rights.

One explanation for the neglect of this vast category of abused women is the assumption that widows are mainly elderly women who are cared for and respected by their extended or joint families. In fact, of course, far from caring for and protecting widows, male relatives are likely to be the perpetrators of the worst forms of widow abuse. If they are young widows, it is imagined that they will be quickly remarried. In fact, millions of widows are very young when their husbands die but may be prevented by custom from remarrying, even if they wish to do so.

But in spite of the numbers involved, little research on widows' status exists (the Indian Census of 1991 revealed 35 million widows, but very little statistical data has been collected for other developing countries). Despite a mass of anecdotal and narrative information, public policies have not developed to protect widows' rights. Despite the poverty that widows and their children experience, organisations such as the World Bank have not yet focused on this hidden section in populations.

LAWS, CUSTOMS, TRADITION, AND RELIGION

Across cultures, religions, regions, class, and caste, the treatment of widows in many developing countries, but especially in the South Asian subcontinent and in Africa, is harshly discriminatory.

Patriarchal kinship systems, patrilocal marriage (where the bride goes to the husband's location), and patrilineal inheritance (where succession devolves through the male line) shore up the concept that women are "chattels" who cannot inherit and may even be regarded as part of the husband's estate to be inherited themselves (widow inheritance). Where matrilineal kinship systems pertain, inheritance still devolves onto the males, through the widow's brother and his sons.

Disputes over inheritance and access to land for food security are common across the continents of South Asia and Africa. Widows across the spectrum of ethnic groups, faiths, regions, and educational and income position share the traumatic experience of eviction from the family home and the seizing not merely of household property but even intellectual assets such as pension and share certificates, wills, and accident insurance.

"Chasing-off" and "property-grabbing" from widows is the rule rather than the exception in many developing countries. These descriptive terms have been incorporated into the vernacular languages in many countries, and even (*e.g.*, Malawi) used in the official language in new laws making such actions a crime.

The CEDAW or "Women's Convention" and the Beijing Global Platform for Action require governments to enact and enforce new equality inheritance laws. Some governments have indeed legislated to give widows their inheritance rights. But even where new laws exist, little has changed for the majority of widows living in the South Asian subcontinent and in Africa. A raft of cultural, fiscal, and geographical factors obstructs any real access to the justice system. Widows from many different regions are beginning to recount their experiences of beatings, burnings, rape, and torture by members of their husbands' families, but governments have been slow to respond, their silence and indifference, in a sense, condoning this abuse.

In India, many laws to protect women have been passed since independence. But it is the personal laws of each religious community that govern property rights and widowhood practices. The world knows of the practice of widow-burning (*sati*), but little of the horrors widows suffer within the confines of their relatives' homes, how they are treated by their communities, or their fate when abandoned to the temple towns to survive by begging and chanting prayers. There are approximately 20,000 widows in Vrindavan, the holy city; Varanasi; Mathura; and Haridwar.

Common to both regions are interpretations of religious laws, customs, and traditions at the local level that take precedence over any modern state or international law. Widows in any case, especially the millions of illiterate widows living in rural areas, are mostly ignorant of the legal rights they have.

MOURNING AND BURIAL RITES

All human societies have sought ways to make death acceptable and to provide opportunities for expressing grief and showing respect to the dead person. In societies where the status of women is low, the mourning and burial rituals are inherently gendered. Rituals are used to exalt the position of the dead man, and his widow is expected to grieve openly and demonstrate the intensity of her feelings in formalized ways. These rituals, prevalent in India as well as among many ethnic groups in Africa, aim at exalting the status of the deceased husband, and they often incorporate the most humiliating, degrading, and life-threatening practices, which effectively punish her for her husband's death.

For example, in Nigeria specifically (but similar customs exist in other parts of Africa), a widow may be forced to have sex with her husband's brothers, "the first stranger she meets on the road," or some other designated male. This "ritual cleansing by sex" is thought to exorcise the evil spirits associated with death, and if the widow resists this ordeal, it is believed that her children will suffer harm. In the context of AIDS and polygamy, this "ritual cleansing" is not merely repugnant but also dangerous.

The widow may be forced to drink the water that the corpse has been washed in; be confined indoors for up to a year; be prohibited from washing, even if she is menstruating, for several months; be forced to sit naked on a mat and to ritually cry and scream at specific times of the day and night. Many customs causes serious health hazards. The lack of hygiene results in scabies and other skin diseases; those who are not allowed to wash their hands and who are made to eat from dirty, cracked plates may fall victim to gastroenteritis and typhoid. Widows who have to wait to be fed by others become malnourished because the food is poorly prepared.

In both India and Africa, there is much emphasis on dress and lifestyles. Higher-caste Hindu widows must not oil their hair, eat spicy food, or wear bangles, flowers, or the "kumkum" (the red disc on the forehead that is the badge of marriage). Across the cultures, widows are made to look unattractive and unkempt. The ban on spicy foods has its origins in the belief that hot flavours make a widow more lustful. Yet it is widows who are often victims of rape, and many of the vernacular words for "widow" in India and Bangladesh are pejorative and mean "prostitute," "witch," or "sorceress." The terrible stigma and shame of widowhood produces severe depression in millions of women, and sometimes suicide.

WIDOWHOOD IN THE CONTEXT OF AIDS

AIDS has resulted in a huge increase in widows, especially in sub-Saharan Africa. For sociological and biological reasons, women are twice as likely to contract HIV through vaginal intercourse as men. In southern Africa, the rates of infection for young women between ten and twenty-four years old are up to five times higher than for young men.

This is significant for widows for a number of reasons. In addition to the normal social practice of older men marrying far younger women that prevails in some communities, there is a belief, held by many men, that having sex with a young girl or virgin will cure men of their HIV infection or protect them from future exposure.

Anecdotal evidence suggests that this myth has significantly increased the incidence of child marriage and child rape. Such early marriage does not bring security but serious risk and vulnerability to infection. Married thirteen- to nineteen-year-old women in Uganda are twice as likely to be HIV-positive as their single contemporaries. These child brides quickly become child widows bearing all the stigma of widowhood, the problems compounded by their youth and helplessness.

Widows whose husbands have died of AIDS are frequently blamed for their deaths because of promiscuity, whereas, in the majority of cases, it is the men who have enjoyed multiple sex partners but return home to be nursed when they fall ill.

These widows may or may not be aware of their sero-positive (infected with the HIV/AIDS virus) status and may reject being tested, fearing the consequences of a positive result, which, with no access to modern drugs, can amount to a death sentence. Besides, the dying husband's health care will, in most cases, have used up all available financial resources so that the widow is unable to buy even the basic medicines or nutritious food needed to relieve her condition.

AIDS widows, accused of murder and witchcraft, may be hounded from their homes and subject to the most extreme forms of violence. A Help Age International Report from Tanzania revealed that some 500 older women, mostly widowed in the context of AIDS, were stoned to death or deliberately killed in 2000.

The poverty of AIDS widows, their isolation and marginalisation, impels them to adopt high-risk coping strategies for survival, including prostitution, which spreads HIV. In the struggle against poverty, the abandonment of female children to early marriage, child sex work, or sale for domestic service is common because the girl, destined to marry "away" at some point in her life, has no economic value to her mother.

But widows are not exclusively victims— millions of surviving AIDS widows, especially the grandmothers, make exceptional but unacknowledged contributions to society through child care, care of orphans, agricultural work, and sustaining the community.

The international community, and especially the UN agencies such as WHO and UNAIDS, need to address the impact of AIDS on widowhood. So far, epidemiological studies have ignored them,

and one can only rely on a few small localized studies, mainly from Africa, to understand the consequences and options for millions of women and their children.

WIDOWHOOD THROUGH ARMED CONFLICT AND ETHNIC CLEANSING

Sudden, cruel bereavement through war, armed conflict, and ethnic cleansing is the shared trauma of hundreds of thousands of women across the globe. Widowhood is always an ordeal for women, but for war widows the situation is infinitely worse. Widows from Afghanistan, Mozambique, Angola, Somalia, Cambodia, Vietnam, Uganda, Rwanda, Sierra Leone, Bosnia, Kosovo, Sri Lanka, East Timor, Guatemala—old women and young mothers— provide testimonies of brutalities, rapes, homelessness, terror, and severe psychological damage.

There are a few actual statistics for individual countries on numbers of widows, but it is estimated that, for example, in Rwanda, following the genocide of 1994, over 70 percent of adult women were widowed. In Mozambique, following the civil war, over 70 percent of children were thought to be dependent on widowed mothers. Widows of war are often uncounted and invisible. Many widows, survivors of ethnic cleansing, have been victims of gang rapes or witnessed the death of husbands, sons, parents, and siblings. They eke out a bleak existence as traumatized, internally displaced persons or languish in sordid refugee camps, having lost not just their bread winner and male protector but also their worldly possessions.

In the postconflict period, they remain in danger. To add to their problems, widows who have survived terrible hardships are often abandoned or ostracized by their relatives who refuse to support them. The shame of rape, the competition for scarce resources such as the family land or the shared house, places conflict widows in intense need. They are unable to prove their title to property and typically have no documentation and little expert knowledge about their rights. They bear all the burden of caring for children, orphans, and other surviving elderly and frail relatives without any education or training to find paid work. Widows in third world nations have the potential to play a crucial role in the future of their societies and the development of peace, democracy, and justice, yet their basic needs and their valuable contributions are mostly ignored. Where progress has been made, it is due to widows working together in an association.

WIDOWS' COPING STRATEGIES

What do widows do in countries where there is no social security and no pensions, and where the traditional family networks have broken down? If they do not surrender to the demands of male relatives (*e.g.*, "levirate," widow inheritance, remarriage, household slavery, and often degrading and harmful traditional burial rites) and they are illiterate and untrained and without land, their options are few. Often there is no alternative to begging except entering the most exploitative and unregulated areas of informal sector labour, such as domestic service and sex work. Withdrawing children from school, sending them to work as domestic servants or sacrificing them to other areas of exploitative child labour, selling female children to early marriages or abandoning them to the streets, are common survival strategies and will continue to be used until widows can access education and income-generating training for themselves and their dependents.

LOOKING TO THE FUTURE: PROGRESS AND CHANGE

When widows "band together," organise themselves, make their voices heard, and are represented on decision-making bodies locally, nationally, regionally, and internationally, change will occur. Progress will not be made until widows themselves are the agents of change. Widows' associations must be encouraged and "empowered" to undertake studies profiling their situation and needs. They must be involved in the design of projects and programmes and instrumental in monitoring the implementation and effectiveness of new reform legislation to give them property, land, and inheritance rights; protect them from violence; and give them opportunities for training and employment.

Widows at last have an international advocacy organisation. In 1996, following a workshop at the Beijing Fourth World Women's Conference, Empowering Widows in Development (EWD) was established. This nongovernmental international organisation has ECOSOC consultative status with the United Nations and is a charity registered in the United Kingdom and the United States. It is an umbrella group for more than fifty grass-roots organisations of widows in South Asia, Africa, Eastern Europe, and East Asia and its membership is constantly growing. EWD is focusing on the plight of millions of widows in Afghanistan—Afghan widows in refugee camps. An offshoot of EWD, Widows For Peace and Reconstruction, was set up in August, 2001 to represent the special needs of war widows and to ensure that their voices are heard in post-conflict peace building.

In February 2001 EWD held its first international conference, "Widows Without Rights," in London; participants, widows' groups, and their lawyers came from some fifteen different countries. EWD represents widows at UN meetings, such as the UN Commission on the Status of Women, and is a consultant to various UN agencies on issues of widowhood. At last, widows are becoming visible, and their groups, both grass roots and national, are beginning to have some influence within their countries.

However, much more work is needed to build up the capacity of widows' groups and to educate the United Nations, civil society, governments, and institutions, including the judiciary and the legal profession, on the importance of protecting the human rights of widows and their children in all countries, whether they are at peace or in conflict.

WIDOWHOOD IN AMERICA

In the United States there are great variations in the lives and identities of widowed women based on the geographical and social characteristics of the communities in which they reside, and the social, service, emotional, and economic support these communities provide. Some communities are active in outreach programmes; others require initiative on the part of a member wishing to take advantage of them.

An upper-class community provides very different opportunities to its members than a lower class or immigrant community. Ethnic and racial identities contribute their share of uniqueness to working within these support systems. Small towns offer different restrictions and opportunities than large cities for continuing and changing one's lifestyle. Personal resources include the ability to analyse a situation for what is needed or wanted and to reach these resources. Personal resources vary from woman to woman, but generally encompass economic support, personal ability to function, and approach to life, the status of the woman's health, and existing and future social and emotional support networks.

THE DEMOGRAPHIC PICTURE

According to the U.S. Census Bureau, there were 199.7 million persons aged 18 and over in the United States in 1999, up from 159.5 million in 1980. In 1999, 95.9 million were men and 103.9 were women, continuing the trend of many decades. Both the number of men and that of women increased by over 20 million between 1980 and 1999. Out of these, 2.5 million men and almost four times as many women were widowed.

To a great extent the difficulties of remarriage by widows can be attributed to this disparity. In 1999 only 8.9 percent of the men and 10.5 percent of the women were widowed. Although both white and black widowed women formed around 10.8 percent of the total of women, only 10.8 of the whites but 37.9 percent of the black women never married. Only 6.5 percent of Hispanic women were listed as widows that year.

Only 2 percent of children under 18 years of age were living with a widowed mother in 1998. Eighty-one percent of female-headed households were headed by widows aged 65 or older. While the percentage of widowed men aged 65 and over remained between 13 and 14 percent from 1980 to 1999, the percent of women decreased from 51.2 to 44.9 percent, mainly due to the increase in the proportion of those who were divorced, from 3.4 to 6.8 percent. Divorced men also increased in percentage, but the vast majority remained married. The older age of widowed women is reflected in their lack of educational achievement. Thirty-seven percent of all widows, compared to 16.5 percent of the total American population, never finished high school and a smaller proportion of the total never finished college or pursued postgraduate education.

Many had been full-time homemakers or held only minimum-wage jobs so that their income in widowhood is dependent upon the husband's Social Security. As widowed mothers or older widows, they have the income of a new husband if they remarry, and informal exchanges of goods and services occasionally offer work for pay. However, many studies indicate that widows are not as poor as expected. Most live in metropolitan areas, while farm women move to small towns and those in retirement communities return to hometowns to be close to their children.

TRADITIONAL, TRANSITIONAL, AND MODERN AMERICA

The situation of American widowed women can best be understood through the prism of social change in this society. Many Americans were socialized into varying degrees of the patriarchal systems, in the family and at large. In fact, as the American society became more complex and industrialized, gender segregation became extended from the home to the whole society. The social world became divided into what has been called "separate spheres," the private sphere of the home under the management of women, and the public sphere, worked in and managed by men.

The latter sphere included the economic, educational, religious, and political institutions. In order to ensure the separation, a whole ideology of separate gender personalities and abilities was created and incorporated into the socialization of children, occupational, and other areas of life. Men were defined as natural leaders, logical, and able to invent complex systems. Women were defined as compassionate, emotional, and natural caregivers. It was therefore a waste to educate them with the tools needed to function in the public sphere. The two-sphere ideology carried the genders throughout life and obviously influenced marital, parental, and other social roles.

THE ROLE OF WIFE

The situation of any widow is heavily influenced by her life as a wife and the circumstances by which she becomes widowed. Even in modern America, and with some of the variations noted, social class accounts for main differences in the role of wife. Lower or working class wives are often tied into family or racial and ethnic networks, affecting relations between husband and wife and affecting members of the social circle associated with that role.

This statement is dependent upon a definition of "social role" as a set of mutually interdependent social relations between the person at the centre of the role and the social circle of all those from whom he or she acquires rights and to whom he or she has obligations because of being the centre of that role. It makes a great deal of difference if a wife's role includes active participation in her and her husband's immediate and extended families, her husband's coworkers and friends, neighbors, and the wider community. The husband's family may offer rights and demand obligations that can even exceed his mutual exchanges when he was living. One of the changes between traditional American families and those striving for new, "modern" lifestyles has been the decrease in importance of the husband's extended family. This means that, although the family has lost much control over the woman's behaviour as both a wife and a mother, it is also less available to provide support. One of the consequences has been an increase in the importance of the woman's family as a support system. In patriarchal, patrilineal, and patrilocal families the daughter moved away from her family of orientation upon marriage, and therefore the family was unable to both demand and supply support. In modern cases in which the mother-in-law is no longer close, the mother-daughter bond often increases in importance.

There are variations in working-class perceptions of the role of wife by social race. When asked how a wife influences her husband's job, white women in the Chicago area stated that a wife should avoid nagging her husband, because that can create problems in his behaviour at work, but expressed resentment over the authoritarian attitude and abuse by the husband. Conversely, African-American women felt that nagging is necessary or the man will not work consistently or take responsibility for the family.

Middle-class wives of America living before the late nineteenth and early twentieth century, when women began to enter the workforce in large numbers, became highly dependent upon the husband—not only in the role of wife, but in all other social relationships. Men freed from educational and economic control of their family of orientation acquired the right to co-select their wives and move wherever they found it necessary. They then joined the "greedy institutions" of the occupational world. This meant that the wife's residence, the amount of economic resources she had available to her, and the people with whom she was likely to associate all became influenced by the husband's job and its geographical and financial situation.

There was an interesting difference in how white and African-American middle-class women responded to the question as to the influence of a wife on her husband's job. The latter were very conscious of the discrimination faced by the man in the outside world and sought to support him at home. Some of the white women stated that they themselves had no influence but that "those women on the North Shore" are influential and that companies insist on interviewing the wife before hiring the man.

The wife's obligations to maintain, rather than raise, the family status is even more important in the case of the mid-century upper-class wife. Her background was often similar to her husband's but she had to make sure that the residence, the children, and her own activities ensured their status within the community. Her voluntary contributions formed a major part of her role of wife, which included making sure that the children went to proper schools and ensuring that her children's marriages did not pull down the family status. At the same time, all this activity could not interfere with the husband as a person, in his job, and in his own community action. Thus, as much as the middle-class wife, she took on the role of protecting the man from distracting family problems, assisting in status-maintaining behaviour, such as the entertainment of important business associates, and sometimes even directly helping with his job in a subsidiary position.

BECOMING WIDOWED

The extent to which the wife in the not-yet-modern times of the mid-twentieth century was dependent upon the husband for economic, locational, and social supports, the family's position in the community deeply affected what happened when the husband became ill or incapacitate and died. It was hard for a widowed woman to retain the status she gained vicariously from the husband or to continue activities that maintained her status. She was often dropped from his associations, and lost mutual friends if marriage to him had been the connecting link. Financial losses might require movement into another community, which was difficult for both her and the children.

If she had been a homemaker without skills for obtaining a job, her social life may have narrowed. Although the husband's family was not likely to have been very important to her support systems, unless upper class inheritance was significant, their involvement in her network would not likely be expanded after his death. Membership in couple-companionate circles was made difficult by the asymmetry of membership, leaving her often out of the loop, or restricting contact to only wives during the daytime. All these changes affected her role as mother, as the social circle of her children decreased or changed due to all the consequences of the death of the husband/father.

Throughout the twentieth century, there was a great deal of scholarly debate whether sudden or prolonged death is more difficult for survivors. Sudden death leaves a lot of "unfinished business," in that all marriages go through periods of conflict or tension that remain unresolved, and can carry over into widowhood. On the other hand, prolonged death usually requires prolonged care by someone, usually the wife. Relatively few people die in hospitals or long-term care facilities, although most usually spend some time in these. The home caregiver experiences many problems, including heavy work, physical nursing, role conflict when there are children, having to support other relatives, or obligations to jobs. The patient can be very demanding and angry, causing tension in the emotional state of the wife. In addition, it is hard for someone to watch a significant other weaken, be in pain and deteriorate, physically and mentally. Prolonged care can also result in social isolation, as the social life becomes constricted and associates cease to visit and offer support. Estate problems or fear of family members can add conflict difficult to deal with in a time of stress.

Certain types of death and dying are especially difficult for survivors. Suicide is difficult because it is easy for the wife to blame herself for creating problems or not providing sufficient support. Others, especially the husband's family, are likely to blame her. AIDS patients provide additional strains, due to both the myths and facts of disease transmission. Some forms of dying provide danger to the caregivers or others in the household, resulting in a protective stance by the wife, antagonizing the patient and other family members. Age of both the dying person and the caregiver is allegedly an important factor, partially due to what the scholar Bernice Neugarten defined as "on" or "off" time. According to Neugarten, people live according to a culturally and privately constructed time schedule.

One is supposed to be able to experience certain events at specified times. Death in the late twentieth and early twenty-first centuries is supposed to occur when people are older, not in youth or allegedly robust middle age. Each ethnic and other socioculturally socialized group has its own interpretation of what is proper death, reason, time, and circumstance, and these notions all affect the grieving process and the widow's life role.

The situation of the actual death can also create problems for survivors and related people, often associated with the type and form of information received by the others. There are definite norms as to the transmission of such knowledge, to be followed by medical personnel, the police, and family members. Often a male member of the family, such as a son, is first informed with the obligation to pass on the news to others. Some hospitals have a special room in which the family is told of the last minutes of life and any messages from the dying. A particular problem exists when the death is not definite, as in missing in action cases during wars or if the body is not found.

Each culture has its own norms for closing off life with ceremonies of mourning in religious or public centers, cemeteries, or funeral parlors. In fact, the taking over of the ceremonies by funeral directors and staff is a relatively new phenomenon; family and religious leaders have served that function in the past. According to Geoffrey Gorer, death has become almost a pornographic subject, hidden from public view and discussion as much as possible, the ceremonies in countries such as America and England shorn down to the minimum (1967).

However, part of every ceremony surrounding death involves protection of those expected to be most affected, such as the children, parents, or spouse of the deceased. In some cultures with strong extended family ties, mothers are always honored as the ones who suffer the most, even before the spouse or the children. Funeral cultures assume that the most affected cannot attend to all the arrangements for the funeral and burial, so that someone else takes over. The "role of widow," in which duties and rights surround the woman with the assistance of circle members, has been narrowed in modern societies into a temporary one. Once it is considered finished, circle members of that role return to their own lives, leaving the widowed woman to work out her "grief work" pretty much on her own. Eric Lindemann, the first psychologist and psychiatrist who devoted himself to an analysis of what the survivors must do to adjust to death, defined this grief work as "emancipation from the bond of the deceased, readjustment to the environment in which the deceased is missing, and the formation of new relationships" (Lindenman 1944). The death researcher Helena Lopata added a fourth necessary accomplishment: the reconstruction of the self-concept and the widow's various identities in relationships with others. All of these are complicated processes, worked through in varying ways and time frames.

An initial study of older widows of the 1960s and 1970s found that the more education a woman had and the more middle class a lifestyle she and the husband built while he was well, the more disorganized her life became after his death. This is true mainly because Americans of this social stratum tend to be emotionally and socially in their various social roles mutually interdependent; so, much of the wife's life depended on the husband as the centre of her various roles. Thus, not only the role of wife, but other roles such as mother, member of both sides of extended families, friend, and neighbour experienced changes that had to be worked out in new ways.

On the other hand, the more the woman had these multiple roles the more personal, especially individual, resources she had to reconstruct her whole self-concept, lifestyle, and social relations.

HUSBAND SANCTIFICATION

One 1970s study of the role changes and support systems of widows dealt with the tendency of some widows to describe their husbands in highly idealistic terms. Certain parts of the interviews would reflect a marriage that was not perfect, often problematic, with which an idealized description did not match. In order to address this discrepancy, the research team developed a "sanctification scale" of two parts. The first asked the respondent for degrees of agreement with polar terms such as *warm-cold, superior-inferior, honest-dishonest,* and *friendly-unfriendly.* The second was a relational segment asking for agreement with such statements as, "Ours was an unusually happy home" and "My husband was an unusually good man." The final statement of this scale was, "My husband had no irritating habits." There was great variation in the scores on the sanctification scale. Women who had a hard time in life, especially those people uneducated and living in poverty, tended to answer with extremes. People belonging to ethnic groups that sanctioned "speaking no evil of the dead" scored high. Those who defined life as hard scored low. Highly educated women would not agree with the final statement, nor did most married women upon whom the scale was pretested.

The process of sanctification performs several important functions for the widow. It removes the dead husband from current life into the safety of sainthood, and thus from watchfulness and the ability to criticize. Besides, if such a saintly man was married to her, then she must not be as bad as her depressive moments indicate. On the other hand, it has some negative effects. It can antagonize friends with living husbands who definitely have irritating habits. It can also discourage potential male companions who cannot possibly compete with the memory of such a saintly man.

MODERN IDENTITIES AND SELF-CONCEPTS

The need to reconstruct the self-concept and the identities given off or imposed by others is a complicated process that often lasts a long time. These concepts must be defined. For the purpose of this entry, identities are seen as those images of the person as she presents the self or as others see her.

According to the scholar Morris Rosenberg, a self-concept is "the totality of the individual's thoughts and feelings having reference to himself [sic] as an object". There is obviously a strong interconnection between identities, as used in social interaction and the self-concept. When life situations change, both of these aspects of the self must be reconstructed. Some identities are carried throughout life and influence one's roles. The self and others use comparisons of how that person behaves and is treated in that role in contrast to others. The person also evaluates the self and all these evaluations and interactions influence the self-concept.

Gender identities are pervasive throughout life, sex determined by others at birth and socialization is aimed at forming and maintaining appropriate gender. The same is true of social race as defined in American society. Other identities such as religion, ethnicity, occupation, community, and organisation are acquired at different stages of life, voluntarily or by others. Finally, many identities arise out of special events, such as graduation or widowhood. Some of these are transformed into social roles, when the person acquires certain characteristics and a social circle from whom rights are granted and to whom obligations are met. In American society, gender—by this definition—is not a social role but a pervasive identity that enters, in more or less significant ways, into various social roles. The feminist and related movements have attempted to prevent gender identity from influencing important social roles, such as physician or astronaut. The traditional and transitional two-sphere ideology is difficult to change so the process of decreasing gender segregation is slow.

In the 1980s the scholar Lynn Lofland concluded that modern society makes the death of significant others, such as a spouse, more difficult than traditional societies, because it has narrowed down the number of persons with whom the self has multiple connecting blocks. Less than a decade later, the scholar Rose Coser argued that modern societies with multiple and complex social structures and relationships free the person, especially women, from dependence upon a small circle of associates who insist on obedience to norms and restrict opportunities to develop multidimensional life spaces. According to this perception of social change,

American society is increasingly modern, in that opportunities for educational and occupational involvement have expanded, not for everyone, but definitely for many women. Although the basic responsibility for the home and children still falls on women, husbands and increasing segments of society are willing to open resources making women less dependent upon spouses for economic and social life spaces. This means that widowhood is no longer faced by women whose whole lives were limited to the home and children, but by women who have developed other abilities and broader social life spaces, enabling the reconstruction of self and life in new ways once the period of heavy grief has waned.

At the same time, if one follows Lofland's argument, individualization and the expansion of the variety of people available for interaction and social roles has been accompanied by the reduction of the number of persons with whom close, intimate building blocks and threads of connectedness of human attachment are developed. This increases the significance of each person who becomes close. Lofland concluded that grief is harder in the modern Western world when one of these few persons dies. This is particularly true if that person is a spouse. According to Peter Berger and Hansfried Kellner, marriage among middle-class couples involves a complex process of self, other, and world reconstruction, carried forth through constant conversation and other forms of interaction.

Relations with others must be more or less transformed with couplehood. This means that the death of the partner necessitates another reconstruction, but the process has to be taken alone, with only partial support from others. The significant partner is not there to comment and either accept or critique the changes of the self and the world the widowed woman is trying to accomplish. The self as a wife exists only in memory and the future self planned before the illness and/or death is not possible. The present may be lonely and beset with other problems, such as shortage of finances, the grief of the children, and other challenges with which the widow may not be able to cope. Friends and relations may start making demands as soon as the role of widow has withered.

The various forms and components of loneliness expressed by women in several of Lopata's studies accentuate the problems of self and world reconstruction. The widow can miss that particular person with whom a unique relationship was formed, having and being a love object, a companion in front of television, a sexual partner, an escort to public events, a partner in couple-companion friendship, someone sharing the household for whom meals and routines are planned, and even just a presence. The widowed woman must also deal with the identities imposed upon her by others. Elizabeth Bankoff's 1990 study of friendship among widows concluded that old friends could become troublesome if they insisted on the widow remaining the same. Many women thoroughly dislike the label "widow," with its traditional implication of an old, helpless woman who is perpetually in weeping grief.

They also find it self-demeaning when associates do not consider them worthy of continued interaction. Thus, as the woman tries to change, often in uncertain and conflicting ways, people around her keep thrusting on her identities she may dislike and refuse to accept. The absence of the late husband may necessitate the survivor learning new skills and areas for building self-confidence—from caring for the family automobile to managing her finances.

The process of change in the self-concept is inconsistent and, like grief, has no clear-cut ending, as new situations and roles affect what has been reconstructed and old images remain in live memory. However, many studies have found widows very resilient. They deal with the pain of caring for a dying husband, the shock of the death, the need to learn to live in a world without the deceased, and the need to change relationships and reconstruct a new self-concept and identities.

FAMILY ROLES IN WIDOWHOOD

The role of mother is obviously changed by the death of the children's father, but many factors affect the form and direction of such changes, including the number, gender, and ages of the children, as well as their prior relationship to the father, and the contributions or problems in the support system from the social circle of that role. The woman may not have complete freedom in relating with her children. Even in the twenty-first century, in-laws may have definite ideas about how the children should be raised, especially if the family is prestigious and inheritance is involved.

Ethnic and people of colour groups may have definite ideas as to the rights of the husband's family over these children and their mother. The financial situation may influence what she can, or wants, to do with and for them. In the historical past of American society "charitable organisations" often interfered with the mother in the absence of father, sometimes even taking the children away from her, as happened to thousands of New York children sent to the Midwest at the turn of the twentieth century. It was not until 1905 that the society decided that children were best off with the mother and even passed a policy of "mother's pensions," which unfortunately were not available in many states. Amendments to the Social Security Act gave widows with minority children special funds, ending when the offspring reached adulthood. Neighbours, schools, even the police can impinge on the rights of mothers, allegedly guaranteeing safety and proper socialisation.

Children can cause work for the mother, but they can also form a major source of support. As mentioned earlier, mother-daughter relationships tend to be closer in America than in some other societies and closer than the mother-son tie. This is particularly true in subcultures with strong gender-segregation norms. As the children and the mother age, role reversal can take place, with the children, and especially one child, taking over some of the household chores, contributing to the family finances, and caring for the parent. These modifications in relationships can be painful, or relatively easy, depending on the kind of bond between parent and child and the behaviour and attitudes of others, especially other children. Children might cooperate by providing support, or withdraw, placing the burden on one offspring.

Lopata's studies found that widowed women received little support from their in-laws. One-fourth did not have such living relatives. Only one-third reported that they were helped by in-laws at the time of death, and only about one-third of the in-laws said that they visited the widow or invited her over. Although in-law contact with the children was more frequent, only one-half said that in-laws gave the children gifts or money. These figures may indicate difficulties in the relationship while the connecting link was still alive, or else that one side or both felt the contact need not be continued. Widows reported that the grandparents were not active in the family. Of course, most of the widows in Lopata's studies were fifty years or older and the children were not of a dependent age.

The two Lopata studies came to one conclusion concerning the contribution of siblings questioned by the scholars Anne Martin Matthews and Shirley O'Briant. Respondents in Lopata's support systems study were given three chances to report someone as contributing to 65 different economic, service, social, and emotional supports, for a total of 195 possible listings. Only 20 percent had no living sibling, but relatively few even mentioned a sister or brother. For example, the highest percent of listings, only 14 percent, was made in response to siblings as givers of food, and 10 percent to siblings who help with rent or with decision making, perform housekeeping or sickness care, function as companions in holiday celebrations, or act as the person to whom they would turn in times of crisis. Twenty percent indicated that they helped a sibling with work outdoors, the highest of service supports. If a sibling appears in one support she (it is usually a sister) appears in several. Martin Matthews studied widows in Guelph, Ontario, which has a low mobility rate and O'Briant in Columbus, Ohio, in which mainly one sibling was active. Chicago is a large city, with high mobility and family dispersal, which may account for the relative absence of siblings in those support systems.

Other relatives do not appear often, especially in the lives of older widows, mainly because of their unavailability. This varies among the studies of various populations. However, more African-American than white widowed grandmothers took care of and even mothered their grandchildren. "Black grandparents were much more likely to take on a parent-like role with their grandchildren.... These grandparents saw themselves as protectors of the family, bulwarks against the forces of separation, divorce, drugs, crime—all the ills low-income black youth can fall pray [sic] to" (Cherlin and Furstenberg 1986, pp. 127–128). Lopata and Jessyna McDonald, who studied African-American families in Detroit, Indianapolis, Los Angeles, and Washington, D.C., in 1987, found many widows living alone. One difference between white and African-American families was the fluidity of housing arrangements. African-American women may have children, grandchildren, even siblings and more distant relatives moving in and out, or she may move into their households more frequently than white women.

WOMEN AND MEN FRIENDS: MEMBERSHIP IN THE COMMUNITY

Many widowed women, especially of the middle class, reported problems with married friends. Social events, whether at homes or in public places, tend to be built around friendships with couples. Respondents complained that they heard about dinner parties to which they were not invited. Some widows explained it in terms of jealousy of married friends who did not want an extra woman around their husband, or having a "fifth wheel" present. More agreed that married friends were jealous of them than that the husbands actually propositioned. Such advances, if they happened, were met with anger. The widows often wanted male companionship, but not a sexual affair with a husband of a friend, endangering the other relationship. Also, many moved after the death of the husband and were located inconveniently to former friends. Bankoff reported that old friends were helpful only early in widowhood. New friends, on the other hand, accepted the widows as they were.

Close relations with men can become a problem for widowed women. Many simply do not want to enter into such interaction, and definitely not to remarry. They like freedom from prior constraints, do not want to take care of another sick man, and fear objections from children. Offspring often do not approve of such changes because of idealisation of the father or inheritance concerns. In addition, of course, there is the ever-present knowledge of the statistical scarcity of available men the same age of most widows. Living men are either married or in poor health.

Sexual relations themselves may be feared, with concern over physical appearance and experiencing emotions or difficulties of physical contact. Some widows do enter cohabitation arrangements, on either a part- or full-time basis, either in home or away. For the most part, widows who remarry desire such a relationship, lack inhibiting influences, are attracted to a specific individual, and feel that they can gain from the relationship, whether economically or from a parenting perspective. Walter McKaine's *Retirement Marriage* (1969) found conservative attitudes among "remarrieds," many of whom had ethnic backgrounds in which marriage rather than personal independence was very important. He notes that success in these marriages involves affection and respect.

American society has created many organisations whose membership is open to participants. Some of these are focused on providing resources, advice, companionship, or social events to the elderly, and some to the widowed. The American Association of Retired People (AARP) has developed the Widow to Widow programme and many communities have variations on such themes. Other groups in which marital status is not a known characteristic attract people with special interests. In the past, widows felt like members of a minority group, with myths and prejudices against them, but active life in the twenty-first century appears to diminish these attitudes.

Becoming and being a wife, and then a widowed woman, involves complex processes of self and other reconstruction and changes in relations with different circle members. These are heavily influenced by many factors, such as the characteristics of the society and the communities in which a woman lives, and her personal resources. Becoming a wife involves relating to the husband but also to a whole social circle of the role, its composition, rights, and duties. An important aspect of American society is its patriarchal and related bases, modified by new forms of complex development, including opportunities and restrictions of resources available to all women, wives, and then widows. Personal resources include the ability to analyse and seek out resources at any stage of life.

Although widows have gone through the trauma of an ill or suddenly dead husband, grief, loneliness, and the need to reconstruct the self-concept and identities, those who had a multidimensional social life space have been able to build independent, even satisfying lives. Others obtain support systems from families, friends, neighbours, and their community's organisations, with varying degrees of satisfaction. There are unknown numbers of widows in modern American society and its communities who live a very restricted life, but their frequency appears to be decreasing as societal resources become available not only in widowhood, but throughout life.

THE ORDEAL OF WIDOWHOOD IN AFRICA

At a recent burial ceremony of a friend in Western Kenya, I came face to face with the ordeal that widows go through soon after their husbands pass-on and that incident is the inspiration behind this piece. Achieng had lived very well with her late husband who was also my friend and renowned journalist. Upon his demise in a grisly road accident, the entire clan rose up in arms against Achieng and we could not help but watch as her rural home was rummaged through and literally all belongings carried away by the husbands relatives. It was a scene to behold yet a lesson for many of us on the African continent. Bereavement is a social fact in any culture but reactions and practices relating to this vary from culture to culture. Although widows constitute a large proportion of the adult female population in African communities, systematic investigation is missing. The result is that much of the scanty pieces of information we have on widowhood practices are mere raw and unprocessed information hence the need to galvanize more public discourse and action on the subject

Solving the problems of widows in Africa means addressing the inequitable power regimes characterised by vulnerability, stigma, discrimination and suffering. We propose that the most crucial interventions should include addressing the role of communities and culture, the socialization processes, practice of polygamy; apathy on the part of the police, the administration, and the judiciary; the absence of any law specifically addressing the problems of widows; and the general avoidance of drafting wills, coupled with the absence of effective means for enforcing wills. It calls in place the addressing of fundamental contradictions inherent in the African legal system where statutory laws coexist with Islamic and traditional customary laws and practices

The problems of widows in Africa cannot be divorced from the larger problems facing many Third World nations and particularly, the problems of women, children, and other marginalized groups within these nations. The plight of widows in Africa clearly implicates the institutional, public, and private actors in the international scene. Economically, whole societies suffer as a result of continuing discrimination against widows. Furthermore, with the current source of HIV and AIDS in Africa, debates about the rights and entitlements of widows take on new meaning. Customary practices of widowhood and widowhood rites also impose special hardships and vulnerabilities on women.

In Africa, one constant feature is widow's disproportionate exclusion from property ownership. This is actualized by the fact that women generally remain a minority (10 per cent) of owners of land and housing and often face discriminatory customs enshrined in patriarchy and negative masculinity, religious laws, and institutional practices that severely restrict their ability to gain and control such property (NACC: Gender technical committee 2010). These trends are true for women in urban and rural areas alike and worst for those infected and affected by HIV and AIDS. Additionally, there is a general lack of data on property ownership disaggregated by sex at national level as acknowledged by the Kenya bureau of statistics thus making it difficult to know the true extent of women's ownership or control of such assets and the realisation of their rights to property and inheritance.

The thinking that we propose is an empowerment scheme targeting the community specifically, cultural practices and traditions generally and widows directly. The thing is the only means through which widows can reduce their helplessness and alienation. In the process, women gain greater control over all aspects of their lives and social environment. The thinking involves attacking all forms of subordination directed at widows. The inhibitions targeted include, psychic, physical, cultural, sexual, legal, political, and economical. We insist that the premise of the project is engaging communities because we hold the notion that resolutions to problems faced by widows require a multidimensional approach that must improve psycho-social, educational, cultural, spiritual and emotional development.

WIDOWS BETWEEN ISLAM AND OTHER RELIGIONS AND CIVILIZATIONS

A widow is the woman who lost her husband who supports her in one of her life stages. This is a circumstantial matter but it does not deprive her of her right of leading an honorable life. The death of the husband does not mean the end of widow's life and does not mean that a widow lives the rest of her life in the chains of this new title.

Reality confirms, in most cases, that when a woman loses a husband, she finds herself alone in front of her tragedy and new responsibilities. In addition to her suffering, another suffering of different kind begins which is suffering the looks of the society to her because she became without a husband, so people count her movements and consonants.

ISLAM AND WIDOWS:

However, the stance of Islam towards widows differs completely from this look and even differs in regard of respecting the feelings of widows after the departure of their husbands.

Since the very beginning, Islam looks with compassion, sympathy, and mercy to them as having special circumstances, needs someone to support them and support their struggle because they have lost their husbands. So, they have to gain the care of the Muslim society which should support them along with their children.

According to the tolerant religion of Islam, it supports the positive image of widows which helps them to associate and interact with others in the society instead of sitting alone recalling the past memories which will be a good soil for Satanic insinuations.

Honoring of Islam to widows emanates from honoring women in general because Islam equates between women and men in rights and duties and it is Shari'ah does not know any distinction between widowed women and others, moreover, Islam granted widows a great status. Allah (Glory be to Him) says in a Divine Hadith: "I only accept Salah from those who do it humbly to My Glory those who spend the day in mentioning me, and takes care of widows, the needy, and the wayfarer."

Widows are included in the commandment of the Messenger of Allah (peace be upon him), moreover most mothers of the believers were widows except *'A'ishah* (may Allah be pleased with her) which was the only one whom the Messenger of Allah (peace be upon him) married as virgin.

Perceptions of Jahiliyyah (pre-Islamic Time of Ignorance):

Widows have nothing to reduce their dignity or their status in the sight of Allah and in the sight of people.

Moreover, any low looks directed to widows is nearer to the perception of the Pre-Islamic Era than the Islamic view because the death of the husband is Allah's decree and they have no fault in that, furthermore many widows give a good example when they rear their children by their own in the best they can.

Widows and the Right of Marriage:

As Islam considers marriage a genuine right for widows, the Shari'ah permitted marriage for them after the end of *'Iddah* (waiting period after divorce of death of the husband) which is four months and ten days or delivering the baby if they are pregnant, especially if they are in young age and have children who need care. In that case, they have the right to protect themselves against adultery and complete their lives in light of a natural family.

Islam maintains the natural disposition of mankind, therefore it permitted widows to marry. Furthermore, most women whom the Messenger (peace be upon him) married were previously married such as *Um Salamah*. Marriage is a shield for women and men together and if there are traditions look badly at widows, they are denied by Islam.

Islam has made benevolence to widows and taking care of them one of the noblest actions in the sight of Allah. The Islamic Shari'ah commended with the good treatment of widows, moreover Islam exhorted people to marry previously married women and not to leave them a subject for accusation and talks.

WIDOWS IN INDIA

This honorable look for widows which Islam grounded its bases and some of them were applied in the Arabian society before Islam differs from the stance of other religions and civilizations. For example, let us take one religion such as Hinduism to see how widows live therein.

In the Indian society where most people are Hindu, there is no voice for widows, where they lose their identity and even their basic rights when they lose their husbands. In some cases, citizens burn widows alive with their dead husbands which is the life which some people described as "the life of *Sati*" in reference to the custom of burning widows with their husbands, but that habit was banned.

Hindu widows face a set of social prohibitions: When a man dies, his widow is expected to give up all joys of life and she has no right to marry.

Her relatives get rid of her by exiling her to rigid Hindu towns such as the town of Vrindavan in northern India, where a study done by the municipality of (Vrindavan) showed that about 3 thousands widows live there, whereas hundreds live in other towns such as Braszbomi and Geoffrdan which are religious Hindu towns.

The Indian widow is called in some cases "*Bram*" or "creature" not a human being because they cannot be described by humanity but in the presence of their husbands. In some Hindu languages, widows are referred to as an absent inanimate pronoun instead of "she".

However, in some other languages they double the sound of the last letter for humiliation or make it similar to the word "whore".

Widows according to them is a source of bad omen, therefore they are prevented to attend ceremonies which form an important part of the Hindu life such as the ceremonies of marriage and birth, moreover in some cases they consider their shadows as impure unlike the pure people of the community.

As a result of these false doctrines, more than 33 million Indian widows suffer poverty, hunger, and need, as they suffer loneliness because of the retarded religious beliefs which dominate their minds, where the Hindu doctrine does not allow widows to remarry again which force them to live alone in the middle of poverty and need. Most widows live on aid, whereas some of them resort to begging. So, there is a big difference between the mercy of Islam and the stance of other religions and civilizations in regard of widows.

MUSLIM WIDOWS IN INDIA

It is necessary to examine the concerns of our society about widowhood, the plight of widows, and the problems that they have to face. The vernacular phrases, idioms, and slang shape the common person's attitude in an unconscious way. The popular movies are an important medium for reflecting and affecting the popular psyche. Here, one is constrained to say that there are rarely novels and stories in Hindi or Urdu that generate the ideas and opinions of understanding and sympathy for the widows: the Bollywood films are a big culprit. They, as if, are always trying to compete in glorifying the state of *'Suhaag'*. *"Mangalsutra"*, nose pin, and jewellery, *i.e.*, the signs of*"suhaag"* is always a grim reminder to the widows of their 'degraded' social status. This is not all; the society is not prepared to listen to the plight of widows even if somebody takes the cudgels to bare it all (the case of shooting of film *Water* is very recent in one's memory). The most neglected are the poor widows, even if the society has a help mechanism.

CROSS-BORDER COMMONALITY IN DISTRESS

The life of a widow and the social practices surrounding widowhood in the countries of the Indian Sub-Continent show a cross-border cross-cultural uniformity. In every culture or religious group widowhood is inauspicious. The life of a widow is marked by suffering and social exclusion, if not destitution. Some cultures have some institutional support systems but, by and large, these support systems also fall prey to misuse and corruption.

Most pathetic is the condition of widows who have to live on their own. The condition becomes worse if they also have some children to support, especially daughters.

The cultural or religious differences surrounding the life of widows and widowhood was brought out in a conference organised by the Guild of Service on *'Capacity Building of Marginalised Women: Widows'* from 1st to 3rd February, 2002 in Delhi.

It was the first South Asian conference on widows, and delegates from neighbouring countries including Afghanistan, Bangladesh, Bhutan, Nepal, Pakistan, and Sri Lanka had come and voiced the problems faced by women, particularly widows in their respective countries. It turned out to be a good background to this study.

INDIAN PERSPECTIVE

India is important not only because it has a large population, but also because this renders India as home to many religions and cultures. Muslim population in India is second largest in the world, more than that in Pakistan. A broad perspective of the plight of Hindu widows serves as a case study of widows. Many littérateurs, historians, and religious authorities have dealt with the customs, and practices followed in the society

The former Supreme Court Judge, Sujata Manohar, addressing the conference, specially mentioned the practice of *Suti*, a significant element of Hindu customs pertaining to women/widows. She, discussing the status of widows in India in the above named Conference, related how the practice of burning of newly widowed woman live on the funeral pyre of her husband was abolished after a campaign by Raja Ram Mohan Roy in 1829 in Bengal; when it culminated into *Suti* Regulation Act of 1829. Bengal, during the period 1815 to 1828, recorded a total figure of 8135 widows burnt alive as Suti. The Dayabhaga system of Hindu law, which prevailed in Bengal, she said, conferred on widows the right to succeed to the landed property of the deceased husband. Changes were effected in Tenancy laws in favour of women. In order to prevent widows from inheriting a share in the land, this inhuman brutality was perpetuated on widows with the ulterior motive of depriving them of a share in land granted by law. So, we have in the 18th and 19th century Bengal, exactly the converse of the anticipated result in giving women, who are otherwise totally deprived, a right to inherit land.

Citing statistics she informed that in India the proportion of widows to the total female population was about 9 per cent, or more than 40 million. Among women above the age of 60, the proportion of widows rises to 64 per cent. And yet little attempt has been made to study this disadvantaged segment of women.

She also talked about prevalent tradition of considering widows as inauspicious and the social stigma they carry with them. She gave the example of Maharashtra where on special occasions like marriage, welcome of a newly wed bride, or wishing a happy and safe delivery to a pregnant woman, five married women whose husbands are alive perform an *aarati*. There are, in orthodox families, customary ceremonies performed at the time of husband's death, which are cruel and verge on the barbaric. Breaking glass bangles, tearing apart the *mangal sutra* from her neck, and in some sections, even the older customs of shaving off the head and wearing a single piece of rough white cloth *dhoti* prevails.

A widow cannot wear *kumkum* nor can she wear nice clothes or ornaments and that she must eat only very frugally the plainest of food so that her senses are under control. These are attempts at controlling sexuality of widows though this does not prevent their being exploited sexually by unscrupulous family members or others. In West Bengal widows, in the name of religion, are abandoned by their families and left at places of pilgrimage such as Varanasi and Vrindavan, ostensibly to lead an austere life in the worship of God. There are approximately 3000 such widows in Vrindavan and surrounding areas alone. The NHRC is actively involved in their empowerment and creation of programmes to prevent abandonment of widows by their families.

In some parts of northern India there is the custom of getting the widow married to the husband's younger brother or she may even be given to a cousin, she said, who has a right to sell her once she has been wedded to him. There are well known novels, stories to depict the plight of such women In the agriculturally rich States, a widow remarried to a younger brother-in-law keeps the land and the worker in the family. "The status of a widow in the family has been closely linked to her illiteracy, her incapacity to earn, and consequent dependence on the family for her livelihood and maintenance; social compulsions in a patriarchical society have ways of keeping a woman's sexuality and property under patriarchical control" she said.

Prior to 1937 the Mitakshara system of Hindu law prevailed in a large region, except Bengal. Under this a Hindu widow had no right to inherit her husband's property. With the Hindu Women's Right to Property Act coming into force in 1937, the law created what is known as a 'widow's estate'. The law gave to a widow the right to a share in her husband's property equal to the share of his son, but she could hold this share only during her lifetime. On her death her share would revert to her husband's heirs. She also got a share in her husband's property on partition of the joint family.

Sujata Manohar also mentioned the property rights of Muslim, Christian, and Parsee widows. With the principles of equality and non-discrimination finding acceptance in the Constitution, some important changes were brought about in Hindu law. The Hindu Succession Act of 1956 made a widow's estate the absolute property of the widow. The share of the deceased husband/ father in case of the property of the joint family came to the widow/ or the daughter under this law. Yet the old practice of only males being coparcener, holding a share in the joint family property, continues. Only in two or three States in this country the law has been changed to give a daughter the right to a share in the joint family property by birth. A Muslim widow under the Shariat Act 1937 got a share in her husband' s property. Yet the social conditions determine the extent to which she can enjoy this right. The same was true of Christian women, but the Christian society offered a better social space to a widow. Christian and Parsee widows also had a right to inherit under their inheritance laws, though some of the local laws were less favourable in case of the Christian women. The greatest problem in this area is in respect of a woman's right to inherit family lands.

The Hindu Succession Act is subject to any customary law to the contrary. Most of the customary laws prevent a woman from inheriting a share in the land. Thus the court upheld a tribal custom that prevented the widow and daughters of a tribal from inheriting land. Similarly tenancy laws in most parts of northern India prescribe an "order of devolution where four generations of men in the main line are preferred to the widow and the daughters". Even for Muslims in undivided India, Shariat Act left out agricultural land from its purview, the inheritance of which was to be governed by local customs and tenurial laws. These laws were highly gender unjust. After independence the Southern States amended the Shariat Act to include agricultural land and thus reduced inequalities in male and female shares. But the law in North India remains highly gender biased.

Justice Manohar mentioned that gradually the world has awakened to the human rights of women and now human rights are rights of women and children as well. This is reflected in the Convention on the Elimination of All Forms of Discrimination against Women, Convention on the Rights of the Child, and various other international instruments dealing with Human Rights in all varieties and all their manifestations. Yet in the Convention that deals directly with discrimination against women, there is no direct reference to the condition of a widow, possibly because the severity of discrimination against widows is an Asian problem not sufficiently articulated in the world fora.

She was of the opinion that the basic catalyst of change was education, followed closely by economic empowerment, which is also crucial.

Meera Khanna, Joint Secretary, Guild of Service, also spoke about widowhood in India. She made the point that widowhood was viewed, not as just a phase in the life cycle of a woman, but as a personal and social aberration, to be totally eradicated. There are deep social, cultural, and even economic implications of widowhood. In Indian psyche, there is acceptance of the inevitability of the death of a person. But in the case of death of the husband this fact is often glossed over. This inherent contradiction motivates the cultural non-acceptance of widowhood. Hence the blessings given to a woman are replete with suggestions of eternal wifehood. *"Akhand saubhaagyavati bhava"* (may your *saubhaagya*, *i.e.*, Life with husband, never terminate), *'sadaa suhaagan raho'* (May your husband live for ever). She rightly emphasised that though the death of a spouse, or of any person, for that matter, is an inevitability, there is a taboo and a hesitation to discuss it between husband and wife and even between parents and children. This leaves anyone including widows unprepared for the change in status and the consequent adjustments to be made in life.

In her opinion widowhood was both a crisis and a problem. In the suddenness and in the sea change that it wrought in the life of a woman, it was a crisis. As the woman tries to cope with the implications it becomes a problem. Yet, very few women are prepared to face the crisis and even fewer are mentally equipped to grapple with the problem. Above all, "a widow is doubly traumatized as a woman and as a widow. She is victimized as a woman and because she is a woman she is marginalised as a widow". The system makes the widow a hapless victim of degrading deprivation.

She mentioned the fact that the widow in some parts of the country is called*raand* while a prostitute is called a *randi*. The derivative relationship of the two words reflects the degradation ascribed to widowhood. It also indicates that social psyche. A widow's sexuality becomes suspect and a source of menace once her husband is no more. And also once she is a widow it is a small step to become a *randi* from a *raand*. Both words are used as common abuses. The colloquial saying in parts of Haryana *"Jawaan raand to boorhaa saand"* (a young widow would turn even an old man into a stud) is a crude allegation of a widow's supposedly wayward sexuality.

Efforts for A Support System

Dr. Hamida Naveem mentioned the special conditions prevailing in Kashmir. The gross violation of human rights at the hands of the extremists and the State both had resulted in 25,000 orphans, and 20,000 widows, besides other devastating consequences

There was now beginning a movement to build a support system. There used to exist an organisation known as Hilal-e-Ahmar (Red cross). However Hilal-e-Ahmar ceased to exist as most of its members were harassed and arrested by the State. After Hilal-e-Ahmar fell, Kashmir witnessed the rise of Public Relief Trust (PRT) that in fact preceded the making of the separatist alliance of 22 parties, the All Parties Hurriyet Conference (APHC), almost on the debris of 13 parties Tehreek-e-Hurriet-e-Kashmir. Unlike Hilal-e-Ahmar, it operated in the countryside with a grand network of known faces. The Government did not allow this too to function for more then three years.

She said that one Abdul Rasheed and some other friends of his floated Human Effort for Love and Peace (HELP). This orphanage offered regular financial support to widows.

In 1993 the Rajiv Gandhi Foundation started functioning. It started financial help on bi-annual basis. But it abruptly stopped functioning after sometime.

Initiative for Women and Children was started in 1997 by Dr. Hamida along with some friends to cater especially to the needs of orphans and widows. They provide immediate help to widows and orphans informally.

She emphasised that there was an unbroken chain of widows in the lanes and by-lanes of the valley that needed and deserved selfless help and care from both, the social institutions as well as the Administration. She described Kashmiri society as a conservative one, ridden with hypocrisy. Conventionality places chains on a widow's personal liberty; she loses the freedom to interact with males as she is held in suspicion.

Though she is not an outcaste, yet the "sin" of being a young widow follows her everywhere. She is not normally accepted in marriage because of social stigma attached to her widowhood. It was an albatross round her neck, as if she was an accused. The condition of those who became a widow within a few days of marriage or before the consummation of marriage, is much more heart rending as the force of social stigmas is so strong that they cannot get re-married to the right persons but, at the most, could be thrust on some unwilling or undeserving man to support her. In border areas like Baramullah young widows have been given in marriage to men who are old enough to be their father and who already have many children by their first wife. Widows with children are hardly accepted in marriage and alas this happens in a society of Muslims whose Prophet had married mostly widows and divorcees to set an example for his followers and instructed them time and again to be kind to orphans in word and deed and to give a respectful place to widows by preferring to marry them.

She pointed out that the appalling problem of growing number of widows was so grave that even if the State government seriously launched rehabilitation projects, these will not be able to make much of a difference.

According to Muslim Personal Law if the father-in-law of the widow is alive, neither she nor her children can claim any share in the family property and there are numerous instances where widows have been thrown out along with children from their husband's house. Half the widows do not know how long they have to wait to get religious sanction to re-marry.

According to religious scholars and clergy, the wait period varies from four years in *Malikia* school of thought to ninety years in *Feghai Hanfiya* (religious laws of *Hanfiya* school) although now even *Feghai Hanfiya* in India has decided to adopt the *Malikia* practice of allowing re-marriage after four years' wait. She said that women whose husbands have disappeared have to live in constant trauma and uncertainty. They have to try to locate the disappeared husband, which is an uphill task in the prevailing circumstances. On the one hand, they live in constant pain of the separation of the husband and on the other hand, they do not know whether he will return at all.

In Kashmir, she explained, there were villages where majority of the men folk had been killed; interestingly one among these villages, Sheikh Mohalla, was in the Chief Minister's constituency of Ganderbal. The ten family strong hamlet had 11 widows, 31 orphans and just three men. They have yet to receive any ex-gratia amount as relief, which accrues to the wife of one killed in militant fire.

Another village is in Bandipora where at least 70 per cent women have been widowed, and 90 per cent orphaned. They feel so scared as night approaches that they leave their homes for safer abodes where there are men folk around. These women are forlorn and have nobody to depend on; their homes have turned into hell for them as these are devoid of any sense of security as well as any comfort.

PAKISTAN: NO DIFFERENT

Rukhshanda Naz and Salma Murad are two prominent activists of the Pak-Afghan region. Rukhshanda Naz, putting forth the ideas of Salma Murad, observed that a widow is usually avoided in any social gatherings as she is considered to be a threat to the other wives. She usually loses most of her friends of her husband's time and she has a hard time warding off the advances of other men. She finds herself completely insecure and usually has to look for new friends. If she is young she would like to dress up well or use a little makeup but she hesitates to do so for fear that it would be a cause of adverse comments. If she goes to work she is looked at suspiciously. In the work place she is usually faced with sexual harassment. "Majority of Asian women are found in jobs with low security, lower pay, low conditions of work, low status, having no bargaining power in a narrow range of occupations". Fear of loss of job, loss of source of livelihood, or a feelings of shame, inhibit their expression of natural reaction to exploitative attitudes.

Many men try to make advances to divorcees or widows considering them to be easy targets. There is no law or rule to check issues of harassment of women in Pakistan. It is proposed that either a law should be devised or clauses be incorporated in service rules to check such immoral practices. Launching a media campaign is also necessary to change the mindset of the people. Men also try to offer their help to widows for ulterior motives. She is treated as public property; if she does not work, she is told to go and earn a living.

Either way she is not left in peace. All the happiness in her life is dampened. Some widows, out of desperation, take their lives and their children's, or they take to degrading activities, such as prostitution, alcoholism, or drug abuse.

THE AFGHANISTAN CASE

Rukhshanda Naz spoke about Afghanistan also. The condition of Afghan widows is no different from that of widows in other neighbouring countries to the East and South, no matter whether they are in Afghanistan or in camps inside Pakistan. They are supposed to have a share in property (as decided by Islam), but the common practice is like the one prevalent in Pakistani Pakhtoon society where people deny every right to their daughters and sisters. In case of marriages, women do get property under dower, but men exercise the ownership right. The issue of second marriage also depends on the tribal custom. In some areas (the settled areas), particularly in the educated middle class, women can remarry.

The condition of the Afghan widows in camps is alarming. In the Jalozai camp alone, it is alleged, their number stands at 5000. In the same camp, there are said to be more than 2500 widows in one ward alone. Most of them have been found disabled. The problems start appearing for them when they reach the Pakistan border from their country. On the border, they first encounter the officials of the administration before crossing over into Pakistan. The males on duty fleece widows in return for enabling them to enter the country. They are forced to pay the border guards even for the entry of their male family members. When in camps, for most of the time, they are exploited by their own family and community male members in the form of sexual harassment, bonded labour, and trafficking. The men misuse the widow's identification cards to get rations.

As for the *Loya Jirga* and participation of women in decision-making, they have no role. *Loya Jirga* is an assembly of elders who are called to decide specific issues and whose decisions are binding on parties in conflict. In a situation where there is no written or formal law the importance of such an assembly is crucial, especially in preventing the situation on ground from collapsing into anarchy. The *Jirga* regulates life through decisions ranging from the location of a mosque to the settling of conflict within sub sections to larger issues such as regulating foreign relations, relation with other tribes, and even conveying decision of the tribes to the Government. Decisions are based on a combination of Islamic law and push to custom. The participation of women in public life or mainstream politics is not new, nor are women of Afghanistan confined to house, as shown in Western media. They had a history of *Loya Jirga* and women organisations, although in private sector (NGO) there is no such model like South Asian Women's movements. All in all, Afghan widows today are not much different as far as their social status goes.

BANGLADESH: THE SAME STORY

Traditionally, in Bangladesh society also, girls are married off at an early age. Regional, pre-partition, as well as historical Urdu literature, depicts such a societal picture. In the traditional Hindu literature one comes across males getting more than one or two wives. According to Salma Ali, a Bangla activist, in many cases it is found that there is a wide difference in the ages of the bridegroom and the bride. The bride is younger by a wide margin. But, this is probably more due to poverty and male dominant attitudes in the society. Naturally, the number of widowed women was much higher in the traditional societies of the sub-continent. Bangladesh constituted an important part of this region. Ruled by various regimes in the past, Buddhists, Hindus, Sultans, and Mughals or Muslims, the historical record shows a grim picture of women's state in the region.

Particularly, the condition of ancient Hindu widows was simply unspeakable. The custom of *Shaho Moron* (burning alive with the deceased husband) was deemed to be a great virtue for her. Barriers to remarriage were another restriction imposed upon a Hindu widow, which still persists in some parts here also. In the Muslim communities, widows were treated as dependent on their sons.

Though their conditions were not as bad as that of the Hindu widows, they too came under heavy burden of societal, familial, and other restrictions. As far as the ground situation today goes, a Muslim widow's status in the society defrauds her of many elements of empowerment. A Muslim woman's right to inheritance is observed more in breach than in compliance. In most of the cases, daughters are not given their due share in father's property. What generally is practiced is that the brothers give her a token amount as 'generous gift' and insist that she will not claim for her lawful share in father's property. The paradox lies here.

The sister hardly goes in for litigation against the brother(s) for fear of losing a cordial familial relationship. Maintaining such relationships is always the responsibility of the 'weaker' party (read sex). She, however, claims her share in crisis moments or in cases when the husband demands dowry, and approaches her brothers.

It is only the sweet will of the brothers that they allocate a little share to the helpless sister as of 'mercy'! Studies reveal that 48.24 per cent of the widows were knowledgeable about Sharia Laws that provides them the right to inherit parent's and husband's property. But in reality women do not claim share from such property.

In the case of widows, it is harder and sometimes impossible to claim their lawful property rights when they are without any adult male to provide them the social, moral, and economic support.

Thus widows lose their right to property and land, even when a proper application of the law would have protected them. Widows at a time of loss and grief, are vulnerable and cannot counter traditional barriers to seek legal help outside the family.

NEPAL: AGAIN THE SAME

Lily Thapa, Chairperson, Women for Human Rights, Nepal agreed that the Nepalese society is also a male dominated society where men make all decisions and choices and women are viewed as household workers and child bearers. There is widespread lack of education and knowledge. This worsens after a Nepalese woman is widowed.

The society divides women into married and widowed. Married status confers a certain social recognition where as widowhood is a state of deprivation. A widow is pitied. There are strict social norms and values. In most of the families, widowed women are held responsible for the death of the husband. It is common for living relatives of the deceased husband to view the widow as an ill omen.

It was a revealing fact that in a recent survey, out of fifty young widows interviewed, very few preferred parental home in comparison to their late husband's family despite their troubles. Some may entertain a hope of a share in husband's property, but not all.

Widows are denied rights on their own body in that wearing red and bright clothes and to put on make-up is frowned upon. In some parts of Western Nepal widows are forced to shave their heads and wear white clothes. In most parts, widows are made to eat vegetarian food and have some restriction on spices, *etc.* Widows have to cook for themselves and cannot eat food touched by others. Due to these rules and their weak economic status widows are denied a healthy life. There is some dilution of these attitudes in urban areas.

SRILANKA: STORY REPEATED

Sunila Abeysekra repeated almost the same scenario from the Srilankan society - discriminatory practices against women, more so against widows. In Tamil and Muslim communities, there are a number of rituals of seclusion and purification that widows must go through before they can be reintegrated into the family and the community. Srilanka is also a society in which a woman without male 'protector' is seen as abnormal. Unmarried women are considered to be unlucky and a burden on their families. A single woman or a widow is especially vulnerable. Many women who have been widowed by the on going socio-political conflict have complained of the problems of sexual and other harassment they have to face. As young and single women, they are seen as 'available', and subject to all types of undue advances when seeking help in government offices, banks, *etc.*

As for the role of religious bodies it was observed that these have played a marginal role in providing support for widows. It appears that since social stigma and level of public ostracisation of widows is less in Srilanka than in other South Asian countries, there has been no real focus on the issue as a priority. It is only within the Muslim community that through the Baithulmal

Fund there has been some support extended to widows. However, the problem of widows has not yet received the priority that it should, it is increasingly clear that there are a large variety of problems facing widows that need to be addressed at many different levels - legal, administrative, social, cultural, emotional, psychological, and spiritual.

In particular the issue of widow remarriage remains as a very critical one in Srilanka because of the large numbers of young women with very young children who are widowed and left dependent on family goodwill as a result of the ongoing strife. Many of these women fear remarriage because they feel the children of the first husband would be neglected or ill-treated. Widows of men who served in the armed forces are granted benefits only if they do not remarry. This pressure not to remarry in turn creates a range of situations in which such young widows are exploited economically and sexually by men who enter into relationships with them and harass them for any number of reasons.

BHUTAN - THE UNCOMMON CASE

Pem Wangdi from Bhutan was proud that her experiences as an activist in matters of rights of women in Bhutan, especially those of widows, were different from many of her compatriots from across the borders of her kingdom country. In the midst of listening to so much narration about the pain and anguish suffered by women, particularly widows, Bhutan stands out as a case where the scenario appeared different. Women in Bhutan seem to enjoy social, economic, and political equality with their male counter parts. They are spared the numerous burdens and afflictions, which women normally endure in other societies, in countries to the South and Southwest.

The position of widows in the family and society was strong. They are protected and remarriage of both widowed and divorced women was accepted. There is no loss of status for a remarried woman.

Women in Bhutan partake in every sphere of community life and enjoy a high degree of freedom and rights. Besides fulfilling their traditional roles as wives and mothers, women also constitute a great supply of workforce especially at the farm level. And although Bhutan belongs geographically to South Asia, its society, social structure, gender relations, and attitude towards women all combine to make it very different from every other South Asian nations.

Obliterated Borders, Uniform sufferings

The above detailed narration from different countries brings out one fact: in this entire region, by and large, the scene is the same. There are differences but these are differences of degree. Hindu, Muslim, Baudh, Tamil, Singhal, Pathan tribal all cultures and sub-cultures have same attitudes towards women, especially women who have lost their 'life partner'. One thing, however, has to be noted: these remarks do not refer to the Christians. Christianity as a separate regional culture does not figure in this area, though the number of Christians in India and other countries is not small. The status of Christian widows needs special treatment.

The plight of widows seems to have obliterated international borders. There is a uniformity of suffering.

PLIGHT OF FAMILIES OF THE WIDOWS INTERVIEWED

This is not meant to be an exhaustive study. It is a preliminary attempt to see if such a study, on an expanded scale, is possible in a Muslim dominated area of Delhi. It has been conducted at a mini-scale in Chandni Chowk as a case study, selecting Muslim Widows at random. It covers 37 widows. The case study is confined to two areas in the Walled City, *i.e.*, Jama Masjid and Kucha Pundit. The study attempts to cover the socio-economic conditions of Muslim widows residing in these areas. The interviewees were chosen at random. It turned out that some respondents called themselves as widows although they later revealed that they were divorcees. It was due to social stigma that they preferred to be known as widows or single women rather than divorcees. However, they have not been included in the study.

Our first visit was to Jama Masjid area. It is a very thickly populated area with a large network of lanes and by lanes (*chattas*). It is a difficult task to search for the concerned houses unless one is familiar with the place. The best way is to ask from the nearby shopkeepers or catch any other gray haired person and make inquiries.

We found during the visits to the houses of the widows here that most of them were living in families jointly with widowed daughter, grand children, *etc.* The houses were mostly congested with each family having one room of their own and a common loo or bathroom to use, with no proper kitchen. It was noticed in many families that the stove was kept on the floor of the living room and the side-shelves (*taaq*) used for kitchen equipment (tea leaves, cups, etc). Majority of these houses had broken floors and smoke-stained walls, these can be better described as overcrowded hovels, thick with grime.

Visits to some of the respondents highlighted the miserable living conditions, individual compromises with them and the bleak future of the families. The individual pattern was repeated case after case, compelling us to conclude that there were only shades of difference. An aged or a little younger woman with daughters at home and male, if any, out for work. No facilities for a sheltered bath, in some cases even no water in the room of habitation or nearby. Most of the women were not clear about the years or dates due to illiteracy and old age. Daughters were found to be slightly vocal, though they also appeared to be suppressed. In some cases where there were no males, the families were victims of harassment from neighbours. We also got the impression that a widow and her family were always under observation and lived in an atmosphere of suspicion, though sometimes they were eager to say that the 'neighbourhood was good'. We had a lurking hunch that may be they did not want to make any negative comment about the neighbours. There was no family that told us that the neighbours were helpful, though there were hints that sometimes, especially during *Ramazaan*, they received help.

The overall impression gathered during the visits to this area was that these were the widows belonging to the poorest urban sections. Neglected, deprived, and condemned to a life of penury, with droplets of aid from the State. Other relatives came into the picture here and there. In almost all the cases, the in-laws, if living, were never mentioned as being a helping hand. It was as if they had turned their back on the daughter-in-law after the death of their son.

Our next visit was to Kucha Pundit, another very thickly populated area. Like the Jama Masjid area, this area and its surroundings are also crowded with a web of lanes and by-lanes. Though divided into different *gulis*, the entire area is connected and one can enter from Lal Kuan, and emerge near Ajmeri Gate. This sprawling area is very thickly populated and congested. An old woman resident of Ballimaran told us, on Enquiry about the residences of some widows, *"Beti tumhein kis sey Milnaa hai? Yahaan to bhari hui hain."* (Dear, whom do you want to see? This place is full of them).

In this area we discovered that there were smaller areas organised into 'Committees'. A Committee is a type of neighbourhood *Panchayat* and embraces all the residents of its territory. This Committee sits in decision on disputes concerning the members. Its membership is probably restricted to males. There was a case where one respondent's married daughter was living with her mother as sometime ago when she had delivered a son in the hospital, her husband had taken away the newly born infant and this girl had to come back to her mother as she had some chronic health problems. In this case, the local Committee met and forbade her from filing any complaint. In another case a widow told us that her grown up son was living with her and it was he who had the control of finances and family affairs and she had no idea of income, *etc.* Whenever she needed money for household affairs, she had to ask her son for it.

We felt one difference between the widow residents of the above two areas. The respondents of the Jama Masjid area were more forthcoming and vocal as compared to those in the Kucha Pundit area. Otherwise, in the living conditions, in the surroundings, in the level of poverty, education and illiteracy, *etc.*, there was no marked difference between the two areas.

However, we came across one question repeatedly, *i.e.*, "Why are you conducting this survey? Are you going to help us?" This almost made one feel guilty of raising false hopes in their hearts.

Role of State Agencies

Since Delhi has a support system for widows introduced by the Municipal Corporation of Delhi, details of the schemes were sought from the Corporation office. Two prominent Municipal Councilors of the area, one male and one female, were also contacted. It was found that the monetary support is distributed through the elected representatives. They were supposed to keep their own records.

It was observed that these two were not always willing to make available their records; the female councilor though was more forthcoming on many counts. The male councilor either did not take the investigator seriously or had no interest in the working of the scheme.

As far as the government functionaries in the offices were concerned some of them did not seem to be familiar with the schemes or with information in their files. They did not appear to be involved in their work with a sense of responsibility. We might emphasise here that this type of responsibility requires a human and helping mindset.

It may be a good idea to involve people's representatives in a work that aims at welfare of the constituents. How much interest they would take depends upon their orientation, attitudes, and pressure from the beneficiaries. The fruitful working of a democratic system depends upon the commitment to the essence of democracy on the part of the people's representatives. The bureaucracy cannot be expected to replace the people's representatives in such a schema. As far as the universe studied is concerned, the beneficiaries of such schemes have to be made aware that they are not getting alms from the State or from the people's representatives. It is the duty of the State to look after them and to provide for their welfare. When they start understanding this, they will become conscious of their right and they may become vocal, and may not lose their self-respect by receiving such help from the State.

Government Schemes

The Municipal Corporation of Delhi started the scheme of old age pension in February 1964. This grant of stipend began at Rs 25/- per annum to persons of the age of 65 and above, who did not have any support nor any source of income. Certain conditions were also prescribed for the purpose of giving this stipends to persons residing in Delhi who were 65 years old and above.

However, the amount has been revised by the Corporation over the years and the increased amount now stands at Rs 200/- per month with effect from April 2001. This old age stipend or *Wazeefa* includes not only people who are above 65 years but also blind persons, widows, insane persons, crippled persons, and widowers irrespective of their age.

Certain guidelines have been issued regarding the distribution of this stipend in different wards and the necessary submission of application forms.

Usually it's the area Councilor of different wards who looks after it. Earlier, a numerical quota of 300 persons per ward for receiving the *Wazeefaa* was fixed but presently the number has been increased to 400 because of the constantly increasing demands. Recently the amount has been further increased to Rs 300/-, as was reported on 25th January 2002 in the *Asian Age's Delhi Age* supplement.

It was reported that the Delhi Social Welfare Minister, Raj Kumar Chauhan, has announced that senior citizens with an individual income of Rs 22,000 per annum and who were getting Rs 200 per month by way of old age pension would benefit from the increased rate. It was reported that the pension for the fourth quarter would be remitted in the bank account of the pensioners at the rate of Rs 300 per month at the end of March. The minister said that the eligibility criteria for old age pension of individual income have also changed.

Another recently published report in *The Hindu* clarified that the Delhi Social Welfare Department had taken a new initiative with regard to disbursing old age pension. Social Welfare Minister, Raj Kumar Chauhan informed that from the next financial Year onwards, forms concerning the Widows' pension and those relating to financial assistance given to widows for the marriage of their daughters would also be distributed through the MLAs. Earlier, the Department issued the forms and it often led to allegations of bribery and corruption. It was alleged that these officials often took money to issue the forms In order to eliminate this element of corruption; it had been decided to issue the forms through the MLAs and Members of Parliament from Delhi as per the report.

To sum up, this turns out to be the story of the poorest urban segment of Muslim widows in Delhi. Forsaken, deprived, neglected, and may be even despised and looked-down upon, they are some of the Muslim widows of*Chandni Chowk* living a life of darkness.

8

Reforms of Widow Remarriage

But Vidyasagar pressed on and urged the British to pass legislation that will allow Hindu widows to remarry. To support his request, Ishwar Chandra Vidyasagar collected almost 1000 signatures and sent his petition to the Indian legislative council. The council received thousands of signatures for and against this measure but the members finally decided to support the enlightened minority, The Hindu widow remarriage act was passé in 1856. Although, the value of this act for improving the lives of woman has been questioned, one cannot doubt Ishwar Chandra Vidyasagar's desire to create a more humane society.

Vidyasagar lived in a world where the males among the Kulin Brahmins, an aristocratic caste with rigid marriage rules were highly sought after as bridegrooms and able to marry as many women as they wished. As Vidyasagar collected data on this custom, he became horrified by the magnitude of the problem. Using as a sample 133 Kulin Brahmins of Hooghly district, Ishwar Chandra Vidyasagar revealed the abuses inherent in polygamy.

One fifty-year old man had married 107 times; Bholanath Bandopadhyaya (age fifty five) had eighty wives; Bhagaban Chattopadhyaya (age sixty-four) had seventy-two wives, and so the documentation continued. Arguing that the practice of Kulinism was inhuman, Ishwar Chandra Vidyasagar presented the government with a petition signed by 2,500 persons requesting the legislative prohibition of polygamy.

No action was taken and ten years later he presented another petition signed by 21,000 persons requesting the legislative prohibition of polygamy. The government cautious after the 1857 mutiny, declined to act. Vidyasagar continued his campaign and although he produced anti-polygamy tracts in 1871 and 1873, the issue was dead. Vidyasagar's third campaign focused on mass education for girls and boys.

He had been appointed Special Inspector of Schools for the Districts of Hooghly, Midnapur, Burdman and Nadia and was able to use his influence to establish a system of vernacular education in Bengal, including forty schools for girls. J.E.D. Bethune, legal member of the Governor Generals council, had set up a girls school in 1849 and it became Vidyasagar's responsibility to guide it through its difficult years. He remained associated with it until 1869.

HINDU WIDOWS' REMARRIAGE ACT, 1856

The Hindu Widows' Remarriage Act, 1856, also Act XV, 1856, enacted on 25 July 1856, legalized the remarriage of Hindu widows in all jurisdictions of India under East India Company rule.

In order to protect both what it considered family honour and family property, upper-caste Hindu society had long disallowed the remarriage of widows, even child and adolescent ones, all of whom were expected to live a life of austerity and abnegation. The Hindu Widows' Remarriage Act of 1856, enacted in response to the campaign of Pandit Ishwar Chandra Vidyasagar, provided legal safeguards against loss of certain forms of inheritance for a remarrying Hindu widow, though, under the Act, the widow forsook any inheritance due her from her deceased husband. Especially targeted in the act were Hindu child widows whose husbands had died before consummation of marriage.

"Second marriages, after the death of the husband first espoused, are wholly unknown to the Hindu Law; though in practice, among the inferior castes, nothing is so common."

— William Hay Macnaghten (1862)

"The problem of widows—and especially of child widows—was largely a prerogative of the higher Hindu castes among whom child marriage was practised and remarriage prohibited. Irrevocably, eternally married as a mere child, the death of the husband she had perhaps never known left the wife a widow, an inauspicious being whose sins in a previous life had deprived her of her husband, and her parents-in-law of their son, in this one. Doomed to a life of prayer, fasting, and drudgery, unwelcome at the celebrations and auspicious occasions that are so much a part of Hindu family and community life, her lot was scarcely to be envied.

On the other hand, the lower, particularly Sudra, castes and the (so-called) 'Un-touchables'—who represented approximately 80 per cent of the Hindu population—neither practised child marriage nor prohibited the remarriage of widows."

— Lucy Carroll (1983)

THE LAW

The preamble and sections 1, 2, and 5:

Whereas it is known that, by the law as administered in the Civil Courts established in the territories in the possession and under the Government of the East India Company, Hindu widows with certain exceptions are held to be, by reason of their having been once married, incapable of contracting a second valid marriage, and the offsprings of such widows by any second marriage are held so be illegitimate and incapable of inheriting property; and Whereas many Hindus believe that this imputed legal incapacity, although it is in accordance with established custom, is not in accordance with a true interpretation of the precepts of their religion, and desire that the civil law administered by the Courts of Justice shall no longer prevent those Hindus who may he so minded from adopting a different custom, in accordance with the dictates of their own conscience, and Where it is just to relieve all mach Hindus from this legal incapacity of which they complain, and the removal of all legal obstacles to the marriage of Hindu widows will tend to the promotion of good morals and to the public welfare;

It is enacted as follows:

1. No marriage contracted between Hindus shall be invalid, and the issue of no such marriage shall be illegitimate, by reason of the woman having been previously married or betrothed to another person who was dead at the time of such marriage, any custom and any interpretation of Hindu Law to the contrary notwithstanding.
2. All rights and interests which any widow may have in her deceased husband's property by way of maintenance, or by inheritance to her husband or to his lineal successors, or by virtue of any will or testamentary disposition conferring upon her, without express permission to remarry, only a limited interest in such property, with no power of alienating the same, shall upon her re-marriage cease and determine as if she had then died; and the next heirs of her deceased husband or other persons entitled to the property on her death, shall thereupon succeed so she same....
3. Except as in the three preceding sections is provided, a widow shall not by reason of her re-marriage forfeit my property or any right to which she would otherwise be entitled, and every widow who has re-married shall have the same rights of inheritance as she would have had, had such marriage been her first marriage.

THE REALITY OF REMARRIAGE AFTER WIDOWHOOD

A few months ago, a well-known and much respected actor mentioned in an interview that he still thinks about his late wife. People were shocked at this "stunning revelation", as the same actor has been happily remarried for a number of years.

This sort of "shocked" reaction begs an obvious question. Since when did remarriage become an equation formula that reads:

Remarried = Forgetting

This latest in a long line of widowed-myths implies that once remarried, the life previously lived somehow fades into oblivion because the widowed has now found new life with new love in it. Because of this new life, the remarried widowed is apparently never again sad or wistful because their late beloved is no longer here.

Conversely and equally perplexing is the companion myth that once a spouse has passed away, the widowed should assume an attitude that they have "caught their limit"; that once their beloved has passed away, a widowed's destiny is to remain alone and longing for a life that is no longer here to live. A widowed should thereafter resign themselves to functioning in life with grief and mourning as their core and living a destiny that they did not choose.

The reality of spousal loss that is so important for both the widowed and those who surround them to understand is that:

You can honour your past You can treasure your past You can and should love your past You do not have to live in your past

When it comes to love, our hearts are truly without capacity or limits — if this were not the case, we would each have only one child because how could our hearts*possibly* expand to love more than one? We all have an infinite capacity to love and should that be a widowed's choice, finding love in a new life can and should absolutely be part of their dynamic.

Love is also not mutually exclusive one of the other. Loving again does not mean that the love for a late beloved somehow goes away. It doesn't. Furthermore, loving again does not dishonour or disrespect the person who is no longer here, nor does it disrespect the *memory* of that person. This is a concept that can create a fair amount of discord (especially within families) when a widowed finds companionship or love once again.

People who surround the remarried or re-partnered widowed can also interpret newfound happiness as not grieving "right", not having experienced grief at all, completely "forgetting" the past (as if *that* is even possible) or believing that we have collectively dusted off our hands and are glancing around as if to say, *"OK, that's done and over with.... who's next?"* The fact is that even in a wonderful new life, things like holidays, birthdays, anniversaries, "angelversaries" (the date of a late spouse's death) and children realizing various life milestones can all serve as painful reminders that someone who a widowed loves without measure is no longer here to celebrate, witness and in general, be a part of a life that was built with love

Almost thirteen years after losing my late husband, I can tell you without reservation that I still love him and I still treasure the life that we had together. However, I have also moved forward into a beautiful new life. Eleven years old when her daddy passed away, our daughter Kendall is now a young adult who enjoys a thriving career. After seven years of widowhood, I met and fell in love with a wonderful man in 2007 (who actually fell in love with me too), we married in 2009 and together, with my fantastic English daughter Michelle, we have built a beautiful blended family. To top it all off, I have the privilege of being on a mission of service and support to others in need. Now, by living this incredible new life, does that mean that I have forgotten about or betrayed my past life? Absolutely not. Does it mean that after Mike died, I should have stayed inside the house in my pajamas and kept the blinds closed forever? What would that have accomplished? I chose instead to grieve in my way, in my time, help my daughter with and through her own grief recovery and slowly, yet steadily, move into a life of my own design - a design that happily included new love and new adventures to go along with that love.

The love that you have for your late beloved will never go away. Not ever. Not with the passage of time. Not with the introduction of a new person into your life and into your heart. Not with the 8 jillion people around you saying things like, *"Well you should be over it by now"*. I am honoring Mike's legacies of love and service by continuing to move forward; by modeling the best example that I can for my daughters, by serving a community that I love and by building a family and living a life with my Dave, whom I love deeply. By doing all of these things, I am indeed honoring the legacies of love and service that Mike left to us to carry forward.

You can do the same, if and when you choose to do so.

Remarriage does *not* equal forgetting — let no one tell you otherwise. Loving again does *not* imply lack of or the end of love for the past. You are *not* destined to remain in mourning forever... that isn't why you are here. Embrace and carry forward the legacies that were entrusted to you by your late beloved. If you choose it, living your new life can include companionship... and love. Choose carefully, choose wisely — and love again abundantly.

STATUS OF REMARRIED HINDU WIDOW

Mr V. S. Anjaria has written a very instructive article in the Supreme Court Cases, dated April 1, 1973 (1973) 1 SCC (Journal 17, pointing out an anomaly in the Hindu Succession Act, 1956, and suggesting certain amendments to Sections 15 and 16 of that Act in order to bring about the intended object to retain the property in the fold of the family to which it originally belonged. According to him the problem arises because the estate taken by Hindu female under Section 14(1) of the Act of 1956, is not defeasible under any circumstances and because the High Courts have rightly decided that a remarriage of a Hindu widow is now no longer a ground for divesting her of her right to the property converted into an absolute estate under Section 14 of the Act.

But it seems to me that the High Court opinion on the point of divestment on remarriage, which the learned author has in view, itself may require a consideration, having been based on an incorrect reading of the law. The contention in a nutshell can be stated thus.

Under Section 2 of the Hindu Widows' Remarriage Act, 1856, a Hindu widow, on remarriage, shall forfeit her right to the property which she has inherited from her husband. That Section 2 has not been repealed by the Hindu

Succession Act and Section 24 of the Hindu Succession Act itself shows that the legislature was conscious of the effect of Section 2 of the Act of 1856. Therefore, the forfeiture clause enacted by Section 2 still holds good and obtains.

This question came for decision before the Division Bench in AIR 1971 Mad 453, but the learned Judges did not seem to have examined the question in any detail being bound by the reasoning in the Full Bench case of AIR 1951 Mad 954.

They also followed the view in AIR 1958 Raj 159, which was a case under the Hindu Succession Act. The Rajasthan case, no doubt, deals with the problem in some detail, but the learned single Judge who decided that case seems to have been overwhelmed by what he considered to be the object behind the amendment of 1956, which object he calls the amelioration of the lot of the females vide Para 9. No attempt has been made, if I may say so with respect, to analyse the nomenclature used in Section 2 of the Act, and that, according to me, is the only proper method for resolving the controversy.

Shri S. V. Gupte had to say the following in his Commentary on the Hindu Law of Succession, 1963 Edn.:

"It is, however, still possible to urge as a matter of construction of Section 2 of the Hindu Widows' Remarriage Act that she would forfeit her estate, though full, especially as the Act has not been repealed. If an estate is liable to forfeiture it should make no difference whether the estate is converted into a full estate by Section 14 or not. Any estate either absolute or limited may in law still be liable to forfeiture in certain circumstances and situations by an independent rule such as the rule in Section 2 of the Hindu Widows' Remarriage Act which has not been repealed.

Referring to the difficulty arising on account of the absence of any rule in the present Act providing for the devolution of the property so forfeited as also on account of the Act not contemplating succession opening a second time except to a very limited extent the author says:

'But Section 2 of the Hindu Widows' Remarriage Act in fact provides for devolution on forfeiture. Neither the said provision nor the scheme of succession indicated in that section is repugnant to the scheme of the succession under this Act.' " The opposite view is provided for by Mulla's Hindu Law, 1966 Edn., p. 796, in the following words:

"The rule laid down in that enactment cannot apply to a case covered by the present Act and a widow becomes full owner of the share or interest in her husband's property that may devolve on her by succession under the present section. Her remarriage, which would evidently be after the vesting in her or her share or interest on the death of the husband, would not operate to divest such share or interest. The Hindu Widows' Remarriage Act, 1856, is not repealed but Section 4 of the present Act in effect abrogates the operation of that Act in the case of a widow who succeeds to the property of her husband under the present section and Section 14 has the effect of vesting in her that interest or share in her husband's property as full owner of the same."

The High Court of Patna in AIR 1962 Pat 65, went a step further and held in a case of remarriage before the Hindu Succession Act, that the forfeiture of widow's right on remarriage is based upon general principles of Hindu law apart from the provisions of Section 2 of the Act of 1856.

Section 2 of the Hindu Widows' Remarriage Act reads as under:

"Rights of widow in deceased husband's property to cease on her remarriage — All rights and interests which any widow may have in her deceased husband's property by way of maintenance or by inheritance to her husband or to his lineal successors, or by virtue of any will or testamentary disposition conferring upon her, without express permission to remarry, only a limited interest in such property, with no power of alienating the same, shall upon her remarriage cease and determine as if she had then died: and the next heirs of her deceased husband or other persons entitled to the property on her death, shall thereupon succeed to the same."

On a proper analysis of the aforesaid sections, it is clear that it deals with four types of properties *viz.*—

(*a*) Property held by way of maintenance,

(*b*) Property held by inheritance to her husband,

(*c*) Property held by inheritance to husband's lineal successors, and

(*d*) Property held by virtue of a Will or testamentary disposition conferring upon her without express permission to remarry only limited interest in such property.

It is submitted that the language used does not permit reading the words "conferring upon... in such property" as qualifying all the above classes of property *i.e.* (*a*), (*b*), (*c*), and (*d*). These words qualify only the last category of property, namely (*d*). Reading the section in this manner, it seems that there is no conflict between Section 24 and Section 14 of the Hindu Succession Act on the one hand, and Section 2 of the 1856 Act on the other.

In the Rajasthan case, it was pointed out that if the above was the intention, then Section 24 would have been differently worded. It seems to me that the contrary reasoning would be correct. Section 24 is worded in its present form because it would have been a superfluity to refer to the result of forfeiture on remarriage of a Hindu widow when the legislature thought of leaving Section 2 of the Act of 1856, untouched.

It is because of this reason that no reference to remarriage of a widow resulting in forfeiture of the property on her remarriage has been repeated in Section 24.

But the above view is meant only to set the legal profession a thinking about the controversy and is not meant to be a final word about it.

RIGHT TO PROPERTY, WIDOW REMARRIAGE, MERRAIH AND INFANTICIDE BY LORD DALHOUSIE IN INDIA

Within Lord Dalhousie, one finds a die-hard imperialist as well as progressive reformer. If he is criticized for aggressive policy of imperial expansion; he is also commended for his progressive attitude by bringing a series of socio-cultural reforms. He is the one among pioneers who modernized India. Introduction of railways, posts and telegraphs, spread of modern education, legislation for widow remarriage *etc.* were some of the memorable steps taken by him. For Indians, he is still a love-hate man.

His reforms in the fields of transport and communication have already been discussed earlier under this chapter. Introduction of rail ways, renovation of existing roads, creation of Public Works Department *etc.* are the carrier of modernism in India. Establishment of the network of communication through electric telegraph, and postal system are the milestone of his reformative zeal. He contributed greatly by preparing the Indians to march for modern age.

His educational reforms are the bright examples in this regard and those are discussed in the following pages under this chapter. He stands among the champions of new age in India.

At times it appears that he was worthy successor of Lord William Bentinck. He carried social reforms from where Bentinck left. He was the Governor General of Indian from 1848 to 1856. During his tenure as the Governor General he took some bold steps to uplift the status of women to settle the issue of inheriting property *etc.*

RIGHT TO PROPERTY:

By this time, there were debates and controversies over the law of inheritance. Law of inheritance was strict one and Hindus, who were converted into Christians, were deprived of the rights of ancestral properties.

The converts were considered as the social out-cast. On this issue, there were instances of social tension and very often religions were dragged into controversies. Dalhousie took a historic step by promulgating the law in 1850. By this law, one can not be deprived of the rights to inherit ancestral properties if converted into Christianity.

Their claim over ancestral property was protected by this law. No doubt, this law created reactions in the Hindu society. However, this law is criticized as an instrument to protect interests of the Christians and to encourage conversion into Christianity. But the law appears to Bengal noble one to protect the rights of man from a different angle.

WIDOW REMARRIAGE:

Bentinck abolished the Sati system and that was not enough to protect the widows from torture and atrocity. Lot more was needed to ameliorate the distress of the widows. As discussed earlier, the widows continued to live a deplorable life as the most unwanted member of the family and society.

A widow did not have right over the property of her deceased husband. In the meantime, intellects like Iswar Chandra Vidyasagar waged a long struggle against the child marriage and for widow remarriage. Dalhousie took the clue from the need of the time and, passed "Widow Remarriage Act" in 1856.This Act enabled the Hindu widows to remarry and widows inherited the share from husbands' property.

Though the effects of this act were negligible, it provided the foundation for all future reforms in this direction. The first lawful Hindu widow remarriage was celebrated in Calcutta in December 1856. If Vidyasagar is revered as the emancipator of the widows, Dalhousie is remembered for the historic law.

MERRAIH AND INFANTICIDE:

The laws introduced by Bentinck for prohibition of infanticide acted slowly. Dalhousie enforced the laws with rigours to check the barbarous practice. However, abolition of human sacrifice or 'Merriah' system was a great leap in the direction of social change. In the hilly tracts of Orissa and Madhya Pradesh the tribal offered human sacrifice in the fields of turmeric *etc.* with the belief of increasing fertility of the soil.

The human to be offered as sacrifice is called "Merriah". Earlier Bentinck had taken the first step to prohibit the practice and it had little impact on the tribals. But Dalhousie ordered to stop this system in to. Under his directives, Campbell conducted rescue operations in tribal areas like Ghumsur, Baud, Ganjam, Udaygiri *etc.* and saved the lives of a number of merriahs.

Even persons either practicing or encouraging the Mariah system were punished severely. Thus, the bold step of Dalhousie changed the life style of the tribal. All apart, Dalhousie had the desire to bring intellectual change among the Indians.

He wanted the Indians to respond to the changes positively. Therefore, he thought Western education and English language as the medium to educate the people. For this vernacular education was promoted, English education encouraged, universities established, and a series of recommendations put forth in the form of "Wood's Despatch,"In short, Bentinck dawned a new era and Dalhousie saw it full grown.

SOCIAL REFORM MOVEMENT IN INDIA AND ROLE OF WOMEN!

There are two distinct groups of progressive movements aimed at emancipation of Indian women. Both groups recognised the restrictive and coercive nature of the social customs and institutions. One group opposed these customs and institutions as they contradicted the democratic principles of liberty and freedom. This group was called the Reformers.

The other group demanded the democratisation of social relations and removal of harm-ful practices on the basis of revival of the Vedic society in modern India, which according to them, was democratic. This group came to be known as the Revivalists.

The social reformers believed in the principle of individual liberty, freedom, and equality of all human beings irrespective of sex, colour, race, caste, or religion. They attacked a number of traditional, authoritarian, and hierarchical social institutions and launched social reform movements to liberate the Indian women from their shack-les. Though many of the reformers were mainly men, the reform movement aimed at improving the status of Indian women.

Raja Ram Mohan Roy was one of the greatest social reformers of India. He was con-cerned about a number of evil customs planning the Indian society. These included "saha marana" or Sati, female infanticide, polygamy, infant marriages, purdah, absence of educa-tion among women, and the Devadasi system. Raja Ram Mohan Roy led a crusade against the evil and inhuman practice of Sati, in which a widow was forced to immolate herself on the funeral pyre of her deceased husband. Sati was in practice in many parts of India.

It was accepted and condoned on the grounds that it would secure "Moksha" for widows. It was also felt that a woman could be led astray if she continued to live after the death of her hus-band. This feeling was disproved by Raja, who felt that a woman could be led astray even during her husband's lifetime.

In fact, after the death of her husband, a woman is under the protection of her family, so she can be watched over with greater vigilance. Raja strongly refuted the contention that Sati was a free, voluntary act of the widow, and called it a mon-strous lie. Raja's arguments and anti-Sati activities led Lord William Bentinck to legislate for the prohibition of Sati, which resulted in the passing of the Prohibition of Sati Act in 1829.

Ishwar Chandra Vidyasagar was another great social reformer who sought to improve the condition of widows by legalizing widow remarriages. Since he felt that his own life should set an example for others to follow, he took a pledge that he would allow his daughters to study, and married all his daughters after they were 16 years of age. He also pledged that if any of his daughters were widowed and they wanted to get remarried, he would allow them to do so. He was also against the prevalent custom of polygamy.

Justice Mahadev Govind Ranade was instrumental in laying down the foundation of an all Indian organisation to carry on the struggle for social reform—the Indian National Social Conference. This organisation was the first national institution to carry on collectively, in an organised way, and on a national scale the social reform movement.

He took up the problems of widow remarriages and was an active member of a society, which worked for widow remarriages. In fact, the Shankaracharya had excommunicated him for attending the first widow remarriage in 1869. Ranade worked towards educating women. He and his wife started a school for girls in 1884.

Maharishi Karve showed great concern for the plight of widows and the problem of widow remarriages. He revived the Widow Remarriage Association and started the Hindu Widow's Home Karve also made efforts to improve the education levels of girls as well as widows.

He created the Kane Women's University. His efforts in the movement to liberate the Indian women are of great significance, and the extensive and successful work brought about a change in the attitudes of people towards widows.

In order to set an example for others, he married a widow after the death of his first wife. As a result of the social reform movement, a number of institutions and organisations were established. The institutions started by the reformers covered the whole country with their activities.

The institutions established during this period are as follows:

THE GUJARAT VERNACULAR SOCIETY:

This social institute was established in 1848. The aim of this institute was to decrease the large-scale illiteracy and superstitious beliefs that was a feature of the Gujarati society. It was associated with all social reform activities concerning women in Gujarat.

The society worked for the cause of women through edu-cation. It started a number of co-educational schools. It published literature on women's issues in the vernacular press. It tried to organise elocution competitions and provide a platform for women to talk about their issues and problems.

The Deccan Education Society:

This society was formed in 1884. The society started girls' schools and encouraged education of women in Maharashtra.

The Ramakrishna Mission:

The Ramakrishna Mission was established in 1897. It set up homes for widows and schools for girls. It also gave refuge to invalid and destitute women, ante- and post-natal care for women, and provided training for women to become midwives.

The Arya Samaj:

Though started as a revivalist organisation, the Arya Samaj emphasized women's education. Girls received instructions in home science and domestic affairs. Fine arts were also included in the curriculum for girls. It also included instructions in religion and religious ceremonies for women. It provided shelter to distressed women in times of difficulty.

The Hingne Women's Education Institute:

This institute was started in 1896 to meet the demand of women, whether married, unmarried or widowed. By imparting training to young unmarried girls in various fields, it tried to prevent early marriages. It tried to impart skills and education to married women to enable them to carry on domestic life efficiently and economically. It also gave training to widows to make them economically independent.

S.N.D.T. Women's University:

This university was established to meet the needs for higher education for women in such a manner that women's requirements were satis-fied. It provided education in the mother tongue. It was established exclusively for the education of women.

The Seva Sadan:

Seva Sadan was started in 1908, with a view to bringing together enlightened women of different communities who desired to work for the upliftment of backward women. Its main activity was to provide social and medical aid to women and children of the poor classes, irrespective of their caste or creed. It also established a home for destitute and distressed women and children.

It also provided training to poor women in domestic crafts to enable them to earn a livelihood. The Seva Sadan in Poona was established to educate women in religious, literary, medical, and industrial subjects. It also emphasized on all-round development of a woman's personality. It stressed on economic self-sufficiency of women.

The Indian National Social Conference:

Some of the activities taken up by this organi-sation were—to deal with disabilities of child marriages, sale of young girls, the practice of polygamy, and the issue of widow remarriages. It also took up the problem of access to education for women.

All India Women's Conference:

The primary focus of this organisation was women's edu-cation as well as social reforms. Its aim was to work actively for the general progress and welfare of women and children. It passed various resolutions in different sessions in order to elevate the status of women.

It also dealt with the evils of early marriages, polygamy, and prohibition of divorce. It advocated complete equality for women in property matters. It sought to improve working conditions for women. It also agitated against immoral traffic in women and children, and against the inhuman custom of Devadas.

WIDOW REMARRIAGE:

The Brahmo Samaj had the issue of widow remarriage high on its agenda and did much to popularise it. But it was mainly due to the efforts of Pandit Ishwar Chandra Vidyasagar (1820-91), the principal of Sans-krit College, Calcutta that the Hindu Widows' Remarriage Act, 1856, which legalised marriage of widows and declared issues from such marriages as legitimate, was passed by the Government. Vidyasagar cited Vedic texts to prove that the Hindu religion sanctioned widow remarriage.

Jagannath Shankar Seth and Bhau Daji were among the active promoters of girls' schools in Maharashtra. Vishnu Shastri Pandit founded the Widow Remarriage Association in the 1850s. Another prominent worker in this field was Karsondas Mulji who started the Satya Prakash in Gujarati in 1852 to advocate widow remarriage.

Similar efforts were made by Professor D.K. Karve in western India and by Veerasalingam Pantulu in Madras. Karve himself married a widow in 1893. He dedicated his life to the upliftment of Hindu widows and became the secretary of the Widow Remarriage Association.

He opened a widows' home in Poona to give the high caste widows an interest in life by providing them with facilities for vocational training. He crowned his work by setting up an Indian Women's University at Bombay in 1916. The right of widows to remarriage was also advocated by B.M. Malabari, Narmad, Justice Govind Mahadeo Ranade and K. Natarajan among others.

WIDOW REMARRIAGE IN INDIA

In Ancient Hindu Society widow re-marriage was considered as a sin because a widow was expected to mourn the death of her husband throughout her life. On the other hand, a widower; a man who has lost his wife was expected to marry again. Hindu society by all means maintained double standards when it came to justifying the rights of a man and a woman.

The case was such that a widow was not only expected to lead a single life, but she was also expected to eat simple food that was devoid of all spices. It was only after the accession of the British Raj in India that widow remarriage came into existence.

Why a woman should be derived of the right to remarry when a man was allowed to do the same?

In some cases a 60 year old man married a 13 or 14 year old girl, in such a case it is but obvious that the girl will turn out to be a widow sooner or later. Widow re-marriage is essential because men and women both are equal to each other in each and every field and most importantly, a woman is as much entitled to happiness as a man is. She also needs a partner who supports her through the ups and downs in life. Staying happy is the birth right of each and every citizen and women are no exception. But the happiest change that has occurred in this 21st century India is that not only is widow re-marriage legal but Indians in general today support the institution of widow re-marriage.

This change is largely the result of Westernization and advancement in the field of education. Any educated individual today does not believe in blind faith and superstitions as a result of which, India as a nation is progressing vehemently.

In most of the cases, widows are not considered as a menace to the society as a matter of fact; men today whole heartedly accept a widow as their wife and understand the fact that even she is entitled to all the happiness in the world.

But still a section of orthodox citizens prevail in the societies who are strictly against the custom of a widow marrying again.

Before raising fingers to other women in the society these men should think that how they would feel and react if something similar happened to their own daughter. Most of the men who are asked such a question remain speechless. Their speechlessness prove a fact, it is easy to point a finger at someone else but when it comes to one's own self, the difficulty is hard to digest. Whatever this orthodox section of the society may think, one thing is for sure; modern India gives a widow the same status as it gives to any other woman and this is a matter of pride for all the citizens.

WIDOW REMARRIAGE TO DEVAR (HUSBAND'S BROTHER)

According to the figures available with her Ministry, there are 33 million widows in the country. As per the 1991 census, widows account for 9 per cent of the female population and only 40 per cent of them are over 50 years of age.

In ancient Indian literature, one can find several references of widow marriage. During the Vedic age, widow marriages were allowed among all the castes. According to Narad Purana, there exist three forms of widow marriages, which are as follows:

For a married woman, who fulfilled the rituals of marriage, but did not live with her husband for a single day.

For a woman who after leaving her first husband, comes back to him after parting with her second husband For a woman, who has been given to any sapinda after her husband expires. Rig-veda prescribes that the widow should give up thinking of her late husband and should accept the marriage proposal of the person who wants to marry her.

The tradition of a widow marrying the brother-in-law of the expired husband is very common. When the dead body of the late husband, is about to be cremated, the dead man's brother take the widow in his custody and marry her soon after. This principal is fully supported in the Yaska's Nirukta. "Arise, woman, than art lying by one, whose life is gone, come to the world of the living, away from the husband, and become the wife of him, who grasps thy hand, woos thee as a lover'", is quoted in the Hindu Vedic texts.

Vashishtha and Kautilya in Arthashastra have allowed widow marriage. During the Epic era, the marriage of widows was not restricted. According to Manu Smriti, the women who do not experience sexual intercourse with their first husband can remarry. During the middle ages, Chandragupta Vikramaditya married the wife of his dead brother. However, Vashishta and Prashar Smriti are far more liberal in their approach, they believe that if their husband dies, disappears, becomes a saint, is impotent or becomes penniless, the wife can remarry".

From the beginning of 10th to 11th century AD, widow marriages were not encouraged and they were universally prohibited. The sati custom sustained and the condition of the widows in the Hindu society became terrible. Hard line widowhood led to illegitimate sexual relations, kidnapping, prostitution and illicit children. Thus, no woman should be enforced to lead a life of widowhood against her wishes.

Every woman wishes to be a mother and therefore child widows and widows without children should be encouraged to remarry. From the humanitarian point of view, for womanhood, the mass should be compassionate about the widows. They too are allowed to lead a happy and complete life. For the freedom of child widows and as a check on immorality widows the government became aware and initiated them to remarry.

The Hindu Widow Remarriage Act of 1856 legalized validity of widow's remarriage. Moreover, Hindu Succession Act, 1956 and Hindu Marriage Act, 1955, also features provisions of remarriage of the widows.

DIVORCE, WIDOW REMARRIAGE ALLOWED BY VEDIC HINDUISM

The Eight Types of Marriages ,Vivaha.

1. Brahma Vivaah:Brahma vivah is considered the best marriage. In this the boy and girl belonging to good families and the same varna get married. The boy should have completed his Brahmacharya Ashram (studenthood). There is no dowry involved and the girl enters the boy's house with two sets of clothes and some ornaments. In this marriage, the boy's family approaches the girl's family. "Kanyadaan", which is the handing of the bride by her father to the groom, is an important ritual of the Brahma Vivah..
2. Prajapatya Vivaah: This type of marriage is the same as the Brahma vivaah in all respects, except that the bride's father gives her away as a gift, not to the groom, but to the groom's father. This type of marriage is resorted to when the groom and bride are both very young. Thus, the protection of the bride or daughter is handed over by her father to the groom's father during the *Panigrahan* (hand-receiving) ceremony. The wedding ceremony involving the young bride and groom may take place immediately afterwards, but the

wedding may not be consummated for several years, until the bride and groom are old enough.

3. Daiva Vivaah: In this type of wedding, there are no feasts or celebrations that are specific to the wedding, but the wedding of the daughter of a poor family is held as an act of charity by wealthy people. It was customary for kings, landlords and rich merchants to hold religious ceremonies and sacrifices where many gifts would be given and charities performed for the benefit of learned Brahmins and the poor. During these great events, a poor man would sometimes approach the wealthy host and seek the charity that his daughter's wedding be performed at this time. This type of marriage may take place if the girl's parents are unable to locate a suitable groom within a reasonable period (several years) after the girl has attained puberty. Often, the reason for this would be that the parents of the bride cannot afford the expense of their daughter's marriage. It was considered improper or unsafe to keep a girl unwed past her teens, and anyway the chances of an aging girl getting a good husband were not better than the same girl getting a good husband at a younger age. So the girl would be bedecked with flowers and whatever small ornaments the parents could provide and taken to the venue of the religious ceremony or sacrifice being performed by a rich magnate. She would be offered in marriage to any willing man and generally this would be one of the priests, young or old. The wedding ceremony would be performed in short order and the feasts which were anyway being hosted as part of the festivities would suffice for this extra wedding also. According to the Dharmashastra, Daiva marriage is considered avoidable but is still respectable since poverty is not culpable; lack of virtue is reprehensible but honest poverty is acceptable.
4. Arsha Vivaah: In this type of marriage, the family of the groom pays *kanya-shulkam* or bride-price to the parents of the bride. According to certain texts, the prescribed bride-price is a cow with a calf and a pair of bulls. The sacred texts provide various lists of specific communities where this custom prevailed and imply that it is unfitting in general society. However, several instances are found in the puranas of marriage between a man from mainstream communities and a woman from one of the bride-price seeking communities (Pandu-Madri; Dasharatha-Kaikeyi, *etc.*). In nearly all cases, the man willingly pays the bride-price and brings his bride home. Also in nearly all these cases, the woman thus obtained comes to dominate her husband and causes havoc and ruin in his family.
5. Asura Vivaah: In the Asura type of marriage the groom is not at all suitable for the bride. In no way is he a match for the girl but he

willingly gives as much wealth as he can afford to the bride's parents and relatives. In Arsha type cows are given in exchange for the bride but there is no such limitation in the Asura type of marriage. Generally the groom is of lower social rank or caste than the bride. This type of marriage is highly disfavored.

6. Gandharva Vivaah: When a man and a woman marry for love and without the consent of their families, that marriage is called Gandharva Vivaah or 'love marriage.' This type of marriage is considered impious and degrading because it is motivated by lust. In Hinduism, a man is supposed to marry a woman who will aid him in performing his duties towards his parents, clan and society, and to have sons to perpetuate his lineage. Love marriages are seen as taking a man away from all these duties and making him besotted to a beautiful, lustful woman, mindful only of his own selfish pleasures and unmindful of his duties. Hence this form of marriage is reprobated.
7. Rakshasa Vivaah: This is essentially marriage by abduction. In cases where the girl is willing to marry the boy but her family is against the alliance, the girl may be abducted and married. It is essential that the girl be willing, because otherwise, the *puranas* and *shastras* simply treat the incident of abduction as rape, with consequent vengeance and retribution. Instances of such marriages include Krishna-Rukmini and Arjuna-Subhadra, in all of which cases the girl was willing and the results were good.
8. Paishacha Vivaah: In the case where the bride is intoxicated, possessed or not in a conscious state of mind when being married and thus is married unwillingly, is an example Paishacha vivaah, and which has been outlawed by Manu.

Of these eight, in the first Two Case, Brahmana Vivaha and Prajapati Vivaha, Divorce and Remarriage and Widow Remarriage were not allowed.

This is because of the elevated status these two groups, which perform these types of Marriages belong to.

Normally these were performed by the Brahmana, Kshatriya and Vaisya Communities. What is important to note is that the 'Caste' is determined based on wedlock and Wedlock is not determined by the caste, in the sense that those who marry other than these two types of Marriages no longer belong to the Group and are not constrained by their original groups laws.

An example is the marriage of Asura Guru,Sukra's daughter's marriage.

Sukracharya, a Brahmin was the Guru of Asuras.

His duty was to get his daughter married in the style of Brahmana Vivaha.

Since it he did not do it, for no fault of his, he separated himself from his daughter, who later married a King. In these cases, the Laws of Manu ,proscribing remarriage or Divorce do not apply. The Laws of Manu forbidding

Remarriage and Divorce are related to the two types of marriages and not to other Varnas. In all the other six cases, laws of Manu do not apply and there is no bar for remarriage. As has been the vein of Sanatana Dharama, stricter laws are applied to Barhmains, Kshatriyas ans Vaishyas.

Therefore Divorce and Remarriages were allowed except in the case of the Brahmanas ,Kshtriyas and Vishyas, In case people from these groups decide to marry in a form other than what is prescribed, Namely Brahman Vivaha and Prajapati Vivaha, tey acn, but they are no longer controlled by the laws that were applicable to them earlier. The which group do they belong to and what rules should they follow? This will be dealt with separately in another post, where I will be discussing how many so-called caste groups came into being.

WIDOWHOOD AND REMARRIAGE

Before beginning the analysis, it is useful to explore the broad patterns relating to widowhood and remarriage across various groups. To do so, we make use of data from the 1998–99 National Family Health Survey (NFHS),a nationally representative survey of 90,303 ever-married women aged fteen to forty-nine (which can be weighted to generate sta-tistics representative at the state and national levels). The survey collects data on a range of demographic, social, and (to a lesser extent) economic variables for the household and its various members, as well as a village-level survey with information on agricultural, economic, and social condi-tions and infrastructure. These data do not contain a great deal of detail on elderly persons, but data from the household roster can be used to describe the patterns of widowhood.

At all ages the incidence is much higher for women than men. About 40 percent of women aged sixty are widowed compared to 12 percent of men, and the gap grows to 69 and 19 by age sev-enty. The large disparity at each age is the result of the large average hus-band-wife age gap (six years) and the greater incidence of remarriage among men.Despite popular perception, remarriage is not prohibited by any caste or religious group in India. Unfortunately, the NFHS only collects more information on marital histories for female re-spondents aged fteen to forty-nine, including whether they have had a previous marriage (but not separately indicating whether the rst marriage ended due to marriage or divorce).We focus on women aged forty-ve to forty-nine, to capture the oldest population available. The incidence of widowhood and remarriage, disaggregated by re-ligious and caste groupings. The data reveal that 15 percent of women of this age have ever been widowed or divorced, and 11 percent of ever-widowed/ divorced women are currently married. The greatest incidence of ever-widowhood is among women of scheduled tribes, at nearly one in ve.

Reecting underlying economic dierentials, there is a gradient by caste, with the higher (forward) castes having only two-thirds the widow rate of the scheduled tribes. However, the rate of remarriage is signicantly higher for the scheduled tribes, at nearly three times the rate among the higher castes, and almost twice that of scheduled castes and other backward castes (OBCs). Thus, in terms of current widowhood, there is not a signi-cant gradient by caste. Muslims and Christians have similar widowhood and remarriage rates as the scheduled tribes.

For Hindus, within castes,two general factors are thought to aect the likelihood of remarriage. First, the likelihood of remarriage (and social ap-proval of remarriage) declines with age, and becomes extremely rare after age forty. An additional important factor is whether the woman has had any children, in particular sons, in her rst marriage. In general, even con-trolling for age, those who have no children and especially no sons will be more likely to remarry. This distinction is motivated in part by choice (for example, a woman may fear a new husband would treat her children poorly, or she may feel less of a need to remarry because the son can help support her) and in part by constraint (no one will remarry a widow with children, or society may not condone it). The NFHS data reveal that con-ditional on having been ever widowed or divorced, having had a child from the rst husband decreases the likelihood of remarriage by about 43 per-cent, and conditional on having had a child, women with at least one son are 23 percent less likely to remarry than women with only daughters.

SOCIOECONOMIC STATUS, CASTE, AND WELL-BEING

Given the widespread incidence of widowhood, especially among older women, it is important to examine the well-being of widows. Unfortu-nately, the NFHS provides only very limited data on SES; while there is some information on employment status and assets owned, there is no in-formation on income or expenditure. Further, even if household income were available, the measurement of poverty among the elderly is very sen-sitive to assumptions on economies and scale and costs of children, as well as assumptions on the intrahousehold allocation of resources.

However, as an initial investigation, the NFHS data do provide information on whether individuals work, either outside the household for pay or in self-employment. The informa-tion on female employment for both widows and nonwidows aged forty-ve to forty-nine, with a distinction drawn between land-owning and land-less households. Female employment rates among nonwidows are low overall, at 20 percent among those owning land and 40 percent among the landless. In general, employment rates are higher among the scheduled tribes and castes relative to the OBCs and forward castes (even though land ownership is highest among the scheduled tribes).

For all castes and reli gious groups, employment rates are higher among women currently wid-owed, for both landed and landless households. Over one-half of widowed scheduled tribe women work, compared to only one-third among the for-ward castes (though, in percentage terms, the dierence between nonwidows and widows is greater for the forward castes). Of course, selection into widowhood is nonrandom, and that selection may dier across these groups, and we don't have panel data to examine the prewidow employ-ment rates of current widows. Therefore, these results should only be seen as descriptive and suggestive.

For a more in-depth investigation of the relationship between caste and well-being, we apply data from the Survey of Aging in Rural India (SARI), a survey of 1,477 households, each containing a person aged fty or older, conducted by the author in 2002 in ve states or Union Territories (Delhi, Jharkhand, Haryana, Kerala, and Tamil Nadu). Several sections of this survey were modeled to be compatible with other demographic surveys for India, including the NFHS. The survey collected information on a range of (current and past) demographic, health, social, and economic variables. In addition, a village-level survey was conducted in each sample cluster, gath-ering information on economic and social conditions and infrastructure, as well as the prevailing customs and norms relating to the elderly.

However, as mentioned above, such data are not entirely indicative of the consumption or well-being of individuals within households. Instead, we explore a reduced-form measure of consumption and nutritional status by examining the body mass index (BMI), constructed from physical mea-surements conducted for all respondents in the survey. BMI across caste groups. Focusing rst on nonwidows, there is a clear gradient in BMI by caste that mirrors that of expenditure per capita, with the scheduled tribes or castes having the lowest BMI and the forward castes having the highest (approximately 10 percent higher than the scheduled tribes).

However, comparing widows and nonwidows within each caste group reveals interesting dierences. In particular, for the scheduled tribes and castes, widows are no worse o in terms of BMI than nonwidows. However, there are large dierences be-tween widows and nonwidows for OBCs and especially the forward castes. While forward-caste widows still have a slightly higher BMI than widows in the scheduled tribes, they no longer dier from the scheduled castes or OBCs. There is no longer any discernible gradient with caste, and in fact none of the across-caste group dierences in BMI are statistically signicant. In part, this lack of a gradient likely reects the fact that there are stronger restrictions on employment among forward-caste women, as sug-gested, and may also indicate that widows in forward-caste households are not given as large a share of total household consumption as they are in lower-caste households. Thus, wealthier, upper-caste widows are no better o in terms of nutritional status than poorer but more equally treated lower-caste widows. Of course, the possibility of dierential selec-tion into widowhood across these groups cannot be ruled out.

RIGHTS AT DISSOLUTION OF MARRIAGE RIGHTS AT DISSOLUTION OF MARRIAGE

Marriages can end in two ways, either by death or divorce. We have chosen to discuss these topics separately since widowhood is more than just a dissolution of marriage, however, the rights at stake for widows and divorcees are similar. Whether the marriage comes to an end because of an action taken by or defended by the woman, resulting in divorce or if it is because of the death of the spouse, where the woman had no part to play, the effects on the woman are not very different. In either case, the woman is single and this status bears its own stigma. Therefore, this chapter contains two sections. As suggested, discuss divorce first since it is more directly related to dissolution.

DIVORCE

Divorce is an initiated action, wherein either the husband or the wife makes a conscious decision to end the marriage. There are many critical issues that are central to the decision and many issues that are to be considered before divorce is initiated. These issues are influenced by the woman's access to finance and the children. As in all other areas, the rights for women are not on par with the rights accorded to men. The personal laws differentiate between the rights enjoyed by women on the basis of the community they belong to. It is critical to examine the status of women in the context of these laws that limit their rights and their access to them.

EVIDENCE OF DISADVANTAGE

India follows a plural system of law and the various religious communities follow their own laws for all matters placed in the 'personal' sphere. The majority of the rights placed in this sphere are related to rights within the family. Access to and exercise of rights in this sphere is important for the empowerment of women. The most critical rights being:

- Right to Divorce,
- Right to Maintenance
- Right to Matrimonial Property
- Right to Custody and Guardianship.

These rights assume greater importance if she has to break a marital relationship while being concerned about her ability to earn and her ability to see or be with her children. These issues are important to a woman, regardless of her religion or community. However, her rights are decided on the basis of her identity as a member of her community.

CONTRIBUTORY FACTORS

The personal laws governing the different communities have provisions for initiation of divorce proceedings by women. However, the related rights of guardianship and custody, of maintenance and control of property, which are critical for a woman to be able to divorce, act as barriers as they are in favour of the husband. Social attitudes and absence of support systems further limit a woman's options to exercise her right to divorce. Placing family law in a religious context allows the state to absolve itself of liability with reference to the rights of women in minority communities.

Arbitrary usage of 'religious sentiment' as opposed to 'human rights' in the context of women has repeatedly served the state to garner electoral benefits with little concern for women as citizens. The plurality of personal laws add to the complexity of the situation, as the provisions for access to the same right differs, being based on the religion of the woman. Like divorce, maintenance is also granted under the different personal laws. The disparity in the laws for the different communities adversely affects the rights of women. For example, the maintenance a Hindu wife is entitled to during a matrimonial proceeding has no ceiling and can be granted at the discretion of the judge, based on the husband's earnings, a Christian woman was not entitled to more than one-fifth of her husbands income. This ceiling has now been removed by the amendment act of 2001. Under the Muslim law there is no provision for maintenance after divorce.

After the Shah Bano case and the passing of the Muslim Women's Act of 1986, Muslim women were denied access to maintenance even under the Criminal Procedure Code. This has been set right to a certain extent by the Supreme Courts interpretation of the Act in a recent case. However, her ability to access and enforce this right is made difficult because of the law's mandate of compromise and settlement. Petitions for maintenance under Section 125 of the Criminal Procedure Code accounted for 51 per cent of the cases filed but only 18 per cent of these petitions were ordered, as compared to 27 per cent of the divorce petitions. Miscellaneous petitions connected to the original suit, accounted for 6 per cent of the cases, of these only 13 per cent were decided. These miscellaneous applications, for the most part, would be applications for interim maintenance.

There seems to be an obvious reluctance on the part of the court to decide issues related to maintenance, which for women litigants is the most critical issue. The whole idea of divorce runs contrary to the idea of chastity, as understood and propounded by the Brahminical order, which has appropriated the right to accord values to practices. Traditionally the practice of divorce was prevalent amongst castes falling out of the "Varna"order but after the passing of The Hindu marriage Act in 1955 it was a right given to all Hindu women. In a society where sati is the ultimate model of a good wife, divorce presents the very anti-thesis of the concept of the good woman. The value attached to tolerating a bad husband and continuing in an oppressive relationship is accepted and justified on the basis of a woman's duty towards her husband. The Personal Laws of all religions make provisions for divorce, however the stigmatisation of the single woman by society contributes to her inability to access divorce. This stigma affects not only her as an individual but also mark her children and her natal family, affecting the chances of marriage of unmarried sisters. These disadvantages are in addition to the major problems of finding a job, access to legal procedures, financial security, housing and safety from sexual harassment as a single woman. Religion becomes a contributory factor to prevent women from accessing divorce. All religions forward the concept of the need to keep the family unit intact and this duty is placed on women.

Religious teachings then accord negative values to divorce, putting single women at a disadvantage for social and religious functions. For example, among Hindus, women who do not have husbands cannot carry out many religious rituals and divorced women are treated on par with widows. The demand of Shah Bano for maintenance, which sparked off a national controversy, was opposed by the community on the grounds of identity and interference with the personal laws of the community, which had no provision for maintenance after divorce. Shah Bano herself was under tremendous pressure and despite a positive order from the Supreme Court, never executed it. Religion and the community put the pressure on women not to access their rights.

SOCIALISATION

In the given social milieu, a divorced woman is seen as a single woman. This single status is stigmatised. The factors in that influence culture and tradition and prevent divorce are essentially the same as those that influence her choices, in the process of socialisation. Lack of support systems and economic resources, which keep women in abusive relationships, also keeps them from exercising their option to divorce. The concept of divorce, unknown under ancient Hindu law was introduced into the community under the Hindu Marriage Act, 1955.

The rising graph of divorce led to the passing of the Family Courts Act, 1984 and the setting up of Family Courts in many cities, focusing on litigation involving divorce, maintenance and custody. The underlying thrust of the Act is to keep the family intact. The government has also set-up Family Counseling Centers, other than those found in the Family Courts and Police Stations. These Centers also work on the same lines of preserving the family. When preservation of the marriage takes top priority and the cases are long drawn out, granting of interim maintenance is not taken up as a priority even though it is of utmost importance to the woman who is forced out of the marital home. A sample from the Lucknow Family Court illustrates the inordinate time taken for the disposal of cases.

At the beginning of February 2001 there were 2483 old cases pending, 24 fresh cases were filed and 53 cases were transferred from other courts, of these only 114 cases were heard and decreed, leaving 2476 cases pending in the court.

Another example is the Family Counselling Centre attached to the court. Of the 2561 cases brought to the FCC between November 1995 and October 1997, a total of 808 were resolved and 1753 were sent back to the courts, as a compromise could not be affected. This means 32 per cent of the cases were resolved while 68 per cent had to be referred back to the Family Court as the FCC was unable to resolve the differences between the parties, adding to the delay in legal procedures. Further, the only agenda of these counselling centres is to keep the family unit intact and enormous pressure is put on the woman to reconcile, without going into the root cause of her problems. The laws governing divorce and its related issues of maintenance and custody contribute to keeping a woman in an abusive situation.

The disparity in the grounds of divorce under the different personal laws leave women of some communities without proper recourse to end a marriage which is abusive. Further, the thought of losing children, even though by precedent the courts do not adhere to statute but looks into what would be best for the welfare of the minor, prevents an abused woman from accessing her right through the court. As stated earlier, long drawn out court procedures not only deprive her of maintenance but also drain her limited finances. Except for a section under the Hindu law, Parsee law, Indian Divorce Act and the Special Marriage Act for divorce by mutual consent, all other grounds are fault grounds. Introduction of irretrievable break down of marriage, as a ground for divorce would go a long way in shortening legal procedures. The Declaration of the Government of India to Article 16 (1) of the CEDAW Convention is on the basis of non-interference with the personal laws of minority communities. As this has no bearing on The Hindu Code and The Special Marriage Act, the provisions of these laws could address the question of discrimination against Hindu women, which the State has failed to do.

Further, the Declaration with reference to Article 16(2) results in the failure to take proactive steps to make the registration of Hindu marriages compulsory. This affects women who have to approach the courts for redressal of matrimonial rights, as the factum of marriage has to be proved before these rights can be enforced. When illiterate Muslim and Christian women have documents to prove their marriage, the stand of the Government that the customs, religions and level of literacy prevent compulsory registration of marriages cannot be accepted.

EFFECTS ON WOMEN

Looking at the disposal of cases there has been a reversal in the figures, with a decrease in the number of divorces granted and an increase in cases were compromises have been affected. This is in keeping with the basic premise of the Family Courts Act, to effect reconciliation and keep the family unit intact. Another reason for this shift is the tendency of the men to file a petition for restitution of conjugal rights when a woman seeks maintenance. If the husband's petition is ordered, the wife is denied maintenance on the ground that she has deserted the matrimonial home without just cause or reason. Given the existing disadvantages faced by women, the issue of economic justice is critical to them when exercising their right to divorce.

The provisions of law pertaining to grant of maintenance and the way that they are implemented, the denial of a share in matrimonial assets and property widens the economical disparity between men and women. The Marriage Laws Amendment Acts of 2001 has made some space for women by incorporating provisions for passing interim orders of maintenance within 60 days. A small survey of the Lucknow Family Counselling Centre indicates a procedure whereby the courts try to effect reconciliation rather than grant divorce. The law provides for monthly maintenance but during the conciliation proceedings many women opt for a lump sum payment.

This protects them from having to take out execution proceedings in the event of the husband defaulting in payment of monthly maintenance. The Below Poverty Line mark in the country is set at ₹1000/- family per month. If we take this as the base for our calculations, the amount sanctioned would last from 9 to 25 months. Another area that is crucial to women when they decide to separate or dissolve the marriage is the question of custody of children. The Courts have repeatedly held that the welfare of the minor is of paramount interest. It has also been held that "a father's natural right must give way where the minor's welfare demands otherwise". It is therefore relevant to examine the statutory position. The personal laws for all communities lay down that the father is the natural guardian of a minor child.

In a recent case, a mother was unable to acquire relief bonds from the Reserve Bank of India for her child on her own initiative. When the matter was taken to the Supreme Court, it held that the mother could act as the natural guardian. The court reinterpreted the existing provisions to mean that the inability or unwillingness of the father to fulfill all the obligations of a natural guardian would construe his absence and the mother was entitled to be the guardian of the child. The position of the mother as the guardian, after the father, is statutory. The judgement has not considered the inherent discrimination in the law, which does not recognise joint guardianship but grants natural guardianship to the father and after him to the mother.

This places the mother at a distinct disadvantage as she has to engage with the complex process of the legal system to get a judicial order appointing her as the guardian, if the father is alive. The man suffers no such handicap leading to the state and private institutions recognising the father as the sole guardian. Custody is a right that is distinct from guardianship. The following chart brings out the position with reference to Hindus, Christians and Muslims, as laws governing these communities have provided for custody and guardianship as separate issues. The person who has custody of the child need not necessarily be the guardian of the child. In cases relating to custody of a child, the Courts view it from the angle of the welfare of the minor and the statutory provisions are not mandatory. In the above situations a woman would risk losing custody of her children in the event of her wanting to leave the matrimonial home.

However, the courts have intervened to ensure that the interest and welfare of the minor is paramount. The woman who wants her marriage dissolved by a decree of divorce or loses an action initiated by her husband has the extra hurdle of court procedures to contend with. Women do not have economic independence nor are they equipped to earn their own living. This dependence on the family or the spouse makes a woman more vulnerable to abuse and also keeps her in a violent domestic situation.

The lack of familial or state sponsored support structures makes it difficult for her to leave an abusive spouse. The woman has to also fight a legal battle for maintenance and custody of children. With long drawn out court procedures, the woman is not able to re-settle herself in a job or another place. The cost of these proceedings is a drain on her limited financial position. The effect of all this is that women have learned to accept domestic violence as their fate and this behavioural pattern is reinforced in the nest generation of men learning to be abusive and the women adjusting to abuse.

GOVERNMENT INITIATI

The State initiative with reference to divorce was to set up Family Courts for quick resolution of family disputes. The Family Courts Act, 1984, in its preamble states that it is "an act to provide for the establishment of Family Courts with a view to promote conciliation in and secure speedy settlement of disputes relating to marriage" These Courts lay a great emphasis on the conciliation clause and have not implemented the directive for speedy disposal. Divorced women are given a very minuscule reservation in admissions to professional colleges and government jobs.

Law and Judiciary

- Section 125 Criminal Procedure Code: This section of The Criminal Procedure Code ensures the right of women to be maintained. The rational behind this section is to give a quick disposal to cases to prevent vagrancy. The maximum amount that could be granted was Rs500/- This ceiling has now been removed by Act 50 of 2001. The definition of 'wife' in this section has been enlarged to mean and include a wife who has been divorced. Implementation: By Family Courts or Criminal Courts when the place of filing has no Family Court. The petition is filed in the court within whose jurisdiction the woman resides, making it easier for women to use this provision of law. As a criminal proceeding, the time taken for disposal is shorter.

A warrant can be issued in case of failure to appear before the court or to pay the amount decreed and the fact that the failure to pay attracts a prison sentence is a deterrent against default. Interpretation: This being a provision under the criminal law, it applies to women of all communities. However, divorced Muslim women were taken out of its purview by the passing of the Muslim Women Act, 1986.This act was promulgated for the express purpose of excluding Muslim women and passed in the face of vociferous opposition by the women's movement. It is seen as a huge step back for the rights of Muslim women. The Act was passed to appease the fundamentalist group which saw the award of maintenance of ₹175/- to Shah Bano, a 72-year old divorced woman, as interference with the Muslim personal law and hence, interference with their identity. Despite the Act, most courts have continued to grant maintenance to Muslim women in their identity as wives. However, as soon as an order of maintenance is passed, the husband comes forward with an unilateral divorce, pays the tiny amount of Mahar, and insists that he has no other obligation. The Supreme Court in Danial Lattifi v Union of India while upholding that the Muslim Women Act as constitutional interpreted the Act in a rather ingenious way making the man liable to "make reasonable and fair provision", for the life time of the woman, during the period of iddat. This provision is in addition to the maintenance paid during the period of iddat. Gaps: This provision did not take into account the earning capacity of a husband and limiting the maintenance to ₹500/- prevented some women from accessing it. With the recent amendment more women are could use this provision but Muslim women are still precluded from its purview. Grant of maintenance is not to prevent vagrancy but enforcement of a right. Critical concern: There must be speedy disposal of maintenance cases and where maintenance has been ordered the recovery of these amounts must be made easier by direct attachment of salary or income generating property so that the woman is not driven to take long drawn out execution proceeding for piecemeal recovery of the maintenance granted. The amendments of 2001 in the provisions relating to interim maintenance, directing the courts to pass orders within 60 days must be strictly adhered to.

9

Status of Indian Women Human Rights and Indian Women and Human Rights

STATUS OF WOMEN IN INDIA STATUS OF WOMEN IN INDIA

The status of women in India has been subject to many great changes over the past few millennia. From equal status with men in ancient times through the low points of the medieval period, to the promotion of equal rights by many reformers, the history of women in India has been eventful. In modern India, women have adorned high offices in India including that of the President, Prime minister, Speaker of the Lok Sabha, Leader of Opposition, *etc.* The current President of India is a woman.

HISTORY OF WOMEN HISTORY OF WOMEN

There are very few texts specifically dealing with the role of women; an important exception is the strIdharmapaddhati of Tryambakayajvan, an official at Thanjavur around c.1730. The text compiles strictures on womanly behaviour dating back to the Apastamba sutra (c. 4th c. BCE).where the term "desire to hear" covers a range of meanings from the devotee's homage to god, or the obsequious service of a slave.

ANCIENT INDIA

Scholars believe that in ancient India, the women enjoyed equal status with men in all fields of life. However, some others hold contrasting views. Works by ancient Indian grammarians such as Patanjali and Katyayana suggest that women were educated in the early Vedic period Rigvedic verses suggest that the women married at a mature age and were probably free to select their husband. Scriptures such as Rig Veda and Upanishads mention several women sages and seers, notably Gargi and Maitreyi. Some kingdoms in the ancient India had traditions such as "bride of the city". Women competed to win the coveted title of the nagarvadhu. Amrapali is the most famous example of a nagarvadhu. Women enjoyed equal status and rights during the early Vedic period. However, later (approximately 500 B.C.), the status of women began to decline with the Smritis and with the Islamic invasion of Babur and the Mughal empire and later Christianity curtailing women's freedom and rights. Although reformatory movements such as Jainism allowed women to be admitted to the religious order, by and large, the women in India faced confinement and restrictions. The practice of child marriages is believed to have started from around sixth century.

MEDIEVAL PERIOD

The Indian woman's position in the society further deteriorated during the medieval period when Sati among some communities, child marriages and a ban on widow remarriages became part of social life among some communities in India. The Muslim conquest in the Indian subcontinent brought the purdah practice in the Indian society. Among the Rajputs of Rajasthan, the Jauhar was practised. In some parts of India, the Devadasis or the temple women were sexually exploited. Polygamy was widely practised especially among Hindu Kshatriya rulers. In many Muslim families, women were restricted to Zenana areas. In spite of these conditions, some women excelled in the fields of politics, literature, education and religion.

Razia Sultana became the only woman monarch to have ever ruled Delhi. The Gond queen Durgavati ruled for fifteen years, before she lost her life in a battle with Mughal emperor Akbar's general Asaf Khan in 1564. Chand Bibi defended Ahmednagar against the mighty Mughal forces of Akbar in 1590s. Jehangir's wife Nur Jehan effectively wielded imperial power and was recognised as the real force behind the Mughal throne. The Mughal princesses Jahanara and Zebunnissa were well-known poets, and also influenced the ruling administration Shivaji's mother, Jijabai was deputed as queen regent, because of her ability as a warrior and an administrator. In South India, many women administered villages, towns, divisions and heralded social and religious institutions. The Bhakti movements tried to restore women's status and questioned some of the forms of oppression. Mirabai, a female saint-poet, was one of the most important Bhakti movement figures.

Some other female saint-poets from this period include Akka Mahadevi, Rami Janabai and Lal Ded. Bhakti sects within Hinduism such as the Mahanubhav, Varkari and many others were principle movements within the Hindu fold to openly advocate social justice and equality between men and women. Shortly after the Bhakti movement, Guru Nanak, the first Guru of Sikhs also preached the message of equality between men and women. He advocated that women be allowed to lead religious assemblies; to perform and lead congregational hymn singing called Kirtan or Bhajan; become members of religious management committees; to lead armies on the battlefield; have equality in marriage, and equality in Amrit (Baptism). Other Sikh Gurus also preached against the discrimination against women.

HISTORICAL PRACTICES

Traditions among some communities such as sati, jauhar, and devadasi have been banned and are largely defunct in modern India. However, some cases of these practices are still found in remote parts of India. The purdah is still practised by Indian women among some communities, and child marriage remains prevalent despite it being an illegal practice, especially under current Indian laws.

Sati

Sati is an old, largely defunct custom, among some communities in which the widow was immolated alive on her husband's funeral pyre. Although the act was supposed to be a voluntary on the widow's part, it is believed to have been sometimes forced on the widow. It was abolished by the British in 1829. There have been around forty reported cases of sati since independence. In 1987, the Roop Kanwar case of Rajasthan led to The Commission of Sati (Prevention) Act.

Jauhar

Jauhar refers to the practice of the voluntary immolation of all the wives and daughters of defeated warriors, in order to avoid capture and consequent molestation by the enemy. The practice was followed by the wives of defeated Rajput rulers, who are known to place a high premium on honour.

Purdah

Purdah is the practice among some communities of requiring women to cover their bodies so as to cover their skin and conceal their form. It imposes restrictions on the mobility of women, it curtails their right to interact freely and it is a symbol of the subordination of women. It does not reflect the religious teachings of either Hinduism or Islam, contrary to common belief, although misconception has occurred due to the ignorance and prejudices of religious leaders of both faiths.

Devadasis

Devadasi is a religious practice in some parts of southern India, in which women are "married" to a deity or temple. The ritual was well established by the 10th century A.D. In the later period, the illegitimate sexual exploitation of the devadasi's became a norm in some parts of India.

Women in British Rule

European scholars observed in the 19th century that Hindu women are "naturally chaste" and "more virtuous" than other women. During the British Raj, many reformers such as Ram Mohan Roy, Ishwar Chandra Vidyasagar,

Jyotirao Phule *etc.* fought for the upliftment of women. Peary Charan Sarkar, a former student of Hindu College, Calutta and a member of "Young Bengal" set up the first free school for girls in India in 1847 in Barasat, a suburb of Calcutta (later the school was named Kalikrishna Girls' High School).

While this list might suggest that there was no positive British contribution during the Raj era, that is not entirely so, since missionaries' wives like Martha Mault née Mead and her daughter Eliza Caldwell née Mault are rightly remembered for pioneering the education and training of girls in south India - a practise that initially met with local resistance, as it flew in the face of tradition. Raja Rammohan Roy's efforts led to the abolition of the Sati practice under Governor-General William Cavendish-Bentinck in 1829. Ishwar Chandra Vidyasagar's crusade for the improvement in condition of widows led to the Widow Remarriage Act of 1856. Many women reformers such as Pandita Ramabai also helped the cause of women upliftment. Kittur Chennamma, the queen of the princely state Kittur in Karnataka, led an armed rebellion against the British in response to the Doctrine of lapse.

Abbakka Rani the queen of coastal Karnataka led the defence against invading European armies notably the Portuguese in 16th century. Rani Lakshmi Bai, the Queen of Jhansi, led the Indian Rebellion of 1857 against the British. She is now widely considered as a nationalist hero. Begum Hazrat Mahal, the co-ruler of Awadh, was another ruler who led the revolt of 1857. She refused the deals with the British and later retreated to Nepal. The Begums of Bhopal were also few of the notable female rulers during this period. They did not observe purdah and were trained in martial arts. Chandramukhi Basu, Kadambini Ganguly and Anandi Gopal Joshi were few of the earliest Indian women to obtain educational degrees.

In 1917, the first women's delegation met the Secretary of State to demand women's political rights, supported by the Indian National Congress. The All India Women's Education Conference was held in Pune in 1927. In 1929, the Child Marriage Restraint Act was passed, stipulating fourteen as the minimum age of marriage for a girl through the efforts of Mahomed Ali Jinnah. Though Mahatma Gandhi himself married at the age of thirteen, he later urged people to boycott child marriages and called upon the young men to marry the child widows.

Women played an important part in India's independence struggle. Some of the famous freedom fighters include Bhikaji Cama, Dr. Annie Besant, Pritilata Waddedar, Vijayalakshmi Pandit, Rajkumari Amrit Kaur, Aruna Asaf Ali, Sucheta Kriplani and Kasturba Gandhi. Other notable names include Muthulakshmi Reddy, Durgabai Deshmukh *etc.*

The Rani of Jhansi Regiment of Subhash Chandra Bose's Indian National Army consisted entirely of women including Captain Lakshmi Sahgal. Sarojini Naidu, a poet and a freedom fighter, was the first Indian woman to become the

President of the Indian National Congress and the first woman to become the governor of a state in India.

WOMEN IN INDEPENDENT INDIA WOMEN IN INDEPENDENT INDIA

Women in India now participate in all activities such as education,sports, politics, media, art and culture, service sectors, science and technology, *etc.* Indira Gandhi, who served as Prime Minister of India for an aggregate period of fifteen years is the world's longest serving woman Prime Minister. The Constitution of India guarantees to all Indian women equality (Article 14), no discrimination by the State (Article 15(1)), equality of opportunity (Article 16), equal pay for equal work (Article 39(d)).

In addition, it allows special provisions to be made by the State in favour of women and children (Article 15(3)), renounces practices derogatory to the dignity of women (Article 51(A) (e)), and also allows for provisions to be made by the State for securing just and humane conditions of work and for maternity relief. (Article 42).

The feminist activism in India picked up momentum during later 1970s. One of the first national level issues that brought the women's groups together was the Mathura rape case. The acquittal of policemen accused of raping a young girl Mathura in a police station, led to a wide-scale protests in 1979–1980. The protests were widely covered in the national media, and forced the Government to amend the Evidence Act, the Criminal Procedure Code and the Indian Penal Code and introduce the category of custodial rape.

Female activists united over issues such as female infanticide, gender bias, women health, and female literacy. Since alcoholism is often associated with violence against women in India, many women groups launched anti-liquor campaigns in Andhra Pradesh, Himachal Pradesh, Haryana, Orissa, Madhya Pradesh and other states. Many Indian Muslim women have questioned the fundamental leaders' interpretation of women's rights under the Shariat law and have criticized the triple talaq system. In 1990s, grants from foreign donor agencies enabled the formation of new women-oriented NGOs. Self-help groups and NGOs such as Self Employed Women's Association (SEWA) have played a major role in women's rights in India. Many women have emerged as leaders of local movements.

For example, Medha Patkar of the Narmada Bachao Andolan. The Government of India declared 2001 as the Year of Women's Empowerment (Swashakti). The National Policy For The Empowerment Of Women came was passed in 2001. In 2006, the case of a Muslim rape victim called Imrana was highlighted in the media. Imrana was raped by her father-in-law. The pronouncement of some Muslim clerics that Imrana should marry her father-in-law led to widespread protests and finally Imrana's father-in-law was given a prison term of 10 years, The verdict was welcomed by many women's groups and the

All India Muslim Personal Law Board. In 2010 March 9, one day after International Women's day, Rajyasabha passed Women's Reservation Bill, ensuring 33 per cent reservation to women in Parliament and state legislative bodies.

WOMEN CULTURE WOMEN CULTURE

Sari (a single piece of a long cloth wound around the body) and salwar kameez are worn by women all over India. Bindi is part of the women's make-up. Unlike common belief, the bindi on the forehead does not signify marital status, however the Sindoor does. Rangoli (or Kolam) is a traditional art very popular among Indian women.

EDUCATION AND ECONOMIC DEVELOPMENT EDUCATION AND ECONOMIC DEVELOPMENT

In 1992-93, only 9.2 per cent of the households in India were female-headed. However, approximately 35 per cent of the households below the poverty line were found to be female-headed.

EDUCATION

Though it is gradually rising, the female literacy rate in India is lower than the male literacy rate. Compared to boys, far fewer girls are enrolled in the schools, and many of them drop out. The National Sample Survey Data of 1997, only the states of Kerala and Mizoram have approached universal female literacy rates. The majority of the scholars, the major factor behind the improved social and economic status of women in Kerala is literacy. Under Non-Formal Education programme (NFE), about 40 per cent of the centres in states and 10 per cent of the centres in UTs are exclusively reserved for females. As of 2000, about 0.3 million NFE centres were catering to about 7.42 million children, out of which about 0.12 million were exclusively for girls. In urban India, girls are nearly at par with the boys in terms of education. However, in rural India girls continue to be less educated than the boys. In 1998 report by U.S. Department of Commerce, the chief barrier to female education in India are inadequate school facilities (such as sanitary facilities), shortage of female teachers and gender bias in curriculum (majority of the female characters being depicted as weak and helpless).

WORKFORCE PARTICIPATION

Contrary to the common perception, a large per cent of women in India work. The National data collection agencies accept the fact that there is a serious under-estimation of women's contribution as workers. However, there are far fewer women in the paid workforce than there are men. In urban India Women have impressive number in the workforce. As an example at software industry 30 per cent of the workforce is female. They are at par with their male counter parts in terms of wages, position at the work place. In rural India, agriculture and allied industrial sectors employ as much as 89.5 per cent of the total female labour. In overall farm production, women's average contribution is estimated at 55 per cent to 66 per cent of the total labour. In 1991 World Bank report, women accounted for 94 per cent of total employment in dairy production in India. Women constitute 51 per cent of the total employed in forest-based small-scale enterprises. One of the most famous female business success stories is the Shri Mahila Griha Udyog Lijjat Papad. In 2006, Kiran Mazumdar-Shaw, who started Biocon - one of India's first biotech companies, was rated India's richest woman. Lalita Gupte and Kalpana Morparia (both were the only businesswomen in India who made the list of the Forbes World's Most Powerful Women), run India's second-largest bank, ICICI Bank.

LAND AND PROPERTY RIGHTS

In most Indian families, women do not own any property in their own names, and do not get a share of parental property. Due to weak enforcement of laws protecting them, women continue to have little access to land and property. In fact, some of the laws discriminate against women, when it comes to land and property rights. The Hindu personal laws of mid-1956s (applied to Hindus, Buddhists, Sikhs and Jains) gave women rights to inheritance. However, the sons had an independent share in the ancestral property, while the daughters' shares were based on the share received by their father. Hence, a father could effectively disinherit a daughter by renouncing his share of the ancestral property, but the son will continue to have a share in his own right. Additionally, married daughters, even those facing marital harassment, had no residential rights in the ancestral home.

After amendment of Hindu laws in 2005, now women in have been provided the same status as that of men. In 1986, the Supreme Court of India ruled that Shah Bano, an old divorced Muslim woman was eligible for maintenance money. However, the decision was vociferously opposed by fundamentalist Muslim leaders, who alleged that the court was interfering in their personal law. The Union Government subsequently passed the Muslim Women's (Protection of Rights Upon Divorce) Act. Similarly, the Christian women have struggled over years for equal rights of divorce and succession. In 1994, all the churches, jointly with women's organisations, drew up a draft law called the Christian Marriage and Matrimonial Causes Bill. However, the government has still not amended the relevant laws.

STATUS OF WOMEN'S SEXUAL AND REPRODUCTIVE HEALTH AND RIGHTS

MATERNAL HEALTH AND SEXUALLY TRANSMITTED INFECTIONS

Each year half a million women die of preventable complications of pregnancy and childbirth and another 18 million are left disabled or chronically ill. Women have a 1 in 2,800 chance of dying from pregnancy-related causes in developed countries, a 1 in 61 chance in developing countries, and a 1 in 15 chance in Sub-Saharan Africa.

Although married women's contraceptive use has risen globally from 14 percent in 1965 to more than 50 percent today, the number of women who wish to space or limit further childbearing but are not using contraception (mainly because of a lack of access to information and family planning services) remains very large. In the mid-1990s the World Health Organisation estimated that some 120 million women had an unmet need for contraception. Among countries with data for both 1990 and 2000 there has been a slight drop in the share of women with unmet need, but the level of unmet need remains high, especially in Sub-Saharan Africa and in the Middle East and North Africa.

Except in the Middle East and North Africa and Sub-Saharan Africa unmet need is higher among adolescents than among adult women of reproductive age and is highest in Latin America and the Caribbean. One result of high levels of unmet need in some regions of the world is a high incidence of unsafe abortions. Of the 20 million unsafe abortions that WHO estimates occur annually, worldwide, an estimated 70,000 result in death, accounting for 13 percent of the overall maternal mortality rate. Evidence suggests that reducing the unmet need for contraception would reduce the need to resort to abortion, thereby improving maternal health and female longevity.

Sexually transmitted infections are another global reproductive health problem. WHO estimates that 340 million new sexually transmitted infections occur annually, and there is clear evidence that the presence of a sexually transmitted infection increases the risk of HIV infection. HIV/AIDS is itself a devastating global health problem. In 2004 an estimated 4.9 million people were newly infected with HIV, higher than ever. At the end of 2004 about 40 million people were estimated to be living with HIV/AIDS, most (95 percent) in developing countries and about half of those 15–49 years old are women. In Sub-Saharan Africa women constitute 57 percent of all adults living with HIV/AIDS. About three-quarters of young people (15–24 years old) infected with HIV/AIDS on that continent are women and girls. Prevalence rates for women are nearing those of men in the Caribbean and in North Africa and the Middle East. Yet, worldwide, fewer than one in five people at risk of HIV infection today have access to prevention programmes. Fewer than four percent of people in need of antiretroviral treatment in low- and middle-income countries were receiving the drugs at the end of 2001. And less than 10 percent of people with HIV/AIDS have access to palliative care or treatment for opportunistic infections.

Nutrition and Reproductive Health

The nutritional status of women and adolescent girls is often overlooked when examining issues related to reproductive health. Malnutrition significantly increases the risk of poor reproductive health outcomes, and multiple pregnancies at short intervals may aggravate women's nutritional status, resulting in poor maternal health overall. Because malnutrition weakens the immune function, malnourished women are less resistant to infection. Chronic malnutrition in childhood leads to stunting, which can increase the risk of obstructed labour.

Data on low body mass index (<18.5 kg/m), a measure of chronic malnutrition in adults, show that 34 percent of women in South Asia and 18 percent in Sub-Saharan Africa are malnourished. By comparison the prevalence is 4 percent in developed countries. Low body mass index is a known risk factor for adverse pregnancy outcomes, including low birth weight infants and infant and maternal death and illness. Iron-deficiency anemia affects 50–70 percent of pregnant women in developing countries. Severe anemia has been shown to be associated with postpartum hemorrhage and is thought to be an underlying factor in maternal deaths, though more studies are needed to substantiate this. Similarly, other nutritional deficiencies with adverse effects on reproductive outcomes are thought to be widely prevalent. Improving the nutritional status of women and girls is therefore a prerequisite for them to achieve health and well-being.

Adolescent Reproductive Health

Reproductive health problems are particularly acute for adolescent girls, because they have the highest levels of unmet need for contraception and are the most vulnerable to unwanted pregnancy and sexually transmitted infections, including HIV. Many sexually active adolescents do not use contraception. Of the roughly 260 million women ages 15–19 worldwide, both married and unmarried, about 11 percent (29 million) are sexually active and do not want to become pregnant but are not using a modern method of birth control. Every year some 14 million young women become mothers and an estimated 1–4 million young women ages 15–19 have induced abortions, many of them unsafe.

An estimated 17 million adolescent girls are married before the age of 20. Rates of early marriage are highest in Western Africa, South Asia, and Sub-Saharan Africa, where 30 percent or more of girls ages 15–19 are married. Early marriage contributes to a series of negative consequences for young women and the societies in which they live. Early marriage usually leads to early childbearing.

In Guatemala, India, Mali, and Yemen, among others, 24–45 percent of women ages 20–24 had given birth by age 18. That compares with 2 percent in France and 1 percent in Germany. Worldwide an estimated 15 million girls ages 15–19—both married and unmarried—give birth each year. The rates are particularly high in developing countries. It is estimated that between one-quarter and one-half of all young women in the developing world give birth before they turn 18. In Bangladesh, for example, more than half of all women have their first child by age 19. Adolescent fertility rates and progress during the past decade in reducing these rates vary significantly across regions. Developed countries have the lowest adolescent fertility rates, at 16 live births per 1,000 adolescents, down from 19 live births per 1,000 in 1990. Adolescent fertility rates are highest in South Asia and Sub-Saharan Africa—and those rates increased between 1990 and 2000.

Underdeveloped physiology, combined with a lack of power, information, and access to services, means that young married women who bear children experience much higher levels of maternal illness and death than do women who bear children when they are older. Severe complications, such as obstructed labour and the fistula that may result, occur most commonly among young women. Women who marry young have little negotiating power and are exposed to greater risk of sexually transmitted infections, especially in the common instance of having partners who are much older and more sexually experienced. In Kenya and Zambia, for example, young married women are more likely to be HIV-positive than their unmarried peers because they have sex more often, use condoms less often, are unable to refuse sex, and have partners who are more likely to be HIV-positive.

THE COSTS OF POOR REPRODUCTIVE HEALTH THE COSTS OF POOR REPRODUCTIVE HEALTH

A recent report by the Alan Guttmacher Institute (AGI) and the United Nations Population Fund (UNFPA) synthesises current evidence on the costs and benefits of sexual and reproductive health care. The health costs are expressed in disability-adjusted life years. According to the WHO's 2001 estimates, sexual and reproductive health problems account for 18 percent of the global burden of disease and 32 percent of the burden among women ages 15–44 worldwide. More specifically:

- Pregnancy and delivery-related complications—hemorrhage, sepsis, obstructed labour, pregnancy-related hypertensive disorder, and unsafe abortion—account for 2 percent of all DALYs lost and 13 percent of all DALYs lost among reproductive-age women.
- Perinatal conditions (low birth weight, birth asphyxia, and birth trauma) account for 7 percent of all DALYs lost.
- HIV/AIDS accounts for 5 percent of all DALYs lost and 14 percent among women ages 15–44.
- Other sexual and reproductive health conditions—sexually transmitted infections other than HIV/AIDS, iron-deficiency anemia among women, genitourinary diseases, and breast, ovarian, cervical, and uterine cancer—account for 3 percent of all DALYs lost and 5 percent among women ages 15–44.

By comparison, respiratory illnesses account for 11 percent of all DALYs lost, cardiovascular diseases for 10 percent, and neuropsychiatric conditions for 13 percent. The report also notes that investing in reproductive and sexual health services is cost effective.

An early study in Mexico found that for every peso the Mexican social security system spent on family planning services during 1972–84, it saved nine pesos for treating complications of unsafe abortion and providing maternal and infant care. Every $1 invested in Thailand's family planning programme saved the government more than $16. An analysis in Egypt found that every $1 invested in family planning saved the government $31. Beyond these savings, reproductive and sexual health services deliver other medical, social, and economic benefits, including prevention of illness and death, improvements in women's social position, and increases in macroeconomic investment and growth.

A MAPPING OF HUMAN RIGHTS ISSUES A MAPPING OF HUMAN RIGHTS ISSUES

This chapter sets out the issues which inhabit the human rights landscape in areas of ordinary governance.

CUSTODIAL VIOLENCE

Custody death, torture in custody and custodial rape have been subjects of much concern. Custodial violence has been on the agenda of civil rights groups for over two decades, and reports documenting instances of violence and its systemic occurrence, have been instrumental in the campaigns against custodial violence. Although custody deaths have found an acknowledgment from the state, and the NHRC has issued directions to the states

- To report of the NHRC any death in custody within 24 hours of the occurrence, and
- To videotape the post-mortem proceedings.

It is difficult to assess if this has resulted in any reduction in the incidence of custody deaths. NHRC reports show a marked increase in the reported cases of custody deaths each year. This is attributed, by the NHRC, to increased reporting and not to increased incidence of the crime; this, however, needs to be further investigated. The incidence of custody deaths demonstrates more undeniably the brutalisation of the processes of law enforcement by the police and armed forces. However, custodial torture is not at the focus of campaigns to reduce custodial violence. There are few places which have taken up the treatment of the victims of torture as victims of torture.

The Indian state, in the meantime, has resisted attempts to have it ratify the Torture Convention. In recent reported cases from the Gauhati High Court, it is 15 and 16-year olds who are found to have been victims of state violence, and the defence of the state has been that they were hardened militants. Custodial rape has found an expanded definition - in terms of power rape - in the Penal Code, 1860.

However, these provisions have hardly been invoked. In the meantime, most often, judicial perceptions of the victim of custodial rape have in significant measure, discredited the victim's version, and blamed the victim resulting in reduction of sentence for policemen convicted of rape to less than the minimum prescribed in law. From Mathura to Rameeza Bi to Maya Tyagi to Suman Rani - these women have become symbols of patriarchal prejudices. Campaigns in the matter of custodial rape have invoked their name, and they are now names that are etched into the history and legend of the women's movement. In the meantime, the legal dictum that the identity of a victim of rape be not disclosed to protect her privacy has been set in place.

PROJECT DISPLACEMENT

Project displacement, for the construction of large dams or for power projects, for instance, have led to protest movements directly involving the affected people. The NBA has utilised strategies and tactics of protest - including jal samarpan, human chains, working on the funders and the contractors to withdraw, participating in the proceedings before, and surrounding, the World Commission on Dams - which have refused to let the issue be drowned out. This has also seen the manufacturing of conflicting forces, such as the pro-dam lobby which is believed to be largely state-sponsored. Human rights issues that arise include

- Displacement, *per se*
- The poverty of rehabilitation, and often, the impossibility of rehabilitation
- The impoverishment that results from displacement
- The non-reckoning of cultural and community identity and of rights.

What constitutes development has come into severe question in this arena. The Land Acquisition Act 1894 has been at the centre of protests. Among the strategies adopted to deal with the coercive nature of the law has been the drafting of alternative legislation. The obduracy of the state in not approving a policy for rehabilitation of the displaced has also been cause for protest.

THE INTERNALLY DISPLACED DUE TO CONFLICTS

The large-scale internal migration caused by political violence has created classes of internal refugees. During the years of militancy in the Punjab, after the anti-Sikh riots in 1984, and the movement of Kashmiri Pandits out of the valley have provided visible evidence of such migration. While the violence that preceded the migration has been squarely addressed in human rights terms, the rehabilitation and return of the migrants after displacement appears to have been only on the margins of the human rights movement.

REFUGEES

India has not ratified the 1951 UN Convention on Refugees, nor has it signed the 1967 protocol. The Indian state has generally resisted visits from the UNHCR to camps where refugees are housed. Activists say that the Indian state has been relatively benign towards refugees. According to one non-governmental source, in 1999, India hosted more than 2,92,000 refugees; which includes more than 16,000 persons from Afghanistan, 65,000 Chakmas from Bangladesh, 30,000 Bhutanese of Nepali origin, 50,000 Chin indigenous people from Myanmar and about 39,000 pro-democracy student activists from Rangoon and the Mandalay region, 1,10,000 Sri Lankan Tamils of whom 70,000 are in camps and 40,000 outside, 1,10,000 Tibetans and around 7000 persons from other countries. The assassination of Rajiv Gandhi in 1991 has reportedly altered the treatment meted out to the Sri Lankan refugees.

According to a fact-finding report of a civil liberties organisation in Tamil Nadu, Sri Lankan refugees fall into three categories: those who are in the 133 refugee camps; refugees who maintain themselves outside the camps; and those who have been identified as belonging to militant groups who were kept in virtual rigourous confinement in the three special camps. In August 1995, 43 inmates of the Special Camp at Tippu Mahal, Vellore escaped and a one-man commission set up by the state describes the structure and administration of the camps.

The refugees were found to be prisoners in these camps and, as even the state appointed commission had remarked, 'admittedly these inmates or most of them are in rigourous confinement in the special camps for five or six years continuously.' The testimony of the two inmates to the fact-finding team also revealed that the camp in Vellore had among its inmates at least 12 disabled persons. The Government of India does not appear to have any policy on how to deal with refugee-prisoners in their camps. The protection of Chakma refugees in the state of Arunachal Pradesh, and their right to have their claim for citizenship considered, was canvassed by a civil liberties group before the NHRC. The Supreme Court, approached by the NHRC, directed that the threats held out to the Chakmas by the local citizens be dealt with by the state. It also asserted that their applications for being granted citizenship be considered under the Citizenship Act. The difficulties besetting refugees even after long years of residence in a state, with state acquiescence, were in evidence here.

LAND ALIENATION

The loss to communities of right over land is widespread, and various movements to recover control over land and related resources have been active particularly in the past decade and a half, though some movements go back many decades. The issue of tribal land alienation was linked with that of displacement, and the judicial system was used to get an order declaring unconstitutional the transfer of land from a tribal to a non-tribal through the medium of the state. Recent efforts to delete this constitutional protection given in Schedule V of the Constitution are being resisted as a denial of basic protection given to tribals, paving the way for their displacement and impoverishment.

The issue of land alienation was one of the primary issues in the struggle for separate statehood for Uttaranchal, and till today is identified as one of the main rights violations occurring in the state. In Kerala, the issue is differently positioned. While the loss of land to the tribal is viewed as a violation of their rights and protection of those rights, the settlers are largely people who are themselves on the economic margins. While groups from within the tribal communities have been demanding restoration of alienated land, and the High Court has supported their stand, other human rights advocates maintain an uneasy silence since the contest appears to be between two vulnerable communities.

RIGHT OVER RESOURCES

The right of the forest dwellers to reside in forests, and for those dependent on forest produce to have access to forests, is contested terrain. Till recently, there were conservation groups which demanded that removing tribals from within forest areas was necessary in the interest of conservation. This stand has softened somewhat, and a more symbiotic relationship between the forest and the dweller recognised as possible. The problems are now spoken of in terms of overpopulation, and over-grazing, in the forest area. State policy is, however, widely perceived as being inimical to the continuance of the forest dweller within the forest. 'Settling' of rights and interests is therefore met with deep suspicion, as is happening in Madhya Pradesh. Activists have therefore been mobilising the grassroots - in MP, it was through a padayatra over a period of six months - to resist the conservation projects which may end up pauperising the dwellers, and, further, may denude the forest too.

There have been attempts in the early '90s to prepare a new Forest Bill that will contain within it the interests of conservation, and of the people. Efforts such as this have stalled the legislation proposed by the state which groups and movements see as being opposed to rights - including the right to livelihood, to culture, to security, to shelter, among others - even while the alternative bills have hardly ever been adopted. An activist identified the problem of land and resources being related to how possession and ownership of land are perceived. There are three kinds of property he said:

- Private property
- Public property
- Common property

What is held as 'public property' by the state, he said, has been treated as property owned by the state, and not held in trust by the state. It is the notion of common property that has to be resurrected and advanced. The entry of mining interests into Orissa has, for instance, brought into the open the problem that is inherent in globalisation when it comes into conflict with local interest. The unequal, triangular contest between multinational mining interests, the state which binds itself to protecting the multinational interest on Indian territory, and the local dwellers - in the case of mining, it is often tribals - manifests itself as a human rights issue. Aquaculture, which brings in corporations to exploit resources through prawn culture, for instance, has been resisted on grounds of loss of livelihood, long-term destruction of marine life and consequent degradation of the environment. Corporatised aquaculture and shrimp farms have been banned. Deep-sea trawlers have also been banned, and the livelihood and lives of fisher communities salvaged. So, too, with prawn culture.

Human rights activists see setbacks to these efforts at preservation of community livelihoods and of the environment in the Aquaculture Bill that has been presented to the Parliament in 2000. The Aruvari Sansad in Ajmer district in Rajasthan, which, with the help of the Tarun Bharat Sangh, an NGO, has wrested control over the river, the check dams it has built along it, the revived rivers and the fish that have sprung into being in the river is an uncommon assertion over water and water resources to the exclusion of agencies of the state. The issue of land reforms and the redistribution of land was encountered in Andhra Pradesh. The Peoples War Group, for instance, avers that land reform is at the root of their attacks against the state.

The problem of professional land grabbers, and the response of land invasion to take possession of land which should rightly belong to the invading community, was also seen in Andhra Pradesh. State response has been to treat the attacks, and invasion, as public order, or law and order, problems. The loss of tribal land through land alienation - something that the law limits - has raised other issues in Kerala, for instance. The land had been bought from the tribals by settlers who are themselves economically and socially marginalised. A prolonged legal battle, where the court had directed the return of the land to the tribals, has not seen a solution to the contending interests of two communities, each in need of protection from expropriation.

URBAN SHELTER AND DEMOLITION

There has been a routinising of the emergency visible in the matter of cleaning up of the cities. In 2000-2001, Delhi has seen a spate of demolitions of 'slums'. The slum dwellers have been divided up into eligibles and ineligibles, with the eligibles being given very small plots of land on which they are required to construct houses within six months on a licence basis. The size of the plot ensures that it is only a 'slum' that develops. The 'ineligibles' are not thereafter considered by state policy. Housing rights activists too do not appear to have been able to identify what happens to the ineligibles when demolition occurs. In Bangalore, housing rights groups have been attempting to demonstrate the effort and money that 'encroachers' expend on the land on which they settle; and that they have worked for their entitlement to alternative plots. In Bombay, and to a lesser extent elsewhere, there have been attempts to involve the slum dwellers in reconstructing the area in a manner which will let the slum disappear, while they are given places in high-rise tenements in the same area with the rest of the space to be used commercially.

In Patna, an order of the High Court in a PIL, requiring the municipal corporation to demolish encroachments, resulted in a demolition spree that an embarrassed court had to step in to stop. The illegal status of the urban dweller who cannot afford to purchase legality has been aggravated by B.N. Kirpal, J saying: 'Establishing or creating slums, it seems, appears to be good business and is well organised...Large areas of public land, in this way, are usurped for private use free of cost... The promise of free land, at the taxpayers' cost, in place of a jhuggi, is a proposal which attracts more land grabbers. Rewarding an encroacher on public land with free alternate site is like giving a reward to a pickpocket.' Unlike South Africa, where the state's obligation to provide shelter before destroying even an illegal habitat was recognised, drawing upon international law, there is no such recognition in Indian law or judicial decisions. Activists and campaigners therefore face an unenviable, if unavoidable, task of combating the anti-poor stand of the state. Pavement dwelling, and houselessness, was raised in the '80s and, though it may never really have disappeared, it has resurfaced more rigourously since the demolitions have begun in Delhi.

Migrant workers living on pavements have been particularly vulnerable to random attacks in areas of militant violence. Newspapers have reported such occurrences in the '90s. This issue affecting migrant labour particularly needs to be addressed. The 'clearing' of pavements by removing hawkers has been a phenomenon visible in most cities. Eviction of hawkers, and of dwellers, is a significant issue, and the demands include recognition not only of shelter, land and monetary compensation, but of livelihood too.

LIVELIHOOD

Apart from issues of rights over resources, and in the context of displacement and relocation, the death of cotton farmers has, for instance, raised questions about protection of livelihood. Liberalisation has resulted in loss of jobs to large numbers in the workforce, and we hear of deaths among the working classes. This is an area that seems to demand closer attention. The withdrawing of protective labour legislation, which is proposed, such as the 'abolition' part of the Contract Labour Act 1970, or the prohibition of night work for women except where specifically attempted, it is feared, is likely to shrink the rights of workers to a great degree. Freedom of association is also being re-cast in a new Trade Unions Bill, which labour leaders and activists believe is meant to stifle the powers of labour to group together and be heard. The casualisation of labour which the changes portend are expected to drastically reduce the bargaining power of labour.

In 1989, a PIL filed by two social/political activists from Orissa, led to the express recognition of starvation as a violation of fundamental rights. In 1994, the NHRC acknowledged that starvation is a violation of human rights and ordered the state to pay compensation to the families of victims of starvation in Kalahandi in Orissa. In March/April 2001, academics/researchers from the Delhi School of Economics and the Madras Institute of Development Studies have asked for distribution of buffer stocks that the government has stored in its godowns, to stem the tide of hunger among those with low purchasing power. The juggling with the public distribution system, and the defining and re-defining of the poverty line and consequently of 'below poverty line' is causing particular concern.

The death of 17 protesters chased by the police into the Tamaraparani river, and over 200 injured in the incident has been compared to the killing of innocent persons by the British at Jallianwallabagh 80 years ago. On July 23, 1999, a solidarity procession organised by several political parties proceeded to the Collectorate in Tirunelveli Town in South Tamil Nadu, demanding an early solution of the wage dispute that had been the cause of discontent and agitation among tea workers in the Manjolai Tea Estate.

The also demanded the immediate and unconditional release of 652 tea estate workers who had been kept in the Tiruchi jail for six weeks following a demonstration before the same Collectorate on June 7 and 8, 1999. Talks on the labour dispute having failed, the political parties decided to present a charter of demands to the Collector. As the processionists neared the Collectorate, the police attempted to prevent the jeep which had the leaders of the agitation in it from proceeding further. As the crowd milled around, the events that ensued included a lathi charge by the police, the lobbing of tear gas and the police also opened fire. A video footage shows an injured person, bleeding, being carried away by four policemen.

This injured person remains unaccounted for. The police then chased the people down the banks of the river Tamaraparani forcing the people to jump into the water to save themselves from the police force. Photographs graphically reveal the pursuit of the people by the police into the river, even pushing the people back into the water. 17 people drowned. There were injuries on the person of the drowned victims, testifying to ante-mortem police brutality. This episode constitutes a new threshold to police violence and brutality in labour related agitation and protest. The 'clearing' of pavements by removing hawkers has been a phenomenon visible in most cities. Eviction of hawkers, and of dwellers, is a significant issue, and the demands include recognition not only of shelter, land and monetary compensation, but of livelihood too.

SEXUAL HARASSMENT AT THE WORKPLACE

This issue acquired visibility with the decision of the Supreme Court in Vishaka. Earlier efforts at having the problem addressed, as, for instance, in the Delhi University, has drawn strength from the guidelines set out in the judgement. It was widely reported, however, that it was still proving difficult to get institutions to adopt the guidelines and act upon it.

The Madras High Court, for instance, was reportedly averring that the guidelines did not apply to the court; and allegations of sexual harassment by a senior member of the Registry were given short shrift. The process of setting up a credible grievance redressal mechanism was reportedly being watered down in the recommendation of a committee to the Delhi University. In Kerala, a Commission of Enquiry was set up after Nalini Netto, a senior official of the Indian Administrative Service, pursued her complaint of sexual harassment against a serving minister of the state cabinet - which is seen as a diversion from a representative investigative and redressal forum. P E Usha, in Kerala, faced hostility in her university when she followed up on her complaint of sexual harassment. There have been allegations of sexual harassment of women employees by senior persons within institutions working on human rights, and in progressive publications, which too have shown up the inadequacy of the redressal mechanisms.

- Translating the guidelines into norms in different institutions and workplaces;
- Finding support systems for women who are sexually harassed
- Breaking through thick walls of disbelief are reckoned to be the priorities.
- This has also been introduced into programmes on gender sensitisation for judicial officers. Sexual harassment accompanied by violence has become a common feature with cases of acid throwing where there is unrequited love, and harassment which has culminated in the murder of a hounded girl.

RAPE

In the '80s and into the early '90s,

- The definition of rape
- The meaning of consent in the context of rape
- Marital rape was widely discussed, and alternative drafts and definitions essayed.

While following Tukaram and Ganpat's case, 'power' rape was partially introduced into the law. The definition of rape, consent and the status of marital rape in law has however not been altered. Again, while the campaign's gains are witnessed in the Supreme Court holding that, as a rule, the victim's version should not require corroboration and that it should be given credence

- The trauma of the trial continues,
- The law's sanction to delving into character evidence concerning the victim remains in the Evidence Act despite the flood of criticism and protest it has provoked.

In Uttaranchal, an issue not uncommon in investigations into, and trial of, rape surfaced. It was reported that women who were raped at Muzaffarnagar are being pressurised not to testify in the criminal cases not only by the police but also by their own community and political leaders, particularly since monetary compensation has been paid. In 1994, the National Commission for Women was asked by the Supreme Court to propose a scheme for establishing Rape Crisis Centres, and for a Criminal Injuries Compensation Board, which could care for victims of crime. This is yet to materialise. In the meantime, the women's movement in Rajasthan has got the administration to provide monetary relief to victims of rape, unconnected with trial and conviction. Though this has, at least occasionally, resulted in the veracity of the accusation being challenged as having been made so as to obtain the sum in compensation, it is seen as a move to helping the woman recover. Rape as reprisal was symbolised in Bhanwari Devi's experience.

Bhanwari Devi, a saathin working in Rajasthan in and around her village, was part of a wider network of women who were involved in a state-sponsored programme of empowerment particularly of women and girls. Her intervention to thwart the practice of child marriage in the community around her is commonly acknowledged as having resulted in the gang rape that was inflicted on her - as punishment, by men of the dominant community who were outraged by her intervention. The acquittal of the alleged rapists, more especially the reasoning of the court, based on caste and hierarchies of belief, accentuates the re-victimising of the woman. The low rate of conviction for rape, and the protest from women's groups, were held out to justify a proposed amendment to criminal law to provide death penalty for the offence of rape. The conflict between provisions of the death penalty and human rights has surfaced, even if gradually, and the groups we met, as well as the National Commission for Women, have rejected the proposal for death penalty for the offence of rape.

DEATH PENALTY

The civil liberties movement has been consistent in its opposition to the death penalty. For a brief while, there were some sections in the women's movement who supported - either vocally, or by their silence - the imposition of death penalty for rape. This too has been retracted, and death penalty for rape opposed. After the period in the early '80s, when the Supreme Court drew up the 'rarest of rare' rule, there has been a downward slide, particularly discernible in the 1990s.

- Multiple death sentences,
- Death penalty to minors, and
- Death sentence while reversing acquittal are not uncommon.

The campaign against execution of two youths in Andhra Pradesh who had been convicted of burning a bus which killed 23 passengers saw concerted action, which resulted in their sentence being commuted by the President. The confirmation of the sentence of death on women is a relatively recent phenomenon. Ramashri's sentence was reduced to life by the Supreme Court, even as the court rejected the right of the NCW to intervene. The sentence of death imposed upon Nalini, convicted in the Rajiv Gandhi assassination case, has been opposed by human rights groups, along with the sentence of death meted out to three others in the same matter. Death sentence confirmed despite dissent among judges of benches of the Supreme Court on the sentence that should be imposed is another, disturbing, occurrence.

Even doubts about the age of the accused - whether he had been less than 16 years of age and therefore a juvenile - were not sufficient to dispense with death sentence where death was awarded by a majority of judges. That the young accused was defended by legal aid lawyers and that 'It is reasonable to presume, in such circumstances, that the amicus curiae or advocate appointed on State brief, would not have been able even to see the petitioner, much less collect instructions from him, during the second and third tiers' was noticed only by the minority judge. Dearth of data, and difficulty of access to data is one obstacle to effectively countering the retentionists. In the meantime, the proliferation of death penalty in recent statutes, *viz.*,

- The Narcotic Drugs and Psychotropic Substances Act 1985
- National Security Guards Act 1986
- TADA 1987
- Arms Act 1950
- Indo-Tibetan Border Police Act 1992
- The Scheduled Castes and Scheduled Tribes Act 1989
- Commission of Sati Act 1987
- S.364 A IPC as introduced in 1993 - 'kidnapping for ransom, *etc.*'

There has been a deafening silence from the NHRC on the issue of the death penalty.

FAKE ENCOUNTERS

In India, extra-judicial killings by the police or the security forces are called 'encounter killings', meaning that the killing occurred during an armed encounter between the police or security forces and the victim. The killing by the state forces is most often declared to be defensive, cases of attempted murder and other related offences are registered against the victims, and the cases closed without further investigation since criminal cases come to an end upon the death of the accused. Despite being 'unnatural deaths', and the victim having being killed, no investigation ensues to determine whether the death was in fact in an actual encounter, nor whether the use, and the extent of use, of force was justified. This is an acknowledged strategy of the state for eliminating certain kinds of opposition to the state and the established order. In Andhra Pradesh, for instance, the naxalites have been the targets; in Punjab, it was the militant; in Mumbai, it is those who are alleged to be part of the underworld. Civil liberties groups, journalists and lawyers have consistently challenged this practice over the past two decades. The demand as it has been articulated after recent episodes has been

- For doing away with state violence in the form of killings in fake encounters, and
- That all cases of encounter killings ought to be registered as first information reports and investigated before the case is closed. The practice of registering cases against the deceased and terminating the proceedings even before it begins is being vigourously challenged. The NHRC too has issued directions endorsing this recommended practice, but to little effect. These court, and out-of-court, battles have carried on throughout the '80s and the '90s to the present.

The Committee of Concerned Citizens, a group of individuals in Andhra Pradesh, has approached encounter killings differently. Addressing both naxalite groups and the state, the CCC has been working at de-escalation of violence. While the naxalite response has taken the CCC to the issue of land reforms as being fundamental in understanding violence of the opposition, the state, it is widely believed, is pursuing the path of unbridled unleashing of the use of encounters.

The numbers killed in encounters have increased in the two years when the process of reconciliation was being negotiated by the CCC, making some of them ask if intervention by the human rights actors was actually prompting the state to escalate the violence. The human rights community has had to contend with the issue of impunity which is immediately seen as arising from thee non-registration and the non-investigation of cases.

INVOLUNTARY DISAPPEARANCES

The Punjab disappearances were brought into the open by two human rights defenders, Khalra and Kumar. Khalra was himself thereafter 'disappeared'. Investigations into these disappearances - which were uncovered when mortuary records in three districts of the Punjab were scrutinised and 'unidentified' and partially identified persons were found to have been cremated without informing the families of the deceased - was handed over by the Supreme Court to the NHRC. The manner in which the matter was reduced to a point where the State of Punjab agreed to pay compensation of ` 1 lakh to the families of 18 persons who had been disappeared and the NHRC's tolerance of this stand of the state, is striking in the general denial of the phenomenon of disappearances. This was after the CBI had found that bodies of several persons had been cremated surreptitiously in the late '80s and early '90s - 585 persons who had been subsequently identified had been cremated after being labelled as unidentified.

Around 330 of them had been partially identified and over 1200 remained to be identified. The deficiency of compensation as a measure of reconciliation is also evident. Disappearances appear to be a pattern where there is militant resistance to the state. Case law speaks of this phenomenon in the Northeast. In fact, the first major case of compensation for disappearance after being picked up by the armed forces was from the Northeast.

On February 27, 2001, newspapers reported that it was alleged in the Lok Sabha, without being effectively countered, that the number of persons missing from the custody of the security forces and the police has risen to 2174 in Jammu and Kashmir; 76 cases had been registered and only one person had been challaned so far.

- Acknowledgment of involuntary disappearances
- Investigation, and seeking to establish what happened to the disappeared so that families and the community can finally know
- Prosecution and punishment, for reasons of deterrence too, and
- Compensation as a measure of atonement are being sought to be worked into the system

It was also reiterated that reconciliation would be impossible to achieve without such acknowledgment, identification of the disappeared and reparation. That Khalra disappeared even while the matter was being taken to the Supreme Court is a statement on impunity. The theme of impunity was laid out when K.P.S. Gill, the policeman in-charge in Punjab through the waning years of militancy, lashed out in protest when a policeman, Sandhu, committed suicide while facing multiple charges of excesses committed during the years of militancy. The schizophrenic attitude of the process which rewarded him when he killed 'terrorists', and later sought to prosecute him for abuse of power even amounting to murder, stood exposed. Gill

- Blamed the judiciary for having been inactive, or of playing safe, when captured terrorists were brought before it, and
- Held out the threat that if pursued by prosecution, the police would be unavailable to deal with militancy another time.

EXTRAORDINARY LAWS

These have been one of the means of routinising the enactment of laws that are normally promulgated in an emergency or in extraordinary situations.

The Terrorist and Disruptive Activities Act 1987 was contested for

- Its denial of fair trial standards - *e.g.*, it reduced the tiers of appeal the provision regarding making confessions to a police officer admissible in evidence
- The broad contours of the law on what constitutes terrorism, and
- Potential and proven abuse - for, *e.g.*, the largest number of TADA detenues were in Gujarat, where militant activity was not present.
- The public condemnation of TADA, political opposition to it, the NHRC's spirited intervention and the state's assessment that it was no longer necessary, led to the law not being re-enacted when it lapsed in 1995. There have, however, been further attempts to revive the law - as in the Prevention of Terrorism Act recommended in 1999 by the Law Commission, for instance. Further, state laws in Maharashtra, Andhra Pradesh and, more recently, in Madhya Pradesh and Karnataka - as a measure against organised crime- have brought the TADA back into their states under a hardly disguised identity. Tamil Nadu has also proposed a Prevention of Terrorism Bill along similar lines. The Armed Forces Special Powers Act 1958 is another law which provides extraordinary powers. It has been in force in the Northeast for these years. The TADA and the AFSPA survived challenge before the Supreme Court in the '90s. This has caused a serious rethink on the courts as a situs for testing the legitimacy of such extraordinary laws that deny fundamental rights, and breach human rights principles. It is evident that it is only vigilance, and resistance, which is keeping the proliferation of these laws in check. The arrest and detention of civilians under extraordinary laws, like the TADA, also appears to be routine. It has been alleged, for instance, that villagers in the vicinity of Veerappan, the sandalwood smuggler's beat are routinely subjected to harassment, search and detention. In the negotiations for the release of actor Rajkumar who was taken hostage by Veerappan on July 30, 2000, the release of 51 detainees being held under TADA since 1992 on suspicion of having participated in the murder of policemen was in issue. Human rights activists claim that many of them were local people who had been roped in as being 'associates' of Veerappan. When a civil liberties organisation moved the court for release of those so incarcerated, the petition was not entertained. But during the negotiations, the government of Karnataka showed a readiness to release them in the interests of law and order, and also, significantly, since others released on bail earlier 'have not repeated the offences and they have not involved themselves in any similar offences and terrorist activity have not been noticed recently in the area.'

PREVENTIVE DETENTION

When the Constitution came into being in 1950, preventive detention laws were avowedly intended to be a transient measure. During the emergency, the Maintenance of Internal Security Act 1971 was among the more infamous laws which allowed for preventive detention of persons in the avowed interest of maintenance of internal security. There are now a number of legislations which permit preventive detention, in the states and at the centre. The National Security Act 1980 is an instance of the latter. The A.P Prevention of Dangerous Activities of Bootleggers, Dacoits, Drug Offenders, Goondas, Immoral Traffic Offenders and Land Grabbers Act 1986 is an example of the former. Public protest against the continuance of these laws is almost inaudible despite

- The long periods, sometimes up to two years, that a person may be kept in preventive detention
- The tardiness of the procedure prescribed - *e.g.*, the executive may be given up to three months to get the opinion of the Advisory Board which may effectively have a person in custody under executive order up to ninety days
- The range of activities that are allowed to be covered by preventive detention laws that are unconnected with public order or law and order.

Unlike the challenge to the TADA, preventive detention laws have not engaged the human rights community in any sustained manner.

DETENTION

A range of detentions including those that were plainly illegal came to light during the course of our work:

- The incarceration of persons deemed to be 'non-criminal lunatics' or the wandering mentally ill in jails was investigated in a PIL before the Supreme Court. These are persons picked up under the Police Acts of the states, or under police powers in other laws such as the Indian Lunacy Act 1912, or its successor law, the Mental Health Act 1987. They are treated as `nuisances', or bracketed as being dangerous, this providing the rationale for putting them away. The term NCL is in contradistinction to `criminal lunatics', that is, those accused of crime but found to be mentally ill or suffering from mental disorder. For years NCLs were received in jails as places of `safe custody' under the Indian Lunacy Act 1912 and later under the Mental Health Act 1987. In the states of West Bengal and Assam, where the Supreme Court sent Commissioners to investigate, it was found that many of those in jails as NCLs were in fact not mentally ill at all, but had been placed there deviously, to serve some completely unrelated purpose. For instance, a 70-year woman was found to have been put away as an NCL apparently because her landlord was using it as a means of evicting her. We heard resonances of this reasoning from a lawyer-activist in Chennai.

- The Supreme Court declared, in August 1993, that using jails as places of safe custody to house non-criminal mentally ill persons is unconstitutional. Apart from the state of Assam, which admitted in an affidavit in the Supreme Court to continuing the practice, the NHRC has intermittently reiterated that NCMI should be housed in places other than jails. It is plain that the practice continues.
- This is an area that has not been widely addressed within the human rights community. NHRC's recognition of the issue too has been desultory.
- There is evidence in law reports, and activists have admitted to have knowledge of, the practice of hostage taking by the police where the person to be apprehended is not within reach of the police. Relatives of the person sought are then picked up and kept in custody till he surrenders. This appears to have happened with some regularity in Punjab, but we also heard of it in Delhi and Andhra Pradesh, for instance. This breach of the law needs further investigation and response.
- There have been reports of people spending long years in jail, which could have been averted if prisons were not as inaccessible as they are. Rudul Sah, the man who spent fourteen years in jail because he had been considered unfit to stand trial, and continued to remain untried despite having been declared fit, is one wellknown instance. Recent instances from Bihar and West Bengal reveal that the neglect that occasions such illegal incarceration continues. The incapacity of a person to follow up on his trial and sentence, and to procure orders in time has been known to keep him in prison long after he was due to have been released. The inability to furnish bail or sureties was reportedly one such reason for the large undertrial population.
- It is evident that systemic changes are imperative if these questions of personal liberty are to be addressed.
- In custodial institutions other than prisons - in 'protective homes' for women, for instance, the problem of custody versus shelter has been raised. Protective homes are established under the Immoral Traffic Act 1956. Since they are the only statutory institutions that can house women for 'protection' as also for 'correction', they act as places of custody, operating within the executive-magistracy system. We met women in 'protective custody' in the Agra Protective Home, who were witnesses in a case to be tried in Jhansi; they desired to leave and they had been in the institution for nearly two years. But

the law would not let them. 'Rescued' women were placed in these institutions, but the purpose of 'rehabilitation' was found to be too inadequate to make the difference.

- Prison jurisprudence since the late '60s recognises that prisoners do not lose all their rights because of imprisonment. Yet, there is a loss of rights within custodial institutions which continue to occur. For instance, it was found that the HIV status of all the women in the Agra Protective Home was public knowledge, and there was no confidentiality attaching to this information. There was segregation within the institutions of those found to be HIV positive, and, for a while, the Supreme Court too endorsed this. The rules governing women in these institutions uncannily resemble prison rules - such as those concerning visitors, letters, and even punishment for conduct within the institutions.
- Persons working in this area said that this was an area which called for an injection of human rights experience and perspectives.
- The non-release of persons cured of mental illness from institutions was also reported to be a problem. We repeatedly met the need for halfway homes and support services which could help a person be restored to liberty.
- In Delhi, we heard of persons who had been picked up as being persons of Bangladeshi origin, who were kept in custody in a night shelter till they could be repatriated if they were, in fact, found to belong to Bangladesh and the Foreigners Act 1946 could be invoked to effect this move. There was concern that even the basis of identifying them as possible foreigners was not clear and that dispelling suspicion of nationality could well be more difficult for the poor and the dispossessed.

It is also found that it is common practice to pick up people for questioning, and not record their presence in the police station till the police is ready to present them before a magistrate - a way of thwarting the constitutional requirement that every person taken into custody be produced before a magistrate within 24 hours. Apart from the illegality of such detention, it also makes difficult proving torture in custody during the period of illegal, unrecorded, detention. Human rights activists suggest that telegrams be dispatched to the Chief Minister, the Director General of Police, the Superintendent of Police, and the Governor for instance, when information about such illegal detention is obtained, to establish the time of detention. The conditions of persons with mental illness in institutions have been cause for human rights concern.

In Gwalior Mental hospital, for instance, it was found that persons with mental illness were left in nakedness; the explanation was that they tore their clothes if they were given them. The press raised the issue. Chaining of mentally ill patients was also a practice, and this was outlawed by an order of the court. One difficulty in ensuring that such violations do not occur, and in getting the law implemented, is access. The human rights community has not engaged with the problems faced within the walls of custodial institutions. Imaginative answers which will make open institutions of what are now bureaucratic, and closed, institutions is an imperative. The hysterectomy controversy in the early 1990s in Pune represents another aspect of the control and decisionmaking within custodial institutions.

The hysterectomy of girls below 18 years of age, who were mentally retarded, raised controversy about the decision made by the professionals. The professionals involved in making the decision neither denied that the hysterectomy was being done, nor did they did see it as a violation. It was justified as being in the best interests of the hygiene of the mentally retarded girl, as making practicable the care of the mentally retarded. The response did not rule out the possibility of sexual abuse when within the institutions, but said it would protect the girls from pregnancy in the event of such an encounter. The persons responsible for the decision responded angrily to the charges of human rights violations. The Medical Council of India, however, distanced itself from this position, and declared the practice as being against their norms. The intervention of the media and the human rights community precluded further hysterectomies from being done.

MISSING WOMEN

There are various situations which throw up the issue of 'missing' women. The lopsided sex ratio in many states, and the juvenile sex ratio in even a state such as Kerala is one area where women, and girls, go `missing'. In Orissa, we heard of the phenomenon of 'Jhansi' marriages and 'Gwalior' marriages. Girls from very poor homes were escorted by a 'broker' to be married to men in Jhansi or Gwalior, and he would bring back a bride price of ₹10,000 to ₹25,000 to be given to the girl's family. While some of these marriages had been found to be genuine, the possibility of some of these women being trafficked was not ruled out. Also, what a girl/woman did if deserted or ill-treated was not clear. There was therefore an attempt by activists to keep track of women who had not been heard from for over a period of three months, so that their whereabouts could be verified and their safety ascertained. In July 1999, activists had begun the process of documenting the 'missing' woman. In Delhi, we were informed that missing persons reports when women go missing from their marital homes were hardly ever related with unidentified bodies of women who were declared to have committed suicide by drowning, for instance. The paucity of information, and the difficulties in follow up, has kept this issue in the margins of human rights concerns.

HOMICIDE IN THE MATRIMONIAL HOME

Often identified as being dowry-related deaths, unnatural deaths of women in their marital home has acquired prominence. Like encounter killings, acknowledgment has not led to a reduction in the incidence of such homicide. In Andhra Pradesh in 1990 a civil liberties organisation raised the issue of violation of women's rights as a human rights issue by comparing the number of dowry deaths and the number of encounter killings during one time period - about 2000 dowry deaths, and 300 deaths in encounters. In Bangalore, a women's group keeps a watch in the Burns Ward of the leading government hospital, and also scrutinises newspapers for reports of deaths of young women, which they then follow up.

They also had a 'Truth Commission' where a tribunal heard the narratives of the families of girls/women who had been the victims of dowry deaths. The inadequacies of investigation, and the many slips in the judicial process which results in a low rate of prosecution and a lower rate still of conviction, was observed everywhere. The definition of 'dowry death' in the Penal Code, based on preponderance of probability and a shifting of onus represents a significant shift in criminal law and jurisprudence. In the meantime, the Dowry Prohibition Act has been hardly at all implemented.

Most states still have no Dowry Prohibition Officers. The maintenance of list of things given and received is still not mandatory. S.498 A, which was brought in to deal with cruelty in the matrimonial home, has suffered criticism as being abused, sending the family of the man to prison till bail is procured.

Some women's groups, however, contended that the abuse was only marginal, and that this was the only provision in law which could hold the perpetrator of domestic cruelty accountable. Some also spoke of bringing into law the notions of right to matrimonial home and matrimonial property as other approaches of protecting women on whom cruelty is practised.

DOMESTIC VIOLENCE

In locating domestic violence in the terrain of human rights, one point of view was that it is not the identity of the perpetrator alone which can be allowed to determine whether a victim has been subjected to a human right violation or not: that it is a man or his family who exercises their power to harass, assault and injure a woman, and not the state which is the perpetrator, should then make no difference to the place for this violence in human rights discourse.

Also, it is state practice, and endorsement, of patriarchy that keeps such violence in the home, we were told.

- Crime against women cells in police stations
- Counselling centres
- Help lines
- Short stay homes - which, though, are few in number have been set up in many cities.

There has also been a concerted effort to bring in a law to deal with domestic violence. A Bill prepared, debated and presented to the government by a women's organisation has been adopted by Parliament for discussion, which is a significant step in a non-governmental role in law making. Section 498 A was introduced into the Penal Code in 1983. It makes cruelty to a woman within the matrimonial home punishable with imprisonment up to three years and fine. It is a cognisable, non-bailable, offence. Widespread violence against women, and increasing evidence of women dying unnatural deaths in the matrimonial homes provoked the women's movement to demand a change in the criminal law. The offence is non-bailable, that is a complaint under Section 498 A, once registered as an FIR, would result in the arrest of the members of the matrimonial family of the woman. They would have to be granted bail by a court before release, and this could keep them in custody for varying periods of time. In matters of remission of sentence, too, offenders convicted under Section 498 A may be excluded.

On the one hand, there have been complaints of the misuse of this provision, and the consequent harassment, often incarceration, of many members of the family complained against. On the other, there is little scope to deny that the incidence of cruelty, including physical cruelty, which leads even to death, is extraordinarily high. This is an issue yet unresolved; the Domestic Violence Bill may have some impact on it.

In the meantime, an activist lawyer asserts that the phenomenon of violence and death in the matrimonial home should not need to be linked invariably with the phenomenon of dowry; violence and cruelty are independent entities within many homes. An activist also told us: when a man beats his wife regularly, and the wife gets him soundly thrashed by the police, civil liberties groups are sometimes confused on what stand to take.

SATI

The burning of Roop Kanwar on the pyre of her husband in Rajasthan in 1986, has reintroduced sati into mainstream discourse. Questions of volition, custom and communal pride have been raised justifying the practice. State inaction has been at issue. In 1987, the Commission of Sati Act was enacted making abetment of sati an offence; and the death penalty was introduced as an alternative sentence. The attempt to commit sati was made punishable with imprisonment for a term up to six months or with fine, or both; this has been contested ever since its inception as punishing the victim. The 'glorification' of sati, where a temple is constructed and a dead woman worshipped bringing in money to the family, has also been made punishable.

This last is constantly under contest - as denying the right to practise a religion. Women's groups in Rajasthan see this as a particularly important provision in taking away the material incitement in the commission of sati. The communal violence of much of the protest against this law, and of the practice itself, is a telling statement of the capacity of patriarchy to deny a place for human rights.

CHILD MARRIAGE

Though a law prohibiting child marriage has been in the statute books since 1929, it is still performed in many parts of India. For instance, the practice of performing child marriages on Akas Teej, it is reported, has not stopped in Rajasthan. It is widely believed that the gang rape of Bhanwari Devi was intended as a lesson, since she was active in preventing child marriages. Another aspect of child marriage was revealed when Ameena, a girl of about 12 years, was married to an old man from Saudi Arabia who was to take her out of the country as his bride.

CHILD LABOUR

Apart from the employment of children in work, including those classified as hazardous, it was reported that

- Children continue to be sold into labour. The parents of a young girl from Assam were paid a sum of money for the girl to be brought to Delhi as a domestic worker. Her plight came to light when she ran away from the ill-treatment she suffered, and she was given shelter by a social activist.
- Child workers employed in homes and in commercial workplaces, were subjected to ill-treatment. The chaining of bonded child labour in the carpet industry near Varanasi so that they could not escape was reported. Injuries on the person of domestic child workers in Delhi sometimes resulting in death, have been reported intermittently in the press. In Maharashtra, a civil liberties organisation took the state and a contractor to court when the latter ill-treated, resulting in death, one of the young boys he had brought with him from Tamil Nadu.

These manifestations of violence against the child disguised as child labour calls to be addressed. The vulnerability of the child has also been seen in Delhi, for instance, where child domestic workers have been accused of killing their employers, or in being accomplices to outsiders. The 'social clause' on child labour does not result in doing away with child labour, we were told, but causes segregation. There were dissenting voices on the ILO Convention on the Elimination of the Worst Forms of Child Labour. The provisions which speak of child prostitution and child pornography as labour are unacceptable, they said.

'These are crimes, not labour,' we were told. Further, when Indian law is so strict that it says that non-payment of minimum wages amounts to bonded labour - a provision that is not found in any international convention - what use is one more convention, we were asked. In 1993, the Supreme Court declared that education is a fundamental right till a child reaches the age of 14 years. Education for the child has got tangled with the issue of child labour; sending the child to school is projected as a necessary step to ending the practice of child labour.

In Andhra Pradesh, an organisation working in the area of education for children has done away with the uncertainties of definition by working on the premise that every child out of school is child labour. They have therefore arrived at a non-negotiable: that every child must belong in a school. In this view, NFE centres, for instance, would be a means of perpetuating child labour.

So, too, with the adjusting of school timings to accommodate the working child. In the meantime, this 1999 Convention is being canvassed for signature, and ratification by the Indian State. The convention defines 'the worst forms of child labour' as comprising:

- All forms of slavery or practices similar to slavery, such as the sale and trafficking of children, forced or compulsory labour, debt bondage and serfdom;
- The use, procuring or offering of a child for prostitution, for the production of pornography or for pornographic performances;
- The use, procuring or offering of a child for illicit activities, in particular for the production and trafficking of drugs as defined in the relevant international treaties;
- Work which, by its nature or the circumstances in which it is carried out, is likely to jeopardize the health, safety or morals of children.'

This is in consonance with the recent trend among UN organisations to directly involve human rights in standard-setting, and the creating of binding obligations of states in their area of operation.

THE 'NEGLECTED' CHILD

- Street children have their peculiar vulnerability. In Bangalore, a study reveals that almost every street child has been sexually violated at some time or another. They are also specially susceptible to drugs. Street children, however, take care of themselves, and often of each other. It does not appear that institutionalising them is an answer to their needs, nor do they seem willing to trade their liberty for a life off the streets. In Bangalore, Bombay and Delhi, we heard of drop-in centres: places where children could drop in for a wash, some lessons, to keep their savings and to discuss their problems with others, if they so chose. They were, however, reported to be vulnerable to being 'rounded up' and sent periodically into state institutions from where they would need help to emerge, or from where they would 'escape'. Women in prostitution have faced the possibility of their children being forcibly separated from them, following an order of the Supreme Court in Gaurav Jain v. Union of India. A 'raid' conducted by Delhi Police in 1990 in which 112 'children' were picked up from the GB Road area was an indication of what such a power being given to the police could mean to the women and their children. The recent changed law on 'children in need of care and protection' even prescribes adoption as an option that may be enforced by the state.

CHILD ABUSE

There has been increasing evidence of child abuse, and more particularly child sexual abuse, being pervasive. The perpetrator is often a near relative or someone close to the family. This adds to the vulnerability of the abused child, and, apart from the confusion and sense of shame which the child experiences, it is also that there is a problem with a refuge which the child can access.

The dependence on the family as a support structure in times of abuse breaks down when the offending event occurs in the home. Following what is widely considered as a useful intervention in the Supreme Court in the Vishaka guidelines regarding sexual harassment in the workplace, the matter of child abuse has also been taken to the court, and the Law Commission has been inducted into setting the parameters for care and action in cases of child sexual abuse.

THE 'UNWANTED' GIRL CHILD

The declining sex ratio, particularly the declining juvenile sex ratio, even in Kerala which is celebrated in economic writings and in state policy for having achieved a high rate of literacy and negative population growth, has begun to seriously engage, among others, researchers and women activists. The low status of women continues to be reflected in

- The practice of infanticide including in some parts of Tamil Nadu,
- Foeticide,
- Sex-selective abortion which the amniocentesis technology has made common, and
- Mal-nourishment among girl children.

In Usilampatti Taluk, reportedly, the ratio of female: male is 879:1000. Since 1986, the issue of female infanticide has been in focus in this area. More recently, scanning centres have mushroomed in the area, and female foeticide is rampant among those who are able to afford it. We were told that, in Tamil Nadu, there are around 2000 scan centres, most of which are unregistered. A researcher reported his encounter with the sale of girl children by communities in Andhra Pradesh to persons who then placed them for adoption. He drew attention to the astonishing fact that there is, as of now, no law to control, or punish, the sale of children. The involvement of adoption agencies in A.P. in what is allegedly the sale of children has since come to public attention, in April 2001.

PROSTITUTION

The fear of AIDS, it is perceived, has given the issue of prostitution a visibility. This has, however, led to attributing to women in prostitution the trait of being a 'high risk group', even as it has been contended that it is high risk behaviour and not high risk groups that should be targeted. It appears that patterns of funding have impacted on this identification of the prostitute woman as belonging to a high-risk group. The demand for prostitution to be recognised as 'sex work' has been raised, with dignity of the woman in prostitution as its basis. There are differing perceptions about prostitution - one which sees it as exploitative of women, and another that views it as representing the 'agency' of the women in the profession. There are various shades of meaning given to 'exploitation' and 'agency' which lies in the spaces between these two positions.

Decriminalisation is also proposed, and disputed, on differing understandings of what decriminalising will mean, and do. Most of the people we spoke to on the issue of prostitution, however, felt after a discussion emphasising the difference, that the practice of prostitution should be delinked from the issue of trafficking.

In this context, trafficking is seen to be the sale and purchase of women and girls, and, more recently, boys, into prostitution. While 'voluntariness' is a term with graded meanings, especially since economic compulsions and social exclusion are not uncommon causes for entering into the practice of prostitution, it is the distinctly involuntary nature of trading in human beings that is at the hub of trafficking. Trafficking in minors is a scourge that is commonly referred to as a crime to be curbed. We encountered the issue of organising women in prostitution in two different ways.

In Calcutta, a 'samiti' of sex workers are articulating their position, and taking a pro-active lead in matters of preventing the entry of minors into the profession in their area of operation. They also said that, if trafficking be seriously dealt with, they be allowed to, legally, participate in curtailing trafficking - for who else was more likely than the people already in the profession to know when women and girls were bought and sold, they asked. In Mumbai, a respondent working among prostitute women for over a decade, advocated 'collectivisation' but had a problem with adopting the norm of forming unions of women in prostitution. While she did find that the state was doing very little about trafficking, she was convinced that if sex work were seen as 'real work' under the law, all efforts to curb trafficking would cease.

It was also suggested that 'sex work is real work' is a funderdriven agenda, and, that those who do not adopt this line were being deliberately excluded. In Kerala, however, a different perspective emerged where a distinction was drawn between the demand that persons in sex work should get all labour rights and the rights based approach. As a feminist, our respondent espoused the rights based approach. There was a recognition that most feminist ideologies oppose commercial sex workers coming together; the commercialisation of the body was identified as the problem.

Also, most people do not believe in the agency of commercial sex workers, it was explained. There was an opposition to licensing since that would only lead to further exploitation. The issue has been invisibilised over the years, and with people in high places being involved, it has helped to send it further underground. The Surinelli and Vidhura cases have however increased confidence to complain; and people are now listening differently. Another women's activist opposed the use of the term 'commercial sex worker': prostitution is not productive work, she said. But her main problem was that she saw prostitution as reinforcing patriarchy, and that endorsing prostitution as work would fall into the snare patriarchy has set for the women's movement. In the matter of trafficking, it was pointed out that proposals for checking all women travelling on their own, particularly across borders was a move detrimental to the interests of women and could end up curbing their right to free movement and achieve little else.

PRISONS

The conditions in jails; solitary confinement; the refusal to make condoms available in Tihar jail on the ground that homosexuality is an offence in law, and this would be seen as fostering an illegality; the inhuman treatment of prisoners, including their being kept in leg irons, for instance; overcrowding of prisons; the right of prisoners, including undertrials, to vote are issues that have been raised repeatedly over the years.

The courts have been the arena of contest. The inadequacy of medical services in prisons, often resulting in the death of prisoners has been much in evidence. Apart from the inconclusive enquiry into the death of Rajan Pillai, when he was in jail, High Courts and the NHRC have been confronted repeatedly with this issue. Statistics in the Annual Reports of the NHRC reveal that there are a much larger number of deaths in judicial custody than there is in police custody. Given the frequency and seriousness of the complaints about medical services in prisons, it would bear investigation to find out how many of the deaths in judicial custody are, in fact, occasioned by medical negligence.

The condition of persons on death row does not appear to have been investigated so far. Nor the effect that execution of prisoners has on their families. The inaccessibility to legal services that is endemic in most prisons, has been identified as a human rights issue, but has not been resolved yet. There are reports of prison riots which were allegedly caused by the poor conditions in prisons including insufficient provision of food, and the maltreatment, including the brutalising, of prisoners. On November 17, 1999, for instance, a riot broke out in Chennai Central Prison. It left at least nine persons dead, and one more succumbed to injuries on November 19, 1999.

There were at least seven prisoners with bullet injuries who were referred to the government general hospital. The figures of those injured and dead in the riots varies, but it appears to be around 100 prisoners. The deputy jailor was killed in the riots. The simmering discontent seems to have had to do with inadequate food, the meagre water supplied to the prisoners, and the torture meted out to them by the prison staff. The death of a prisoner tortured and killed in the Central Prison in July 1999, which was explained away without an enquiry as being a suicide, seems to have caused resentment and anger among the prisoners.

It was the death of Boxer Vadivel, a prisoner believed to have been tortured for over three days between 12th and 15th of November, and the torture of two other prisoners by the Deputy Jailor which sparked off the riots. Jeyakumar was burned alive. The prisoners claimed to a fact-finding team that the rebellion had already come under control when antiriot police were brought in and prisoners were indiscriminately targeted. For instance, a prisoner who was physically disabled, and could not have posed any threat to the police, was shot at point blank range. The anatomy of a prison riot, and what it means in the context of human rights, and of punishment, calls to be investigated in full, and addressed.

Prison riots have been erupting sporadically, leaving little reason to doubt that they are symptomatic of a systemic malaise. The condition of medical care in prisons is woeful, and cases before the High Courts and the NHRC testify to this fact. The inordinately large number of deaths in judicial custody, as reflected in the figures set out in the Annual Reports of the NHRC, is also an indicator. That prisons are death traps becomes apparent. Overcrowding of prisons, with a large population of undertrial prisoners spending extended periods in jail - a recent press report cites a survey conducted by the State Department in Bihar which shows 154 undertrial prisoners in Bhagalpur jail for over 20 years awaiting trial and they are now over 70 years old - only strains the system further. Systemic changes and bold initiatives are imperative. So far, the Supreme Court's directive in 1979 to release undertrial prisoners on personal recognisance bonds, and periodic intervention thereafter by the Supreme Court, has provided *ad hoc* relief. There is little to indicate that there has been any fundamental re-thinking on this matter.

On the other hand, recent legislation is severe in matters of bail, and persons arrested under the NDPS Act 1985, for instance, regardless of the nature of their participation in the offence, are not entitled to bail. In Mumbai, social workers reported that they have been allowed access to prisoners to help them re-establish, and maintain, contact with their families, and to provide related support services to the prisoners.

They admitted to shutting their eyes to human rights violations in prisons since any intervention of that nature would jeopardise even the services they are now able to provide. In Chennai and in Mumbai, the '80s and a part of the '90s saw active provision of legal aid to prisoners; in Chennai, the High Court legal aid board was engaged in this process. In Delhi, legal literacy, literacy, meditation and yoga and legal aid has reached Tihar jail. The setting up of the NHRC appears to have had some impact on the accessibility of prisons, as have the many PILs which challenged the conditions within.

WAGES TO PRISONERS

The work that prisoners do has been devalued in a decision of the Supreme Court in State of Gujarat v. High Court of Gujarat. A judge in the case has held that

- Prisoners are not entitled to minimum wages, particularly where they have been sentenced to rigourous imprisonment, and it is part of their sentence to do hard labour
- The non-payment of wages in prison will not amount to a violation of the constitutional dictum on the right against exploitation
- Where they do earn a wage, apart from deductions for their maintenance in the prison, monies may be taken from it to pay to the victim as compensation.

There is a complete negation of the rehabilitative potential of work and wages, and a re-introduction of the purely punitive in this judgement of the court that human rights advocates and activists will have to contest.

SEXUALITY

Discrimination against, and harassment of, those with a sexual orientation different from the heterosexual is being more openly addressed in the past ten years than it was earlier. Yet, coming out openly is still an act of courage. And we were told how homosexual couples were susceptible to arrest and extortion. Just the knowledge that a person is a homosexual would render him vulnerable, they said. The lesbian groups that we met spoke about the difficulty of coming out, and the support services that were needed to help resist, principally, the families. One of the ways of providing that support is in the initiation of 'help lines'.

FREEDOM OF EXPRESSION

- The rise of communalism has been accompanied by an assault on free expression. The vandalising of M.F. Hussain's paintings because he had painted a nude Saraswati many years ago; the destruction of the exhibition organised by SAHMAT in Varanasi because it depicted Rama differently from how the vandals believed he should be depicted;

the protests, and their vulgarisation when the protesters paraded in their underwear in front of Dilip Kumar's house, against the film 'Fire'; the concerted attacks on the filming of 'Water' - all these are instances of intolerance, which have denied free expression, with the implicit - sometimes explicit - support of the state. The banning of the play on Nathuram Godse following protests and disturbances are part of a pattern. More recently, there have been reports of a government circular that conferences, seminars, workshops...which include participants from abroad require clearance from the government, including the External Affairs Ministry. Human rights are specifically in the list. And it is particularly applicable to people from Pakistan, China, Bangladesh, Sri Lanka and Afghanistan.

DALITS

The practice of untouchability has persisted, and dalit activists and unions have been making efforts to demonstrate its pervasiveness and variety, even while they contest its practice. In Andhra Pradesh, in a study done by dalit activists, 46 ways of practising untouchability have been documented. In Kerala, there was collaboration underway between caste groups and dalits in combating caste and brahmanism. In Gujarat, a study of the practice of untouchability has been recently done. Some groups working among dalits, and including some dalit groups, have been lobbying to place caste as an agenda in the World Conference against Racism. The definition evolving in the conference, which includes discrimination based on descent and occupation is seen as an acknowledgment of caste discrimination.

This is an avowed effort to internationalise the issue of caste-based discrimination and oppression. This issue permits an exploration into the relationship between a movement - in this case, the dalit movement - and groups working with dalits and/or dalit issues in terms of their respective politics and priorities. Police firing on a group of dalit villagers in Nadunalumoolaikkinaru in Tamil Nadu in 1991 is believed to have occurred to put down a young leadership that was emerging in the village. A chain of circumstances from the support given to the villagers by activists, to filing the matter as a case in the Supreme Court, to three committees which investigated the matter, to the awarding and disbursement of compensation to the injured villagers and the court order which prohibited the indicted policemen from being posted in the vicinity appears to have empowered the village. It has also bolstered their confidence that help could well come from beyond the village. In Melavalavur it was a different story. This is a panchayat which is reserved for dalit leadership within the panchayat system. When elections were first to be held

- The dalits were chastised, subjected to a community fine of ₹2000 and warned to withdraw their nominations.

- In the second round, the administration urged the dalits to file nominations, which they did. The ballot boxes were taken away by the non-dalit villagers.
- The third time around, the administration promised protection and conducted the elections amidst threats and tight security. About a month after the elections, the dalit panchayat leader, Murugesan, and five of his comrades were waylaid when they were travelling in a public bus, and brutally hacked to death on the highway.

This was in June 1997. Since then, another election has nominally installed a dalit as panchayat head. But the village lives in a state of permanent terror. A police outpost has been set up, but in that part of the village from where the threat to the dalits emanates.

A memorial has been constructed to the memory of the six dead men. The Scheduled Castes and Scheduled Tribes Act has been on the statute books since 1989. There are however hardly any convictions under this Act. Dalit activists say that there are many loopholes in the law which help offenders slip out of both the Atrocities Act as well as the Penal Code. An activist made particular mention of Section 3 (iv) and (v) of the Act in illustrating the non-user of this law. Studies on the working of this Act have been started in some states. Manual scavenging, and the disinterest of the state in putting an end to this inhuman practice which involves the carrying of excreta manually, and which additionally aggravates caste-based exclusion has been identified as a priority for action in Andhra Pradesh and Tamil Nadu.

MEDICAL RESEARCH

- The connection between abortion, *in vitro* fertilisation and gene manipulation was drawn to ask how the question of human rights could be considered in this context. The poser was: ought it not to be the primary question whether neo-eugenics through gene manipulation should be resisted, or was it to be asked in terms of the mother's choice to have a 'blue-eyed baby girl'? Depo Provera, a contraceptive drug, was introduced into the Indian market without conducting Phase IV trials, which meant that the Indian state conducted no research specific to Indian users before deciding to introduce the drug in the market. The issue in Phase IV trials of Net-oen was of informed consent. In the pre-liberalisation phase, we were informed, all research was to be undertaken by the ICMR. But post-liberalisation, there has been a dramatic change, and the trend has been for pharmaceutical companies, or the NGOs funded for the purpose, to conduct research; their agenda is not beyond suspicion. Pharmaceutical companies have been attempting to dilute the guidelines for scientific research on human subjects. The Nuremberg Code was very strict. The later Helsinki declaration, we were told, relaxed these rules. And efforts are underway to further relax the notion of informed consent for the greater common good. These efforts have been stalled at the international level. But ICMR's 'Ethical Guidelines for Biomedical Research on Human Subjects' has been amended in 2000 to allow proxy consent in some cases, such as in epidemiological situations or in the larger public good. In 1997, the Indian government signed an agreement with the USA that would allow Indian citizens to be used as research subjects in an international research project on human genome for furthering 'international good'. Since this became known, there have been protests - that the bodies of Indian citizens do not belong to the state that it can sign them away. Court battles around banned drugs being sold in the Indian market have sometimes resulted in prospective banning. But the plea of the pharmaceutical company that the stocks be not destroyed, but that they be allowed to transport it to another jurisdiction outside India has been allowed. Sharing information with other potential markets becomes of importance, and ways of doing this may have to be established.

POPULATION POLICIES

There has been a deliberate re-introduction of 'incentives' and 'disincentives', and of punitive measures into state policy.

- The birth of a third child beyond a period of gestation from the commencement of state laws on the subject will disqualify a person from standing for elections to the panchayat, or to continue in office.
- Medical termination of pregnancy and tubectomy has been included in the Maternity Benefit Act 1961 for 'benefit' under the law. The threatened denial of 'maternity benefit' for the birth of the third child and thereafter was, however, shelved after concerted protest, The new provision puts an onus on the woman to keep the size of her family low.
- There are private proposals pending in various state legislatures including Delhi and Andhra Pradesh to disentitle the third child to ration under the Public Distribution System, and for the parent to be penalised in their jobs if they hold a government job. The Delhi proposal even included provisions that the family could not be allowed to procure a house if there was a third child! These have not yet become law, but they have not disappeared from the public debate altogether.
- 'Social marketing' of contraceptive drugs, supported in Uttar Pradesh by large grants from funders, has been the subject of protest from, particularly, women activists. Social marketing, which includes across-

the-counter sales, would inevitably lead to ill-informed use of the contraceptives, without an understanding of the sideeffects, or of the meaning of symptoms that may manifest upon use. The prioritising of reducing population at the cost of women's health is being stoutly resisted.

ORGAN TRANSPLANT

A racket in the sale of kidneys was exposed in Karnataka in the late 1980s and early '90s. There were allegations that the 'donor' was duped and his kidneys were removed and 'donated'; or that the donor had sold his kidneys as a commodity may be sold to raise resources - poverty was the characteristic that distinguished the donor. A series of exposés confirmed that there was a pattern to the sale and purchase of kidneys, which implicated, among others, doctors and hospitals.

The dust refused to settle, and in 1994, Parliament enacted the Transplantation of Human Organs Act 1994, which allowed organ donation either only after death, or where the receiver was a near relative of the donor, or it is actuated by 'affection, or attachment towards the recipient.' In the last-mentioned case, an Authorisation Committee has to approve the donation. The Act, in its prefatory text, says it is 'to provide for the regulation of removal, storage and transplantation of human organs for therapeutic purposes and for the prevention of commercial dealings in human organs.' The issue seems to have acquired a subterranean residence since. This may be an area which must be regularly revisited to prevent exploitation, and worse. In a different context, the issue of surrogacy has entered Indian parlance; but the human rights, and legal, implications have not been pursued with much rigour.

TRAFFICKING

While trafficking in women is rampant in many parts of the country, and also across borders, it is Kerala that the sexual exploitation of women and trafficking has been exposed, and the accused brought to trial and conviction. The Surinelli case, the Ice Cream Parlour case and the Vidhura case are undiluted narratives of sexual exploitation. In the Surinelli case, forty persons, including prominent political figures and persons from the establishment among them, were convicted after a prolonged trial in 2000. They are now on bail while their appeal is pending. Some women's activists have been studying the issue of migration and trafficking - whether for prostitution, labour in sweat shops, domestic work which is often ill-paid and oppressive, or as mail order brides - while recognising that while migration makes women vulnerable to exploitation - and violence, migration is often not wholly involuntary. Women, for instance, migrate to escape violent domestic situations too. Shorn of its moral content, activists say, the law regarding trafficking could actually help women trafficked into situations for which they did not bargain.

BONDED LABOUR

Though the Bonded Labour Act is of 1976 vintage, it was not till the Supreme Court's judgement in December 1983 that the recognition of bonded labour acquired a national reach. As the champion of the bonded labour said it, it is

- Minimum wages
- Minimum guarantees of employment
- Child labour
- Land rights and
- Alcohol

Identification, release and rehabilitation of bonded labour have happened essentially by court supervision. In Tamil Nadu, there is a separate ministry that has been set up to deal with bonded labour; this was following a report given to the Supreme Court of the extent of bonded labour prevalent in the state.

The issue of bonded labour has been handed over by the court to the NHRC, which has set up a committee including activists, advocates and bureaucrats with experience, to find a means of dealing with the issue. We watched while a political activist working among bonded labour discoursed with a body of bonded labourers from Rajasthan. They were seeking his help in getting free, and getting land which could help them retain their liberty.

The advice was that they get together a mass of similarly positioned people before launching a campaign in their district.

The confidence they exuded that bringing together 25,000 people in the district would not be an unmanageable task was an indication of the dimensions of the problem of bonded labour.

ANTI-LIQUOR MOVEMENTS

There is a connection that seems to exist between liquor and violence, particularly domestic violence. Many parts of the country have witnessed anti-liquor movements in assertion of the women's right to be free of violence. This includes Andhra Pradesh, Himachal Pradesh and Orissa. Apart from the factor of state interest - particularly in terms of revenue - in the proliferation of liquor, the liquor mafia also has a long reach.

There have been reports of women leading anti-liquor movements being killed, in an apparent attempt to stifle protest and resistance. Illicit liquor and the deaths of those who drink the brew - the 'hooch tragedy', as it is termed - is oft-experienced, and it is common to find people wielding state power, including ministers, being implicated. Last year, for instance, Kerala reverberated with reports of deaths in just such a hooch tragedy. In Uttarakhand, the demand for prohibition was closely linked to the struggle for statehood and is a challenge before the new government.

HIV AND AIDS

The right

- To privacy
- To confidentiality between doctor and patient
- To informed consent
- Against discrimination have been issues that have been raised in the context of AIDS, particularly since the AIDS Bill which was in circulation in the mid-1980s.

The identification as 'high risk groups' or as 'high risk activity' has been considered both in pragmatic and rights-related terms. While categorising people as 'high risk' on the basis of the class to which they belong has been rejected by rights activists, it has in fact been adopted in practice.

The question of confidentiality has been adjudicated in the 'right to marry' case in which the Supreme Court held that the right to marry is not an absolute right. Referring to the provisions in the Penal Code,the court held that, apart from making a person punishable under the law if he marries and transmits AIDS to a woman, there was duty upon him not to marry. And the doctor, aware of the HIV status of the patient had not disclosed it to persons he knew were likely to be affected by it, he would be a participant in the crime,' the court said. Till a disease/ condition is cured,the right to marry will be 'suspended', the court has held.

There are two points of view in this position of the court on the 'right to marry'. A rights group advocating the cause of people with HIV/AIDS, and of persons with a positive status, contend that the right to marry is part of the right to life. A woman activist lawyer has taken the stand that the disclosure mandated by the court is necessary to protect the interests of women. The former group contests this expectation, and holds that this will result in denial of rights to positive people without empowering women.

A respondent further located it in the context of 'personhood' - that even while conceding that there may be no right to marry, there would be a violation of the rights of the HIV+ person where there is disclosure without any of the protections that an HIV+ person may need, and to which they would be entitled - particularly given the rejection and discrimination that is known to ensue. The right to treatment, and discrimination - in the workplace, in custodial institutions and in places like hospitals - of positive people are centrally in the human rights arena.

DENOTIFIED TRIBES

British India notified specified tribes as 'criminal tribes', with all members of the tribe tarred by the same brush, and all of them classed as criminals or potential criminals. The Indian Parliament passed a law in the early years after independence repealing this categorisation of tribes. The 'ex-criminal tribes' are now referred to as 'denotified tribes'. While the status of these tribes has changed in law, the prejudices attaching to treatment of these tribes seems relatively unchanged. The attribution of criminal characteristics to a tribe has not abated. That they continue to be called `denotified tribes' freezes their status. Rampant discrimination, and criminalisation was reported. The neglect of land reforms, and of improving their conditions of life, was reportedly allowing for the perpetuation of stereotypes about these communities. The very construction of identity was said to be responsible for the human rights violations that they faced, and was acknowledged as a violation on its own.

TOURISM

Tourism's contribution to the violation of human rights has become an area of increasing concern.

- The growth of the sex industry, including the use of children for sexual pleasure, is associated by activists with tourism.
- The displacement and exclusion of people from forest areas, and the introduction of elite tourism is said to be passed off as 'eco-tourism'; activists find this contradictory
- The taking over of agricultural land to create hotel resorts, as is happening in the Diamond Harbour area in West Bengal, is opposed as being inherently unjust and environmentally unfriendly.
- The images of the reservoir in the Tehri and at the Sardar Sarovar being converted into lake resorts, militates particularly against equity.

Destruction of culture, sometimes through showcasing culture, is another issue. An instance is the Todas in Tamil Nadu. The non-involvement of local communities in making choices about whether, and what kind of, tourism would be brought into their midst was also reported.

RIGHT TO INFORMATION

The Mazdoor Kisan Sangharsh Samiti. It has caught the imagination of activists and groups across the country, particularly as a tool for preventing and challenging violations as well as asserting the right to development. A norm of transparency has been given prominence, including transparency of the government as well as the group working in the area.

The irresistible force it has generated has moved the government, albeit reluctantly, to table a Freedom of Information Bill 2000. Meanwhile, the right to information has been introduced into the law following the Bhopal Gas disaster. Among the persons now entitled to receive information about potential hazards in a factory are

- The workers
- the local authority
- People living in the vicinity of the factory as also the Inspector appointed under the Factories Act 1948.

The information is to include the means of disposal of hazardous substances, and the arrangements for their storage or transportation. Information on what should be done to limit damage in the event of a disaster is also to be disseminated; the onus is on those running the factory. We did not, however, hear of anyone having used these provisions. The rights inherent in these provisions demand to be asserted.

POLITICAL VIOLENCE BY NON-STATE ACTORS

Variously termed as 'militancy', 'terrorism', 'non-state violence', the use of violence in pursuing political ends has been in existence for over a couple of decades at least, in a number of states. The state response has been varied including

- The enactment of the TADA, and other extraordinary laws, including the treatment of political violence as 'organised crime' as has happened in Andhra Pradesh, Madhya Pradesh and Maharashtra
- The identification of such political activists as 'enemy' of military forces - as in the ITBP Act which defines 'enemy' as including 'all armed mutineers, armed rebels, armed rioters, pirates and any person in arms against whom it is the duty of any person subject to this Act to take action.'
- The unleashing of state violence, as happened in the Punjab particularly in the late '80s, and the beginning of the '90s. Or, again, as being witnessed in the encounter killings in Andhra Pradesh.
- The implicit equation of state violence with non-state violence in placing both in the agenda of the NHRC, while yet leaving violations by the Armed Forces beyond the NHRC's direct reach

The question of political violence has gone through phases in the civil liberties movement. In the 1970s, a political journalist told us, he had walked out of a civil liberties organisation because they had taken a decision to focus on state violence, and not speak to condemn violence by non-state actors. In the 1980s, silence about the violence of the militants in Punjab, which included the deliberate and often indiscriminate killing of civilian targets, was held out as evidence of the partial and one-sided image that the civil liberties movement conjured up; there was an uncertainty that crept in among civil liberties groups too. In the 1990s, there was an open debate, most specifically in the context of Andhra Pradesh, where one point of view held that political violence to overpower and alter systemic violence could not be condemned; and another point of view emerged that revolutionary violence was not equal to, or the same as, people's response, and that sustained violence over decades injured the weak and the vulnerable the most. 'Systematic and calculated violence begins with the enemy, ' a civil liberties activist says, 'but soon turns to agents of the enemy within and among one's friends.'

There is also the question of congruence between means and ends, he adds. The abduction and disappearance of Sanjay Ghosh at the hands of the ULFA in 1997 did lead to re-appraisal of the presumptions about revolutionary violence and the latitude that should be permitted it. A civil liberties group, for instance, spoke of its position as opposition to 'systematic, significant and sensitive killing by armed opposition groups.'

An activist said: 'unless a revolutionary movement develops a tradition of human rights, there is a problem.' The ranks of 'surrendered' militants has raised human rights issues - not only in terms of their rehabilitation but also for how they are used by the state. Caught between the cadres that they have walked away from, and the police or security forces who are now their protectors, it has been noticed that an inordinately large number of 'surrendered' militants die violent deaths. It also appeared evident to civil liberties groups that the surrendered militants are set up as stooges to carry out 'executions, which would then be passed off as a clash between the cadres and the deserters. Their position is plainly vulnerable. In Andhra Pradesh, we heard that cases against surrendered naxalites are never dropped, leaving them open to blackmail and to being manipulated.

Recent brutal killings of civil liberties activists, often in broad daylight and open to public gaze, are suspected to have been engineered on order of the state government, using surrendered naxalites. Political violence in North Kerala and West Bengal seems to claim victims with regularity. It is an occurrence about which activists in both states spoke. In West Bengal, activists spoke of 140 CPM workers having died in 1999-2000. This is concentrated mainly in the Hooghly, they said, but had spread to Calcutta too. It has percolated to the grassroots and, they said, it has ceased to have ideological basis. Peace talks, and mediation, seem to be ways in which intervention has been attempted by human rights activists.

Bibliography

Bernier, François. *Voyages de F. Bernier (Angevin) contenant la description des Estats du Grand Mogol, de l'Indoustan, du royaume de Kachemire.* Amsterdam: D. P. Marret, 1699.

Durkheim, Émile. *Suicide: A Study in Sociology,* translated by John A. Spaulding and George Simpson. Glencoe, NY: Free Press, 1951.

Hawley, John Stratton. *Sati, the Blessing and the Curse: The Burning of Wives in India.* New York: Oxford University Press, 1994.

Nandy, Ashis. *"Sati As Profit versus Sati As a Spectacle*: *Sati: The Blessing and the Curse.* New York: Oxford University Press, 1994.

Narasimhan, Sakuntala. *Sati: A Study of Widow Burning in India.* New Delhi: Viking, 1990.

Sharma, Arvind. *Sati: Historical and Phenomenological Essays.* New Delhi: Motilal Banarsidass, 1988.

Thompson, Edward. *Suttee: A Historical and Philosophical Enquiry into the Hindu Rite of Widow-Burning.* London: Allen and Unwin, 1928.

Wadley, Susan. *From the Margins of Hindu Marriage: Essays on Gender, Religion, and Culture.* New York: Oxford University Press, 1995.

Weinberger-Thomas, Catherine. *Ashes of Immortality: Widow-Burning in India,* Chicago: University of Chicago Press, 1999.

Chen, Marthy, and Jean Dreze. *Widows and Well-Being in Rural North India.* London: London School of Economics, 1992.

Dreze, Jean. *Widows in Rural India.* London: London School of Economics, 1990.

Owen, Margaret. *A World of Widows.* London: ZED Books, 1996.

Potash, Betty, ed. *Widows in African Societies: Choices and Constraints.* Stanford, CA: Stanford University Press, 1986.

Berger, Peter, and Hansfried Kellner. , *Patterns of Communicative Behavior.* London: Collier-Macmillan, 1970.

Bernard, Jessie, *Family in Transition.* Boston: Little, Brown, 1983.

Bernard, Jessie. *Remarriage.* New York: Holt, Rinehart and Winston, 1956.

Cherlin, Andrew. *Marriage, Divorce, Remarriage.* Cambridge, MA: Harvard

University Press, 1992.

Daniels, Arlene. *Invisible Careers: Women Community Leaders in Voluntary Work*. Chicago: University of Chicago Press, 1988.

Lopata, Helena. *"Widowhood: Reconstruction of Self-Concept and Identities.*, *Studies in Symbolic Interaction,* Vol. 23. Stanford, CT: JAI Press, 2000.

Lopata, Helena. *Current Widowhood: Myths and Realities.* Newbury Park, CA: Sage, 1996.

Lopata, Helena. *Journal of Marriage and the Family*, New Brunswick, NJ: Transaction, 1991.

Lopata, Helena: *Widows: North America.* Durham, NC: Duke University Press, 1987.

Lopata, Helena: *Women As Widows.* New York: Elsevier, 1979.

Lopata, Helena: *Widowhood in an American City.* Cambridge, MA: Schenkman, 1973.

Lopata, Helena: *Occupation: Housewife.* New York: Oxford University Press, 1971.

Matthews Martin: *Widows: North America.* Durham, NC: Duke University Press, 1987.

McDonald, Jessyne: *Widows: North America.* Durham NC: Duke University Press, 1987: 139-157.

McKaine, Walter. *Retirement Marriage.* Chicago: University of Chicago Press, 1969.

Neugarten, Bernice. *Middle Age and Aging.* Chicago: University of Chicago Press, 1968.

O'Bryant, Shirley. "Sibling Support and Older Widows' Well-Being." *Journal of Marriage and the Family* 50 (1988):173–183.

Papanek, Hannah.

Index